NOT PASSION'S S[

Happy Birthday Kev

Heres to 2008

... A year of transformation!

love Alex

THE PASSIONATE LIFE
A Series on The
Philosophy of Emotions
by Robert C. Solomon

Not Passion's Slave: Emotions and Choice

Not Passion's Slave
Emotions and Choice

ROBERT C. SOLOMON

UNIVERSITY PRESS

2003

OXFORD
UNIVERSITY PRESS

Oxford   New York
Auckland   Bangkok   Buenos Aires   Cape Town   Chennai
Dar es Salaam   Delhi   Hong Kong   Istanbul   Karachi   Kolkata
Kuala Lumpur   Madrid   Melbourne   Mexico City   Mumbai
Nairobi   São Paulo   Shanghai   Taipei   Tokyo   Toronto

Copyright © 2003 by Robert C. Solomon

Published by Oxford University Press, Inc.
198 Madison Avenue, New York, New York 10016

www.oup.com

Oxford is a registered trademark of Oxford University Press

All rights reserved. No part of this publication may be reproduced,
stored in a retrieval system, or transmitted, in any form or by any means
electronic, mechanical, photocopying, recording, or otherwise,
without the prior permission of Oxford University Press.

Library of Congress Cataloging-in-Publication Data
Solomon, Robert C.
Not passion's slave: emotions and choice / Robert C. Solomon.
p. cm.—(The passionate life)
ISBN 0-19-517978-1
1. Emotions (Philosophy) I. Title.
B105.E46 S67   2003
128'.37—dc21   2002066237

9 8 7 6 5 4 3 2 1

Printed in the United States of America
on acid-free paper

Give me that man
That is not passion's slave, and I will wear him
In my heart's core

Shakespeare, *Hamlet* Act III, Scene ii.

Preface

> For the idea which I have never ceased to develop is that in the end one is always responsible for what is made of one. Even if one can do nothing else besides assume this responsibility. For I believe that a man can always make something out of what is made of him. This is the limit I would today accord to freedom: the small movement which makes of a totally conditioned social being someone who does not render back completely what his conditioning has given him.
>
> Jean-Paul Sartre

The idea that we are in some significant sense and to some significant degree responsible for our emotions is an idea that I, too, have never ceased to develop, following Sartre's philosophy. That was the thrust of my earliest publication on the subject, "Emotions and Choice," in 1973, and of my first book, *The Passions*, in 1976. In both publications, the thesis was polemical (which is to say a bit overbold and unnuanced) and it inevitably required considerable rethinking and revision. Thus I have watched with decided discomfort as I am quoted from my earliest work, as if I haven't written anything since or developed my admittedly polemical view on emotions beyond the scope of such bumper slogans as "We choose our emotions" and "Emotions are judgments." Here, in a single volume, I trace the development of this theory of emotions and develop it in detail. To preserve the historical development, I have not altered the older pieces, except to correct minor but intolerable errors and to occasionally refer to more recent work in the field. The later essays (those written since 1990) have gone through several revisions over the years but now reflect my current view (along with my remaining reservations).

Two themes run through all of my work, and I have not backed down on either of them. The first is the responsibility thesis, "emotions and choice," the idea that we are (at least sometimes, to some extent) responsible for our emotions and our emotional responses. The second is that emotions are "cognitive" in nature, which means that they are something more than mere feelings or sensations and something more than physiological reactions (although I have never denied that both feelings and physiology are pervasive ingredients in emotion). When I first introduced this "cognitive" thesis in philosophy, it was greeted with considerable disbelief. Since then, I am happy to say, it has become the standard of most philosophical discussions. In the 1980s, Steve Leighton called it "the new view" of emotions. By 1997, Paul Griffiths could treat it as the Goliath that utterly dominated the field and so had to be defeated. I take very seriously the arguments that Griffiths and others have advanced against the cognitive theory, mainly from the perspective of evolutionary biology and neurology, but I have not felt the need to revamp, as opposed to simply expand, my thesis that "emotions are judgments" on account of them. The first thesis, however, has not fared so well. To the contrary, the new emphasis on biology and neurology has reinforced the ancient prejudice I have always been fighting, namely, that emotions "happen" to us and are entirely beyond our control. Researchers like Joe Le Doux have argued that most of emotion precedes cognition, and, indeed, even feeling is mere "icing on the cake." Emotions are first and foremost neurological "affect programs" (Sylvan Tompkins's and Paul Ekman's term) to which questions of choice and responsibility are wholly inappropriate.

Accordingly, the themes that dominate the chapters which follow are all attempts to develop and clarify my "cognitive" view of emotions as judgments and my existentialist insistence on choice and responsibility regarding our emotions. But as I have developed these themes, other issues have become more prominent as well, for instance, the social nature of emotions and the fascinating challenge of cross-cultural and linguistic comparisons of emotions in different cultures and the temporal nature of emotions as processes. To put this last thesis bluntly, I take an emotion to be a process and not a mere reaction, much less a more or less automatic and instantaneous neurological reaction or "affect program." To be sure there are such reactions, for instance, the startle reflex that some researchers have confused with emotion or the burst of physiology and feeling in embarrassment that the ancient Stoics recognized as "first movements," preceding the appearance of the actual emotion (which is defined by judgments). But by "emotion" I mean not those momentary phenomena but those long-lasting complex experiences such as Othello's love and growing jealousy, Iago's insidious and dangerous envy, Frantz Fanon's escalating rage, and Lily Bart's fateful pride. Emotions involve social narratives as well as physical responses, and an analysis of emotions is an account of our way of being-in-the-world. Thus a full account of our emotions is nothing less than an account of human life.

This holistic view of emotions suggests a further thesis, which provided both the original context and the ultimate framework for my research. There is a paradigm of emotions research (presented by William James) that is strictly scientific, which is to say "nalue-neutral," and essentially a "third-person" account. That is the context within which a great deal of emotions research is carried out today, and I find a great deal to learn from it. But there is another, larger context for the study of emotions, and that is *ethics* (still best represented, I think, by Aristotle). These two perspectives are not opposed. Indeed, they are thoroughly entangled and require one another. But moralists who do not pay attention to empirical research and ordinary experience and common sense have caused a great deal of suffering in the world through unrealistic and even cruel moral imperatives, however backed-up by "reason." On the other hand, science-minded philosophers have created a stunningly cold approach to emotions research by ignoring or even ridiculing ethics. Thus two of the best recent studies, by Paul Griffith and Jon Elster, both attack the "moralizing" of emotions. I think that this is a bum rap. The emotions themselves are "moralized" through and through, and to think otherwise is to misunderstand their fundamental nature.

We are responsible for our emotions because of the central roles they play in our moral and social life. If we were those perennial fantasy figures of the philosophical literature, marooned and miraculously living alone on a desert island, we would have no need for and no opportunity to learn most complex emotions. But we do need emotions and we do need to learn them and to learn how to "do" them. In Kenneth Branagh's *Mary Shelley's Frankenstein*, the monster complains to the titular mad scientist, "You gave me these emotions. You did not tell me how to use them." Indeed. The idea of emotions without learning, without an "upbringing," or without a context is no idea of emotions at all.

But with context and learning and, most important, with reflection, we do have an impressive amount of choice as to what our emotions will be. This is true not only of those states of character and psychological dispositions which can clearly be cultivated (although die-hard psychological determinists may deny even that) but also of what Elster calls "occurent" emotions, or "episodic" ongoing emotional states and processes. The relationship between responsibility and choice is complex, as are the connections with passivity and spontaneity and freedom. It is sometimes said that it is a "harsh" view which would hold people responsible for not only what they do but also for what they feel, but I would argue that some such "moralizing" lies at the very heart of our Judeo-Christian tradition (and other traditions as well). We do not divorce morals from motives and intentions, and we do not or should not divorce our actions from our "feelings." To "command" people to "love their neighbor" may be a bit far-fetched (depending on the neighbor), but it is by no means nonsense or inappropriate. It just turns out to be rather difficult to do.

In the chapters that follow, I begin with "Emotions and Choice" from 1973, and a few brief selections from *The Passions* from 1976. I am not one to hide or deny my previous excesses and errors, and so I include two of the most rabid sections of my book, one rejecting what I then saw as the overtight association of emotions with neurology and physiology more generally, and the other rejecting even more vehemently what I saw as the uncritical identification of emotions and feelings. One of the best things to come out of that publication at the time, I should mention, was the fact that it so infuriated or amused several prominent social psychologists, James Averill and Joe Campos in particular, that they became good friends and also set me on the interdisciplinary path that I have followed ever since. (In the second edition of *The Passions*, I apologized for the indelicate way I had treated my social science friends.)

The discussion of neurology and physiology, I should say, came well before the explosion of work on emotions and neurology that has taken center stage. Most of my references are archaic, focusing on the overly materialist claims that I rejected and still reject insofar as they ignore the psychological and ethical. It also anticipated at least some of what has come to be called "eliminative materialism" (by Paul Churchland and others), namely, the idea that the absence of neurological knowledge in our ordinary ("folk psychological") conception of emotion was simply a contingent matter and surely would change as our knowledge of neurology increased and became more widespread. My inclusion of these sections here, however, is much more a way of doing penance and providing amusement than it is a continuing uncompromising insistence on a narrowly "cognitive" theory of emotions.

The essays from the 1980s mainly develop themes briefly introduced in *The Passions*, for example, concerning the nature of emotion's "intentionality" and further elaborating the notion of "judgment." In the two essays on intentionality (unusually, unbearably scholastic for me), I develop my contentious distinction between the *object* of an emotion and its *cause*, and begin a campaign (still continuing) against "components" analyses of emotion. The "components" analysis is the idea that an emotion has different components, like an automobile transmission or a stereo set, which can be disassembled and examined independently. Of course an emotion has different *aspects* or *dimensions*—behavioral, experiential, neurological, cognitive, social, its object, its causes, its intentionality—but the fact that we can *abstract* these from the emotion is not at all the same as saying that the emotion is built or "constructed" out of components or can be "broken down" into such components. The standard philosophical treatment of emotions in terms of intentionality all too easily falls into this trap.

The essay "On Emotion as Judgments" is in fact an amalgam of three different essays, one from a philosophy journal, one from a book on personality theory and one from a book on social psychology. With some temerity, I have tried to integrate these three very different (and sometimes mutually hostile) approaches. The 1980s also saw my early efforts to apply the theory to the cross-cultural comparison of emotions, first in a piece called "Emotions and Anthropology" (*Inquiry*, 1978) and then through the auspices of the Social Science Research Council in New York, where I again had the very fruitful pleasure of meeting a number of prominent social scientists who became both friends and colleagues. That essay is included here. "The Politics of the Emotions" grew out of my growing realization of the importance of the social nature of emotions, not only as the context within which we learn and exercise our emotions but as the very structure and content of the emotions themselves.

The final four essays have been written and rewritten since 1990, first as various lectures and presentations to philosophy and psychology groups, then as contributions to interdisciplinary conferences and books. "Back to Basics" was written in response to a raging debate in psychology in the early 1990s, but it took several more years of gestation before the increasingly swollen piece was ready to take on a life of its own. The "Thoughts and Feelings" essay was the outgrowth of years of debate and attempts to defend the idea that emotions are judgments as opposed to other candidates for "cognition" such as beliefs and thoughts. It finally was forced to completion with an invitation to join an American Philosophical Association symposium on Jerry Neu's book *A Tear Is an Intellectual Thing* and by a wonderful conference, "The Philosophy of Emotions," at the University of Manchester in 2001. In "Against Valence: On the Positive and Negative Emotions" I pursue a claim that I have made offhandedly for many years, and reject the ancient and seemingly commonsense tendency to reduce all emotions to "positive and negative affects," to pleasure and pain, what psychologists (borrowing from physics and chemistry) codify as "valence." Finally, "On the Passivity of the Passions" represents my latest attempt to say what I mean—and what I do not mean—in my insistence that we are responsible for our emotions. It is the culmination of the thirty-year campaign that I inherited from Jean-Paul Sartre.

The essays thus arranged present a kind of intellectual memoir as well as the development of an idea. I do not apologize for the inevitable repetition that follows as a matter of course. Nor do I apologize for the inevitable conflicts and contradictions that emerge as well. It is not as if I never changed my mind. As Sartre said toward the end of his own career, "The idea which I have never ceased to develop is that in the end one is responsible." When I am told that the idea that we are responsible for our emotions is both harsh and implausible, I agree, but I then contrast that with the too-easy alternative of using our emotions as excuses and refusing to take responsibility for them. Even if it were untrue that we are responsible for our emotions, it would still do us a lot of good to seriously consider this. Thinking that we have control often makes it so, and the world, as we now know, is too fragile a place for unexamined, and uncultivated emotions.

I have retained the original style of the notes and references for the various pieces that follow. The result is inconsistencies and repetitions that I have not tried to correct. In chapter 6, for example, the references are included on a separate "References" page.

Acknowledgments

Chapter 1, "Emotions and Choice" (1973; Appendix 1980), originally appeared in *Review of Metaphysics*, 28, no. 1 (September 1973). Appendix from Amélie Rorty, ed., *Emotions* (Berkeley: University of California Press, 1980).

Chapter 2, "On Physiology and Feelings" (1976), originally appeared in *The Passions* (New York: Doubleday-Anchor, 1976; paperback ed., 1977; Notre Dame, Ind.: University of Notre Dame Press, 1983). Revised and reissued as *The Passions: Emotions and the Meaning of Life* (Indianapolis and Cambridge: Hackett, 1993).

Chapter 3, "The Rationality of Emotions" (1977), originally appeared in *Southwestern Journal of Philosophy*, 8 (Summer 1977), pp. 105–114.

Chapter 4, "Nothing to Be Proud of" (1984), originally appeared in F. Miller et al., eds., *Understanding Human Emotions* (Bowling Green, Ohio: Philosophy Documentation Center, Bowling Green State University, 1980).

Chapter 5, "Emotions' Mysterious Objects" (1984), originally appeared in G. E. Myers, and K. D. Irani, eds., *Emotion: Philosophical Studies* (New York: Haven Books, 1984).

Chapter 6, "Getting Angry: The Jamesian Theory of Emotion in Anthropology" (1984), originally appeared in R. A. LeVine and R. Shweder, eds., *Culture Theory* (Cambridge: Cambridge University Press, 1984).

Chapter 7, "On Emotions as Judgments" (1988), previously appeared in *American Philosophical Quarterly*, 25, no. 2 (April 1988), and as "Emotions as Judgments: A Phenomenological View," in Joseph de Rivera, ed., *Studies in Personality* (Worcester, MA: Clark University Press, 1988), and "Phenomenology, Emotions, and the Self," in L. Cirillo, B. Kaplan, and S. Wapner, eds., *Emotions in Ideal Human Development* (Hillsdale, N.J.: Lawrence Erlbaum, 1989).

Chapter 8, "Back to Basics: On the Very Idea of 'Basic Emotions'" (1993, rev. 2001). This is the original publication.

Chapter 9, "The Politics of Emotion" (1998), originally appeared in P. French and H. Wettstein, eds., *The Philosophy of the Emotions, Midwest Studies in Philosophy*, no. 22 (Notre Dame, Ind.: University of Notre Dame Press, 1999).

Chapter 10, "Against Valence" ("Positive" and "Negative" Emotions) (2001). This is the original publication. A social science version of this essay has been prepared with Lori Stone, of the University of Texas at Austin.

Chapter 11, "Thoughts and Feelings: What Is a 'Cognitive Theory' of the Emotions and Does It Neglect Affectivity?" (2001), appears in A. Hatzimoysis, ed., *The Philosophy of Emotions* (Cambridge: Cambridge University Press, 2002).

Chapter 12, "On the Passivity of the Passions" (2001), appears in A. S. R. Manstead and Agneta Fischer, eds., *Feelings and Emotions* (Cambridge: Cambridge University Press, 2002).

Contents

1. Emotions and Choice (1973), 3
2. On Physiology and Feelings (1976), 25
3. The Rationality of Emotions (1977), 34
4. Nothing to be Proud of (1980), 42
5. Emotions' Mysterious Objects (1984), 57
6. Getting Angry: The Jamesian Theory of Emotion in Anthropology (1984), 76
7. On Emotions as Judgments (1988), 92
8. Back to Basics: On the Very Idea of "Basic Emotions" (1993, rev. 2001), 115
9. The Politics of Emotion (1998), 143
10. Against Valence ("Positive" and "Negative" Emotions) (2001), 162
11. Thoughts and Feelings: What Is a "Cognitive Theory" of the Emotions and Does It Neglect Affectivity? (2001), 178
12. On the Passivity of the Passions (2001), 195

Notes, 233

Bibliography, 247

Index, 253

NOT PASSION'S SLAVE

1

Emotions and Choice (1973)

I

Do we choose our emotions? Can we be held responsible for our anger? for feeling jealousy? for falling in love or succumbing to resentment or hatred? The suggestion sounds odd because emotions are typically considered occurrences that happen to (or "in") us: emotions are taken to be the hallmark of the irrational and the disruptive. Controlling one's emotion is supposed to be like the caging and taming of a wild beast, the suppression and sublimation of a Freudian "it."

Traditionally, emotions have been taken to be feelings or sensations. More recently, but also traditionally, emotions have been taken to be physiological disturbances. Accordingly, much of this century's literature on emotions is dedicated to mapping out the relationship between sensations and correlative occurrences. William James, for example, takes consciousness of emotions to be consciousness of physiological occurrences. Other philosophers and psychologists, for one reason or another, have tried to reduce the emotion to a physiological occurrence, or, alternatively, have focused on the feeling of emotion and denied any conceptual role to the physiological occurrence. But these traditional worries should be quite irrelevant to any analysis of the emotions, for an emotion is neither a sensation nor a physiological occurrence, nor an occurrence of any other kind. "Struck by jealousy," "driven by anger," "plagued by remorse," "paralyzed by fear," "felled by shame," like "the prick of Cupid's arrow," are all symptomatic metaphors betraying a faulty philosophical analysis. Emotions are not occurrences and do not happen to us. I would like to suggest that emotions are rational and purposive rather than irrational and disruptive, are very much like actions, and that we choose an emotion much as we choose a course of action.[1]

Emotions are intentional; that is, emotions are "about" something. For instance, "I am angry *at John for stealing my car*." It is not necessary to press the claim that *all* emotions are "about" something. Kierkegaard's dread may be an emotion which is not "about" anything, or, conversely, may be "about" everything. Similarly, *moods*, which are much like emotions, do not have a specific object. Euphoria, melancholy, and depression are not "about" anything in particular, though they may be caused by some particular incident. We might wish to say that such emotions and moods are "about" the world rather than anything in particular. In fact, Heidegger has suggested that *all* emotions are ultimately "about" the world and never simply "about" something particular. But we will avoid debating these issues by simply focusing our attention on emotions that clearly seem to be "about" something specifiable.

"I am angry at John for stealing my car." It is true that I am angry. And it is also true that John stole my car. Thus we are tempted to distinguish two components of my being angry; my feeling of anger and what I am angry about. But this is doubly a mistake. It requires that a feeling (of anger) be (contingently) directed at something (at John's having stolen my car). But feelings are occurrences and cannot have a "direction." They can be caused, but to say that I am angry "about" John's having stolen my car is very different from saying his stealing my car caused me to be angry. John's act might cause me to be angry "about" something else, for example, my failure to renew my insurance. It might be false that John stole my car, though I believe that he did. Then it is false that John's stealing my car caused me to be angry, but still true that what I am angry "about" is John's stealing my car. Once might suggest that it is not the alleged *fact* of John's stealing my car that is in question, but rather my *belief* that he did. But what I am angry "about" is clearly not that I believe that John stole my car, but rather *that John stole my car*.

Feelings do not have "directions."[2] But I am angry "about" something. The relationship between my being angry and what I am angry about is not the contingent relation between a feeling and an object. (Though it is surely contingent that I am angry at John for stealing my car.) An emotion cannot be identified apart from its object; "I am angry" is incomplete—not only in the weak sense that there is more information which may be available ("Are you angry about anything?") but "I am angry" requires that there *must* be more information available ("*What* are you angry about?") But feelings have no such requirements. Anger is not a feeling; neither is anger a feeling plus anything else (e.g., what it is "about").

Neither can "what I am angry about" be separated from my being angry. Of course, it makes sense to say that John's having stolen my car is something different from my being angry at him for doing so. But it is not simply the *fact* that John stole my car that is what I am angry about; nor is it, as I said above, my *belief* that John stole my car about which I am angry. I am angry about the intentional object "that John stole my car." Unlike the *fact* that John stole my car, this intentional object is opaque; I am not angry that John stole a vehicle assembled in Youngstown, Ohio, with 287 h.p., though that is a true description of the fact that John stole my car. I am not angry that someone 5'7" tall got his fingerprints on my steering column, yet that is a true description of the fact that John stole my car. Sartre attempts to point out this feature of what emotions are "about" by saying that their object is "transformed"; D. F. Pears points to this same feature by noting that it is always an "aspect" of the object that is the object of an emotion. What emotions are "about," as in beliefs, can be identified only under certain descriptions, and those descriptions are determined by the emotion itself. This does not mean that what emotions are about are beliefs—only that emotions share an important conceptual property of beliefs. "Being angry about . . ." is very much like "believing that . . ." To be angry is to be angry "about" a peculiar sort of object, one that is distinguished by the fact that it is what I am angry "about." Husserl describes this peculiarity of mental acts in general by insisting that an intentional act and an intentional object are "*essentially* correlated." For our purposes, the point to be seen is that emotions cannot be discussed in terms of "components," by distinguishing feeling angry and what I am angry about. (Pears, e.g., begins by making this distinction.) In Heideggerian phrase, I am never simply angry, but there is always "my-being-angry-about- . . ."

If there is no legitimate distinction between feeling angry and what I am angry "about," or, to put it in a different way, if the connection between my being angry and what I am angry "about" is a conceptual and not causal connection, then it is easy to explain a feature of emotions that has been pointed out by many analysts. A change in what I am angry "about" demands a change in my anger; if I no longer feel wronged by John, who only bought a car that looks like mine, I cannot be angry at John (for stealing my car) any longer. One cannot be angry if he is not angry "about" having been wronged. Similarly, one cannot be ashamed if he does not accept some responsibility for an awkward situation, nor can he be embarrassed if he does not find the situation awkward. If emotions were feelings, it would be a peculiar coincidence that the feelings were so faithful to our views of our situation, that they did not hold onto us with a momentum of their own after opinions had passed, that they were not so "irrational" as to pay no attention to our opinions at all. But emotions are not feelings, nor feelings plus what they are "about"; the format of an emotion is ". . . -about-. . ." And so it is no surprise that emotions change with our opinions, and so are "rational" in a very important sense.

Emotions typically involve feelings. Perhaps they essentially involve feelings. But feelings are never sufficient to differentiate and identify emotions, and an emotion is never simply a feeling, not even a feeling plus anything. Moreover, it is clear that one can have an emotion without feeling anything. One can be angry without feeling angry: one can be angry for three days or five years and not feel anything identifiable as a feeling of anger continuously through that prolonged period. One might add that one must have a disposition to feel angry, and to this, there is no objection, so long as being angry is not thought to *mean* "having a disposition to feel angry." I do not know whether it makes sense to suppose that one can be angry without ever feeling angry. But I do know that it does not even make sense to say that one feels angry if one is not angry. This might seem mysterious, if we accept the traditional view that anger has an identifiable feeling attached to it (for then, why could one not have the feeling without whatever else is involved in anger?). And this might seem obvious on the traditional view that anger *is* a feeling (for then being angry is nothing but having the feeling of anger). But on our account, anger is not a feeling, nor does it involve any identifiable feeling (which is not to deny that one does feel angry—that is, flushed, excited, etc., when he is angry). One can identify his feeling as feeling angry only if he is angry. It is true that I often feel something when I become angry. It is also true that I feel something after I cease to be angry. I am angry at John for stealing my car. Then I discover that John did not steal my car: I cease (immediately) to be angry. Yet the feeling remains: it is the same feeling I had while I was angry (flushing, etc.). The feeling subsides more slowly than the anger. But the feeling, even if it is the same feeling that I had while I was angry, is not a feeling of anger. Now it is just a feeling. Sometimes one claims to feel angry but not be angry. But here, I would argue that the correct description is rather that one does not know exactly what one is angry "about" (though one is surely angry "about" something); or perhaps one is angry but does not believe he ought to be. One cannot feel angry without being angry.

A familiar move in the analysis of emotions subsequent to the discovery that emotions are not feelings or occurrences, is the thesis that emotions are conceptually tied to behavior; that is, the ascription of an emotion to a person is the ascription to him of various sorts of behavior. Thus, to be angry is necessarily to "anger-behave." Of course, it is evident that one can *pretend* to be angry, that is, anger-behave without being angry, and so pretending has become a major topic in the analysis of emotions. (More on this in part II.) What is generally agreed is that a single piece of behavior is never conceptually sufficient to identify an emotion, or to distinguish emotions from pretense. E. Bedford, for example, suggests that what is always needed is at least "more of the same." Since Ryle's *Concept of Mind*, this "more of the same" is provided by the suggestion that ascribing an emotion to a person is not to simply describe one or more episodes of behavior but rather to ascribe to him a disposition to behave. But there is considerable confusion about the nature of such disposition ascriptions, and the suggestion is clearly unsatisfactory as an analysis of *my* having an emotion. The behavioral analysis does maintain one important feature of emotions, their intentionality, though authors (e.g., Ryle, Armstrong) who favor this analysis are often intent to reject "intentionality" as well. But for our purposes, we can remain uninvolved in these issues that have become virtually definitive of "philosophy of mind." We can agree that it is undeniably true that if a person is angry, he has a disposition to anger-behave and leave it entirely open whether this connection between emotions and behavior is conceptual, or causal or something else. The purpose of this essay is to show that emotions are very much like actions, and if it should turn out that emotions are actions in any such straightforward sense, this can only make our task easier. And so, we can simply say of the behavioral analysis: insofar as it is true, it supports our thesis.

"Emotions are caused." The idea that emotions are occurrences naturally gave rise to the idea that emotions are caused. Many philosophers would argue that, if emotions are occurrences, then they must be caused, and conversely, that if emotions are caused, they must be occurrences. But if, as I am arguing, emotions are not occurrences, then they cannot be caused.

But surely this is wrong. We do speak of the cause of anger, the cause for sadness, a cause for fear. And surely emotions, as intentional, are typically if not necessarily *reactions* to something that happens to us. Sometimes this cause is manifest in what the emotion is "about"; for example, I am angry about your hitting me; your hitting me is the event which caused me to become angry. But sometimes the cause for an emotion is *not* what the emotion is "about." The cause of my anger might be too little sleep and too much coffee. The cause of my love might be sexual deprivation. But I am not angry "about" lack of sleep and hyperstimulation, and I am not in love with my sexual deprivation (nor is my love "about" a cure for my sexual deprivation).

The cause of an emotion is a function in a certain kind of explanation. The cause must in every case be distinguished from what my emotion is "about" (its "object"). The cause is always an actual event (or state-of-affairs, etc.). The object of my emotion is always an intentional object. The cause is subject to certain lawlike generalizations in a way that objects of emotions are not. If I claim to be angry because of a harsh review of my book, pointing out that I have not become angry at previous harsh reviews of my book is sufficient to show that the cause of my becoming angry is not (my reading of) the review of my book, but it is not sufficient to show that I am not angry "about" the harsh review. I am not in any special position to know the cause of my emotion (though only I know, as a matter of fact, that I did not sleep last night, that I have had four cups of coffee); I am always in a privileged position to identify the intentional object of my emotion. This is *not* to say that my knowledge of the object of my emotion is "immediate" or "direct," nor is it to claim that my identification of the object of my emotion is "incorrigible." It is possible and not unusual that I should misidentify—sometimes in a gross way—what I am angry about, or whom I love, or why I am sad. I may identify the object of my anger as John's having stolen my car, but I am really angry at John for writing a harsh review of my book. I may think that I love Mary, when I really love my mother. And I may think that I love Mary when I am really angry about the harsh review of my book. The problem of "unconscious emotions" would take us far beyond our current argument. For now, it should suffice for us to insist that the difference between identification of the cause of an emotion and its object is not a difference between direct and indirect knowledge—as traditionally conceived—or a difference between corrigible and incorrigible identification. The cause of an emotion is an occurrence (state-of-affairs, etc.) of a type that stands in a lawlike connection with emotions of that type. The object of an emotion is simply "what the emotion is about," whether or not it is also the cause, whether or not it is even the case, and whether or not the subject himself knows it to be the object of his emotion.[3]

We have noted that emotions are interestingly similar to beliefs. We can now explain this similarity by claiming that emotions are judgments—normative and often moral judgments. "I am angry at John for taking ("stealing" begs the question) my car" *entails* that I believe that John has somehow wronged me. (This must be true even if *all things considered*, I also believe that John was justified in taking my car.) The (moral) judgment entailed by my anger is not a judgment *about* my anger (although someone else might make such judgments to the effect that my anger is justified or unjustified, rational, prudent, foolish, self-indulgent, therapeutic, beneficial, unfortunate, pathological, or amusing). My anger *is* that judgment. If I do not believe that I have somehow been wronged, I cannot be angry (though I might be upset, or sad). Similarly, if I cannot praise my lover, I cannot be in love (though I might want her or need her, which, traditional wisdom aside, is entirely different). If I do not find my situation awkward, I cannot be ashamed or embarrassed. If I do not judge that I have suffered a loss, I cannot be sad or jealous. I am not sure whether all emotions entail such judgments; moods (depression and euphoria) surely present special problems. But emotions in general do appear to require this feature: to have an emotion is to hold a normative judgment about one's situation.

The idea that an emotion is a normative judgment, perhaps even a moral judgment, wreaks havoc with several long cherished philosophical theses. Against those romantics and contemporary bourgeois therapists who would argue that emotions simply *are* and must be accepted without judgment, it appears that emotions themselves are already judgments. And against several generations of moral philosophers who would distinguish between morality based upon principle and morality based upon emotion or "sentiment," it appears that every "sentiment," every emotion is already a matter of judgment, often moral judgment. An ethics of sentiment differs from ethics of principle only in the fact that its judgments are allowed to go unchallenged: it is an ethics of prejudice while the latter is typically an ethics of dogma.

We can now see why "what an emotion is about" is not simply a fact; nor is it even a fact under certain descriptions. The object of an emotion is itself "affective" or normative. It is not an object *about* which one makes a judgment but is rather defined, in part, by that normative judgment. The peculiar emotional object, *that John stole my car*, can only be fully characterized as the object of my anger. "That John stole my car" is also the name of the object of my belief, of course, and perhaps of any number of other propositional attitudes I hold. But the object of my anger, that John stole my car, is an inseparable piece of my being angry. This sounds strange, no doubt, if the intentional object of the emotion is thought to be a fact or a proposition. But my anger-at-John-for-stealing-my-car is inseparable from my judgment that John in so doing wronged me, while it is clear that the *fact* that John stole my car is very different from my anger or my judgment. My anger *is* my judgment that John has wronged me.

It has always been recognized that there is some difference between our ascriptions of emotions to ourselves and our ascriptions of emotions to others. I know that I am angry and what I am angry about very differently than I know that John is angry and what he is angry about. (This first-person privilege remains the presupposition of, and is not undermined by, either the Freudian concept of "unconscious emotions" or by recent philosophical attacks on "incorrigibility.") On the traditional view in which emotions are feelings, this difference has been explained by appeal to the peculiar "privacy" of sensation-like occurrences. But emotions are not feelings and not occurrences, we have argued, but rather judgments. Yet the difference between first- and other-person cases can still be made out, and in a far more convincing way than on the feeling-analysis of emotions. *You* can say of me,"He is angry because he thinks John stole his car, which he did not." *You* can say of me, "He is angry about the review, which actually was favorable, but only because of his lack of sleep and his having drunk too much coffee." *You* can say of me, "He doesn't really love Mary, but rather a mother-surrogate." But *I* cannot say these things of *myself*. "I am angry at John because I think that he stole my car, which he didn't" is nonsense. If emotions are judgments, then the sorts of "pragmatic" paradoxes that have long been celebrated regarding judgments in general will apply to emotions also. "I am angry about x, but not x" raises the same problems as "P, but I do not believe P." No feeling-account of emotions can account for such paradoxes. But, if emotions are intentional, emotions must partake in conceptual relationships in a way that mere occurrences, feelings, or facts do not. If I am angry about John's stealing my car, there are certain beliefs which I logically cannot hold, for example, the belief that John did not steal my car.

The difference between first- and other-person ascriptions of emotions lies in the realm of the "pragmatic paradoxes." Given that I have a certain emotion, there are certain beliefs which you can have (including beliefs about me) but which *I* cannot have. The most interesting set of beliefs in this regard are those which pertain to the *cause* of an emotion. Earlier, we argued that the cause of an emotion is a fact (state of affairs, etc.) which can be variously ("transparently") described and occupies a role in lawlike generalizations. The *object* of an emotion, however, is limited by certain judgments (is "opaque") which are determined in the subject's having that emotion. But this distinction, we can now add, breaks down in the first-person case. If I am angry *about* John's stealing my car (the object of my anger), then I cannot believe that the sufficient *cause* of my anger is anything other than John's stealing my car. *You* can attribute my unjust anger to my lack of sleep. *I* cannot. If I attribute my anger to lack of sleep, I cannot be angry at all. And this is not simply to say that my anger is "not reasonable." (I cannot say that of myself either, except perhaps in extremely peculiar circumstances, for example, following extensive psychoanalytic treatment, which here, as elsewhere, confuses all distinctions as well as the patient regarding first- vs. other-person ascriptions of emotions, motives, intentions, etc.) I can only be angry so long as I believe that what has caused me to be angry is what I am angry about. Where the cause is different from what I am angry about, I cannot know that it is.

One can argue that the person who is angry (or in love, or sad) is in the worst position to pick out the cause for his anger (or love or sadness) *as opposed* to its object.[4] We can only add that this thesis marks out a conceptual necessity. We earlier pointed out the familiar phenomenon that our emotions change with our opinions and argued that this was not a causal matter and not a coincidence, but a consequence of the thesis that emotions are themselves judgments. We can now add that our emotions change with our knowledge of the causes of those emotions. If I can discover the sufficient cause of my anger, in those cases in which the cause and the object are different (and in which the newly discovered cause is not itself a new object for anger, as often happens), I can undermine and abandon my anger. It is here that Freud's often debated notion that emotions are "defused" by bringing them to consciousness contains an important conceptual truth too often and too easily dismissed by philosophers. Once one becomes aware of the cause of his emotion as opposed to its intended object, he can indeed "defuse" his emotion. And in those familiar Freudian cases in which one mistakenly identifies the object of his emotion (he thinks he is angry at his teacher: he is "really" angry at his father), correcting this identification can, in those cases where the correctly identified object is also the cause of the emotion, also "defuse" it. Where Freud opened himself to unnecessary criticism, I believe, was in his construing this as a *causal* relationship, a "catharsis" of repressed emotional air bubbles in the mental digestive system. But it is not as if my recognition of the true cause of my anger *causes* the easing of my emotion. Rather, my recognition of the true cause of my emotion amounts to a denial of the judgment which is my emotion. When I see that my anger is wholly a result of my lack of sleep and overdose of coffee, I thereby abandon my anger. Of course, the flushing, pulsing, irritable *feelings* of anger may thus be *caused* to diminish by the disappearance of my anger, but these are, as we have argued, in no case my anger.

If emotions are judgments and can be "defused" (and also instigated) by considerations of other judgments, it is clear how our emotions are in a sense *our doing*, and how we are responsible for them. Normative judgments can themselves be criticized, argued against, and refuted. Now if *you* criticize my anger at John by maintaining that he has not wronged me, you may conclude that my anger is unreasonable, unfair, and perhaps unbecoming. But if you should convince *me* that John has not wronged me, I do not simply conclude that my anger is unreasonable, unfair, or unbecoming. *I cease to be angry.* Similarly, I can make myself angry at John by allowing myself to be convinced that he has wronged me. I can dwell on minor behavioral misdemeanors on John's part, building them into a pattern of overall deceit and abuse, and then become angry at any one or any number of these incidents.

Since normative judgments can be changed through influence, argument, and evidence, and since I can go about on my own seeking influence, provoking argument, and looking for evidence, I am as responsible for my emotions as I am for the judgments I make. My emotions *are* judgments I make. Now one might argue that all we have shown is that one can take steps to *cause* changes in his emotions, such as one can take steps to diminish a pain by pulling out a splinter or take steps to prevent being hit by a bus by crossing only on the proper signals. And it is true, of course, that one cannot *simply* choose to be angry or not to be angry, but can make himself angry or cease being angry only by performing other activities. But this is true of judgments in general: I cannot simply choose to judge a situation fortunate, awkward, or dangerous.[5] It is worth noting that I cannot *simply* perform most actions either: I cannot simply assassinate a dictator. I must do something else (pull the trigger of a rifle, let slip the string of a bow, push the button activating the detonator). Yet, although it is also true that I cause the death of the dictator (I do not cause the killing of him), I kill the dictator. Similarly, making judgments is something *I do*, not something that happens to me and not something I simply cause, even though I cannot *simply* make a judgment in many cases. (Legal judgments by an appropriately empowered judge or judiciary should *not* be taken as paradigm cases here.)

I must be in appropriate circumstances to pass judgment, have some evidence, know something of what the judgment is about. Of course, one can make judgments rashly, with minimal evidence and with superficial knowledge of what the judgment is about. Emotions, we can now see, are rash judgments, something I do, but in haste. Accordingly, the evidence upon which I become emotional is typically (but not necessarily) incomplete, and my knowledge of what I am emotional about is often (but again not necessarily) superficial. I can take any number of positive steps to change what I believe and what judgments I hold and tend to make. By forcing myself to be scrupulous in the search for evidence and knowledge of circumstance, and by training myself in self-understanding regarding my prejudices and influences, and by placing myself in appropriate circumstances, I can determine the kinds of judgments I will tend to make. I can do the same for my emotions.

II

Against the near-platitude "emotions are irrational," we want to argue that emotions are rational. This is not only to say that they fit into one's overall behavior in a significant way, that they follow a regular pattern (one's "personality"), that they can be explained in terms of a coherent set of causes. No doubt this is all true. But emotions, we have argued, are judgments, and so emotions can be rational in the same sense in which judgments can be rational. (Of course, judgments can be irrational, but only within the context of a rational activity.) Judgments are actions. Like all actions, they are aimed at changing the world. But, although the expression of a judgment may actually produce such a change, the judgment itself is more like the winding of the mainspring of an intention to change the world rather than the overt activity which will do so. But if emotions are judgments, and judgments are actions, though covert, then emotions, too, are actions, aimed at changing the world (whether or not their expression actually does succeed in changing the world). In other words, emotions are purposive, serve the ends of the subject, and consequently can be explained by reasons or "in-order-to" explanations.

Because emotions are usually thought to be occurrences that we suffer, the idea that emotions are purposive actions has not been given sufficient attention. But consider the following very familiar sort of case:

Joanie wants to go to a party; her husband does not. She begins to act bored and frustrated; he watches television. She resigns herself to reading, sighing occasionally. He asks if she has picked up some shirts from the laundry; she says "no." He flies into a rage. He needs shirts (he has hundreds). He needs one of *those* (they are all the same). She is negligent (she was busy). She takes advantage of him (she stays with him). Naturally, she rebels, but she is upset, with mixed guilt and anger. She thinks him unreasonable, impossible, and slightly neurotic. Their encounter is short-lived. She goes off to read; he settles back before the television. The party is out of the question.

What are we to say of this familiar sort of case? It appears to be given that the husband's anger is inappropriate to the incident. His being angry about his wife's failure to pick up his shirts seems unreasonable; and the *intensity* of his anger is most surely unwarranted. To this, the standard response, since well before Freud, has been to suppose that the husband is really angry about something else; perhaps he is redirecting anger from his day at his office—anger which could not be expressed as safely toward his superiors as it could to his wife. Or perhaps the anger is accumulated anger from weeks or months of minor marital frictions. Or perhaps, it might be suggested, the anger is caused by the fact that the husband is tired.

But, in this case—and many other cases—there is an alternative sort of explanation that is available and persuasive. The anger can be explained, not in terms of what it is "about" or what causes it, but in terms of its *purpose*. The husband, in this case, has *used* his anger to manipulate his wife. He has become angry "about" the shirts *in order to* get his wife's mind off the party and in order to stop her irritating reminders. His anger is not a disruption of his activities (watching television, refusing to go to the party) but a part of it, its winning strategy. The best explanation of his anger is not that it was caused by anything (although that is not precluded) and not that it was "about" anything in particular (although that is surely true), but that he got angry at his wife *in order* to continue watching television and in order to ensure that his refusal to go to the party would be successful.

But if emotions are rational and purposive, why is it that emotions are so often counterproductive and embarrassing to us, detours away from our aspirations and obstacles blocking our ambitions? Why do emotions so often appear as disruptions in our lives, threats to our successes, aberrations in our rational behavior? We can outline three distinct accounts of the apparent "irrationality" of emotions.

First, it is the situation in which one becomes emotional that is disruptive, a detour, an obstacle, a threat, and not the emotional response. Emotions are urgent judgments; emotional responses are emergency behavior. An emotional response occurs in a situation in which usual intentions are perverted or frustrated; and unusual response is necessary. The normative judgments involved in having an emotion are inseparable from the overall network of our motives, beliefs, and intentions. The fact that emotions typically lead to apparently "pointless" behavior is not a consequence of emotions being irrational, but a natural consequence of the fact that emotions are responses to unusual situations in which usual behavior patterns seem inappropriate. The intentions of an emotional reaction are not infrequently impossible. The angry or sad man may wish to undo the past; the lover may want to possess, and be possessed by, his loved one. This is why Sartre calls the emotions "magical transformations of the world." One can always reduce the range of his emotional behavior by developing stereotyped responses, by avoiding all unusual situations, or by treating every situation as "usual." These are common but perhaps pathological ways of choosing our emotions. But such common "control" is not the avoidance or the suppression of a wild psychic beast; it is simply the avoidance of situations (or recognition of situations) where one's usual behavior patterns will not suffice. Emotions are rational responses to unusual situations. They differ from "cool" judgments and normal, rational, deliberate action in that they are prompted in urgency and in contexts in which one's usual repertoire of actions and considered judgments will not suffice. An emotion is a necessarily hasty judgment in response to a difficult situation.

It must be added that the "hastiness" of a judgment does not entail that it is made quickly. For example, one can make a hasty judgment after weeks of halfhearted deliberation. Similarly, although emotions are typically urgent and immediate responses, one can become increasingly angry over a period of time, or one finds that an emotion that is formed in urgency is then maintained in full force for weeks or even years. But what distinguishes emotions from ordinary judgments is their lack of "cool," their seeming urgency, even after weeks of simmering and stewing. There are no cold emotions, no cool anger, no deliberate love. Emotions are always urgent, even desperate, responses to situations in which one finds oneself unprepared, helpless, frustrated, impotent, "caught." It is the situation, not the emotion, which is disruptive and "irrational."

Second, and consequently, emotions are short-term responses. Emotions are rational in that they fit into a person's overall purposive behavior. But this is not to say that a person's various purposes are always consistent or coherent. Short-term purposes are often in conflict with rather than a means toward the fulfillment of long-term purposes. My desire to drink at the reception may tend toward disaster regarding my meeting of the celebrity who is my reason for going to the reception. My desire to visit Peking may undermine my ambition to become an FBI agent. Similarly, emotions often serve short-term purposes that are in conflict with longer-term purposes. I may be angry with John because I feel I have been wronged, but this may be inconsistent with my desire to keep a close, unblemished friendship with John. I may love Mary, but this might be totally inconsistent with my intention to preserve my marriage, to remain celibate, or to concentrate on my writing. Thus, the husband in our example might succeed in staying home from the party by becoming angry, but break up his marriage in so doing. It is in this sense that emotions are "blind";

more accurately, they are *myopic*. Emotions serve purposes and are rational; but because the purposes emotions serve are often shortsighted, they appear to be nonpurposive and irrational on a larger view. For the sake of passion, we destroy careers, marriages, lives. Emotions are not irrational; people are irrational.

Third, there is an anthropological response to the idea that emotions are irrational In a society that places taboos on emotional behavior—condemns it in men and belittles it in women—it is only to be expected that emotions will be counter to ambitions. A society that applauds "cool" behavior will naturally require strategies that are similarly "cool." In such a society, emotional behavior appears as "irrational" because it is bad strategy, not because it is not purposive. Perhaps it is not at all difficult to envision a society in which *only* emotional behavior would appear rational—where only short-term emotional responses had any meaning at all. But it is surely not Anglo-American society, in which "reason is and ought to be the slave of the passions."

Against our view that emotions, as actions, are purposive and that a person chooses his emotions rather than being victimized by them, there is a uniquely powerful objection. A person cannot identify at the time the purpose of his emotion. The husband who uses his anger to manipulate his wife cannot identify the purpose as opposed to the object-cause of his anger. If he were to identify the manipulative function of his anger, the effect would be the destruction of his anger. One cannot be angry and know that his anger has a purpose.

This is much more, of course, than a mere pragmatic claim. It is certainly; true that the husband cannot tell his wife that his anger is purposive, for the very purpose of the anger is to distract his wife from that purpose. But the claim here is that the husband cannot even think to himself, "I am being angry in order to . . ." If the husband is unusually self-aware, he may know that he, in general, uses his anger to manipulate people; but he still cannot entertain that thought at the time of his anger and remain angry. If he does, he ceases to be angry and continues, at most, only to act angry—to feign anger.

One's inability to see the purpose of his emotion is a conceptual matter, just as before we pointed out that one cannot (conceptually) make certain judgments, such as the judgment the what he is angry about is not the case, or that the cause of his anger, where this is different from the object of his anger, is a sufficient explanation of his anger. We can now add to this list of conceptual inabilities the inability of one to suspect the *purpose* of his emotion. Now many philosophers would argue that, regarding intentional actions in general, one cannot fail to be aware of his motives and intentions at the time of acting. It would take us too far astray to argue against this view here but notice that this inability to notice one's purpose is not limited to emotions. Consider, for example, Nietzsche's account of belief in God as a belief whose function is to serve certain purposes (achievement of salvation; a basis for "slave-morality" and self-righteousness; to seek power). Yet, even if a purposive analysis of belief in God is true, this neither denies that people do in fact believe in God nor need it suggest that believers could state these purposes. To the contrary, we can add, if they were to think seriously that their belief was held to serve a purpose rather than because it was true, we would have to conclude that they did not believe at all (A conclusion that Nietzsche too easily comes to on the basis of an argument from the third-person to the first-person case). To believe is not to believe for a purpose; yet beliefs can still be purposive.

Judgments in general, not only emotions, can be purposive but cannot be recognized (by the person who makes them at the time that he makes them) as purposive. If I judge, calmly and deliberately, without a hint of that urgency and intensity that characterizes anger, that John has wronged me by stealing my car again (he does it all the time), I may be rationalizing an opportunity to take out John's wife. In fact, I may even say to myself, "Since he has wronged me so, I feel justified in taking out his wife." But I cannot believe that my judgment that John has wronged me has been made for this purpose. I can at most believe that since he has wronged me, I am justified. . . . Similarly, I may judge, calmly and deliberately, that Mary is a magnificent woman, attractive and intelligent, strong-willed and sensitive, but without the slightest hint of that urgency and intensity that characterizes love. But, knowing that Mary is John's wife, I may be so judging as a way of rationalizing an opportunity to run off with John's mistress. Now I may openly judge that John does not need his mistress, since his wife is so magnificent, and so I can feel justified in running off with his mistress. But I cannot believe that my judging that Mary is magnificent is made for this purpose. In other words, judgments, no matter how calm and deliberate, when they are made for some purpose (leaving open the question whether all are so made), cannot be recognized as having been made for a purpose. In this sense, all judgments are "blind." To recognize the purpose for which a judgment is made is to undermine the judgment. One cannot judge that he has been wronged and at the same time recognize that he has judged that he has been wronged only in order to. . . .

One must also consider apparently "unintentional" actions, to which emotions bear a striking resemblance. Some act-types allow for only intentional acts, for example, murder, fishing. Others allow for only unintentional acts, for example, forgetting, slipping, stumbling, tripping, losing—in short, most of those actions that make up the subject matter of what Freud calls the "psychopathology of everyday life." Yet Freud demonstrated that such "unintentional" actions function in a remarkable accordance with a subject's overall purposes and intentions. Freud surely does not want to say that these simply *appear* to be intentional (as some authors have argued, e.g., R. S. Peters, A. MacIntyre), but rather that they truly are intentional, the difference being, in his terms, the "inaccessibility" of the intention to the subject. The status of such actions remains a matter of controversy, but we feel reasonably confident that most philosophers and most everybody else would agree that such "actions" are indeed actions and can be demonstrated in at least some cases to be done for a purpose; yet the subject cannot state their purpose. And once again, the "cannot" is a *logical* "cannot," since a man who knows that he is losing his wedding ring in order to show his opinion of his marriage is making a gesture, not losing his ring. And a man who knows he is forgetting to call his office in order to avoid extra work is not forgetting but refusing to call his office. Thus we can see in what senses such actions may appear to be both intentional and "unintentional." They are intentional insofar as they clearly fit into the purposes and intentions of the subject; they appear to be unintentional insofar as they cannot be stated as purposive or intentional by the subject. Similarly, anger is purposive and intentional insofar as it can be clearly shown to fit into the structure of the subject's purposes and intentions; it appears to be "unintentional," and thus differs from many straightforward actions, in that these purposes and intentions cannot be known by the subject at the time. Emotions, when they are purposive and intentional, are essentially devious.

Can one feign anger? One might think, "Of course, act angry when you are not angry." But what is it that constitutes the anger apart from acting angry? The traditional answer to this is simple enough: a feeling. To feign anger is to act angry but not feel angry. To feign love is to act lovingly but not feel love. To feign an emotion would be, in general, to pretend one has a feeling which one does not have, as a child pretends—usually badly—to have a cramp in order to stay away from school. But we have seen that an emotion is not a feeling. This traditional analysis does lend support to our contention that to have an emotion in order to . . . is not to have that emotion. But, on our account, the difference is not due to the presence or lack of a feeling. Rather, to have an emotion is to make certain judgments; to feign an emotion, then, is to pretend that one holds certain judgments which one does not hold.

But this makes the notion of feigning emotion much more difficult than has been supposed on the simple "feeling" analysis. André Gide has written that feigned emotion and "vital" emotion are indistinguishable, and in this there is an often unseen giant of a truth, one that would appear absurd on the thesis that emotions are feelings. Miss Anscombe, replying to J. L. Austin, has distinguished between mock performances and real pretenses. The most obvious difference between the two is that one is intended to mislead others, the other not. Accordingly, the one should be more cautiously consistent and prolonged than the other: a successful mock performance may be announced as lasting only thirty-five seconds, a real pretense must go on as long as it must go on. But the most important difference between mock performances and real pretenses is the *context* (what we have been calling "the situation"). A mock performance may be performed on a stage, in any context in which it can be announced or in which it is evident that this is a *mere* pretense. A real pretense, however, requires that the context of performance be appropriate; anger can only be feigned in real pretense if the situation is one in which anger is appropriate. One can only pretend to be in love with someone whom it is plausible that he should love. But the appropriateness of the situation is not a causal determinant of a feeling of love or anger. Rather it is the context in which judgments of the requisite kinds make sense and are plausible. But if to feign anger is to act angry in a context in which the anger-related judgments are plausible, it is easy to see how one could, upon prolonged pretense, come to accept those very judgments. If, over a protracted period of time, I pretend to love a woman whom I have married for her father's wealth, it is more than likely that I shall grow to love her (if I do not first come to openly despise her). And if I pretend to be angry about a political issue in order to be accepted by my friends, it is not at all unlikely that I shall come to be really angry about that same issue. Perhaps there is no better way to choose to have an emotion than to decide to pretend that one has it. As Sartre has said, the best way to fall asleep is to pretend that you are asleep. And here, I think we may say that Gide's theory has a plausibility which cannot be explained on the idea that what one pretends to have is a feeling.

Emotions are intentional and rational, not disruptive and "irrational." Emotions are judgments and actions, not occurrences or happenings that we suffer. Accordingly, I want to say that emotions are choices and our responsibility. Yet I am never aware of making such a choice. Emotions, we argued, are hasty and typically dogmatic judgments. Accordingly, they cannot be made together with the recognition that they are dogmatic and not absolutely correct. What distinguishes emotions from other judgments is the fact that the former can never be deliberate and carefully considered. Emotions are essentially nondeliberate choices. Emotions, in this sense, are indeed "blind" as well as myopic; an emotion cannot see itself. Few things are more disconcerting than suddenly watching one's angry reflection in the mirror, or reflecting on one's anger to see its absurdity in media res.

If emotions are judgments or actions, we can be held responsible for them. We cannot simply have an emotion or stop having an emotion, but we can open ourselves to argument, persuasion, and evidence. We can force ourselves to be self-reflective, to make just those judgments regarding the causes and purposes of our emotions, and also to make the judgment that we are all the while *choosing* our emotions, which will "defuse" our emotions. This is not to opt for a life without emotions: it is to argue for a conception of emotions which will make clear that emotions are our choice. In a sense, our thesis here is self-confirming: to think of our emotions as chosen is to *make* them our choices. Emotional control is not learning to employ rational techniques to force into submission a brutal "it" which has victimized us but rather the willingness to become self-aware, to search out, and to challenge the normative judgments embedded in every emotional response. To come to believe that one has this power *is* to have this power.

In response to our argument, one might conclude that we have only argued that one can choose and is responsible for his *interpretation* of his situation and his emotions. But then I simply want to end by once again drawing Nietzsche to my side and quipping, with regard to emotions, "There are only interpretations . . . ."

Appendix (1980)

Against Plato and the rhetoricians (e.g., Gorgias), Aristotle defended the view that some emotions were both practical and intelligent (righteous anger, for example), *essentially* involving both goals and cognition.[6] Anger, for example, was a desire for vengeance because of an unjustified offense or slight.[7] Aristotle also developed a theory of the intentionality of emotions and understood the linkage between logic and rhetoric in changing emotions.[8] Centuries later, Seneca defended the view that emotions are judgments, within our power.[9] He then went on to chastise emotions as *irrational* judgments, incompatible with reason, and so promoted his Stoic concept of *apatheia*, in direct contrast to Aristotle, who took at least certain passions as essential to moral virtue and the *eudaimon* life.[10] The idea that emotions are akin to judgments and within the bounds of human responsibility is thus a very old theory. How pathetic, then, that the emotions have been so removed from their cognitive and activist moorings by modern philosophy, from Descartes's "animal spirits" to James's visceral spasms and Freud's "id." How this has happened is not my concern. But what does concern me—passionately—is to resurrect and defend the older view, with a decided existentialist twist.

"Emotions and Choice" (1973) was a polemic. It hit some raw nerves, but it soon became obvious that its bolder claims had to be qualified and defended by a far more detailed analysis of emotions, which I developed in *The Passions* (1976).[11] Subsequent discussions and criticisms convinced me that some of these claims require still further defense and modification, but I remain convinced that no noncognitive view of emotions will ever allow us to understand them[12] and no view that does not involve the idea of responsibility will have any but a deleterious effect on both moral philosophy and psychology. But let me review the arguments.

Emotions are Intentional

In "Emotions and Choice," my defense of the distinction between the object and cause(s) of emotion had to take priority over a careful analysis of intentionality. At the time the notion of intentionality was under severe attack, and several articles and books have straightforwardly attempted to eliminate this notion altogether by reducing all talk of "objects" to accounts in terms of causes.[13] The motivation behind this attack has turned in part on well-known historical abuses of "intentionality" and a recent fetish for extensional accounts, as well as a reaction against the still platitudinous obscurity surrounding that sacramental concept in the writings of some phenomenologists. But more importantly, it was a reaction against the now classic account of the intentionality of emotions suggested by Anthony Kenny in his *Action, Emotion and Will* (1963).[14] Kenny analyzed emotions as intentional feelings: what he did not provide was any way of understanding how it might be possible for a "feeling" to be intentional. Kenny argued, following a tradition that stretches back to Aristotle (if not Plato),[15] that there must be a *formal* connection between the feeling and its object; but again he provided us with no understanding how this might be possible.[16] And, finally, pointing out that some emotions clearly have "inexistent" objects (for example, emotions concerning the future), he disastrously concludes that the objects of *all* emotions must be understood in terms of "a special non-causal sense." Kenny rightly insists on the distinction between objects of emotions and their causes, but he gives no adequate analysis of "a special non-causal sense." Thus he provokes one recent critic to accuse him of rendering the connection between emotion and object, and the notion of "object" itself, both "otiose" and "mysterious."[17]

What is needed is an account of the intentionality of emotions which avoids these obscurities. Accordingly, the opening move of *The Passions* is one of ontological frugality; the distinction between cause and object is made to be functional, not a distinction between two types of entities. The traditional emphasis on existence and "inexistence" of emotional objects is replaced by a phenomenological concept of "subjectivity," where the emphasis is wholly on the idea of an object *as experienced*.[18] Whether an experience also provides an accurate account of the world is not part of an analysis of either emotions or their intentionality, although it may enter into discussions of their rationality or their justification. Whether the description of the object can also function as a description of the cause of an emotion, in other words, in a causal explanation, is also something other than the analysis of emotion requires. But this is not to say anything about the identity of cause and object. The notion of intentionality is ontologically innocent.

The simpleminded disjunction between the existence or "inexistence" of emotional objects and discussions thereof has a more disastrous consequence. Consider, for example, the Freudian claim that a certain young man, Dorian, does not in fact love his wife but his mother. Whether or not this claim is defensible in general, whether or not it is defensible in this particular case, it is clear that here we have a critical test case for any analysis of the emotion of love: What characteristics are essential for the love of a particular "object"/person? But what is clearly not at stake is any question about the ontological status of the disputed object, only its phenomenological ("subjective") identity in the eyes of Dorian. In this way, the concept of intentionality opens up a rich field of new investigations: to ontologize is to forfeit them.

To account for the fact that emotions are intentional, I reject Kenny's claim that emotions are a species of feelings and insist that emotions are a species of judgments. This explains, as no "feeling" analysis could, how it is that emotions are "about" the world in a "noncausal sense." It also explains, in a nonmysterious way, why so many authors (Aristotle, Hume, and Kenny, for instance) have felt compelled to insist upon the "formal" connection between emotion and object and the "essential" or "natural" connections between emotions and beliefs. What a judgment is about defines the judgment. Similarly, what an emotion is about defines the emotion.

In "Emotions and Choice," I attack what I call a "components" analysis of emotions, for just this reason. As soon as one distinguishes between the "feeling" of emotion and its object, as Kenny does, for example, there is no way to understand either how emotions intend their objects or how their objects define emotions.[19] In *The Passions*, I counter this "components" view by developing a (quasi-Heideggerian) notion of what I call "surreality," a theory of intentional structures, given conceptual shape by judgments of a number of specifiable types which I there describe in detail. In "Emotions and Choice," the nature of these intentional structures is not discussed, and so my attack on the "components" view and the analysis of intentionality remain dangerously incomplete.

Emotions Are Judgments

This is the key slogan of my entire campaign, but as a slogan, it should not be taken as a theory as such. I repeatedly insist that emotions *essentially* involve desires, expectations, purposes, and attitudes. Emotions are motivated by desires, sometimes distinguished by desires, and in virtually every case some desire is essential to an emotion. But I take this claim to be so widely accepted—even by Descartes, to whom I am most vehemently opposed[20]—that I saw little point in defending it. But it certainly does not follow that by so "opening up" my analysis beyond the "emotions are judgments" slogan I am thereby bound to include also dispositions to behave and feelings and all sorts of things.[21] It is the heart of my argument that "feelings" and physiology and, with qualifications, dispositions to behave, do *not* play an essential role in the constitution of emotions and cannot be used in even the most rudimentary account of the definitive properties of either emotions in general or particular emotions. My central claim is that emotions are defined primarily by their constitutive judgments, given structure by judgments, distinguished as particular emotions (anger, love, envy, etc.) as judgments,[22] and related to other beliefs, judgments, and our knowledge of the world, in a "formal" may, through judgments. No alternative theory, it seems to me, has ever made the slightest progress in explaining the central features of emotion, as opposed to their red-in-the-face and visceral cramp symptomatology.

We often think of "making a judgment" as a distinctively deliberate act; to counter this, I argued in "Emotions and Choice" that emotional judgments are essentially nonreflective and prior to deliberation. This was, however, an overreaction, and in *The Passions* I discussed several examples of deliberate emotions, for example, making oneself angry. In the book I also stress the affinities between my notion of judgment and Kant's concept of "constitutive judgment," but what is "constituted" in emotions is not knowledge but meanings. In my more recent work, I prefer to talk more in terms of emotions setting up "scenarios," within which our experiences and our actions are endowed with personal meaning. Each emotion, so characterized, is a specifiable set of judgments constituting a specific scenario. Anger, for example, is to be analyzed in terms of a quasi-courtroom scenario, in which one takes the role of judge, jury, prosecuting attorney, and, on occasion, executioner. ("I'll be judge, I'll be jury, said cunning old fury."—Lewis Carroll, *Alice in Wonderland*.) The object of anger is the accused, the crime is an offense,[23] and the overall scenario is one of judgmental self-righteousness. (One might add that the court is almost of the kangaroo variety, with self-esteem taking clear priority over justice.) The scenario helps to explain, among other matters, the tendency to self-righteousness in anger, which in turn can be used to explain the motivation of petty anger and "bad tempers" and provide, in general, the beginning of a functional account of emotions. In the context of "Emotions and Choice," the scenario analysis provides a far more complete portrait of emotional experience than the bald claim, "Emotions are judgments."

With these additions, it is possible to map out a refutation of the most common objection to my theory, which is that it is possible to make a judgment, the same judgment that I claim to be constitutive of an emotion, and not have that emotion. If that is true, then emotions cannot be judgments.[24] But an emotion is never a single judgment but a system of judgments, and although one might well make one or several judgments of the system without having the emotion, my claim is that one cannot make *all* of them and not have the emotion. To make all essential judgments is to create the relevant scenario and take one's part in it. Of course, one might simply act *as if* one were taking part, but the distinction between pretending and really taking part is none too clear, as I argued in "Emotions and Choice," and insofar as one is merely acting, the set of judgments, and thus the scenario, cannot possibly be completed (This example shows why it is so important that the scenario be understood as a way of experiencing a situation and not as the situation itself—as it might be described by others, for example.) Finally, to have an emotion requires not only a specifiable set of judgments but certain desires as well. One might make a judgment—or even much of a set of judgments[25]—in an impersonal and uninvolved way, without caring one way or the other. But an emotional (set of) judgment(s) is necessarily personal and involved. Compare "What he said to me was offensive" (but I don't care what he thinks) and "He offended me!" Only the latter is constitutive of anger. (The first is a judgment about the perlocutionary act potential of a certain utterance; the latter is, in part, a judgment about my own self-esteem.)

Emotions and Choice

My most cavalier move in "Emotions and Choice" was my easy inference from "emotions are judgments" to the idea that we "choose" them. The suppressed sequence of moves was something like this: emotions are judgments and we "make" judgments; ergo emotions are activities, and activities are "doings"; "doings" are voluntary and what is voluntary is chosen. So, emotions are chosen. I agree with my critics that this is much too glib, much of it unsound, and I tried to weaken the argument accordingly in the book. I do insist, even in the essay, that emotions, like many activities, cannot "simply" be done. (One cannot "simply" decide to love someone.) But this is not enough.[26] I still insist that emotions, as judgments, are a species of activity, and thus to be included on the "active" side of the all-too-simple "active–passive" disjunction according to which we evaluate most human affairs. This means, too, that emotions fall into the realm of responsibility, so that it always makes sense, at least (as it does not, for example, for headaches, heart attacks, and hormones) to praise or blame a person, not just for contributing to the situation that caused the emotion but, in some sense to be worked out, for having the emotion itself, as one blames a person for bigotry, for example, or praises them for their courage. What I now question is the once seemingly innocuous move from "activities" to "doings," and I reject the subsequent moves to "voluntary," then to "chosen." Perception, for example, is an activity: I am not sure that it is something "done," and (as opposed to an activity such as "looking for") I am sure that it makes little sense to ask whether perceiving something is voluntary, much less a matter of choice. Intractable emotions[27] must be treated similarly; they are still matters of judgment, and as such, activities and matters of responsibility. But they are surely neither voluntary nor chosen. My account in *The Passions* is in terms of emotional "investments," the "cost" of giving up certain emotions.[28] But what this shows is that the whole question of choice and voluntariness, outside of the overworked realm of intentional action, has yet to be pursued successfully.

In the essay, and even in the book, I say far too little about the sociocultural determinants of emotions, the extent to which the essential sets of judgments and desires are shared, restricted, suppressed, or encouraged within a given society. Accordingly, some of my most recent work has been more anthropological apprenticeship than philosophical analysis.[29] From this, I want to add to my thesis the sense in which emotions are cultivated responses, within whose limits one is responsible even if they were learned in childhood and so seem entirely "natural." This certainly places harsh restrictions on my original "choice" thesis, but I still take the notion of responsibility as inescapably central.

Emotions Are Purposive

In "Emotions and Choice," I insist that emotions can be accounted for in terms of "in order to" type explanations. This is suggested by the fact that desires are part of emotions. What I do not do in that essay, but attempt in the book, is to provide an overall theory about the function of emotions. In a phrase, it is the *maximization of self-esteem*.[30] The concept of self-esteem serves two very different purposes in my theory. First, it is part of my characterization of emotions as judgments that they be personally involved judgments, and this can be further elaborated in terms of self-esteem. Second, I offer an empirical hypothesis about the motivation of emotions—emotions serve self-esteem. This is not the place to pursue these claims, since they play a relatively negligible role in "Emotions and Choice." But it is necessary to point out that (1) to say that emotions have a certain purpose or function does not require that there always be an intention as such. Often, even usually, emotions do include such (implicit) intentions; sometimes they clearly don't. (2) To say that the purpose of emotions is to maximize self-esteem is not to say that they always—or even usually—succeed in this. Resentment and spite, for example, can be easily argued to be desperate attempts at self-esteem, but it can also be argued that they usually fail. (3) Emotions are ready candidates for self-deception, and sometimes the goal of an emotional strategy is exactly the opposite of what it seems to be. Resentment, guilt, and depression (a mood) are examples. (4) There are examples that raise difficulties for the claim, for example, grief.[31] A man who loses his son in an accident does not grieve to increase his self-esteem, to be sure, but the difference between an appropriate sense of loss and the emotion of grief may be considerable, and it is in this difference that self-esteem plays a weighty motivational role. After a certain point, grief becomes feeling sorry for oneself, and here the strategy for self-esteem becomes evident.

Much more could be added, but let me just present my minimal claim: every emotion is at least a candidate for a purposive account (which can't even be made sense of on the traditional theories). It always makes sense to ask "What is motivating that emotion?" and, at least usually, part of the answer will involve an appeal to self-esteem.

My preliminary example in part II of "Emotions and Choice" involves a serious error. In the book, I make a point of distinguishing purposive explanations of the *expression* of emotion (e.g., using angry behavior to intimidate someone) and purposive explanations of the emotion itself (e.g., to maximize self-esteem through the self-righteousness of anger). In my example of marital politics in the essay, I conflate the two.

Emotions Are Rational

Emotions require rationality (the ability to manipulate concepts) but they may be said to be rational or *ir*rational (opposed to *non*-rational) in a second sense, according to whether they succeed or fail to satisfy certain purposes or functions. In the essay, I discuss only the coherence, consistency, and completeness of the evidence in the making of emotional judgments. There are also questions about the *warrant* to making certain claims (e.g., a "right" to something in jealousy,[32] or whether something is or is not *worth* getting angry about). What must be added are questions about the maximization of self-esteem: resentment and spite are usually irrational because they fail to maximize self-esteem. Moral indignation, however, succeeds rather well. But one must also add the "external" consideration of social utility; hatred and love might equally raise self-esteem, but the social cost of hatred is considerable—divisive and destructive. Any account of the rationality of emotions must take into account these features as well as others,[33] and by the time we have done this, we will have in effect developed a full-scale moral theory and done a good deal of philosophical anthropology as well.

2

On Physiology and Feelings (1976)

> ... our feeling of [bodily] changes as they occur *is* the emotion
> William James

> ... these [visceral] disturbances cannot serve as a means for discriminating between ... emotions.
> W. B. Cannon

Of course, it is true that every emotion has its distinguishable neurological correlates.[1] Or at least there is utterly no reason to believe that it is not true, at least in some sense.[2] But what does that have to do with *my* having an emotion? Most philosophers would be a little too quick to say "nothing," assuming that our concept of an "emotion" included only those properties which are commonly recognized by virtually all speakers of the language. It is easy enough to show that our everyday concept of "emotion" has no *logical* connections with neurology. For example, Aristotle could identify his emotions perfectly well without knowing the first thing about neurophysiology; he thought their physiological source was the heart, not the brain. The "man on the street" probably knows less about the workings of his brain than Descartes did three hundred years ago; yet he has an adequate conceptual grasp of the language of emotions. But this facile argument is worth far less than many philosophers have thought. It may be a "knock-down" argument where "ordinary" language is concerned, but it arbitrarily excludes the idea of *embellishment* of our present-day conception (something short of a *change* of concepts) by physiological knowledge, an embellishment that has proceeded rapidly in the past decade but which was beginning even with Aristotle. We all know that certain chemicals—alcohol, Dexedrine, barbiturates, hashish, and mescaline—alter our states of consciousness considerably, and we have an idea of how they do this: they affect certain centers in the brain, speed them up, slow them down, open them up. As this admittedly crude knowledge of neurology progresses, there is no reason to doubt that, several generations from now, the man on the street will have a language of emotions heavily embedded in neurological jargon.[3] There is only a difference in the precision of the knowledge now increasingly embellishing our conception of emotions and the knowledge that will embellish the conceptions held by our grandchildren. And the difference between our knowledge and that of Aristotle is a matter of precision, not ignorance versus knowledge. I do not wish to make it sound as if the very recent science of psychoneurology is doing no more than mopping up details, that, from within the scope of that science, there are no "qualitative" leaps in our knowledge—almost yearly. My point is only that the situation is not as if we now have *no* knowledge that affects our conception of our emotions; even Aristotle knew that heavy drink made a man insensitive and potentially brutal, and his thesis that the emotions are "more primitive" than the clarity of reason surely included this essential correlation between drunkenness and the emotions. Similarly, we also know that our emotional lives become much richer with certain drugs, much more "open" with others, and are virtually paralyzed with yet others. It is this knowledge that provides the basis for much of our thinking about the emotions, particularly what we have called the hydraulic theory. These are also precisely the considerations that led James and Lange to their now famous theory of the emotions—to the effect that an emotion is *nothing but* our awareness of these chemical and physiological changes in our bodies. (Lange, in particular, stresses these arguments.) Our problem, therefore, is to understand the role of this "objective" knowledge in the subjective conception of ourselves.

The most tempting thesis, and a most disastrous one, is simply to accept the "objective" findings of neurology as the exclusive truth and to incorporate these findings into one's self-conception, relegating "feelings" and the subjective components of emotion to the role of "illusions" or "epiphenomenal affects." This was the thesis argued by James and Lange, and it dominated psychological thinking for thirty years. That thesis is, in its most basic form, that the physiology of emotion is primary, and the "emotion felt" a secondary consequence; it is, in James's words, "the priority of the bodily symptoms to the felt emotion":

> Our natural way of thinking about these standard emotions is that the mental perception of some fact excites the mental affection called the emotion, and that this latter state of mind gives rise to the bodily expression. My thesis on the contrary is that the bodily changes follow directly the Perception of the exciting fact, and that our feeling of the same changes as they occur *is* the emotion.
> William James, "What Is an Emotion?"

The James-Lange thesis was proven to be incorrect on physiological grounds, primarily by W. B. Cannon (1927), who argued conclusively that the same visceral and neurological changes accompanied very different emotional states and that artificial induction of these changes did not produce the appropriate emotions:

> Since visceral processes are fortunately not a considerable source of sensation, since even extreme disturbances in them yield no noteworthy emotional experience, we can further understand now why these disturbances cannot serve as a means for discriminating between such profound emotions as fear and rage,

why chilliness, asphyxia, hyperglycemia and fever, though attended by these disturbances, are not attended by emotion. . . .

Related experiments have often been repeated since, each time with a sense of "break-through," so entrenched is the *kind* of thinking that the James-Lange thesis represents in contemporary psychology. That thinking is fundamentally to pay close attention to the tangible and mechanical; and to neglect or ignore what is glibly and conciliatory designated as "the emotion felt." It should not come as a surprise that the refutation of the James-Lange thesis almost exactly coincided with the upsurge of behaviorism in America;[4] having lost the warrant to identify the emotions with physiological processes, psychologists turned to the equally tangible equation of the emotions and their behavioral expressions. If decidedly different emotions could not be distinguished on the basis of their physiological correlates, perhaps one could do so on the basis of their behavioral expression, still without entering the forbidden realm of subjectivity.

Since Cannon's discrediting of the James-Lange theory, the particular error of identifying the emotions with the epiphenomenal affects of physiological changes in the body has not been a problem. But the danger of the James-Lange thesis was not dependent on its particular claims so much as on its overall tendency to incorporate into our conception of ourselves and into our own emotions concepts which were wholly neglectful of subjectivity. The opposing position, far more popular among philosophers than psychologists, is no better—that the "emotion felt" *is* the emotion, as if neurology had *nothing* to do with it.

This is why I began by warning that our everyday emotional conceptions are not exclusive of quasi-neurological knowledge and influence. So long as we focus on the technical disputes between those who believe that emotional reactions are centered in the hypothalamus and those who more conservatively defend the role of the thalamus, the relevance of neurology to our conceptions of our own emotions will be negligible. But turn instead to our everyday experiences with neurology, leaving the "localization" and the neural and endocrine mechanisms of these processes for the experts, and the problem is much more interesting. At the present time, narrowly neurological conceptions have virtually no role in our subjectivity, excepting a small number of professional neurologists and hypochondriacs.

Consider: This morning I drank three cups of coffee. (My "limit" is one cup.) I was "wired" and irritable; I growled at my students and bitched to the personnel office; I almost got into a fight with another driver and sent my lunch at Gino's back to the "kitchen" with an angry complaint. My students were innocent; the matter at the personnel office was the usual red tape which I wade through unthinkingly every morning; it was I and not the other driver who had been inconsiderate; and the lunch at Gino's was just another lunch at Gino's. Yet I was angry in each case—or had some related emotion (I was *impatient* with my students but indignant with the personnel office). Now, the philosopher's argument that the charging up of my limbic system is irrelevant to my anger is no doubt correct. But what of these cases? My coffee drinking quite obviously *caused* my anger in each case. The general relationship between my drinking too much coffee and my being "irritable" is well known to me. And afterward, at least with my students, I will surely apologize and dismiss my irritation with them as "just the coffee" or "just irritation," not anger *with them* at all. Was this, because of the cause, not "really" anger at all? What does my knowledge of the *cause* have to do with my conception of my anger?

The answers to these questions can only be anticipated, since I have yet to provide a general account of the nature of an emotion in which the concept of "cause" can be given its place. But the following can be said: *Whatever* the cause, my emotion itself is "real"—I should say "surreal." That is, I am angry with my students *because* of my having had too much coffee, but I am angry nonetheless. My after-the-fact apology is surely justified, but my denial that "I was 'really angry'" or that "I was angry *at them*" is not. That is my *excuse*—my attempt to blame the coffee (or possibly to accept the blame for having let myself be given the second and third cups). I was really angry, but unjustifiably so. It is the *unjustifiability* of my anger that requires the apology. The coffee, the cause, has nothing to do with it. If this were not the case, then one could plead innocence to all his emotions! We all accept, in some form or another, the neurologist's claim that all of our emotions have their neurological causes. And even though we don't have the foggiest notion what such causes might be, we accept the claim that *every* emotion has its sufficient neurological cause, thus allowing us to excuse ourselves from "really" having that emotion in every case. But this is absurd. Whether I am angry or not, in love or not, jealous or not, has nothing to do with whether or not my anger, my love, or my jealousy has been caused. We may presume, in every case, that it has. But my emotion has nothing to do with the fact that it is caused. (With even this simple understanding of this "excuse" system, one can see why the hydraulic model, which is nothing other than a system of providing, in every case, some such causal excuse, will be so well worth our constant opposition.)

To say that physiological cause has nothing to do with emotion or that *the fact that* an emotion is caused by some physiological alteration has nothing to do with the (sur) "reality" of the emotion is not yet to say that my *knowledge* of such causes and facts has nothing to do with the emotion. In retrospect, I remembered the fact that I had drunk three cups of coffee, and knowing the effect coffee always has on my temperament, I then understood *why* I had gotten so unusually irritated that day. But suppose that I had come to that realization during, not after, the period of my anger. What would have happened then? I would have stood in my class, fidgety and cranky, but fully aware that I was likely to find fault where there was none. I would have become impatient when there was no reason for it, and I would accordingly *cancel* all such emotions as they appeared (perhaps warning my students as well). My knowledge of the cause *undermines* my emotion. I am still irritable, but I do not allow myself to be irritable *about* anything or *at* anyone. I am simply irritable. In retrospect, I cannot cancel the "aboutness" of my irritability and deny my anger; but in the process of becoming angry I surely can do so. And so, coupled with the thesis that the cause of my emotion has nothing to do with the emotion, there is a second thesis, superficially contrasted with it: my knowledge of the cause of my emotion tends to undermine the emotion. This is a partial explanation of the fact that apparently any crackpot psychotherapy, no matter how absurd its theories or ludicrous (or lucrative) its practices, tends to have a calming effect on the emotions. It is the attribution of a cause, *any* cause, that does it.

One of the best-known psychophysiological experiments concerning the emotions performed in recent years was that carried out by S. Schachter and J. E. Singer. They injected their subjects with epinephrine—the adrenal secretion that is responsible for the most marked sensations of emotions (flushing, pulsating, anxiousness)— and then provided different subjects with different social situations. What was "discovered" was that the physiological changes and their accompanying sensations had nothing to do with the differentiation of the emotion, a conclusion reached by Cannon thirty years before. In fearful circumstances, the injected subject reported feeling fear; in offensive circumstances, he reported feeling anger. For those who continue to cling to the art of experimentation as the only source of truth, here is an empirical foundation for the claims that I shall be making "subjectively," that the chemistry of the body and the sensations caused by that chemistry have in themselves nothing to do with the emotions.[5] But it is also worth heeding the warnings of equally experimentally oriented critics of that experiment, who rightly comment that the "injection procedure limits the conclusions that can be drawn about emotion in the normal life situation."[6] To put it mildly. Apart from the students' minor trauma of injection and the artificial sterility of the laboratory, there is a logical thesis that is relevant here; namely, the *knowledge* that their emotions have been caused by the injection is already sufficient to undermine the emotions themselves.

There are other causes of emotion besides physiological causes, and an adequate defense of the two theses above should wait for a more general account. (See chap. 8, sec. 2.) My purpose here has been only to show the simplemindedness of the two usual methods of dealing with the relationship between emotions and physiology— reducing the former to the consciousness manifestations of the latter or denying the relevance of the latter to the former altogether. Matters are not so simple. We are not simply hydraulic mechanisms, voltage cells, or boilers who happen to have this curious attachment, consciousness—like a galvanometer attached to the cell or a valve on the boiler—that passively registers the pressures within. But neither are we Cartesian spirits, attached to our pumping and pulsing bodies through a thin passage in a minor gland at the base of our brains, for whom the workings of the physical world are a matter of interest but, so far as our passions are concerned, of no relevance. What we know partially determines what we "feel," and this is as true of the workings of our brains as it is of our circumstances.

2. Emotions as Feelings and Sensations

With or without the hydraulic model, the most common and even unquestionable thesis among nonpsychologists is that emotions are *feelings* of a special kind, typically conjoined with certain specific and readily identifiable sensations.[7] Even our language embodies this identity: we "feel" angry or jealous; love and hate are our "feelings" for other people; disappointments and insults "hurt our feelings." But this linguistic phenomenon is only the result, not the origin, of this familiar and trivially obvious equation. Whatever the hidden "dynamics" of the emotions, their essential manifestation is thought to be *in consciousness as feelings*. (Thus, Freud constantly complained that his view of "the Unconscious" flew in the face of common sense and the usual "way of talking" *(façon de parler)*.

It is obvious that "being in a passion" and "becoming emotional" are regularly associated with certain feelings and sensations, the flushing and pulsing and tightness of the throat, tensions in our arms and legs and mild cramping in the stomach, slight breathlessness and nausea, an over-all feeling of readiness and excitement. But it does not follow from this regular association that these feelings and sensations *are* the emotion. Thus, I have noted that Freud and a great many other psychologists augment the Jamesian claim that an emotion is simply an affect (that is, simply a feeling) with some version of the hydraulic theory that would allow that an emotion also has a role in the dynamics of the personality (for example, as energy or instinct, as motive or cognitive appraisal). However predictable the association of feelings and emotion, the feelings no more constitute or define the emotion than an army of fleas constitutes a homeless dog. They are always there, take the shape of the emotion, but just as easily move from one emotion to another (love to hate, fear to anger, jealousy to resentment). Feeling is the ornamentation of emotion, not its essence.

It is easy to appreciate this in a simple "introspective" way (although it has been given more objective experimental support in the Schachter-Singer experiment discussed in the previous section). What is the difference in feeling between a common pair of emotions—for example, embarrassment and shame? People are rarely, if ever, confused about which emotion they "have," but, when asked to differentiate between them, they find themselves speechless. Of course, one might say that differences in feelings and sensations are typically difficult to articulate, like the slight difference in taste between two bottles of wine that are so easily distinguishable but about which one has no vocabulary to express the difference. But this is not the problem; emotions are not distinguished by discriminating one set of feelings and sensations from another. In fact, the feelings and sensations associated with the one emotion may be, and usually are, no different from those associated with the other. But now imagine two situations. In the first, you are standing in line to board a bus when a crowd behind you pushes you abruptly and you fall, unable to catch yourself, into an elderly woman, knocking her into the rain-soaked gutter. In the second, obeying a malicious whim, you push her—with the same result. Following both incidents, you find yourself confronting an irate elderly woman and suffering from an intense feeling of . . . of what? In the first case, obviously embarrassment; in the second, shame. But how can we even guess what we would *feel* in some hypothetical example? How can we be so sure which is which? Because the feelings and sensations involved in the two emotions are of little relevance to discriminating between emotions. What allows us to do so is what I shall call the "logic" of the situation. Briefly, the first case is one of embarrassment because it is a situation in which, though we find ourselves in an awkward situation, we see no need to take responsibility for that situation. In the second case, we recognize our own action—however "spontaneous" and unthinking—as the cause of the situation: we are responsible. Of course, there are feelings in both cases; they might even, upon close inspection, have some differences between them. (Perhaps shame involves more constriction of the throat, and embarrassment includes more flushing. Physiologists, for example, have separated two distinct adrenal secretions, one more prevalent in "fight" reactions and the other more prevalent in "flight" reactions; presumably there would be some differences in feeling as well.) But the emotions are not merely the feelings, and the feelings are not what distinguishes one emotion from another. (The same sort of argument applies to any number of other emotion pairs—for example, love and hate, anger and indignation, resentment and envy, sadness and remorse, guilt and despair.)

A second objection to this familiar equation between emotions and feelings consists of the simple fact that we often have an emotion without experiencing any particular feeling. Anger or envy may be sufficiently subdued, perhaps with the long discipline of suppression, perhaps simply because it is long-established and familiar—still as powerful as it was in the beginning, but no longer given to "outbursts" of intensity and feeling. In fact, we sometimes find that our passion is so intense that we can feel absolutely nothing. In the most extreme indignation, one finds oneself completely numb. In panic, running from fear, one might find that one feels nothing. Or, more positively, there are those tender moments of love after "making love" when all the feeling has been drained from us, but the emotion is at its peak. Emotions may typically involve feelings. They may even essentially involve feelings. But feelings are never sufficient to identify or to differentiate emotions, and an emotion is never simply a feeling. One can have an emotion without feeling anything, and one can feel anything (including all of the "symptoms" of emotionality, for example, flushing, pulsing) without having any emotion whatever.

The close association of emotions and feelings is symptomatic of a dangerous misrepresentation of the emotions. There are, of course, those impassioned or emotional states of crisis and urgency, in which emotional *feeling* is at its height as a consequence of the preparatory posture we assume, for example, immediately before we allow months of "pent-up" anger to "explode." Such crises are apparent as one approaches an object of fear, ready for the decisive battle, or as I confess an obsessive love to the person I once thought I knew, but who now stands before me in ominous and foreign silence. But having an emotion is not limited to these moments of crisis. A person might be angry for years about some betrayal in youth, for decades at parental offenses in childhood scarcely remembered, for months about a friend's careless insult now stale (but still true). Surely through that duration there are no characteristic and continuous feelings; in fact, one might well feel nothing at all during that entire period and face no situation which would bring matters to a head and force the confrontation within which such feelings typically appear. Anger may "erupt" only in certain isolated moments, but the anger may exist for years, unexpressed and even unrecognized, as one of the defining structures of our existence. Resentment may on occasion manifest itself in the venom of public persecutions and temporary moments of viciousness, but most of the time it hides unobtrusively at the very foundation of our world, giving that all-too-familiar defensive posture and bitter taste to every act and statement. A romance which attempts to maintain itself on the peaks of crisis of uncertainty and doubt is not the prototype of love despite its frequency in "romantic" novels and in our more adolescent adventures. Of course, love at its best does not remain unperturbed and without feeling, but surely it is a serious if not neurotic misunderstanding to think that love is "true" only when it is in a state of crisis. To the contrary, love, like anger and resentment, is most "true" precisely in those moments of calm and continuity, when it is not called upon to defend itself or prove its existence. An emotion is not a crisis; that is, as if one said, continuing our quasi-architectural metaphor, a structure has strength only in those moments when it is threatened with collapse. That indeed may provide the *test* of the structure, but not the structure itself.

Philosophers commonly distinguish between "episodic" and "dispositional" mental concepts, the former designating episodes or occurrences, the latter not designating but rather acting as "inference tickets" to various possible episodes. (For example, the breaking of a glass is an episode, but the brittleness that makes possible the breaking of the glass is a disposition.) But this very influential distinction already contains within it the misunderstanding described above: the idea that an emotion is *either* an "episode" or occurrence *or* a disposition for those episodes or occurrences. To argue that an emotion is an occurrence is surely a misunderstanding of emotions (my anger is not simply my "getting angry"), but so is the idea that an emotion is a disposition to have certain feelings. My emotion is a structure of my world, which may at times manifest itself in certain specific displays of feeling or behavior. But my emotion *is* neither such displays nor the disposition to such displays.

It is worth noting, by the way of a clue rather than a full-blown argument, that we often say of our emotions that they are "reasonable" and "unreasonable," "warranted" and "unwarranted," "justifiable" and "unjustifiable," "legitimate" and "illegitimate," "sensible" and "foolish," "self-demeaning" and "enhancing," and even "right" and "wrong." Yet no such evaluations are appropriate in the realm of headaches and bellyaches, warm flushes and nausea. Headaches are neither reasonable nor unreasonable; there is no such thing as a "sensible" flush; it is never right or wrong to be nauseous. Yet we say without hesitation that "you were wrong to be angry at him," that "he was unjustified in being jealous," that "loving her was the wrong thing to do." And although one wants to be careful about taking ordinary attitudes toward emotions as a philosophical argument (considering how often we are "ordinarily" wrong about the emotions in other ways), these sorts of evaluations should give us a further reason to reject the seemingly indisputable thesis that emotions are mere feelings, occurrences that happen to us beyond our own control. Feelings and occurrences are not "reasonable" or "unreasonable." They simply *are*. Only what we *do* can be so assessed.

A further argument against the identity of emotions and feelings is this: It is obvious that we are frequently mistaken about our emotions. We deny that we are angry when there is every reason to suppose that we are; we laugh at the idea that we are in love when even the laughter itself, hysterical and defensive, is further proof of our affections. We feign anger and fool even ourselves, realize after years of apparent tenderness that what seemed to be love was not love, believe that we are self-righteously indignant when we find that we are envious or resentful. We sometimes think ourselves depressed when we are really angry, sympathetic when we are being vicious, loving when we are jealous and possessive, merely sad when in fact we are guilty or depressed. We think ourselves, perhaps, angry at the cat when we are angry with the policeman who has just given us a stiff speeding ticket; we think we love a wife when (if Freud is right) we really love only our mothers. Such complex and common mistakes would be difficult to understand if they were simply misinterpretations of various feelings or complexes of feelings. One is rarely mistaken about his having a headache or a toothache, about a feeling of queasiness or nausea, the dullness that comes with a hangover, or the giddiness that follows the inhalation of hashish. Of course, there may be mistakes here as well, due to inexperience or a confusion of sensations. But mistakes are neither so common nor so complex as in the case of emotions. This is a phenomenon that will be understood only when we have said something more about the structure of emotions. But as a piece of evidence, it should already give another clue to the conclusion that emotions are something far more sophisticated than mere feelings.

3

The Rationality of the Emotions (1977)

For Frithjof Bergmann

> . . . as if every passion didn't contain its quantum of reason.
> Friedrich Nietzsche

"I didn't mean it; I didn't know what I was doing. I acted without thinking; I acted irrationally. I was emotionally upset." How often we hear that! And, without attempting a refutation, we sense its falsity, the hollow desperation that accompanies a feeble and halfhearted excuse. "I was emotionally upset"; that is the touchstone of a cop-out plea of momentary insanity. But we know better; not only did you "mean it," but that single ephemeral "lapse," as you call it, was more full of meaning than the years of labored inhibition that preceded it. You knew *exactly* what you were doing. You seized the precise moment, and you went straight for the most vulnerable spot. You knew exactly where to cut deepest, how to manage the most, and you knew exactly what the consequences would be. You had planned it for years, brooding and in fantasy, privately rehearsing and envisioning its effects in quick forgetful flashes. And yet you think the seeming spontaneity of that instant negates those years of strategy and rehearsal. "Irrational"? Nothing you have ever done has been more rational, better conceived, more direct from the pit of your feelings, or better directed toward the target. That momentary outburst of emotion was the burning focus of all that means most to you, all that has grown up with you, even if much of it was unacknowledged. It was the brilliant product of a lifetime of experience and knowledge, the most cunning strategy, and it had the most marked sense of purpose of anything you have ever done. Despite the consequences, can you really say that a you wish you hadn't done it?

And yet we hear, "emotions are irrational"—virtually a platitude. The emotions are said to be stupid, unsophisticated, childish, if not utterly infantile, primitive, or animalistic—relics from our primal past and perverse and barbaric origins. The emotions are said to be disruptions, interfering with our purposes in life, embarrassing us and making fools of us, destroying careers and marriages, and ruining our relationships with other people before they have even had a chance to take hold. "It was fine, until you got involved," "it would be all right if you didn't feel so guilty about it," or "it was a fine triangle until he got jealous and spoiled it." The emotions are said to disrupt our thinking and lead us astray in our purposes. This what I call the Myth of the Passions: the emotions as irrational forces beyond our control, disruptive and stupid, unthinking and counterproductive, against our "better interests," and often ridiculous.

Against this platitude, "emotions are irrational," I want to argue that, on the contrary, emotions are *rational*. This is not only to say that they fit into one's overall behavior in a significant way and follow regular patterns (one's personality"), and that they can be explained in terms of a coherent set of causes according to some psychological theory or another. All of this is true enough. But emotions are rational in another, more important sense. Emotions, I have argued elsewhere,[1] are judgments, intentional and intelligent. Emotions, therefore may be said to be rational in precisely the same sense in which all judgments may said to be rational; they require an advanced degree of conceptual sophistication, including a conception of self and at least some ability in abstraction. They require at least minimal intelligence and a sense of self-interest, and they proceed purposefully in accordance with a sometimes extremely complex set of rules and strategies. In this sense, we may well talk of the "logic" of the emotions, a logic that may at times be quite difficult to follow but a logic which is, nevertheless, never merely an emotion's own. Even the most primitive emotions, fear for one's life of love of one's mother, require intelligence, abstraction, purpose, and "logic" in this sense. Most emotions involve much more, strategies for the maximizations of self-interest that would shame a professional confidence man and a prereflective awareness of psychological intrigue that would impress even S. Freud. We often criticize our emotions for their stupidity, their lack of justification, their foolishness, but correspondingly we often acknowledge their right and justification, their astuteness and their effectiveness. Such criticism and praise already presuppose a rational structure, a game of intelligence with strategy and logic, which can go well or badly. It is significant that we make no such attempts at evaluation of our headaches and feelings in general. We simply suffer them, or on occasion, feel lucky that one came along at precisely the right time (in order that we might miss a dull party or meeting). But unlike feelings, emotions are rational, presupposing a system of purposiveness, logic, and intelligence that far more resembles the structures of rational action than the phenomena of bodily feelings. (We know what it means to say that one's anger is unreasonable; what would it be to have an "unreasonable" attack of nausea?)

It is often thought that rationality resides solely in reflective thought, in the articulate calculations of a mathematician or a statesman. But we all know well enough to trust certain rational "intuitions" in ourselves, in a chess strategist, or a Napoleon, which seem to dispense with reflection altogether but yet follow an indisputable logic. "Intuition" is thought to be mysterious only because reflection is so often taken to be the paradigm of rationality. The rationality of the emotions is a prereflective or "intuitive" logic, if you like, but one that can, like all logics, be brought to the surface upon reflection and rendered explicit. This has not been done, of course, only because it has so long been presumed that the emotions had no logic worth investigating, that rationality lay exposed on the surface and needed only formalization, not exploration. But reflection may itself be quite irrational, ponderous and disassociated ramblings which are rational in form only and whose purpose is strictly antirational, to throw us off the track of our investigations and defeat the rationality of the emotions which is proceeding below the reflective surface. Rationality does not mean reflective; it rather signifies intelligent, purposive activity, whether reflective and fully articulated or not. Contrary to their usual image, the emotions are paradigmatic of such activities.

To say that the emotions have intelligent purpose is not simply to say that they play a significant role in our psychological life; this would be admitted by any number of theorists who would wholly reject our view of the emotions as judgments. Emotions have a purpose in the sense in which our actions have a purpose—to get something done, to change something. But, in the case of the emotions, much of this "something to be done" and "something to be changed" lies in the realm of personal experience as well as in reality. An emotion changes our view of the world as well as formulates intentions to change the world (Thus we might say that an emotion is "intentional" in a double sense, "intentional" in the phenomenological sense of "taking an object" and in the sense in which actions are intentional, that is, purposive.) In the case of some emotions, the change that is brought about may be strictly subjective, for example, in envy and resentment, where there is little sense of action but considerable restructuring of one's views and values. In other emotions, for example, fear, the change that is brought about is wholly directed toward reality. An emotion is itself a voluntary changing of one's world. (Thus, Sartre calls them "magical transformations of the world.")[2] The envious person, through "rationalization," changes the status of his loss without "in reality" changing anything at all. The angry man, through his anger, effects the indictment of his adversary that he insists upon. But in this case, the subjective indictment is accompanied by a demand for a real indictment as well. The angry man wishes his indictment to be corroborated by actual indictment and punishment, a bolt from the heavens, preferably, or a punch, or a winning lawsuit more probably. Similarly, a woman in love will not be satisfied with mere attitudes of affection, which constitute only admiration and not love, but she will insist upon demonstrating her love with gifts and attention, and she will want the world in general to corroborate her affections by providing the best for her lover.

An emotion is a demand that one's world, if not the world, be changed. One might say of an emotion, paraphrasing what Marx said of the bourgeoisie, that it "compels all other emotions (and perceptions, judgments, and values) on pain of extinction, to adopt its own mode of perception; it compels them to introduce what it calls Reality into their midst, that is, to become that emotion themselves. In one word, it creates a world after its own image" (*Communist Manifesto*, 1848). An emotion, in other words, is not merely a judgment; it differs from other judgments in its heightened sense of importance and purpose, its intense motivation. It demands the world be changed, and if an objective change is impossible, a subjective change will have to do. It is the necessity for such subjective alterations, often in the face of impossible objective obstacles, that breeds the often peculiar logic of the emotions, which is more often than not a strategy of desperation. That is why it often becomes so devious and so complex. Initially, the intention of every emotion is to change reality, to punish an offender, to caress a loved one, to take away what one thinks is rightfully his or hers, or to vanquish an acknowledged adversary. It is not only because this is sometimes impossible, but even more often because it is self-defeating, that the strategy turns to the subjective. A lover completely won is less demanding than one still in doubt. (Stendhal, for example, emphasizes the absolute need for doubt and intrigue in keeping the passions of romance alive.) An enemy vanquished is no longer an enemy; one's life now lacks a purpose which only a living adversary can fill. An idea realized is a bore, wrote Schopenhauer, and we know how true that is. Accordingly, the emotions rarely consist solely of intentions to act (fear, often taken as paradigm for general arguments to this effect, is an exceptional emotion in this instance). Virtually every emotion consists of both objective and subjective intentions, intentions to change the world and transformation of one's (view of) his world. One cannot imagine anger, for example, that did not consist both of a subjective indictment and an intention, no matter how symbolic, indirect, or ineffective, to punish. The first judgment assigns a status to the offender in one's experiences; the second intends to notify him or her of that status and punish him or her accordingly.

The purpose of an emotion, like the purpose of an action, is a multileveled affair. There are any number of goals in an emotion, from the very specific goals in the emotion ("wanting to see that bastard punished"), to the very general goals of this emotion or the emotions in general. Ultimately, all emotions have a common goal—the maximization of self-esteem. I would argue this to be true even of those emotions that appear to be wholly other-esteeming, e.g., love, worship, gratitude, and those emotions that are ostensibly self-demeaning, such as guilt and shame. Between the particular goals in an emotion and this common goal, one might formulate a crude means-ends continuum; for example, "he got angry about the garbage because he wanted an excuse to punish her for (faultlessly) wrecking the family car, which he was angry about because he was jealous about her affair with the garage mechanic, which threatened him because it made him feel insecure in general." But this admittedly crude device for displaying the "in order to" logic and laying bare the various levels of purposiveness can be misleading if it is taken to be a representation of the complex and sophisticated logic of the emotions, as if this "logic" were merely a sequence of steps from one goal to another. Although all emotions share an ultimate end, their interconnection is a network of intertwined and mutually entailing judgments, more like a web than a chain, which constitute the basic structures of our experience.

The intelligent purposiveness of every emotion dictates a certain "logic," abstract in its form but geared in every case to the particulars and "the facts of the situation." To say that emotions are "abstract" is to say that they are never concerned simply with a particular situation, that, like all strategies, the logic of an emotion keeps continuously in mind its abstract and ultimate purpose—the maximization of self-esteem—and tailors itself to particular objects and situations. The "rationality" of an emotion turns on how well it does this, whether the object of an emotion is an appropriate object for the maximization of self-esteem, whether the emotion is the right emotion, and so on. Without retreating an inch from our basic thesis that the emotions are subjective, we must insist that the logic of an emotion—like all "logics"—is objective and to be objectively evaluated. It is a commonly stated half-truth that each emotion has its own logic; the half-truth is that emotions are subjective, dependent upon the particular perspectives and investments of a particular person. But it is also a commonly stated half-truth that the emotions are shared in common by all people, whatever their differences in languages, customs, religion, etc. The half-truth here (leaving for the anthropologists and future space travelers the dubious universality of that thesis) is that the logic of emotions is in no case simply "own's own," that in every case the logic of the emotion, once its parameters are known, is a public affair. Consider the sense one gets in an inferior film or novel, where the characters are "unconvincing" ("I can't imagine doing that to someone I really loved," or "she wouldn't have reacted that way"). We recognize these breakdowns in the logic of the emotions, and it will do a screenwriter or author no good to protest that "we don't understand the character." Logic dictates the course that emotions will take—the emotion's own logic—and that is where we expect it to go.[3] Similarly, we criticize our own emotions, in reflection or retrospect, for their foolishness and stupidity, for their lack of justification and unreasonableness, and such criticisms make sense only on the basis of an objective logical structure that we expect—and are correct in expecting—our emotions to follow.

Consider any number of Shakespeare's tragedies (compared, for example, with his comedies or with the French classical tragedies that were their contemporaries). Each plot is driven not by the logic of events (there are often surprisingly few events) nor by a preestablished plan or routine, the "fates" in classical drama, for example, or the working through of a complex scheme, but by the logic of the emotions of the leading characters. In *Hamlet*, for example, we find a play in which virtually every action has occurred beforehand, is kept until the final moments of the play, or is hinted at offstage, as if of little importance. The drive of the play, as everyone realizes, is in the character of Hamlet himself. But if one summarizes that drive in the usual way, as the tragedy of a man "who could not make up his mind," both the character and the plot are lost. At no point in the play was Hamlet indecisive; at each point of decision, circumstances combined with his own emotional requirements (for example, that his uncle not be murdered without a public demonstration of guilt, and that he must have an unsalvaged soul before the Heavens).

It is Hamlet's subjectivity that provides the plot of the play, interrupted and given further instrumentation by the drowning of his lover and his murder of her father, incidents which occupy remarkably little of his concern, if we fail to see the obsessive emotional drive of his sense of vengeance. The play moves solely according to the logic of resentful revenge, necessarily subdued and therefore all the more obsessive. One might argue similarly for Othello. Although Othello's own jealousy is uncomplicated and would by itself make either an extremely dull tragedy or a slapstick comedy, Iago's envy is the intelligence that defines the course of the play. (Othello's jealousy is merely its instrument.)

My intention is not to force a somewhat overpsychologized interpretation of Shakespeare, but rather to make a general point about the emotions; the logic and strategy of the emotions, which provide the plot and drive of these tragedies, is extremely "rational" and sophisticated. The emotions are not merely forces or feelings of but a single dimension, like a pleasure or a pain, but rather complexes of judgments with endless logical entailments and complications. In the hands of a genius, these entailments and complications can be articulated so skillfully that we no longer recognize them as merely emotions rendered explicit. In the hands of a grade-B novelist or movie director, the same entailments and complications can become so bungled that we are forced to recognize the breakdown in logic, but we still fail to recognize the essential role of logic *of the emotions* in such cases. (Even some of the better movie critics can be caught saying things like "it's somehow unsatisfying" or "it just doesn't work," without attempting to explicate the emotional logic that has gone awry.)

The emotions are rational. Yet no one can deny that, through our emotions ("out of anger," "out of love for you, I . . ."), we perform some remarkably stupid and destructive acts. And so, despite the rationality of the emotions as judgments, complete with strategies and logic, we should have to say that, at least in a great many cases, the emotions are irrational as well. Thus, there are two different claims involved here. First, I claim that the emotions in general are rational in the sense of *intelligent* and *conceptual*, and a purely *descriptive* sense. Second, there is the *evaluative* question, with regard to particular emotions, of whether their strategies are successful. In the first sense, we can say that all emotions are rational insofar as they are strategies; in the second sense we can say that some emotions are irrational, insofar as their strategies are hopeless or just plain stupid.

It has often been argued that our emotions are not even rational in the first sense. Freud, for example, argued that the emotions were infantile and instinctive, not intelligent or conceptual at all. Gilbert Ryle, in a very different way, considered the emotions to be "agitations," breakdowns in normal behavior patterns. This is not the place to dissect or refute these claims; I want to take it as already argued that emotions are rational in the first sense, so that we can immediately proceed to the second.

An emotion is rational insofar as it succeeds in its purpose; namely, to maximize self-esteem. So considered, we can already see why it may be a mistake to suppose that any particular kind of emotion is categorically rational or irrational. And, in any particular case, we should have to understand much better the complex of judgments that constitute an emotion and the circumstances under which it is to be judged successful in its purpose or not. In every case, the logic of an emotion is to maximize self-esteem in the face of apparently very difficult or insurmountable obstacles in reality. Because an emotion is not a substitute for action, therefore, but sometimes a desperate compensation for impotence, it is unfair to pass a blanket condemnation over them for their "ineffectiveness" (as Sartre, for example, tends to suggest) or "irrationality" in this sense. Some emotions, however, are clearly based on confidence and strength (e.g., love and respect, pride and scorn). The problem with which an emotion must contend is a problem which by its very nature will not submit to direct action. Thus the nature of emotional strategy is clear; it must restructure experience by reordering priorities and investments, making little change, or no change at all, perhaps, in the "objective" order of reality. The criterion for an emotion's success, therefore—or its rationality—is how well it succeeds in doing this.

A familiar argument for the conclusion that all emotions are irrational is based upon a serious confusion. How often the emotions are accused of irrationality on the basis of the sometimes extravagant and inappropriate "outbursts" to which they give rise! But an emotion is not to be confused with an emotional crisis or an emergency situation. Of course, because an emotion consists of judgments of a self-involved and therefore extremely important nature, they are more likely to be prone to crisis than other judgments. But notice that in many cases, it is not the emotion that is disruptive at all. The emotion, as a matter of fact, may have been a durable structure of one's life for a considerable length of time. It may be the situation that spurs the crisis that is disruptive, unusual. It is an emergency situation in which one's normal responses—both subjective and objective—are rendered inappropriate. And so again we want to say that it is not the emotion that is "irrational"; it is the situation that is "irrational," unexpected, and unpredictable, "beyond one's reason" or "unreasonable." Of course, there are "rational" and "irrational" ways of dealing with such situations, but these are not always questions of the rationality of the emotion. The emotions may, through their self-concerned structuring of experience, set us up for such situations, and, moreover, the management of such situations may well be the test of an emotional strategy, but the rationality of the emotion cannot be judged solely on the basis of such situations.

We must also be careful not to confuse the rationality of an emotion with that of its expression. For example, a man may be furious with his boss for the best of reasons, but, given all ill-considered comment on the part of his boss last Tuesday morning, he flies into a rage, loses his job and his recommendations, is forced to go on welfare, move out of his house, separate from his wife, and so on *ad melodramataicum*. In the light of his overall interests, the outburst was clearly "irrational"; The emotion itself, however, was perfectly justified and it may have seemed to him at the time the only possible way in which he could have dealt on a day-to-day basis with a degrading but inescapable reality.

There is an anthropological dimension to this question of the rationality of the emotions; in a society in which "cool" behavior and stereotypic responses are taken to be the paradigms of rationality, it would follow that many emotions, by their very nature, would be deemed irrational. But one can evaluate the rationality of this conception of "rationality" (by the same criterion, the maximization of self-esteem) and see how much it is found wanting by the sense of meaninglessness and absurdity in which it culminates. (Here, Camus's Cartesian origins are exemplary as is the crude American sense of "pragmatism," which sees the emotions as interferences with good business sense and "sound," that is, dispassionate, judgment.) In a society that places taboos on the passions in general, condemns them in men and belittles them in women, it is only to be expected that emotions will run counter to public success and ambitions. There are situations, naturally, where "cool" behavior has a decisive advantage, for example, as opposed to panic in the face of danger. But again, it is a mistake to take the example of "fear in the face of danger" as the paradigm according to which all the emotions are to be judged. "Cool" behavior, our paradigm of rationality, may itself be an example of extreme irrationality, for it may deprive a person of all of those structures which give his life some meaning and self-esteem, leaving him only with the hollow coinage of success and public recognition.

Having thus laid the groundwork for the evaluation of the emotions as rational strategies, we are now in a position to understand both the bad press that the emotions have always received and the often unappreciated wisdom and rationality that they possess. The emotions are subjective strategics for maximizing self-esteem, often in the face of our impotence and inability to change an unappreciative and sometimes downright insulting universe of situations and, particularly, other people. Where the ostensive manifestations of an emotion may seem irrational or foolish, the goals of the emotion may be subjectivity successful to an enormous degree (the self-indulgence of guilt, the self-righteousness of resentment). My defense of the rationality of emotions is not a defense of these particular emotions, I hasten to add, but a plea for a philosophical-logical analysis of them—and all other emotions. They have been denied this in the past, swept out of court with the uncritical, blanket objections of "irrationality." But if emotions are indeed rational (in our first sense), then their structural analysis is just about to begin.

4

Nothing To Be Proud of (1980)

Emotions, according to David Hume,[1] are "simple and uniform impressions," "internal" impressions which are related to other impressions according to an empirically demonstrable set of "laws of association." The notion that an emotion is "simple" and a mere "impression" accounts for the relatively little attention the topic of "the passions" has received in modern philosophy, at least until very recently. Unlike "ideas," to which such "impressions" are usually contrasted, emotions are thought to be preconceptual, unintelligent, irrational, casual products of "animal spirits" of a subhuman nature, mere "feelings" which deserve none of the careful analysis so often dedicated to the structures of perception, knowledge, and reason. In Descartes's treatise on the passions,[2] for example, "animal spirits" and the crude physiology of emotions take priority over his quick and often glib quasi-conceptual analyses of them. His analysis is thoroughly straitjacketed by the dubious dualism that usually bears his name, and ever since, the question whether emotions should be thought of as mere "feelings" or "impressions," or rather conceived of in terms of their physiology and manifestations in behavior has dominated what little study of emotions existed before this century.[3]

Even in the writings of Hume, however, there is another, more complex and more edifying theory of the passions. He recognized the importance of passions as something more than distractions in human life. Hume insisted, in his most often quoted phrase, that passions should be served by reason, not the other way around, and he suggested that the passions "form a complete chain of reasoning by themselves." Buried beneath the sometimes unintelligible rubble of his atomistic sensationalism and quasi-Newtonian casual theory of association, Hume defends a view of emotions in which beliefs, attitudes, intentions and judgments play an essential role.[4] When he moves from his general theory of emotion to an analysis of particular emotions—for example, pride—it is evident that he insists upon analyzing at least some emotions in terms of ideas as well as impressions. Moreover, he insists that these emotions have an "object" as well as a cause. In more contemporary terminology, we would say that he had a notion of the intentionality[5] of emotions.(This is also true of Descartes, who betrays a drastic shift when he moves from his discussion of passions as such [as physiologically induced affects in the soul] to his discussion of the six "primitive" passions, which are intentional [article LXIX ff.].)

What is the relationship between an emotion and its "object"? In other words, what is intentionally? Hume provides us with a wholly unworkable set of answers, typically couched in *casual* terms (i.e., the emotion-impression *causes* us to have an idea of the object), occasionally expressed as a logical relationship (e.g., "as distinguishing character of these passions"), and most often muddied over with the most unhelpful appeal to "natural" and "original" properties. If we turn to the writing of more recent authors on the subject, however, we find ourselves no better informed. Brentano and Husserl, for example, who brought the term "intentionality" into its current prominence, provide only the most simplistic characterizations of their most important concept, for example, the idea that an emotion (or any mental "act") is "directed toward" its object. What follows in every discussion is the usual catechism of examples. "You can't be angry without being angry *about* something," "You can't be in love without being in love *with* someone," "You can't assert without asserting *something*," and so on. But what does this "aboutness" amount to? Can it be analyzed as a casual relationship, a simple association of ideas, as Hume believed? Or is it instead, as Husserl, for example, has argued, some *essential* relation, a matter of necessity? Given the problems that have arisen in even the most superficial attempts to spell out the Humean insistence on the intentionality of emotions, several recent authors have attempted to reject this entirely, reducing the object in every case to the cause of emotion.[6] But even Hume saw the importance of distinguishing cause from object, even if his subsequent analysis of "objects" has casual flaws. In his analysis of the emotion of pride, for example, he distinguishes the "object," which is always oneself, from the cause, which is a belief about circumstances (some achievement or honor, for example, with which one can identify). Taken in conjunction with Hume's theory as a whole, this primitive intentional analysis must be judged to be incoherent.[7] But this does not mean that Hume's insight can be explained away, even if his analysis, and so many glib characterizations of intentionality since, tend more to obscure this insight than to explain it.

Hume's Theory of Pride

At the beginning of book II of the Treatise, Hume offers us the characterization of the passions as "simple and uniform impressions" (277). But this is just a piece of his theory, and, insofar as it is Hume's final word on the subject, it is also a misleading oversimplification of a theory that is anything but simple or uniform. Emotions are complex phenomena, and Hume is well aware of that. Ideas are involved as well as impressions and the former are as important as the latter. In his general psychology, the human mind may be flatly analyzed in terms of "ideas and impressions," distinct psychological entities standing to one another in specifiable casual relationships. This view of the mind, typically characterized as Hume's "psychological atomism," makes the characterization of even the simplest psychological phenomena awkward, at least. In the analysis of particular emotions, it becomes all but impossible, and Hume's analysis of pride, for example, becomes nothing less than a hopeless jumble of casual connections and distinctions, as he tries to characterize what could be a uniform and simply described experience in terms of a grossly over-simplified psychological ontology and a therefore unnecessarily complicated theory.

It is not my intention to make an attempt to sort out Hume's analysis; if it is essentially incoherent, no doubt one could pursue a number of different interpretations. I am interested only in diagnosing the underlying reason for that incoherence and trying to understand the phenomena he appreciated but could not account for in his theory. The underlying problem can be stated in a phrase—Hume's refusal to accept the intentionality of emotions as such. Pride is about something. "Impressions" are not. This profound difficulty leads Hume to an elaborate ruse. He insists that emotions are "impressions of reflection," that is, impressions which are effects of ideas (which are in turn the effects of other impressions). The model, as so often in Hume's psychology, is that of casual "association," and since ideas are intentional, i.e., about something, their effect (the passion) would seem to be as well, by "association." But this is obviously inadequate, given Hume's conception of "impressions," and so he does not pursue this dubious line of argument. Rather he turns to a more ingenious strategy.

If emotions are intentional, and ideas are intentional but impressions are not, then the intentional object of pride, what the pride is about, must lie in an idea rather than an impression. But the passion itself is an impression; "a passion is an original existence" and "contain(s) not any representative quality" [*THN* 415]. But relations between impressions and ideas are causal relations. Therefore, the passion itself, which is an impression, must *cause* an idea in us, which is about something. That "something" turns out to be the self. The self, then, is the intentional object of pride, loosely speaking. Such speaking is "loose" because, insofar as pride itself is a "simple and uniform impression" (about which Hume never even hesitates), it can have no object. But the idea it causes can have an object, and this is called the "object of pride."

Now it may be objected that I have overplayed the Humean distinction between ideas and impressions here, that the two are not nearly so distinct in Hume's *Treatise*. But if this is so, Hume's argument becomes even less plausible than my reconstruction, for any shift towards making ideas and impressions more alike would have to be a shift of ideas towards impressions, and thus intentionality would be further excluded from his analysis. There is also a problem, which Hume explicitly recognizes, in his central theme of causality as the link between pride and its object (i.e., the resultant idea of self): Late in the *Treatise*, he complains:

> There are two principles which I cannot render consistent, nor is it in my power to renounce either of them, viz., *that all our perceptions are distinct existences and that the mind never perceives any real connection among distinct existences.* (THN 636)

The notion of "self," too, is a problem for Hume.[8] But, for our purposes, we can again leave aside such general dilemmas and focus solely on the analysis of passions. Granting Hume reasonably ordinary notions of "self" and "causality," can his analysis of pride, and passions in general, be made coherent?

It is worth mentioning again that Hume did not take pride to be merely an "impression." It is an "impression of reflection," which, we are told, means an impression that is caused by a particular kind of idea. "Pride is a passion placed betwixt two ideas of which one produces it, and the other is produced by it" [*THN* 278]. This idea, too, like the idea which is pride's object, is an idea of self. But the idea of self which is the cause of pride is not identical to the idea of self which is the object of pride. (Thus Hume distinguishes pride as one of the "indirect passions," those whose casual ideas are not identical to their objects-ideas, in contrast to the "direct passions," whose casual-idea are identical [*THN* 276].) The casual-idea involves "other qualities" [ibid.]; the objects-idea is, more or less, the self *simpliciter*. (Hume's analysis is in fact not nearly so, simple, for he has grave reservations about the idea of pride in oneself without qualification, which this oversimplified characterization of the object would suggest.)[9] The "other qualities" required in the casual-idea of pride are recognition of one's own virtue (or virtues on identifies with, for example, one's family or school) and the idea of one's consequent uniqueness and superiority over others in some respect. (It is not clear to what extent this "respect" also enters into the proper description of the object-idea.) It is also necessary that the "qualities" recognized in the causal idea be pleasant, and thus the impression of pride itself being *pleasant* as well ("the very being and essence of pride" [*THN* 286]). It is worth noting, too, that the pleasure(s) in the casual idea and the pleasure of the impression are, as atomistically always, distinct. ("Every cause of pride, by its own peculiar qualities, produces a separate pleasure" [*THN* 285].) There is also pleasure, we may presume, in the object-idea, since the pleasure of pride surely involves taking pleasure in the object of pride. Notice, too, however, that Hume's atomism requires that the pleasure in the causal-idea itself be a separate impression of pleasure distinct from the idea, and one may well at this point feel like throwing away this increasingly complex analysis and insisting simply, "Look, pride is taking pleasure in one's virtue," where "pleasure in" and "pleased about" the object of the emotion. This seems to be, in fact, what Hume wants to say. But his atomization makes extremely complex and implausible that which, on the face of it, would seem to be eminently simple. There are, in addition, severe problems with Hume's concept of "pleasure" itself[10] such that the whole idea of separate impressions of pleasure, whether those involved with the causal-idea or that which constitutes the emotion of pride itself, may be unintelligible.

Price, as Hume rightly insists, is taking pleasure in one's virtue. (He also says that it is virtuous to do so, and taking pleasure in that second-level virtue also warrants pride, but we need not concern ourselves with this possible difficulty.) But pride may also be taking pleasure in someone else's virtue (a parent, a child, one's country)[11] Hume's problems aside, we can say that the object of pride is, which some proper qualifications, one's having a virtue or otherwise identifying with it. The pleasure is also about that same object (for pleasure, too, it would seem, is intentional, at least in this context). But to these simple and convincing insights Hume is forced to add the baggage of his psychology; impressions must be separated from ideas and from each other; relationships among these must be causal and not logical; the object of the emotion itself. And so what emerges is, to put it mildly, bizarrely complicated:

> That cause, which excites the passion, is related to the subject, which nature has attributed to the passion; the sensation, which the cause produces separately, is related to the sensation of the passion; from this double relation of ideas and impressions the passion is derived. [*THN* 286]

Hume's ambiguity between the passion as simply the "sensation" and the passion as much more ("from this double relation . . . the passion is derived") is evident here, as if he saw the wholesale inadequacy of his own continued insistence on the passion as "a simple and uniform impression." To this already too complex analysis, we now have to add attributions of merit, comparisons with others, the concept of "pleasure," and the sense in which "nature has attributed [the object] to the passions," all of which must be divided up between the impression itself, the causal-idea, and the object-idea. As soon as we do this, it becomes evident that the analysis becomes what Hume elsewhere feared as a "monstrous heap" [*THN* 282] of doubled attribution of merit, two concepts of self, objectless pleasures, double ideas, dubious comparisons, and causal confusions. But what is left out of (or hidden by) this "heap" is the simple central theme, that pleasurable pride is *about* its object, namely, one's virtue or achievement. And Hume's causal account, even clarified in this jungle of "relations," is obviously inadequate.

What pride causes is not its object. As a purely contingent and causal relationship, that which is caused by the impression of pride might well be anything—a regular thirst for an extra-dry Beefeater martini, or the idea that one should receive another medal, or the thought that "if only my poor old grandfather should see me now." In fact, pride might well trigger monkish guilt, the very pseudo virtue Hume attacks, and the object of pride would thereby seem to be the very opposite of pride, mortification at one's own alleged egotism, or, in a more modern vein, an acute awareness of one's extremely low self-confidence and self-esteem. Even if it turned out that pride regularly or even universally caused the "correct" Humean idea of self, coupled with pleasure and self-congratulation, this would in no way serve to provide the connection that is needed between emotion and object. That connection must be a *logical* connection, whatever else it may be. That is, the description of the emotion *entails* a description of a certain kind of object. Being proud *entails*, not just causes, the idea that one has or identifies with some virtue.[12]

Hume is aware of this requirement, but his attempts to fulfill it are awkward, doomed from the start by his own earlier arguments. Elsewhere, it is Hume who invokes the notorious principle that two things causally related cannot be described in terms that render them logically related as well. This means that Hume, once he has already insisted on the causal relationship between emotion and object, cannot allow there to be a logical relationship as well. Thus he cannot show how the object-idea *must* (logically) be an idea of a certain kind, namely, an idea of one's having a certain virtue. In place of this, he limply insists on the view of the object-idea as that "which nature has attributed to the passion" [*THN* 286]. What does this mean? At most, it is an appeal to a quasi-innate "association of ideas," which, even if it can be made intelligible in this context, falls far short of the requisite logical connection. Elsewhere, Hume insists that "to this emotion, [nature] has assigned a certain idea, viz. that of self" [*THN* 287]. Elsewhere again, he says that the passion is "originally determined" to have a certain object [*THN* 280], that pride "mediates" between human nature and its object [*THN* 287].All of this is a pathetic attempt to sneak in the logical connection required for any analysis of emotion and object under the guise of casual associations, "original" and "natural" connections.

But why should Hume have to do this? Just because he denies himself the apparatus for accounting for the simple observation that the emotion of pride is *about* one's virtues by his atomization of psychological entities and his insistence on solely causal connections. It is not that he didn't appreciate the obvious facts of intentionally; he just couldn't account for them, given his method. Hume wanted to be the Isaac Newton of empiricist psychology, a misplaced ambition. One might as well strive to be the King Kong of garden party etiquette.

Hume Reconstructed (by Davidson)

To insist that the connection between (the description of) an emotion and (the description of) its object must be a logical connection need not require giving up the idea that it is a causal connection as well. Hume is trapped by his own principle into rejecting the obvious, that whatever else, the connection between emotion and object has a logical basis. But even if Hume were right, that the emotion is an impression which causes the idea which is its object, it does not follow that the relationship between emotion and object (that is, the two descriptions thereof) might not be a logical one.

Donald Davidson has reconstructed Hume's theory of pride on the basis of just this counter-Humean principle,[13] which he himself has amply justified elsewhere.[14] This helps Hume out of his dilemma in the following way: A causal connection is itself the logical essence of "being a parent." So, too, one can say that the Humean impression of pride, in order to be pride (rather than just some pleasant impression or other), must cause an idea of a certain kind as well as be caused by ideas of a certain kind. In other words, certain impressions count as pride (the logical point) only if they have the right kind of causes and effects (the causal connection). Hume's causal thesis remains intact. But it is also a logical point, one that allows the reconstructed Humean to say that pride *must* take as its object, as a matter of logic, a particular kind of object, namely self. And he can do this without retreating to such wholly unhelpful fudge concepts as "natural" and "original."

By rejecting the "causal versus conceptual" dichotomy, Davidson recasts Hume's account of pride as a sequence of logically connected propositions, in fact, in the form of a syllogism. Davidson cautiously warns us, "I do not pretend that this is what Hume meant; it is what he *should* have meant, and did inspire" (744). He attacks Hume's critics as having "gone wrong . . . in rejecting the causal aspect of Hume's doctrine as if it were inseparable from the atomistic psychology" ibid.). I will argue that Davidson himself is still caught up in "atomistic psychology," though boldly reconceived. What he has done for Hume, however, is to give him a way of providing the necessary logical account of the connection between emotion and object. In Davidson's reconstruction, Hume's view of passion as "a simple and uniform impression" is not to be taken all that seriously, whether or not Hume intended it seriously. What is rather more important is the "pattern of elements" which make up the passion (754). This pattern consists of ideas (beliefs) primarily, impressions and sensations (including pleasure) only secondarily. Davidson ultimately even rejects Hume's causal view: "Hume was wrong to suppose that the state of being proud causes the idea of self to which it is directed; that idea is a constituent of the state" (754). Notice Davidson's explicit reference to intentionally here ("to which it is directed," emphatically not a causal notion). Notice, too, the move from pride as impression to pride as idea. In fact, Davidson even adds, "What Hume *called* the passion (i.e. the impression) had no 'representative quality'; . . . So the valid criticism is that what Hume called the passion has no place in the pattern" (ibid.). (One is naturally reminded of Wittgenstein's sensational gear that plays no part in the mechanism.)

Davidson's reconstruction begins with a significant but suspicious revision. Although nearly all of Hume's examples are in the form "proud *of* . . . ," Davidson says that he is "best" interpreted as providing as account of "propositional pride"— "pride described by sentences like, 'She was proud that she had been elected president'" (744). Davidson even admits that this is not Hume's sort of example, and he rightly worries about the possible lack of self-reference in the propositional account; it is not sufficient, for example, to translate "she was proud of being elected" to "she was proud that (her name) had been elected." There is no need to introduce the horribly technical questions concerning the possible need to replace the reflective pronouns with proper names, which, if accepted, would undermine the propositional account altogether. Emotions are nothing if not *personal*, and any reconstruction that does not retain this essential self-reference is wholly inadequate from the start.

Clearly some emotion are propositional attitudes, including some species of pride, but not all are.[15] In a trivial way, it may be that any such non-propositional attitudes can be converted into propositional attitudes, e.g., "proud of . . . ," by the addition of the perhaps awkward but usually grammatically acceptable addition of the appropriate "proud that . . ." clause. But it is worth noting that this cannot always be done with emotion verbs, e.g., "John loves Mary," or "Fred hates spinach" (Dennett's example). And even where it can be done, there are nagging questions of notorious philosophical difficulty. What is a proposition, other than a semantic construction of philosophers? Does it make sense (in general, that is) to say that one is proud that a certain proposition is true? And given what seems to be the experiential content of the emotion, namely that one *feels* proud of oneself, doesn't the shift to prepositional attitudes lose precisely that experiential and personal reference? This is, however, an apparent problem for any "cognitive" view of emotions, and so it is particularly important, for someone who also holds such view, to distinguish Davidson's reconstruction of Hume from other theories, in opposition to Hume, that promote what Hume called "ideas" to definitive status in the analysis of emotions. Why "reconstruct" Hume, if one's purpose is in fact to refute him?

Davidson at one point asserts, as I have argued at length elsewhere,[16] that there is a "judgment that is identical with pride" (751). "A judgment" makes it much too simple. Every emotion is composed of a system of judgments and beliefs, not as causes but as components, and this accounts (among other things) for the "cognitive" features of emotion that Davidson and others have emphasized. But this judgment-belief analysis alone is not sufficient. Every emotion also has its component desires, expectations, and hopes, which give judgments their motivational force. Without them, emotion isn't emotion.[17] Then, too—our main concern here—every emotion has its object. But how does a "cognitive" theory account for this?

First of all, the belief itself, even the object of the relevant belief, i.e., a proposition, cannot plausibly be taken to be the object of the emotion. For example, John's love for Mary is composed of a network of complex judgments and beliefs, but the object of John's love is Mary. In the case of pride, matters are more ambiguous: "She is proud of having been elected president" must be analyzed in terms of a set of beliefs, to be sure, but it is not at all clear, as in Davidson's use of this example, that what she is proud *of* is a proposition or a set of propositions. She could not possibly be proud of having been elected president, of course, if she did not believe (know?) that she had been elected president, that the election was more or less honest, that gaining the presidency was in some sense desirable and an honor, and that she deserved this honor. But is she thereby proud *that* she has been elected president? The first problem is the "she." No translation into the form of a definite description, "the person who . . . ," will capture the fact that, from her view, "*I* was elected." But more seriously, is this pride *just* a matter of belief? What of the experience so badly captured by Hume's "impression"? And why insist on a reformulation in terms of propositions? Not all judgments, and certainly not all of experience, require propositional attitudes. The cognitive theory of pride remains intact without it, so long as beliefs and/or judgments remain essential components of emotion.

Davidson has other things in mind. He is not just after a "cognitive" theory; he is also after a theory which dispenses with the problematic concept of "intentional objects." He is a "Sinnephobe." Extensional analyses only. Accordingly, even if his propositional analysis is not faithful to the wide range of non-propositional examples of pride (and other emotions), he gains another advantage, being able to recast Hume's complex causal relations of impressions and ideas imperfectly yielding objects is not a simple syllogism, a creature well-suited to his own analytical techniques It is not the first time that philosophical method dictates the nature of human experience. (Hume, for example.) Thus recast, Hume appears to be analyzing pride as a sequence of inferences, rather than causal stages:

All who (have a certain property) are praiseworthy.
I (have that Property).
Therefore, I am praiseworthy.

Davidson's strategy seems to be this. He has argued that causal relations do not preclude logical connections, and seen the necessity of tying the emotion to its object in a logical rather than a Humean merely causal way. The syllogism, in which each line correlates with one of Hume's causal atoms, is an apparent way of doing just this. The syllogism, however, does not work, as Davidson points out. The crucial clause in parentheses, that which one is proud about, drops out in the conclusion. Thus what one would be proud about would always be oneself "*überhaupt*," which Hume does suggest but Davidson rightly denies.[18] Furthermore, it is clear that Hume did not hold anything like the first premise of Davidson's reconstruction. To the contrary, he argues at length that pride is based precisely on the uniqueness of one's virtue, and that, were everyone else to have it (e.g., the virtue of "humanity"), it could not be a proper object of pride at all. But then we want to ask, if this translation does not succeed in saving Hume, and it is not even what he meant, why does Davidson attempt it at all? (In fact, he drops it immediately and moves on to the far less committal claim that pride always has its "reasons.") The answer, I think, is this: Davidson sets out to save Hume's atomism, despite his denials. The atomism of causal elements is replaced by an atomism of propositions, but it is the same, the illicit breaking up of a single *gestalt*—"being proud of one's virtue"—into discrete bits which cannot be put together again. Hume needs his atomism to allow for causal connections between "atoms"; Davidson needs his so that he can analyze emotion in terms of propositions and their logical relations. Both, in other words, avoid the analysis of emotional object itself. And neither provides an adequate analysis of emotional *experience*.

What Davidson wants to do with Hume is surely valuable—to shift our focus to Hume's attention to "ideas" and away from his simple minded conception of passions as impressions, and to provide Hume with the needed but missing logical link between the emotion and its object. But his syllogistic interpretation is neither accurate to Hume's intentions nor does it provide an adequate analysis of pride. At this point, Davidson retreats to the meek observation that pride always has its reasons ("someone who is proud always has his reasons," 752). But although this again stresses the "cognitive" aspects of emotion, it adds nothing to the belief analysis already offered, in fact, weakens it considerably. (Davidson says, "giving the belief and attitudes on which pride is based explains the pride in two ways; it provides a causal explanation, and it gives the person's reasons for being proud" [ibid.].) "Reasons" are appropriate in several different senses. "Reasons" might be beliefs, but they need not be. They might also be desires, but there is nothing in Davidson's account to suggest anything like the idea that emotions are purposive. Nor does he seem to allow for the fact that emotions *include* certain desires, as even Descartes had pointed out. There are reasons for holding a belief, all of which need not be further beliefs. Reasons can be argued to be (causal) explanations, and Davidson, like Hume, is easily prone to slip from reasons back into causes (though Davidson, unlike Hume, has an elaborate justification for sometimes doing so). Employing a time-tested formula from his other writings, Davidson says, "the cause of his pride rationalizes it" (752), but here he confuses beliefs as causes and beliefs as components in a gross way. Consider the following example: a man tends to take considerable pride in his own slovenliness. A behavior-modification therapist à la *Clockwork Orange* subjects him to a series of experiences in which sloppiness is accompanied by drug-induced nausea and neatness is rewarded with praise. After a few weeks, the man takes pride in his neatness. What is the reason? The series of artificially induced associations. Those are also the cause of his pride. To be sure, if he is truly proud, he must therefore have certain beliefs concerning his appearance as virtuous (1) those beliefs need have no role in the causal explanation of his pride; (2) the cause of his pride clearly does *not* "rationalize it"; and (3) he need have no reasons for being proud, other than his beliefs which constitute pride. But as they constitute pride, they are hardly *reasons for* the pride in any sense. In other words, someone who is proud need not "always have his reasons." He need only have the requisite beliefs.

Davidson makes good his promise to extract Hume's "Cognitive Theory of Pride," but he fails to do what Hume himself failed to do, to provide an account of the object of emotion and its relationship to the emotion. These elaborate maneuvers from propositions to syllogism to reasons weave a "cognitive" veil around the concept of intentionality. But the object of the emotion is not always (or is it ever?) the same as the object of the component beliefs It is not always a proposition. It is not a "reason for" the emotion but what the emotion is about. It is, in a sense to be explained, a further description of the emotion rather that an explanation for it. But all of this is totally missing from both Hume's and Davidson's accounts. Davidson has provided the web of beliefs tangentially introduced by Hume. He still has given us no account of the intentionality of emotions, and he has dropped out Hume's undeniable reference to the "feeling" of the emotion, the so-called impression.

It is worth taking a closer look at the accusation that Davidson wholly ignores the intentionality of emotions, despite the fact that he attempts to provide just those logical relationships that seem to be demanded by intentionality. His postures of avoidance are at times grotesque. In his initial reconstruction of Hume (before he attempts to recast Hume in syllogism), Davidson rightly argues that,

> What a man takes pride in, that is, the fact that he has a beautiful house, is identical with the content of his belief; one could say that the belief *determines* the object of pride. (745)

The "what" and "the content of his belief" would seem to point unabashedly toward intentionality, and although "determines" is noncommittal in itself, "determining the object" would seem to be a step toward a very Husserlian account of "intentional constitution." But immediately, in an extremely revealing footnote, he comments:

> This is not to say, of course, that the belief is the "object of pride." All this talk is loose. I do not assume that "the object of pride," "what pride is taken in," "the content of belief" refer to psychological entities of any kind. Of course the semantic analysis of intentional [sic] sentences, like those which attribute belief or prepositional pride, may require objects such as propositions, sentences, or utterances. (745 *n*; see also p. 755)

Such "loose" talk is never clarified, however, a rare lapse for Davidson. But the reason that it is never clarified is because it is indefensible. Davidson says that the belief "*determines* the object of pride" (his italics). But here it is obvious that Davidson takes the objects of emotion to be propositions, and, for most cases, this just is not true.

Yet Davidson is right, in a sense not intended. Beliefs do "determine"—or should we say "constitute"?—the objects of emotion. But then how could the object *not* be a "psychological entity of some kind"? Beliefs don't build houses (except in Monty Python skits, perhaps). Beliefs don't convey legal ownership. So it is neither the house nor the ownership that could be constituted by the belief, so what is it? It is the object of the emotion *as experienced* which must therefore be, contra Davidson, a "psychological entity of some kind." This isn't to say that it is not the wood-and-brick house that is the emotional object. It is rather the house *as one is proud of owning it*. The psychological qualifications cannot be eliminated without losing the notion of pride altogether. Does this make the house itself a "psychological entity"? Of course not. But the house as an object of pride has its *essential* psychological properties. It is essentially an object experienced, in a certain way, and it is mixture of the psychological and tangible "objects" that the notion of intentionality tries to capture.

The ontology of intentional objects raises serious questions of identity; in what sense can we say that the object of pride, which has certain essential psychological properties, is identical to the house "in itself"? In what sense is the object of pride identical to the object of component and accompanying beliefs about the house? (And what about the object of frustration, where it is exactly "the same" house that now needs a new roof after only four months?) Such questions as these have scared more than a few philosophers away from the notion of intentionality altogether. But problems of identity are not unique to questions of intentionality, and regarding the analysis of emotions, such ontological questions can be avoided altogether.[19] On the other hand, if one restricts one's choice to the intolerable ontological dichotomy of "in the mind" or "in the world," then the notion of an "object" of emotion can make no sense whatsoever, and one should try at almost any cost to avoid it. But it is that ontology that is intolerable, not necessarily the notion of "intentionality."

We can now see too clearly why Davidson takes the trouble to shift Hume's analysis of pride to an analysis of propositional pride. If the idea of an emotional object as such is a matter of ontological hysteria, a proposition can be analyzed away in any number of familiar quasi-Quinean ways. A man who is proud *that* he owns a beautiful house can be reconstructed as a man who believes a certain set of propositions, who thereby tends to utter certain sentences and act in certain ways, and—poof—the mystery is dissolved. But a man who is proud of his beautiful house does not only believe a certain set of propositions: he also has a distinctive *experience*, which cannot be reduced to mere Humean impressions, and his experience has an object, which is neither a proposition nor an idea. It is, in some sense, *the house* that he is proud of, and no manipulation of causes, beliefs, and propositions will account for this.

What is wrong with Hume's account is not merely his atomistic psychology, nor even the causal account that Davidson defends. The essential feature of pride, that it is experiencing of something (including oneself), escapes Hume altogether, and Davidson too. One might too easily conclude, from this indictment, that it is "intentionality" that is missing, but "intentionality," too, has its problems. In fact, it might even be that this now fashionable notion embodies more than it wishes of the same atomism of emotions and their objects that we have rejected in the above accounts.

Taking Emotions Seriously: Beyond Intentionality

"Intentionality" is a concise but hardly precise way of characterizing the fact that emotions are always "about" something. But what emotions are "about" are always putative objects in the world (including myself, of course[20]). They are not (except rarely) about ideas. (I might be proud of my brilliant idea.) They are not (except rarely) about beliefs. (I might be indignant that you *believe* that *I* did it, or sad that I can believe that you might have done it.) But neither is it the case that ideas and beliefs are merely the causes or the cognitive presuppositions of our emotions. Davidson is surely right, and Hume wrong, that ideas and beliefs are themselves constitutive of emotions, an intrinsic part of them. But Hume is surely right, and Davidson wrong, that some kind of *experience* (though not a "simple impression") is essential to emotion, but Hume has his hands on the wrong kind of experience, while Davidson ignores the experience of emotion altogether.

How does any cognitive theory of emotions capture the essential experience of having an emotion? Since I, too, have defended such a theory at length, namely the theory, over-simply stated, that emotions are basically judgments of certain specifiable kinds, this question applies to my own analysis as well.[21] Furthermore, how does either a cognitive or an experiential theory—and I do not want to imply that these will turn out to be different—account for the so-called "intentionality" of the emotion? The main problem seems to be this: If one accepts anything like the empiricist account of experience, as an "inner impression," for instance, then the question how this "inner" experience connects up with an "outer" object—person, state-of-affairs, or situation in the world—seems to be insurmountable. And the word "intentionality" only hides this rather than solves it.[22] Hume solves the problem by making the object out to be an idea, which is still "inner" (though the "aboutness" question arises for the idea, too, thus not really solving the problem at all). Davidson substitutes a sequence of propositions—a sort of computer model of emotion—thereby leaving the work ascribed to "intentionality" to his unstated theory of reference. What Hume inherited from Newton, and Davidson from Quine, is a method that systematically distorts or dismisses experience to fit models and methods derived from elsewhere. But can any judgment-type theory of emotion capture both emotional experience and what is indicated, if not clarified, by the notion of intentionality?

Intentionality, perhaps unintentionally, retains Hume's atomism, just as Davidson does. There is still the emotion, on the one hand,, and its object, on the other. And if one were to claim that emotions are judgments, understood as some purely "inner" episode, the same problem would emerge once again.

It is for that reason, in *The Passions*, that I place such enormous emphasis on "subjectivity" and in re-doing, without the jargon, the work of the phenomenologists (not so much Husserl as Heidegger and Merleau-Ponty), before I even begin to introduce my theory. An emotion, as a system of judgments, is not merely a set of beliefs *about* the world, but rather an active way of structuring our experience, a way of experiencing something. In place of the psychological atomism of Hume, Davidson, and in the early phenomenologists, I want to substitute an organic molecule, in our case of pride, the irreducible complex *being-proud-of-my-house*. The "being proud" is not an "act" or episode or a feeling "in" consciousness, mysteriously related to an "outside" object, namely, my house. *Being-proud-of-my-house* is, in Heidegger's terminology, a "unitary phenomenon." The so-called object is not simply *the house* but is defined by the emotion of which it is part. Neither is being proud a distinctive psychological entity, "directed toward" or possibly even looking for an object. *Being-proud-of-my-house* is a complex and irreducible experience, not divisible into components or individual atoms.

Here, too, we can understand Hume's uncertainty regarding the proper object of pride. He says that it is one's Self, but he hedges with the restriction that it may not be the Self wholly unqualified. But there is also a sense, which Hume misses, in which the object of pride, in this example, is not a Self but a house, or, one might argue, not merely the house (which was not an object of pride before I bought it, though it was indeed "the same" house) but my ownership of the house. Here one could launch, as the literature has demonstrated, into a lengthy debate, but one that proves to be wholly beside the point. Neither Self nor house nor ownership as such is what the emotion is "about," but rather pride is, to continue the atomic metaphor, an experiential molecule, whose inseparable ingredients are judgments of a certain kind (for example, those which form the steps in Davidson's syllogism, amended by Baier).[23] Some of these pertain particularly to the house, others to self, and still others to the virtues of ownership. But what is most important is that these judgments are components of the emotion only insofar as they structure a certain experience, a certain way of experiencing the house, and oneself, and one's ownership. One might even say, with some reservations, that every emotion is a worldview, a distinct perspective within which certain aspects of one's world (namely, the "object" of the emotion) receive special attention.

An emotion is a system of judgments, through which we constitute ourselves and our world. This does not mean that an emotion is a set of beliefs *about* the world, but a way of experiencing, shaped by concepts which need not, and often are not, made fully articulate. In anger, for instance, we review another person (the "object" of our wrath) through judgments constituting him as an offender, as offensive, as deserving of punishment. In pride, to use Hume's example, we view the house *as* beautiful, *as* beautiful because of some achievement on our part, *as*, therefore, a reflection on ourselves. Pride is a species of *seeing as* (as are all emotions), and it is the analysis of the judgments which define the "seeing as *what*" that form the proper analysis of the emotion. This is where ideas and beliefs enter into the analysis, not as causes or effects, but neither as a sequence of abstract propositions. They are the skeletal structure of a distinctive experience, in this case, the emotional experience of pride.

With this analysis, it is time to give up the notion of "object"—except perhaps as a kind of shorthand for the focal point of an emotion—for the very idea of emotion *and* object ("act" and "object," "*noesis*" and "*noema*") already sets up a dualism that no further tinkering will put back together. (Husserl, for example, insists that "noesis and noema [act and object] are essential correlates." Too late.) So, too, it is time to say that the now favored concept of "intentionality" serves only to antagonize the

Sinnephobes and too easily soothe those who employ it so freely. The very idea of an "object," as a distinctive ontological entity, raises infamous paradoxes, but more important for our interests, to remove the "object" from its emotional context is, in phenomenological fact, to destroy it as an "object." Of course, one could proceed to discuss one or more features of the emotion (e.g., the house one is so proud about) as an ontological entity wrenched from its emotional context (much, for example, as my girlfriend's gynecologist examines her), but this is by no means any longer what the emotion was about. The "object" of an emotion is such only as viewed through the judgments that make up that emotion, and so the problem to which "intentionality" is supposed to be the answer (or at least the name) cannot even arise. One could wax Sartrean here, and say that the object of an emotion is not what it is, but I trust the point has been made without the need for new confusion. Not only is the "object" necessary to the emotion, but the emotion is equally essential to the subject. Hume in his fashion fully appreciated the complexity of emotional experience, but denied himself the apparatus for talking about it.

Of course, there is still a problem: I have not said a word about what was once called "intentional inexistence," the nasty habits some emotions have of directing themselves toward "objects" that don't exist. But the first (and only) comment to make here is that the problem is overrated, that most of its instances can be simply translated into instances of false belief, and the more interesting cases are not matters of "inexistence" at all but the far more fascinating phenomenon of "willful seeing," for example, two ugly, even grotesque people who, because they are in love, see each other *as* beautiful. But it is not their existence that is in question; rather, their judgment. But emotions are judgments, after all. And if there is a problem here, it is not a problem of ontology, a matter of phantom or "subsistent" objects. At most, we have to account for ugly people, or houses, judged to be beautiful, perhaps an aesthetic problem, but not a Meinongian nightmare.

Neither have I said much of anything about the often intricate connections between emotional "objects" and the *causes* of emotion, which Hume anticipated too. But these topics will require another paper.

5

Emotions' Mysterious Objects (1984)

Emotions are distinguished, at least in part, by what they are "about," their so-called intentionality. This has not always been appreciated in the classical literature on emotions, in which emotions are more often than not taken to be mere "feelings" or "impressions" or aimless "motivations," perhaps the stirrings of some physiological apparatus of arousal, without reference to causes or objects. And yet, Aristotle argued quite clearly 2500 years ago that anger, for example, is "about" an offense, "real or merely perceived" (*Rhetoric*, book ii, chap. 2). Spinoza and even Descartes grappled awkwardly with this aspect of emotions, Spinoza successfully by taking emotions to be "thoughts," Descartes unsuccessfully because the "animal spirits" that defined emotions in his theory left little room for intentional reference. It is David Hume, however, who deserves credit for opening up the question of "intentionality" (though not by that name) in his complex analysis of "pride" in book II of his *Treatise of Human Nature*.[1] Pride, he argues, is distinguished by its object, which is the Self. It is thereby distinguished from love, for example, whose object is another person. According to Hume, the object of an emotion is, in part, what defines that emotion; it is not just an external cause or an effect, however regularly conjoined with it.

Hume's theory, however, is inconsistent. The emotion itself, he tells us, is an "impression," "an original existence," and "contains not any representative quality" (*THN* 415). How, then, is the emotion, an impression, "about" its object? Hume utilizes his causal theory of ideas to tell us that the impression-emotion *causes* an idea of self, which is its object, and it is also *caused by* another idea (which in pride, for example, also contains reference to the Self). This analysis of emotion as an impression sandwiched between two ideas strikes Hume himself as overly complex and a "monstrous heap" (*THN* 282), and he recognizes that his causal analysis fails to capture the *conceptual* dependency of emotion to object and subject to emotion. He tries to compensate for this inadequacy by speaking somewhat murkily of an "originally determined" and "natural" connection between the two, thus sneaking in the importance of the conceptual connection under the guise of causal association. Given the Newtonian model of the *Treatise*, Hume simply could not account for the essential fact of intentionality, the fact that what an emotion is "about" is not just its associated effects and not its causes either.

Hume's analysis has been updated in a clever but truly perverse way by Donald Davidson.[2] Rejecting Hume's atomism, he reinterprets the Humean text by converting causal atoms to propositions in a logical syllogism. In accord with arguments he has made well-known elsewhere, Davidson rightly insists that two elements might stand in both a causal and a specifiable logical relationship (as in "X is the father of Y"), and that the essence of Hume's analysis is this logical reconstruction. ("I do not pretend that this is what Hume meant; it is what he *should* have meant" [744].) Davidson simply rejects Hume's "impression" analysis of emotion, and translates his causal relations between the ideas into logical relations; "what Hume called the passion has no place in the pattern" (754).

Davidson captures the conceptual connection between emotion and object, but it is clear that in doing so, he (willingly) sacrifices Hume's original insight, that an emotion is not just a series of associations of ideas, but something more, a "feeling" about something (about oneself in pride, for example), *experience* of some kind which is not to be considered merely tangential to the emotion but rather its essence. Davidson asserts at one point a thesis I have argued at length elsewhere, namely, that there is a "judgment that is identical with pride" (751). This thesis should not be taken to mean, as Davidson interprets it, that an emotion is just a logical (or illogical) sequence of propositions. Nevertheless, the more routine semantic sense in which judgments, too, are "about" something provides at least a partial clue to the intentionality of emotions.

Hume tried to develop a theory of emotions in which intentionality is an essential feature, but he left out the all-important conceptual connection and, in some important sense, leaves out the emotion. In fact, it could be argued that the point of Davidson's analysis is to deny the intentionality of emotions altogether, a conclusion Hume resists, despite his theory. For Davidson, the problem of intentionality is converted into the more manageable question of the intensionality of certain kinds of sentences. The content of the judgments that make up the emotion are propositions, and the propositions are "about" the object of the emotion in a sense that has been rather rigorously analyzed in a variety of contemporary semantic analyses. But however well this captures the formal aspects of the intensionality of emotions, it fails to satisfy our sense that an emotion is "about" its object in some further sense, a phenomenological sense, in which pride, for example, requires an experience of a certain kind, pertaining to the house. This experience is something much more complex that Hume's simple, pleasant "impression," but so, too is it something more than a sequence of propositional attitudes. Davidson, too, insists that the object of an emotion must be a "psychological entity of some kind," but his analysis provides us with an incomplete account of this "entity." I think that he is right in suggesting a "cognitive" analysis of emotions, in which judgments play an essential role. But not all judgments are propositional attitudes, and the intentionality of emotions requires an account of perception as well as conception, of the way we emotionally experience objects as well as the way we talk about them. This is traditionally, but misleadingly, summarized as the "feeling" component of emotion, the ill-analyzed notion that to have an emotion is to have an experience of a certain kind. But how are we to understand this? And is "intentionality" in fact the proper vehicle for such an account?[3]

A. What Is an "Object"?

"Intentionality" is a concise but not sufficiently clear way of marking off the special properties of emotions (and other "mental acts") which are "about" something. Among those who use this concept the most, there is infamous lack of precision, a few stock phrases and examples which too often serve as the full explication, e.g., "one is never merely afraid, but always afraid *of* something? . . ." But how do we identify this "object," as distinguished, for instance, from the *cause* of an emotion (e.g., "What caused one to be afraid?")? There are two traditional answers, both apparently true but neither of them wholly acceptable.[4]

The *phenomenological* answer emerges in a cramped (if not exactly vicious) circle: the object of the emotion is the essential content of the emotional experience. In other words, it is what the emotion is "about." In Edmund Husserl's writings, this circle is developed in an elaborate and painstaking way; the central feature on his analysis is that the object of experience (he does not discuss objects of emotions as such) requires a description that may be significantly different from a description of the object as such. For example, a tree "as perceived" may lack essential features of the tree described as a plant by a botanist. Husserl underscores this distinction by insisting that his phenomenological descriptions do not yield up any ontological claims, and, more technically, that the object of experience (or "noematic correlate") is to be analyzed as an essential aspect of the mental act (or *noesis*), thus bypassing all ontological questions about what the object in question is "really" like. We shall see that this treatment of intentional objects is of immense value in what we shall say about objects of emotion. But it is also evident even from the brief description here that the ontological status of such objects is not resolved but simply ignored on the phenomenological analysis. It also suggests (though Husserl argued against this) that the object of an emotion (or of any "mental act") might be something *other* than the object itself, a suggestion which leads to grave problems and misunderstandings.

The *analytic* answer begins with the notion of an "opaque" (as opposed to a "transparent") context in the *description* of the emotion (thus providing us with an account of intensionality, not intentionality as such). An "opaque" or "intentional" context is defined in terms of substitutivity and the peculiarities of certain sorts of truth conditions. For example, the sentence form "S believes that A is P but (although A=B) S does not know that B is P" signals such a context. In the realm of emotions, "Sam is angry at the man who stole his umbrella, but he is not angry at his best friend Joe (because he does not know that it was Joe who stole the umbrella)" would mark such a context too. In both the phenomenological and the analytic account, it is essential that an intentional object *need not exist* (or, if it is a state of affairs, need not be actual). One version of the phenomenological account borrows from its progenitor Franz Brentano the scholastic conception of "intentional inexistence," though the ontological status of such "inexistent" objects has long presented philosophers with puzzles and paradoxes. The analytic account more modestly settles for an account of the truth and falsity of certain sentences, although this leaves the question of the status of the intentional object in a true proposition (e.g., "She was proud that she had been elected president"), there is some plausibility to the Humean-Davidsonian paraphrase, "She was pleased because she believed (truly) that she had been elected president." But where the object is of the sort indicated by the problematic phenomenological notion of "intentional inexistence," however (e.g. "John is still in love with Mary, even though she's been dead ten years"), there is a sterile silence. To be sure, certain sentences about John's (propositional) attitudes regarding Mary will be true under some descriptions of Mary and false under others. But the analysis of tragic emotions can hardly be reduced to instances of false existential belief.

The phenomenological account presents us with mysteries; the analytic account seems to miss the emotion. Worse yet, the two accounts are often confused, providing us with the worst of each. The notion of an "opaque" context, as a semantic concept, includes the context of interpretation as well as the context of the sentence, and, as such, is too easily confused with the *content* of the emotion, a phenomenological concept. The conceptual connection that is required to link the *descriptions* of the emotion and its object is mistaken for an intrinsic connection between the emotion and the object themselves. And certain formal aspects of the analytic account are mistaken as properties of the emotion itself. Anthony Kenny, trying to capture the essence of both accounts, relies on a formal description of emotion language but tries to capture the experiential element as well by taking the emotion itself to be a "feeling," although this is never analyzed in any way.[5] Moreover, Kenny simply asserts that some "feelings" are intentional (e.g., emotions) and others are not (e.g., sensations). But how can any "feeling" be intentional? And what is the difference between those which are and those which are not? Here Hume's insistence that the "impression" that is the emotion "contains not any representative quality" comes back to us. What is a "feeling" in this context? And what possible properties of the "feeling" (described phenomenologically as a certain kind of experience) account for the peculiarities of description which are summarized by the notion of intensionality? How, between the two, does that peculiar entity called "the intentional object" fit into the analysis?

The confusion of the two accounts becomes evident most of all in the move from the analysis of belief—in which the analytic and phenomenological accounts are much the same, to the analysis of emotion, in which they are not. Insofar as an emotion can be reduced to a set of beliefs—which is precisely what Davidson tries to do—this confusion can be disguised, if not avoided. But the objects of belief—propositions—are quite different from the intentional objects of most emotions. Propositions can be either true or false; a false belief can be analyzed as a relation between a person and a false proposition. In every case, however, a belief is a relation between a person and a proposition, whether true or false. But this same mode of analysis has absurd consequences when applied to those cases in which the intentional object of an emotion does not exist, as in false pride, unwarranted anger, of misguided love (that is, *really* misguided love, in which the person putatively loved does not exist at all). Since *some* emotions are "about" objects that do not exist, it is argued, then—on the model that *all* beliefs are "about" propositions—*all* objects of emotions must be something other than the things, people, events, or states of affairs which appear to be their objects. Kenny, for instance, argues,

> There are many cases in which it is natural to think of the object of emotion as its cause: e.g. "I was angry because he burst in without knocking," and "Her behavior made me most embarrassed." But there are other examples that show that the relation of an emotion to its object cannot be one of effect to cause; e.g., "I dread the next war," "I hope Eclipse will win." So despite appearances, the ostensibly causal expressions in the earlier examples must be understood as having a special non-causal sense.[6]

The confusion between the two modes of analysis becomes most obvious when Kenny refers us to the Aristotelian concept of a "formal object" of emotion, a bastard mix of intentionality talk and intensional analysis. The notion of "a special non-causal sense" is left unexplained, and the nature of the "objects" themselves remains a mystery, too. Of course, one thing he means by "special non-causal sense" is that there is a logical ("non-contingent") connection, but this seriously confuses the relation between an emotion and its object, on the one hand, and the connections between their descriptions, on the other, as if "causal" and "non-contingent" applied equally to both. Kenny skips as lightly and quickly as possible over the ontological horrors his account suggests, preferring to stay on the safe empirical ground of descriptive semantics ("grammar"). But even so, he saves the intentionality of emotions only at a costly price. He implicitly opens the door to the old ontological zoo of Meinong and Brentano, with "subsistent" (or whatever) intentional objects which need not exist in order to perform their semantic functions. He reintroduces Brentano's conception of "intentional inexistence" and the disastrous generalization mentioned above, such that, since *some* intentional objects are not real objects, *all* objects of emotion must in fact be "inexistent." Causes of emotion are real, but objects are never causes. Thus "objects" are not real objects, but something else ("formal objects"). This is Kenny's "special non-causal sense." He explains the difficult cases only by making the normal cases equally difficult.

Robert Gordon has rightly objected to Kenny's making "otiose . . . the mysterious non-causal connection between an emotion and its object."[7] Gordon, following some of Davidson's earlier suggestions, suggests that intentionality talk (as opposed to intensional talk) be dispensed with and replaced, as in Hume's original attempt by straightforward causal analysis. In other words, the so-called intentional object of the emotion is simply to be understood as its *cause*. Causes, unlike "objects," must exist, or they wouldn't be causes. Nothing can *make* me proud unless it happened. "I am proud." "I am furious at John" translates into "John makes me furious." What of those cases in which the "object" doesn't exist? They will be treated as degenerate cases, misdescriptions, or else not really emotions at all.

A similar analysis defines J. R. S. Wilson's *Emotion and Object*.[8] His arguments (many of them well-directed against Kenny's analysis) deserve extended discussion, but their main thrust can be easily summarized here, the first part of the book utilizes Davidson's arguments to explode Kenny's familiar insistence that, if the connection between emotion and object is a "non-contingent one," then it cannot also be causal (chaps. iii–v). His own analysis, accordingly, is based on the thesis that "the relation of an emotion to its object is indeed causal" (7). An emotion, Wilson tells us (chap. ix) is essentially a *reaction to* something, a reaction *caused by* something, and that something, properly qualified, is its object. What is this reaction? It is, primarily, to *feel* something (78), which is distinctively passive ("to feel is for something to happen to one") (ibid.). He further insists that "involved in a person's state of feeling are spontaneous, undeliberated impulses or inclinations to behave" (79). "Spontaneity" is emphasized as Wilson (wrongly) insists that "one cannot reason one's way to an emotion" (80). (Not even Hume held that!) An emotion, in other words, is a feeling caused by something, and that something is its "object."

The claim that the cause is the object clearly won't do. Obviously any cause isn't the object: physiological causes, for example, aren't the objects of emotions. I can be angry *because* I have had too much coffee, but I am not angry "about" drinking too much coffee. And where in this account is the logical connection between (descriptions of) the emotion and its object? Given that Wilson is not so crude as to say that *the* cause is always the object (he rather emphasizes the "causal story" of an emotion), he does not fall easily to the objection that "what caused me to be angry was my headache, but what I was angry *about* was the barking of the dog." But if it is the barking of the dog that also causes me to be angry, does that *entail* that it is what I am angry about? And couldn't I be angry about the god's barking without hearing the dog's barking (perhaps being told, falsely, that the dog is barking)?

Suppose I am caused to be angry by the dog's barking but what I am angry about is the fact that he has not been kept in the house? What I react *to* is a situation that can be described in a great many ways; what I am angry *about* can be described correctly in only a limited number of ways. What *causes* my emotion is a situation, my entire genetic-cultural-social-psychological background; the object of my emotion is one particular aspect of that situation. Thus Wilson is forced to make a vital concession:

> What someone feels in a particular situation is closely connected with how the situation seems to him, how it strikes him, what particular aspects of the situation impress themselves upon him, and so on. Thus the expression of the feeling often takes the form not of an introspective report, but of a description or characterization of the situation itself. (79)

And again, he emphasizes "what kind of event or action the reactor takes it to be" (82) and that there is "a connection between what someone feels and the way things seem to him" (83). The shift from mere reaction to active interpretation marks an all-important shift from cause and psychological effect to the phenomenologically distinctive notion summarized as "seems to him." Intentionality is slipped in through the language of "relevance," by insisting that "his response must be relevant" to the situation (84). Despite the strained use of the passive voice, it becomes evident that the "reaction" language is superseded by its qualifications, and the "response" that supposedly constitutes the emotion is *logically* tied to a "way of seeing." Now this does not undermine the causal connection between a situation and one's emotional reaction to it; both Davidson and Wilson are right on this point and Hume and Kenny wrong. But the relation of object and emotion is not just the causal connection between a situation and a person's emotional reaction to it. Here I want to defend Kenny, despite his problematic and ontologically suspect separation of object from cause. We need not talk about a "special non-causal sense"; not need we deny the appropriate causal relations as we describe the essential logical connections. But the function and nature of the description of the object of emotion are always independent of the function and nature of causal explanations of that emotion, even in the cases where those descriptions and explanations are seemingly identical.

B. The Cause of an Emotion—and Its Object

The cause of an emotion is whatever event, state of affairs, thing, or person incites the emotion, whether or not this has anything to do with what the emotion is about. Thus the cause of an emotion might be a physiological disturbance or state, an incident which "jogs one's memory" and sets off a sequence of associations, one which has emotional import, a situation which evokes a certain emotional response (whether or not the emotion is about that situation). One might add that there is probably never a single "cause" as such but rather many elements in a complex "causal story," one of which is singled out in an explanatory context, the other causal factors being presumed. One might also add that what justifies a causal explanation and, consequently, what is implied by it, is a regular law-like connection between the occurrence of the cause (with appropriate qualifications and given certain standing conditions included in the total causal story) and the occurrence of the emotion. The scope of such laws is controversial, but this is a controversy concerning causal explanation in general, and it is no less problematic in the explanation of the boiling of this pot of water than that of my getting angry because I had too much coffee this morning. (Under what conditions do I *always* get angry after having had too much coffee? And what must be the frequency of this reaction among *other* people in order for it to be an acceptable explanation of *my* getting angry? Under what conditions could my anger be explained by my having drunk too much orange juice?) Finally, one must insist that the cause of an emotion must be an *actual* occurrence (state of affairs, etc.) and that it need not be recognized by the person who has the emotion. For example, there is no need that the situation which is the cause of the emotion "seem to him" to be a certain way. It need not "seem to him" at all. (Here is where Wilson confuses cause and object.) Where the cause of the emotion is a physiological occurrence, it is possible that the person may not know about it under any (non-trivial) description (e.g., "the cause of my emotion"). Where the cause is a situation, the person may know that such situations cause him to get angry, but he need not. A miserly businessman may always get angry whenever approached by a beggar, yet refuse to acknowledge that this causes him to be angry (whatever he then gets angry *about*). Where the cause of emotion is a belief, perception, or other psychological state or occurrence (including other emotions), it may be that the person must, in some sense, know it, but just because it is psychological, not because it is the cause of the emotion. The causes of emotion are not all psychological; they may be physiological or, for that matter, astrological. When the cause of an emotion is psychological (a Freudian wish or an impulse, for example), it need not be explicit in the experience. And when the cause of an emotion is in fact an experience (for example, a trauma), that experience need not be what the emotion itself is about.

The object of emotion, unlike the cause of the emotion, is always distinctively psychological and always part of experience. In our brief discussion of Davidson's reconstruction of Hume, we quoted his comment that the object of an emotion is always "a psychological entity of some kind." Now we must explain that pronouncement. The object, as Wilson insists of the cause, is always something as "it strikes" a person, as "it seems," as he or she "takes it." The intrusion of the beggar causes the greedy businessman to become angry; but what his anger is about is some specific aspect of that situation: the invasion of his privacy, the appeal to his guilt feelings about success, the resemblance of the beggar to his elder brother. The fact that the beggar was wearing a tattered Robert Hall suit coat is a proper part of the description of the cause; unless the angered businessman has some specific reaction to Robert Hall suits, however, this fact plays no role in the description of the object of anger. Like the objects of imagination (as William James argued long ago), the objects of emotion are underdetermined. There are certain essential properties which define that object, but others are undetermined. The horse that one imagines has no particular weight; the person at whom one is angry wears no particular brand of underwear (unless, of course, one happens to be angry about the underwear). The object of anger is circumscribed by the experience of the angry person, whatever the facts, and, moreover, it is circumscribed by those aspects of the experience germane to the anger. Thus the angry businessman might notice the Robert Hall suit coat, but it is not in any way part of (the object of) his anger. Thus, according to the analytic account, descriptions of causes are (more or less) "transparent";[9] descriptions of objects are "opaque." Descriptions of objects are determined by the way the person (who has the emotion) perceives (imagines, thinks about) those objects *through that emotion*. (The importance of this qualification will became apparent later.)

Regarding the object of the emotion, there need be no generalization to other cases, actual or merely possible. Causal explanations always require such generalizations. If I am caused to be angry by too much coffee, even just once, that explanation requires corroboration with other cases involving other people, coupled with some semblance of a physiological account of the effects of coffee. But if I am angry about something, just once, comparisons with other persons in similar circumstances are neither necessary not appropriate. Of course, it is perfectly appropriate to ask me for the reasons for my anger, and you may expect that they will tie together in some coherent set of beliefs. But even if you find my reasons incomprehensible, you may not have sufficient ground for denying either that I am angry or that I am angry about what I say I am angry about. In causal explanations, my say-so is of no special significance. In the description of what my emotion is about, my say-so is prima facie authoritative. This is *not* to say that I might not be wrong about what I am angry about, or that you might not, in some instance, even convince me that I am angry about something else. But what is at stake in such assertions and corrections is only the coherence of my own way of seeing things. You (or a good analyst) might convince me that what I am *really* angry about is something else (or that the woman I *really* love is my mother) but this *supplements* the description of the object; it doesn't refute or replace it. Causal explanations are intrinsically generalizations; descriptions of emotional objects are not, and when they are generalized (as in some Freudian theory), it is often with the danger of serious distortion and lack of phenomenological acumen.

The function of causal explanations is to *explain*, to tie this emotion to other occurrences of similar emotions. ("This always happens when . . . .") The function of object descriptions is to *make explicit* the experience of the person who has an emotion.[10] ("Here is how I really feel. . . .") These functions are very different, but it does not follow that the descriptions of the cause and the object will be different. In many cases, of course, the descriptions will appear to be identical, and so "he became angry because . . ." serves as *both* the description of the cause and the description of the object. For the sake of economy, why not? But one context is intensional; the other is not. The cause can be described in any number of ways (the description being more or less "transparent"), and some of these ways are appropriate as descriptions of the object, too. Thus, in a single phrase, one can both explain the emotion (assuming the rest of the causal story to be understood) and describe what it is about. But this is not always possible, and it must not be supposed that, because it so often is possible, that descriptions of the cause and descriptions of the object are the same and serve similar functions. They are always different, and, in this sense, we may say (not falsely but misleadingly) that the cause and the object are never the same. This is Kenny's claim, crudely interpreted. But, to be fair to him, his "special non-causal sense" might be interpreted instead in terms of the two different "functions" I have described here. Ontologically, the cause and the object are often the same. Their descriptions often appear to be the same. But the function of their descriptions is always different, and, in this sense, it is always wrong to confuse philosophical accounts of the objects of emotion with causal explanations.

C. Objects of Emotion and Objects of Belief

When beliefs, perceptions, or other psychological states or occurrences are the causes of emotion, the systematic ambiguity between descriptions of causes and descriptions of objects becomes even more complex. Beliefs, for example, often have built into them a "way of seeing" a situation. It is thus that Hume's theory (and Davidson's reconstruction of it) have some immediate plausibility. If I am angry at my friend John for stealing my car, it is essential to my anger that I believe that John has stolen my car. It is plausible to suggest that I am angry because John has stolen my car. But it has often been objected that the fact that John stole my car isn't sufficient to cause my anger; I must believe that John stole my car. Thus I am angry because I believe that John stole my car. In fact, both of these formulations are correct, for both the fact and the belief are ingredients in the causal story of my anger. If John in fact did not steal my car, then the belief alone would be the cause (together with the reasons for my coming to have that belief). What I am angry *about*, however, is another matter. I may be angry about the fact that John stole my car, but it is never simply the fact that I am angry about. It is John's stealing my car viewed by me in a certain angry way. This must be spelled out in detail and the evident circularity must be explained, but for now, we can simply say that what I am angry about is not simply the fact but the *offense*. Similarly, although it is my belief that John stole my car that is the cause of my anger, what I am angry about is not the belief. Furthermore, what I am angry about is more than what that belief is about. One might alternatively suggest that the belief that causes me to be angry is not just the belief that John had stolen my car, but rather the belief that John has offended my by stealing my car. Now, it is clear that the description of the causal belief is such that it serves as well as a description of what pride is about. But it is still of the utmost importance to keep distinct the very different functions of causal explanations of emotions and descriptions of what those emotions are about, for it is not at all generally the case that the object of an emotion can be properly described as the object of certain beliefs (or other emotions) which are its cause.

D. The Existence of Objects: Actual and Possible

The object of an emotion is a situation, thing, person, etc., as viewed in a certain way. In a complete account, it will be necessary to specify, for each emotion as well as for emotions in general, what this "certain way" is. In pride, for example, the "certain way" is, as Hume rightly argued, seeing the object as signifying one's own virtue. This "seeing in a certain way" is Kenny's special "non-causal sense" demystified. But notice that our way of approaching the concept of intentional objects of emotion is just the opposite of Kenny's, in the following sense. He makes the disastrous move from the fact that some objects of emotions don't exist to the general claim that the objects of emotions must be understood in a "non-causal" way. Now as we have argued, this is correct in one sense (accounts of objects are always different from accounts of causes), but it is incomprehensible if it means that the objects themselves are never real (and part of the causal story). The mistake is taking the odd cases as paradigms and then supposing that all objects of emotion have some peculiar ontological status. What distinguishes the objects of emotions (and intentional objects in general) is not any peculiar ontological status as such but rather the fact that they are essentially specified by the way in which they are "viewed." An "object-as-viewed" has distinctive phenomenological, not peculiar ontological, status. But the primary case must nevertheless be the case where the object actually exists. Those cases where it does not, must be treated as special cases. This is a move Wilson also anticipates against Kenny, but he goes too far. He says, "I restrict the term 'object' to items existing in the world" (7). Objects whose emotions do not exist, he argues, are "malfounded" (97) and merely "aspirant cases of emotions" (97–98). But when I am (wrongly) angry at John for stealing my car (which he didn't), I am angry despite the fact that my emotion is unjustified by the facts and based upon a false belief ("malfounded"). I am still angry at John for stealing my car. Furthermore, Wilson's position becomes patently absurd for emotions directed toward the future (or past). It becomes logically impossible to hope for anything; indeed, in one sense, it would be impossible even to be afraid (since the event feared, as distinct from the being that will cause that event, is in the future). The objects of emotion clearly need not be "items existing in the world." Nevertheless, it is nonsense to suppose that, in most cases, the objects of emotion are anything else.

"Intentional inexistence" is not the paradigm case; the paradigm is the case in which the object of emotion is part of the causal story, viewed and described in a certain way. If we return to Davidson's domestic example of the man who is proud of his beautiful house, we can say, without ontological catastrophe, that the object of his pride is the house. On the other hand, the house as the object of his pride is distinctively "psychological" in that it has properties which can only be identified by reference to the proud person's attitudes towards his house. Yet these are not properties of his attitudes; they are properties *of the house*. It signifies his virtue and *it* satisfies his ego. The house as the object of pride, in other words, is the house *as-it-is-viewed-by-the-proud-person*. This becomes absurd if the only properties ascribed to the house (as object of pride) are "natural properties"—made of wood and brick, four bedroom, etc. It becomes more absurd if psychological properties are given some special "non-natural" status, as if, being accepted as properties, they have to be accepted as properties of the house "in itself," without reference to the proud person. and what is most absurd of all appears as soon as our simple phenomenological model of "the house as viewed" is rendered as ontology, viz. that in addition to the wood-and-brick, four-bedroom house and the proud person's attitudes toward it there is a peculiar intentional object, i.e., *the house as viewed*.[11] We need not deny that in some sense the house exists "in itself." And we can insist, commonsensibly, that the house one is proud of and the house "in itself" are one and the same house. The house is an ontological item; the house-as-viewed is not. But as the object of pride, the house is *essentially* viewed in a certain way, and that, in turn, is what makes that emotion pride.

To insist that our paradigm must be "the object as viewed" does not, however, relieve us of the responsibility of accounting for those cases in which the putative object of an emotion does not exist. Consider the unfortunate fellow with the fine house, which alas, either has burned down or has been repossessed, even while he was bragging about it to his colleagues at work. His pride in his owning a fine house is still intact, but either his house or his ownership is not. Such is the kind of case that forces the introduction of "intentional inexistence" into our discussion. This does not mean, as for Kenny, that such a concept is necessary in every case, but neither does it allow us to simply dismiss such cases, as Wilson does. What it does mean is that we have to enrich our phenomenology (whether or not our ontology) to include not only "items existing" but entities which have existed or might exist in the world (or out of it). The objects of emotion may be the objects of imagination, memory, and contemplation as well as those of perception.

Inexistent objects, whether they are part of a future-oriented emotion, or objects which once existed and now do not, or objects that never existed, seem to create problems insofar as we want to say the the relation of an emotion to its object is a relation between the person who has the emotion and the object. Our analysis of the object of emotion as the object as viewed, for example, is such a relation. "Proud of x" means "viewing x in a certain way." But what if there is no x? The first thing that must be said is this: nothing need be different, from a phenomenological point of view, between the case in which x exists and the case in which x does not. The experience of the man who is proud of his house is exactly the same whether his house in fact still exists or not, and whether he in fact owns it or not. What is essential, first of all, is that he *believes* that he still has and owns it. This is emphatically not to say that the object of emotion is reducible to a set of beliefs. But the experience of emotions and their objects is constituted by these beliefs, and so we can say that many cases of "intentional inexistence" can ultimately be reduced to ways of viewing the world which are *predicated upon* (but not reducible to) false existential beliefs. An "inexistent object" is not a peculiar kind of object; it is an object which is falsely believed to exist. And although one cannot have an experience of an object which does not exist, one can clearly have experience based upon the false belief that a certain object exists and thus say, intelligibly but misleadingly, that those experiences are experiences *of* that object.

E. The Phenomenology of Objects

The mystery of "intentional inexistence" is provoked by the insistence, such as Kenny's, that *all* emotions (and all intentional "acts") involve such objects, even when existent objects are involved. The mystery is also aggravated by the image of such objects, even when existent objects are involved. The mystery is also aggravated by the image of such objects on the model of hallucinations, as if still being angry at John (after John has disappeared) is being angry at some phantom representative of John. The misleading idea is that one cannot be angry at John (as grammar and common sense would indicate) since John is not present to be angry about. but the object of anger is John, whether he exists or not, the same John of such and such properties who would be instantiated in the world if he existed in exactly the way he is now exemplified in the emotional experience of anger.[12] There is no peculiar object other than John which exists whether or not he does.

Philosophers are often prone to talk about objects "in themselves," allowing ontology to infiltrate phenomenological description to disastrous degree.[13] In discussing emotions, we are *concerned with phenomenology*, the way the world (and certain objects in it, including oneself) are viewed. Phenomenologists distinguished the evidence for certain claims from the "things themselves," but it is essential to remember that "the things themselves," described phenomenologically, are still functions of experience. One's contact with the objects of emotion, for example, is often by way of evidence rather than direct confrontation. To be angry at John, for example, need not involve contact with John; the conclusive evidence for anger might consist of the notable absence of one's car coupled with several "eyewitness" reports about its last driver. What one is angry about, of course, is not this evidence but about its meaning, namely, John's having stolen the car. But where John no longer exists, perhaps murdered by Mexican bandits, or where the evidence is only circumstantial and John did not in fact steal the car, what goes wrong is the inference from the evidence to its alleged meaning. There is no mysterious "object" that is required to stand in for John. There is only the faulty inference and false belief, upon which the remainder of one's emotional experience is allowed to persist.

All of this is further complicated in the following way. We have been speaking in the (usual) clumsy way about objects existing or not existing. In fact, matters are rarely so simple. The object of emotion as object as viewed is not an ontological particular but an opaque cluster of essentially defined properties as well. So it is not simply a question of John's existing but also of his being the thief who took my car, his being the same friend I graduated college with, and whose personality is not now so deranged that I might say "he's a different person." And if it is John's love for Mary that concerns us, it is clear that it is not just any version of Mary that will serve as the object of John's love. His love need not be so fickle as to fizzle when Mary dyes her hair, but, nonetheless, it is not (to use the usual ontological obscenity) Mary as "bare particular"[14] that turns John on, but Mary dressed in a substantial outfit of personal properties. The ontological complication here is this: John loves Mary, who exists. But he loves her for her brilliance (perhaps she is in fact a mediocre wit) and for her voluptuousness (apparent only to him) and for her genealogy (which she has lied about). The question can be raised, therefore, whether it is in fact Mary whom he loves after all. The case can be generalized via Freud and Jung; suppose it were true that what every male loves is in fact his mother or a mother archetype? What are we to say of the intentional object of a man's love? Existence isn't in question; existence *as* a certain kind of person is. It is clear that some of the most interesting questions of intentionality have been left out of the traditional ontological formulations.

This kind of complexity arises along another dimension. Sometimes the existence of the object and all facts about it are accurately perceived, but yet something else goes wrong which also makes the emotion inappropriate. A husband is violently jealous because his wife has gone out for coffee with a male friend, innocently enough. The husband is completely and correctly informed about the situation, but his jealousy is inappropriate for other reasons having to do with the legitimacy of claims and rights rather than his perception of the facts of the case. Now we may say, although we cannot defend it here, that all emotions involve such non-epistemic considerations, and so we may say that the object of every emotion is never simply a fact, person, event, or state of affairs, but a network of values, expectations, and claims as well. Thus we have said that the object of anger is never simply a deed; it is an *offense*. The object of pride is never just a house, but the ownership of the house as a sign of one's virtue. Now what one wants to say about the ontology of values is, again, not our concern here. But, whatever one says, the simple ontology of objects of emotions as simply "objects themselves" is undermined by the recognition that emotional objects are partially defined by the concerns of ethics, aesthetics, politics, religion, and all sorts of personal tastes and preferences as well as matters of ontology. In this sense, emotions never view objects as they are "in themselves," but always as they are "for us."

But let us not push too far in this direction. If the object of emotion is never exactly identical with the object "in itself" (and therefore never identical with its cause either), this does not mean that the object is something *other than* the object "in itself" (and, sometimes, the cause). The extreme paranoid does not simply imagine the objects of his unreasonable fear; in fact, what is most disturbing is our realization that all of the paranoid's allegations do have some truth to them. It is what he *makes of* these that constitutes the paranoia. Lovers rarely imagine the "objects" of their love; the wandering knight may never see his "beloved," but he still requires a few golden locks or a scattered shoe or two to "represent" her. So we can see that "inexistence" isn't such a simple matter. The object of emotion is constituted by a complex system of beliefs and evaluations, only some of which involve "existence" in its crude and oversimplified ontological sense. The analysis of emotions requires far more subtlety. But, at the same time, it requires far less ontological mystery than many of the traditional accounts would suggest. The object of an emotion is in virtually no case simply "the thing itself," not is it ever anything else.

F. Emotions, Descriptions, and Objects: Beyond Atomism

In our preceding discussions, we have left unchallenged one major assumption, shared by virtually every author on the subject—namely, the assumption that an emotion and its object are distinct entities, however each of them is to be analyzed. Thus Hume sharply distinguished the impression that is the emotion from the ideas which are its cause and object. Kenny sharply distinguishes the emotion, which is a "feeling," from the object, the thing, event, or state of affairs to which this feeling has a "special non-causal" relationship. Wilson, flatly rejecting Kenny's analysis in general, still begins his analysis with the same flat-footed distinction: "If I am afraid of a dog, the dog and my fear are distinct items in any sense of the word."[15] This assurance immediately follows a short discussion in which he suggests that proponents of the "non-contingently connected" view of emotions and objects (namely, Kenny) might really mean "a contrast between situations where two items are causally connected, and situations where there are not two distinct items at all." This would account for the logical relationship between emotion and object very simply, but Wilson pursues it no further: "I shall not consider this possibility any further, since fairly clearly it will not do in the case of emotion and object."[16] I want to argue exactly the position dismissed: The relation of emotion to object is in effect one of *identity* (or more accurately, something like Spinoza's "dual aspects" of one and the same phenomenon). The confusion surrounding the intentionality of emotion and the nature of emotional objects is a product of the same atomistic thinking that undermined Hume's theory—the need to distinguish and treat as separate "components" what in fact must be viewed as a unitary phenomenon.

We have continuously stressed the importance of the logical connection between an emotion and its object. But we have also insisted that this isn't quite right. Logical connections are connections between descriptions, and the crucial logical connection between the emotion and its object is rather a tie between certain descriptions. Anger in no sense entails its object. But neither does the statement "He is angry" entail "He believes that the National Bank has repossessed his house," despite the fact that what he is angry about is the repossession of his house. In this case, the necessary connection can be supplied by insisting upon a full description of the emotion, namely, "He is angry about the National Bank having repossessed his house." But a "full" description need not be an ontologically complete description. An ontologically complete description might also include mention of the new roof just purchased, the fact that the dog no longer has a yard, the fact that the bank gave insufficient notice, etc. If the "object" is (wrongly) considered independently of the emotion, it would seem that the description might include anything that is true about the house, the bank, the repossession, and so on. But what is appropriate for the "full description" requirement depends entirely on the emotion. The description must be appropriate to the object *as viewed* in the emotion, and therefore, to the emotion as fully described. Thus it may be true that the National Bank is also the bank that suffered a severe financial loss in October, but this has no place in the description of the object of anger. (This may be true even if one also *knows* of the bank's loss.) This "opacity" condition requires that as the emotion and the object are described more "fully," the two descriptions merge together. This is not yet to say that they are the same; but it is a large step in that direction. Much of the illusion of independence is bound up in the usually incomplete descriptions of the emotion and inproportionately detailed descriptions of the object.

It is worth pointing out that what is usually called the "object" of the emotion is in fact only its *focus*.[17] A man is never proud of just his house; he is also proud of himself (as Hume argued) not just in respect of his owning the house but by virtue of any number of implicit qualities which have earned him that ownership. Thus it would not be unreasonable to argue what Davidson denies and Hume argues too quickly, that pride typically involves a sense of self *überhaubt* after all, a sense of one's overall worthiness, even if, other things considered, one might find oneself unpraiseworthy.[18] Moreover, it might be far-fetched but still plausible to suggest that the proud man also adopts a certain vision of the universe as recognizing (his) virtue, as therefore just and fair (the very antithesis of the "indifferent" universe bemoaned and celebrated by Albert Camus in his *Myth of Sisyphus*). Or the proud man might see the universe as indeed hostile, and so see himself as a bold spirit who has managed to introduce some justice in its midst. (Enter Camus.) In either case the point is this: it is literally true to say that the man is proud of his house, but the view that marks pride may be—and perhaps must be—much more than this. It is a *world* view. To counter the atomistic view of objects as isolated and precisely delineated, we might counter by saying that the object of every emotion is ultimately the world. What we call "the object" is its minimal description, only its primary focus.[19]

How does the distinction between emotion and object arise in the first place? The most obvious answer lies in traditional conceptions of emotions as "internal" states or occurrences, Humean "impressions," for example. Since the emotion is something wholly psychological—a sensation or feeling—it is clearly distinct from what it is "about," another person or a state of affairs, for example. Modifications of this traditional view, no matter how radical, leave this conception intact. The view that emotions are ultimately physiological occurrences or states also makes necessary the unquestionable distinction of emotion and object, although, on both the feeling and the physiological views, the very possibility of such "about" relationships ought to be highly doubtful. (Headaches and gout attacks are not "about" anything, though they surely may be from [be caused by] something.) Even modern behavioral views leave the separation between the disposition to behave and what the emotion is about, although behavioral views might sneak in the notion of intentionality by talking about behavior "toward" others. The general erroneous scheme, then, is this: an emotion is a property, state, disposition, or something that happens to a person, while the object is some item or event in the world, which stands in some curious "about" relationship with the emotion. Given such conceptions of emotion, no wonder the emotion-object relation raises such difficulties. But what if we reject these conceptions of emotion?

A second part of the account of the emotion-object distinction is the idea that an emotion is *explained* by its object—causally, presumably. Then the question is *how* the object explains the emotion, burdened with the difficulty that the description of the object often seems logically tied to the description of the emotion. Hume is largely responsible for this explanatory-causal view, but he has been followed by many philosophers, who are not so concerned with explanation as such, just because of the ontological advantages of causal accounts. They seem not to require nasty intentional notions and can be satisfied purely extensionally. Which means, of course, that their ontology must be neatly divided into quantifiable bundles—emotions on the one hand, objects on the other. But, as we have seen, such causal accounts cannot make sense of intentionality. Descriptions of objects of emotion don't *explain* the emotion; rather, they further *describe* it.[20] There are not two entities, one explaining the other. There is no distinctive item which is the object of emotion; rather, to describe the so-called object is simply to further describe the emotion.

A third part of the account is more pedestrian. We often ascribe emotions to people without saying what they are about, "he's angry today" and "she's madly in love." It can be insisted that such incomplete ascription can always be followed by "about what?" or "with whom?," but the point is that, incomplete as they may be, such ascriptions are perfectly legitimate and often, in context, all that one wants to know. But such incomplete ascriptions leave a sense that there are two components to the emotion which can be described separately, the emotion itself and what it is about—some situation or person. And philosophers, grasping onto the handles of ordinary grammar, begin their accounts on the basis of this vernacular indifference to accuracy.

The fourth part of the account—and no doubt there are more—is more of a general challenge, which I will not pursue here. Much of contemporary philosophy involves the rejection or neglect of experience, in this case, concentration on the grammar, ontology, and causal etiology of emotions and wholesale neglect of what we call "the emotional experience." Kenny, for example, discharges his obligations to human experience by using the word "feeling," which remains totally unanalyzed as he goes on to a detailed examination of the grammar of emotional ascriptions. Davidson hardly gives "experience" a role in his analysis of pride, although one can be sure he would shruggingly accept that there is an experience of pride, but not of philosophical interest. When experience enters into analyses of emotions, it is usually, at most, à la Humean impressions, "simple and uniform" blips on the *tabula psychologica*. Even phenomenologists, one hesitates to suggest, have not always given fair attention to experience as such, despite a methodology that ostensibly could not be more dedicated to experience. But that is a long and complex story, for another time.

This four-part account involves four errors, some slight matters of inattention, other serious defects in philosophical methodology. Their joint result is the impossibility of understanding emotions. The traditional conceptions of emotions have been attacked often and convincingly, but what has rarely been offered is an alternative. I would argue that emotions can be understood as systems of judgments, which constitute a particular kind of world view.[21] The details are unimportant for purposes here, but the upshot of the theory is a quasi-phenomenological account of emotional experience, in which an emotion is viewed as a way of *seeing* something *as* a thing of a certain sort in a certain kind of context—a person as offensive in anger, a situation as awkward in embarrassment, and event as dangerous in fear, a thing as rightfully one's own in jealousy, an accomplishment as a sign of one's virtue in pride. The emotion is this "seeing as," structured by judgments of various specifiable types which constitute the different emotions. In this account, however, the distinction between the emotion and what it is about all but vanishes. Of course, one can always pry an object away from the emotion through some incomplete description, but, insofar as it is the object of the emotion that is pried away, rather than a mere description of an object in the world, one will find that one has taken the characterization of the emotion along with the object. Similarly for the emotion: it is not an internal occurrence or state which can be clearly distinguished from what it is about. If one wishes to continue talking about "objects" at all, it must be understood that the emotion as a way of seeing "the object" and "the object" as what is seen in this way are neither components nor distinct items, but a unitary gestalt, which can be atomized only at the cost of being incomprehensible.

This allows us to see clearly why reference to the object is not an explanation of the emotion but rather a further description of it. To say "he is angry" is to say that he sees something in that certain way essential to anger. The description of the "object" of anger is then a description of the anger, that is, the way that particular thing is seen in anger. As for the ontology of the matter, that is a matter of phenomenological indifference. The person who is angry describes what he is angry about without any problematic ontological commitments.[22] Intentionality-phobes (*Sinnephobes*) should not find their nightmares manifested here, and if they like, the entire emotion complex can be simply described as the property of a person, so long as it is also insisted that it is a description that cannot be broken into components without systematically misleading consequences.

Conclusion

The concept of "intentionality" captures an essential but misleading property of emotions. It points to the fact that emotions are not merely "feelings" but ways of seeing, ways of directing one's experience of the world. But the concept of intentionality also suggests some too extravagant ontological projections, and it suggests, too, that an emotion and its object are two distinct phenomena, with a problematic if not downright "mysterious" connection between them. It leads us to think of the object as an independent particular, when in fact it is virtually always embedded in a larger context—a world—in which it has the special meaning essential to that emotion. Accordingly, while we should resist those theories of emotion which deny or attempt to reduce intentionality, we must also insist that "intentionality" is a misleading way of modeling emotions, and that a quite different analysis must be offered up in its stead.

6

Getting Angry: The Jamesian Theory of Emotion in Anthropology (1984)

> The Tahitians say that an angry man is like a bottle. When he gets filled up he will begin to spill over.
> Tavana, quoted in Levy (1973:285)

The metaphor is so pervasive, it so dominates our thinking about our feelings, that we find ourselves unable to experience our emotions without it. We find it in philosophy and medicine as well as in our poetry, and we find it, too, in other cultures. Consequently, we believe what the metaphor tells us instead of recognizing it as a metaphor, a cultural artifact that systematically misleads us in our understanding of ourselves and, in anthropology, our understanding of other peoples.

The metaphor, captured succinctly in the Tahitian simile that an angry man is like a bottle, is the *hydraulic metaphor*. It presents the image of emotion as a force within us, filling up and spilling over. Rendered as science, the same metaphor is made respectable in physiological garb. The medieval physicians theorized at length on the various "humours" that determined the emotions. And in this century, the metaphor has been elegantly dressed in neurology and presented as a scientific theory—indeed, the only theory that has thoroughly dominated the subject over the past century. The theory is that an emotion is an "inner experience," based on a physiological disturbance of a (now) easily specifiable kind plus, perhaps, some outward manifestation and an interpretation according to which we identify this feeling as an emotion of a particular kind.

The theory received its classic formulation by William James (1884), in "What Is an Emotion?" James answered his question with his theory: an emotion is the perception of a visceral disturbance brought about by a traumatic perception, for example, seeing a bear leap out in front of you or coming across a bucket filled with blood. The theory (developed simultaneously by C. G. Lange in Europe) is now appropriately called the "Jamesian (James-Lange) theory of emotion." It is, I shall argue, as misleading as it is pervasive.

Emotions in Anthropology

> Emotions as biological events are the same the world over. (Lindzey 1954; also see 1961)

The Jamesian theory has special appeal, and is particularly damaging, in anthropology. There is an obvious problem, given the nature of the theory. An emotion as an "inner feeling" is unobservable and inaccessible to the anthropologist, thus leaving any attempt at describing emotion in other peoples at the mercy of obviously anthropocentric "empathy." And yet, the theory (scientific or not) has been accepted as apparently useful for interpreting not only the emotional life of other peoples but also the language used by other peoples to describe their own emotions, thus suggesting a kind of double confirmation. The theory that emotions, as feelings based upon physiological disturbances, can be understood in strictly biological terms, results in this familiar but fallacious consequence: Emotions can therefore be taken to be more or less universal human phenomena, the same is everyone, making allowances for certain minimal differences in physiology and, consequently, temperament. (In fact, I would argue that there is little reason to suppose that such differences or their emotional consequences are minimal, but that is not the thesis I wish to pursue here; see, e.g., Freedman 1974.)

Even if the emotions were essentially the same in all people, however, it is evident that the language and interpretation of emotions, as well as their causes, expressions, and vicissitudes, vary widely from culture to culture. The effects of epinephrine may be identical in angry people from Borough Hall in Brooklyn to the beaches of Bora Bora, but there are, nevertheless, differences in the emotional lives of various peoples, and this is where anthropology enters the picture.

The anthropological appeal of the Jamesian theory is obvious: It divides the phenomenon of emotion into two comprehensive components, a physiological feeling component, which can be presumed a priori (and falsely) to be more or less the same in all human beings, and a cultural component, which can be described by the anthropologist, using the same techniques of observation and interview that are appropriate for almost any other cultural phenomenon. Any mystery surrounding emotion is thus dispelled: the difficulty of "getting inside another person's head," without which which one cannot understand another's feelings, is rendered unnecessary. Emotions are to be understood in the realm of physiology, not phenomenology, thus circumventing the hard problem of "empathy." The interpretation of emotions (including the basic interpretive act of naming and identifying one's emotion) is quite distinct from the emotion itself, thus leaving the emotion proper outside the realm of anthropology.

My argument turns on two related objections to the Jamesian theory. First that the theory is not only incomplete but quite mistaken. It trivializes, rather than captures, the nature of emotions.[1] Second, the distinction between an emotion and its interpretation is faulty and misleading in a variety of ways. The consequence of these objections is to insist that emotions themselves are the proper province of anthropology. My thesis is that emotions are to be construed as cultural acquisitions, determined by the circumstances and concepts of a particular culture as well as, or rather much more than, by the functions of biology and, more specifically, neurology. There may be universal emotions, but this is a matter to be settled empirically, not by a priori pronouncement.

The Variability of Emotions

> Take aggression as an example. A distinction must be made between the instrumental acts that are indices of aggression (e.g., hitting, insulting, nonco-operating) and the hypothetical "goal response" of the aggression motive (perceiving another person's reactions to injury). It is the latter that one would expect to find transculturally. The aggressor's instrumental activities that serve to hurt someone else—and thus enable him to perceive reactions to injury in his victim—will differ from one culture to another. The form of an insult, for instance, depends on the values held by the insulted one. Or to take another example: automobile racing and football can be instrumental activities for competition only if the society has automobiles and knows how to play football. (Sears 1955)

The cultural specificity and variability of several dimensions of emotion are not in question. For instance, the various causes of emotion are clearly cultural in their specifics (whether or not there are also some causes of some emotions that might be argued to be universal or even "instinctual"). What makes a person angry depends upon those situations or events that are considered offensive or frustrating. A New Yorker will become infuriated on standing in a queue the length of which would make a Muscovite grateful. The same action will inspire outrage in some societies and not others: consider, as examples, failing to shake hands, kissing on the lips, killing a dog, not returning a phone call. The same objects will provoke fear in one culture but not in others, for example, snakes, bewitchment, being audited by the IRS, not getting tenure, and being too rich or too thin. Causes of emotion vary from culture to culture; it does not follow that emotions do, or do not, vary as well.

The *names* of emotions clearly vary from culture to culture, along with most vocabulary entries and names for virtually everything else. But this obvious point hides a subtle and troublesome one: How do we know whether it is *only* the names (i.e., phonetic sequences) that vary, rather than their reference? The problem here is what W. V. O. Quine calls "radical intranslatability," do the words "anger" in English and *"riri"* in Tahitian refer to "the same" emotion? How would we tell? Even if the causes are commensurable and the behavior seems to be similar, how do we gauge the similarity of the emotions? Names of emotions are clearly cultural artifacts, even "arbitrary" in the sense that it is now said as a matter of Paris-inspired cant that "all signs are arbitrary." But the identities of the phenomena that those names name are yet an open question, not obviously the same references for quaintly different vocabularies but clearly not entirely different either. We are, after all, identifying a shared reference to *something*.

A similar point can be made about the various *expressions* of emotion. Clearly some expressions, at least, differ from culture to culture as learned gestures and more or less "spontaneous" actions. Clenched fists are expressions of anger in one culture, not in another. Banging one's head on the wall is an expression of grief in one society, not in others. And the *verbal* expressions of emotion vary not only along with the language (of course) but also according to the familiar images and metaphors of the culture. (Not everyone would understand what we so easily and now clumsily refer to as "heartbroken.") There may well be emotional expression that vary very little from culture to culture, particularly certain minimal facial expressions, as Paul Ekman (1975) has recently demonstrated. But that there are such universal expressions, if there are any, no more demonstrates the universality or "nature" of emotions that the wide variety of more complex expressions proves the variability of emotions. Again, this must at least start as an open question, for which the observation of emotional expressions may serve at most as a preliminary. Indeed, the more fundamental question—of what are these expressions expressive?—will have to wait for an account of the emotions themselves.

Finally, there is the series of metaphors to be found in almost every culture with any vocabulary of psychological self-description that are essentially explanations and diagnoses of emotions, rather than merely names for them. The Tahitian gentleman quoted at the start of this essay, for example, is expressing a theory, the hydraulic theory, which has long been dominant in discussions of emotion in our culture, too, in part because of (but also culminating in) Freud's "dynamic" and "economic" models of the psyche in terms of various "various "forces" within. Metaphors and theories of emotion are often related and even interchangeable. They also influence the experience of the emotions themselves. To believe that anger is a force building up pressure is to experience the physiological symptoms of anger as a force "inside," just as believing that "falling in love" is bound to have a certain irresponsible influence on one's loving.

It is a matter of no small interest that the same metaphors—the hydraulic metaphor in particular—can be found in societies of very different temperaments. But such metaphors are by no means universal. Catherine Lutz (1982) describes an emotional vocabulary among the Ifaluk that is relatively devoid of references to the hydraulic metaphor or the Jamesian theory.[2] The prevalence of James's metaphor by no means proves the Jamesian theory to be true. Nevertheless, the variability of emotion metaphors and theories can be counted among the various dimensions of variability of emotion, if, that is, it is true that beliefs about emotions influence or determine the nature of the emotions themselves. (On the Jamesian theory, it is hard to see how or why this should be so; on the alternative view I shall propose at the end of this essay, the mutual influence of beliefs and emotions should be quite transparent.)

Names of emotions do not yet entail metaphors or theories, but even so rudimentary a psychological activity as "naming one's feelings" already stakes out a network of distinctions and foci that are well on their way to extended metaphors and crude theories. The fact that one language has a dozen words for sexual affection and another has fifty words for hostility already anticipates the kinds of models that will be appropriate. A culture that emphasizes what David Hume called "the violent passions" will be ripe for the Jamesian theory, but a culture that rather stresses the "calm" emotions (an appreciation of beauty, lifelong friendship, a sense of beneficence and justice) will find the Jamesian theory and the hydraulic model that underlies it patently absurd. A culture that bothers to name an emotion pays at least some attention to it, and it is hard to find a culture with named emotions that does not also have theories about them, however primitive. In some cases, the theory might consist simply of the warning "anger is dangerous." In theory-enthusiastic cultures such as our own, the theories surrounding an emotion might more resemble the theology of the Druids, thus prompting more or less perennial cries about emotional simplicity and "getting in touch with your feelings." But whether the theory at stake is the labyrinth of Jungian typologies or the homilies of Joyce Brothers, the beliefs people have *about* emotions vary considerably, and it remains to be seen just how this reflects—or doesn't reflect—the cross-cultural (and intracultural) variability of the emotions themselves.

(Not) Getting Angry: Two Examples

> My intestines were angry. (quoted in Levy, 1973:214)

Anger is an emotion that would seem to be universal and unlearned if any emotion is, however different its manifestations in various cultures. John Watson chose anger as one of his three "basic" emotions (fear and dependency were the other two). It is one of those emotions most evident even in infants, and Watson suggested that it is one of the building blocks for all other emotions. More recently, Robert Plutchik (1962) has developed an evolutionary model of emotions and emotional development in which anger again emerges as one of the (this time eight) basic building blocks of emotion. Anger is one of the most easily observable emotions: we might debate its nuances (outrage or indignation) and perhaps surmise its etiology (jealousy, frustration, or moral offense). The causes of anger might differ from culture to culture, and the expressions, at least the verbal expressions, might vary, too. But it is too easy to assume that anger itself and its basic manifestations—the reddened face, visible irritability and what William James properly called "tendency to vigorous action"—are much the same from the Philippines to the Lower East Side, from Bongo Bongo to the more boisterous committee meetings of the Social Science Research Council.

Getting Angry: The Jamesian Theory of Emotion in Anthropology (1984)

Everyone gets angry—at least at some time and for some reason. Or so it would seem.

But let us consider two quite different accounts of anger, in two quite different societies. I want to discuss later in this chapter some of the methodological problems to which any such account is subject. But, as a first, superficial observation, let us make clear certain gross differences—or at least claims about certain gross differences—in two cultures: the Tahitian (Levy 1973) and the Utka (Utkuhikhalingmiut) Eskimos (Briggs 1970) in the Northwest Territories. In both cases, these people do not get angry. Some of this may be emphasis rather than substance, but that, too, constitutes a significant difference in emotional life. It might be argued, for instance, that Americans give far more importance to the emotions of anger and moral indignation than do the Russians or Japanese, for example, whether or not the emotions themselves are so significantly different. But having pointed out this difference in emphasis, have we not already indicated vast differences in temperament and emotional constitution as such? For both the Tahitians and the Utka, however, anger is as rare as it is feared.

The Tahitians, according to Levy, place an unusual amount of emphasis on anger. They talk about it and theorize about it extensively: it is "hypercognized," he tells us, in that "there are a large number of culturally provided schemata for interpreting and dealing with anger." Other emotions, sadness, for instance, are "hypocognized" and, Levy suggests, virtually unrecognized. Anger, however, is rare, no matter how much the object of concern. Does this mean, however, that it is indeed present but unaccounted for or, rather, that in circumstances in which *we* (for example) would most certainly have an emotion, they do not?

A partial answer to this crucial question can be couched in terms of the Tahitian theory of emotion, which is distinctively Jamesian. Emotions have a "place" in the body, the intestines, for example. Indeed, the language of emotion is often "it" rather than "I," although one must quickly add that this grammatical feature of the Tahitian language is not to be found only in the realm of emotions (Levy 1973:213). He quotes an informant:

> "In my youth, [it was] a powerful thing, very powerful, very powerful 'it' was [sic], when it came, and I tried to hold it down . . . there was something that was not right. That was the cause of a lot of bad anger inside one . . . after a time . . . that thing, 'it' would go away." (ibid., p. 212)

Levy adds that "people will say 'my intestines were angry'" (ibid., p. 213). This locution may seem slightly odd but certainly not unfamiliar; it indicates, however, a much deeper difference between our conception of anger and the Tahitian conception and, consequently and more important, a deep difference between Tahitian anger and our own.

Throughout the literature on Tahiti, Levy tells us, one message above all keeps repeating itself: "These are gentle people" and there are "extremely few reports of angry behavior." Morrison noted two centuries ago that the Tahitians are "slow to anger and soon appeased" (in Levy 1973:275). Levy quotes a contemporary policeman who talks of "the lack of a vengeful spirit" (ibid., p. 276), and though Levy reports some forty-seven terms referring to anger, he adds that the Tahitian concern with and fear of anger and its violent effects are "in the face of little experience of such anger" (ibid., p. 285). The pairing of so much attention and theorizing with so rare an emotion points to a curious relationship between the having of an emotion and the understanding of it, but it is clear from Levy's descriptions and reports that this relationship is not to be construed (as we might be likely to construe it in ourselves) as one of "suppression" or social "control" as such. It is the gentleness, the lack of anger itself that seems to be learned, not the inhibition or suppression of anger. Part of this learning experience, ironically, is the acquisition of an enormous number of myths and metaphors about anger through which this rather rare emotion is explained—and feared.

In Jean Briggs's (1970) descriptions of the Utka Eskimos, they do not, as her title *Never in Anger* indicates, get angry. Not only do they not express anger; they do not "feel" angry, and, unlike the Tahitians, they do not talk about it. They do not get angry in circumstances that would surely incite us to outrage, and they do not get angry in other circumstances either. The Utka do not have a word or set of graded distinctions for anger, as we do and as the Tahitians do; indeed, the word with which they refer to angry behavior in foreigners and in children is also the word for "childish." There is no reason to suppose that, biologically, the Utka have any fewer or more impoverished epinephrine secretions than we do, and Dr. Briggs's descriptions show that, on occasion, they get just as "heated up" as we do. But they do not get angry, she assures us. They do feel annoyed, even hostile, and they can display raw violence, for example, in the beating of their dogs (in the name of "discipline," of course). But is this to be considered merely a nuance of terminology? Or something more significant?

There have been some severe objections to the observations and conclusions of this research, but the central claim remains intact, at least by way of a plausible hypothesis not yet refuted. Michelle Rosaldo, for instance, has argued that Briggs confuses lack of anger with fear of anger, the sense—to be found in Tahitian society as well as in Filipino society and in our own—that anger is dangerous and can even destroy a society. But here again, we meet that suspicious and too-neat distinction between the essence of the emotion itself and talk *about* emotion, as if it can be assumed that the emotion remains more or less constant while our thoughts and feelings about the emotion alter its expression and its representation. But even if Briggs is wrong about the absence of anger as such, the context of that emotion and the peculiar absence of (what we would consider) the usual expressions and manifestations of it would have to be explained.

The Problem of Methodology

> I see no reason to suppose that our wondering about the nature(s) of emotional states is any different, epistemologically, from our wondering about the nature of many seemingly natural kinds of phenomona. (Rey 1980)

What warrants an anthropologist's attributing emotion of a specific sort to persons in a very different society? We have already pointed out the obvious need to make allowances for differences in vocabulary and expression, differences in context and cause, differences in theories of emotion and etiology, as well as possible differences in etiology itself. But, assuming that an anthropologist with rapport can see through such differences, how can he or she refer with confidence to Jamesian feelings, themselves unseen and unseeable? A few years ago, in his *Rise of Anthropological Theory*, Marvin Harris expressed shock and professional outrage at the "horrifying confidence" of his colleague Margaret Mead in identifying the emotion of her Samoan subjects. Indeed, where should such confidence come from? Is there any justification for confidence in such matters at all?

Dr. Briggs, a *kapluna* (white foreigner) among Utka, is sensitive to such problem.

> Conscious of the pitfalls of misperception to which such a personal approach is subject, I shall try throughout to distinguish explicitly among the various kinds of data on which my statements are based and not to extrapolate from my own feelings to those of Utku without cautioning the reader that I am doing so. I hope, moreover, to present the material vividly enough so that the reader sharing to some extent my cultural background [middle-class, urban, Protestant New Englander] can also experience empathy and contrast between his feelings and those of Utku. (1970:6).

But the key, despite the caution, is "empathy," and although Dr. Briggs succeeds in her "vivid" presentation, the problem remains: How is she (or are we) justified in understanding Utku feelings (or lack of feelings) on the basis of what she observes? How will she know, on the basis of their varied expressions, that the difference is one of emotion rather than merely expression? For example, she describes one of the dominant personalities of the group, Inuttiaq, in the following way:

> Inuttiaq was, if I have read him correctly, an unusually intense person. He, too, kept strict control of his feelings, but in his case one was aware that something was being controlled. The effort of this control was caught in the flash of an eye, quickly subdued, in the careful length of a pause, or the painstaking neutrality of a reply. Occasionally, when he failed to stay within the acceptable bounds of expression, I learned from the disapproval of others what behavior constitutes a lapse and how disapproval is expressed. (1970:42)

Of the other Utku, she says they "were so well controlled that my untutored eye could not detect their emotions" (p. 42). The problem should be evident. Here she is quite obviously talking about differences in the *expression of emotion*, not the emotion itself. To the contrary, she is noting the difficulty of recognizing the emotion beneath the controlled responses. This thesis, if it is all that is meant by "never in anger," is not enough to cast doubt on the universality of anger, nor does it seem to support the view that the Utku are emotionally different in any interesting way from ourselves. But how does the anthropologist read beyond the expression to the emotion to suggest that something is being suppressed or to deny, as the stronger thesis would require, that the Utku do not get angry? How does one legitimately move from what is observed (the expression) to what cannot be observed (the emotion)? Can one do anything other than "extrapolate from [one's] own feelings to those of Utku" (p. 42), however cautiously?

Let me raise the problem, as philosophers are prone to do, to the level of an explicit paradox: the thesis or hypothesis under consideration is the alleged difference between Utku emotion and our own, particularly regarding emotions like anger. But insofar as the anthropologist assumes that she is capable of understanding the emotional expression of her subject, that is, understanding them as expressions of particular emotions, then she must assume from the outset precisely the hypothesis to be verified, namely, that different people have, and can mutually understand, essentially the same emotions. Insofar as empathy plays a role in these investigations, however cautiously, the paradox remains intact. But if the anthropologist gives up empathy as a tool, what can be left, other than a flat behavioral description of emotional expression into which one is not allowed to "read" or "extrapolate" any emotions at all?

Jamesian "Feelings"

Suppose an anthropologist, having had one too many lunches with a philosophical colleague, came to have the following doubt.

Observing some subjects in Bongo Bongo (the only nonurban anthropological site easily accessible to most philosophers), he or she observed that certain people at certain times appeared to be scratching. Or at any rate, that would be the loose, dubious description. The tighter, more operational description would be that they made certain movements at certain times. A rather more suspicious description—of the sort that recalls Marvin Harris's (1968:410) utter horror in regard to Margaret Mead's confidence in identifying the inner states of others, would be that they are scratching an itch. The philosophical caution is the following: given that all that one can observe is the overt behavior, how can one infer the nature of the "inner" states? In this case, presumptively, an itch. And for the anthropologist, though perhaps not for the philosopher, there are methodological restrictions of a troublesome kind: He or she cannot take at face value the descriptions or reports of the people themselves nor trust the words that are used to supposedly translate the name of one feeling to another.

There is no problem here, one might suppose, because itches and scratching, at least, are bound up together in a physiological package that is wired into the species, indeed, not only the species, and there seems no more room for serious (that is, extraphilosophical) doubt that a dog or cat itches when it scratches than there is for the doubt that a foreign subject itches when he or she scratches. The experience, as well as the behavior, can be ascribed with confidence. To make matters slightly more complex, suppose that these certain people believe that itching is a sign of bewitchment, or, turning to the mythopathology of our own society, suppose a frequent sunbather believes, on the basis of continuous media reports, that itching is a certain sign of skin cancer. Can we continue to say with the same assurance that what he or she feels is the "same" feeling that we feel? One might suppose that, yes, the feeling—that is, the itch—is the same but that the *interpretation* is different. Perhaps, but how does one pry the interpretation from the feeling, at least in the occurrent view of the person who is feeling it? Suppose that because the neurological wiring and chemistry are the same (*if* they are the same, which is by no means a closed question), there is some feeling, the itch, that is common to the various cases and equally inferable in each case of scratching. If we compare the itch that I have, which is merely annoying, to the itch of the bewitched or the forewarned, it would still seem that we would want to say that the inference from their behavior—which would presumably involve much more scratching—is a matter of interpretation with which it may be extremely difficult to empathize. And it is certainly no mere matter of biology and its sensational consequences.

Philosophers might push the argument one step further: Whatever the interpretation of the itch, one could argue, there remains the itch. But Wittgenstein long ago publicized his ill-formulated "private language argument," suggesting that the identification of such "inner" feelings could (logically) be based only upon overt behavior; the feeling itself, he told us, with poetic rather than philosophical insight, was "a wheel that played no part in the mechanism." One might then say that the interpretation is everything; it defines the itch even for the itcher-scratcher as well as for the observing anthropologist.

Emotions, quite obviously, have a physiological basis, though not always the violent visceral disturbance emphasized in the Jamesian theory. But emotions do have typical manifestations in our feelings, based on physiological occurrences. Are these sets of feelings, as James argued, the emotion? From the argument concerning so distinctive a feeling as an itch, it should be evident that the feelings present in emotion, which are not nearly so specific and are often very difficult to identify, cannot alone qualify as the emotion, whether or not one wants to argue that they are an essential ingredient in emotion.

An emotion is not a feeling (or a set of feelings) but an *interpretation*. Sometimes it is an interpretation of a feeling, but not usually so, and when it is, it is often so under the influence of the Jamesian theory. Thus Levy's Tahitians are Jamesian precisely in their insistence that it is their feelings that constitute the emotions they then interpret, as Levy himself is a Jamesian in his acquiescence to their distinction between the intestinal basis of anger and "cognitive" reflection of it. But the distinction between an emotion and its reflective interpretation is not so clear, precisely because an emotion is already a good deal of interpretation. Thus Levy cautiously limits much of his discussion of Tahitian anger to Tahitian conversations *about* anger, whereas Briggs, less cautiously, draws conclusions about her subjects' emotional life even while expressing doubts about the possibility of doing so. But both approaches display the deep problem raised by the Jamesian division between the emotion (as inner feeling) and the interpretations thereof: That the emotion itself is rendered unobservable and quite outside the province of the anthropologist perhaps leads also to the absurd, skeptical conclusions suggested by the Wittgensteinians. There is a way to escape such conclusions, but it involves a radical rethinking about the nature of emotion. It means that an emotion cannot be, in any interesting sense, a feeling. If the wheel so easily drops out of the mechanism, we might well conclude that it never played an essential role in the first place.

The Cognitive Theory of Emotions: Emotions as Cultural Artifacts

Not only ideas, but emotions too, are cultural artifacts. (Geertz 1973:81)

. . . complete rubbish. (Leach 1981)

One need not challenge the obvious—that strong emotions such as rage, at least, include a predictable physiological reaction and its sensory consequences—to reject Jamesian model in all its forms. An emotion is not primarily a physiological reaction-cum-sensations, with whatever embellishments and consequences. A strong emotion may well have as its predictable secondary effects the bodily responses that James identified as primary, but this is neither necessary nor always the case. It has long been argued (see, e.g., Cannon's 1927 reply to James) that the same physiological reactions might be induced without any emotion whatever, that longer-term emotions (e.g., long-standing anger) need not ever "explode" into a physiologically measurable response (though usually it does), and, more subtle but most important, that the physiological reaction itself is virtually never sufficient to distinguish one emotion from another, even in a gross way (anger versus jealousy or hatred but certainly not anger versus irritation or moral indignation). Anger is not just a physiological reaction-cum-sensation *plus* an interpretation, a cause, and certain forms of behavior. It is *essentially* an interpretation, a view of its cause (more accurately, its "object") and logically) consequent forms of behavior. By way of putting disagreement aside, one might yield the point that there is also, as a matter of causal uniformity, a physiological reaction and sensations, although the stronger thesis, which I will argue elsewhere, is that these are samplings from a faulty paradigm, the too exclusive focus on "urgent" emotions in emergency situations, which, quite naturally, involve bodily responses appropriate to such emergencies. But to be angry over a long period of time is certainly not to be any less angry, nor is it to be construed as a discontinuous sequence of angry reactions connected by a dispositional description. The anger *is* the interpretation plus the view of a cause (as well as the "object" of emotion) and consequent behavior. That anger also has biological backing and includes sensation is inessential to understanding the emotion, though no doubt significant in certain measurements, which only *contingently* correlate with the intensity of an emotion or its significance.

The thesis I am invoking here generally goes by the title "cognitive theory of emotions." The strong version, which I support but am not arguing here, is that an understanding of the conceptual and learned appetitive functions of emotion is all that there is in identifying and distinguishing them from each other and from non-emotions. The weaker version, which is all that I am invoking here, is that an understanding of the conceptual and learned appetitive structures of emotion is sufficient for identifying them and distinguishing them from each other and from non-emotions. An emotion is a system of concepts, beliefs, attitudes, and desires, virtually all of which are context-bound, historically developed, and culture-specific (which is not to foreclose the probability that some emotions may be specific to *all* cultures). What we call an emotion is an important function of that part of our emotional life, and so is what we think of it and how we treat it. Here is the problem when the distinction between emotion and interpretation of (and talk about) emotion is too sharp: both are interpretations, and the same concepts often enter into the structure of each. Being angry may be one thing, questioning the legitimacy of one's anger, something else. But the crucial concepts (e.g., of legitimacy, blame, or responsibility) are just as much a part of the anger as they are part of the questioning. If we had no concept of *righteous* anger, there would be no intelligibility, much less any point, to debating the legitimacy of anger, whether in this case or in general. Anger *is* a kind of interpretation, not of a feeling (which may or may not be co-present) but *of the world*. It is, one might say, not an "inner" phenomenon so much as a way of being-in-the-world, a relationship between oneself and one's situation.

Getting angry, so conceived, is not a matter of inner experience—a feeling caused by a physiological disturbance that is, in turn, caused by a disturbing perception. There is, to be sure, an experience, and it may, but need not, be accompanied by certain characteristic physical sensations. But the experience of anger is an experience of interpreting the world in a certain way and is precisely summarized by Lewis Caroll in *Alice in Wonderland*, as a matter of fact:

I'll be judge. I'll be jury.
Said cunning old fury.

Anger, in other words, is essentially a *judgmental* emotion, a perception of an offense (as Aristotle argued in *Rhetoric*). It consists of a series of concepts and judgments that, among other ingredients, involve the concept of *blame*. Getting angry is making an indictment (whether overtly or not). It involves concepts and evaluations that are clearly learned and, in their specifics, learned only in the context of a particular society with certain kinds of ethical views and theories. Again, this is not to deny that one might find anger (or some similar emotion) in every society, but the evidence seems to suggest that this is not the case. At any rate, also again, this should remain an open question for cross-cultural inquiry, not an a priori supposition based on the erroneous Jamesian theory of emotion.

The cognitive theory of emotions takes emotions to be composed (at least as their essential structure) of cognitions—concepts, perceptions, judgments, beliefs. But not only are (most of) these cognitions learned in a particular cultural context. They are themselves *public* phenomena, in the same sense that language and knowledge are public phenomena. One can mutter sentences to oneself in private, and one might well know what no one else does, but the shared concepts and cognitive structures that allow for mutual understanding also make possible the sentences and the knowledge in the first place. So, too, with emotions. Privacy may be a practical problem for the anthropologist, but it is not a logical problem. Feelings may be private in exactly the philosophically troublesome sense, but emotions are not. We might not understand a particular case of anger ("Why are you angry about your winning a Jaguar in the lottery?"). We might not understand the intensity of anger ("Why kill him just because he looked at you oddly?"). We might not understand the absence of anger ("How could you let him do that to you, and not even care?"). But these failings are in every case open to explanation, whether or not that explanation is acceptable or rational. What we do not find is a case of emotion, certain romantic pretensions aside, that is so different, so personal, so individual, that no one else could understand it or share it, if only the circumstances, the concepts, and the evaluations involved were known.

This becomes enormously complicated when the other person involved is from a different culture, with a language and a life we do not share. But the paradox, remember, was formulated not with just cross-cultural descriptions in mind but for *any* attempt to understand emotions in others, even one's husband or wife or best friend. Deflating the paradox, we now find the ascription and description of emotions in others on epistemologically firmer ground, problematic perhaps, but not logically impossible. We want to know whether the word (Tahitian *riri*) is used in precisely the same contexts and with the same reference and significance as our own word (anger). But if there is no inaccessible private reference, then this problem is just part of the general translation problem in anthropology and no more difficult (but no easier either) than translating religious or domestic language whose references are attitudes and circumstances rather than concrete objects and actions. We have to be able to compare and contrast attitudes and circumstances, and this, in turn, already presupposes some familiarity with the language and views of the community. Our observation of behavior helps establish this familiarity, but, of course, informed observation already requires some sense of the proper interpretation of behavior, which presupposes some knowledge of the attitude and circumstances of the community, as well as some sense of the emotional life of the people. To understand an emotion, in other words, one must understand much more about a person or a people than their behavior in an isolated incident. It may be reasonable to suppose that a man who gnashes his teeth and shakes his fist—after he has been sideswiped by an ox—is angry. But that supposition is reasonable only insofar as we assume that he shares a substantial set of concepts with us, this is not always reasonable, and it is often incomplete.

Indeed, where emotions are in questions, this is the essential point, for it has too long been presumed that emotions, unlike the more clearly cultural acquisitions of the community, have their own "inner" independent existence, based on biology and individual eccentricity, perhaps, but isolated from, and not to be understood in terms of, the rest of the culture, its language, and concepts. But what the cognitive theory of emotions implies and requires is that the concepts that make up virtually all emotions are essentially tied to the community and its conceptual apparatus. One cannot leap from the observation that we share *some* of the concepts constituting anger with another people to the conclusion that we share them *all*, that is, share the same emotion. One learns to identify the emotional life of a people along with learning everything else, including, not least, what they *say* about their own emotional life. But this is not a matter of taking their self-descriptions at face value (a suspicious business, in any case). It is rather understanding that what people say about their emotions and what they actually feel, though not precisely correlated (as Levy's Tahitians show so dramatically), are part of the same cultural, conceptual package.

It was Suzanne Langer, I believe, following the long tradition back to Rousseau and Hume, who suggested that the distinction of the human species was not so much reason as certain sorts of emotion and sentimentality. Thomas Hobbes, only partly in that tradition, pointed out that whereas animals might appreciate "damage," only humans had any sense of "injury." But this tangential wrinkle in the perennial dispute between reason and the passions can be settled—as all aspects of that dispute can be settled—by seeing that we are not here dealing with two dramatically different parts of the human soul but a single (not always integrated) system of concepts and attitudes, some of which enter into our calculations but most of which are built right into our immediate perception and conception of the world, seeing things, events, people, and actions as ugly or odious, offensive or enviable, lovable or admirable. But not only *what* these things, events, people, and actions may be, but the conceptions themselves, vary from culture to culture, community to community (whether or not from person to person within a community). The more obvious fact is that the causes, circumstances, and expressions, as well as the vocabulary of emotion, vary from place to place. The less obvious fact, in part because of the popularity of the Jamesian theory, is that emotions may vary from place to place as a matter of *kind*. The emotion may have a physiological-sensory base, but very little of anthropological interest follows from this. The fact (if it is a fact) of transspecies physiological similarity no more points to the uniformity of emotions than the universality of thirst points to uniformity in drinking habits from Dublin to Pago Pago. Emotions are conceptual constructions, and as go the concepts, so go the emotions as well.

Conclusion: Emotions, Concepts, and Culture

> The affective component of human information processing appears to be deeply imbedded in cultural representations. . . . What advertising tries to do with problematic success, culture does with great effectiveness. (D'Andrade, Chapter 3, *Culture Theory*)

My purpose in this limited essay has been to deflate (once more) a popular but pernicious theory of emotions, and with it, an old and vicious dichotomy between intellect and emotion. To develop the constructive theses that emerge from this, it would be necessary to turn to a piece by piece investigation of the concepts that make up our various emotions and their complex permutations, side by side with more holistic investigations of a number of other societies, such as those offered us by Levy (1973) and Briggs (1970). The flat-footed question "Do these people get angry or not, and if so under what circumstances?" would be replaced by a broader inquiry into the overall evaluative-conceptual schemes of appraisal and and self-identification that give structure to emotional life, including especially such concepts as blame and praise, status and responsibility, and all those other concepts that are so much a part of anthropological investigation but not, usually, a part of the analysis of emotions, except, perhaps, as an aspect of their causes or interpretations. But variation in emotional life is a very real part of cross-cultural differences and not only in the more obvious variations in circumstances and expression. Or at any rate, this should be an open question for investigation and not an a priori pronouncement based on an unacceptable philosophical theory. Indeed, Clifford Geertz has described anthropology as the desire to understand what it is to *be* a member of another culture. If emotions are ruled out of the investigation or simply assumed to be all alike, it is hard to imagine what content that desire might have or whether anthropology could give it any satisfaction at all.

References

Briggs, Jean L. 1970. *Never in Anger.* Cambridge, Mass.: Harvard University Press.
Cannon, W. B. 1927. "The James-Lange Theory of Emotion." *American Journal of Psychology,* 39:106–124.
Ekman, Paul. 1975. *Unmasking the Face.* Englewood Cliffs, N.J.: Prentice-Hall
Freedman, D. G. 1974. *Human Infancy.* Hillsdale, N.J.: Erlbaum.
Geertz, Clifford. 1973. "The Growth of Culture and the Evolution of Mind." In C. Geertz, *The Interpretation of Culture.* New York: Basic Books.
Harris, Marvin. 1968. *The Rise of Anthropological Theory.* New York: Crowell.
James, William. 1884. "What Is an Emotion?" *Mind,* 9:188–205.
Langer, Suzanne. 1953. *Feeling and Form.* New York: Scribner's.
Leach, Edmund. 1981. "A Poetics of Power" (a review of Geertz's *Negara*), *New Republic* 184 (April 4, 1981):14.
Levy, Robert I. 1973. *Tahitians.* Chicago: University of Chicago Press.
Lindzey, Gardner. 1954. Psychology. Cleveland, Ohio: Worth. 1961. *Projective Techniques and Cross-Cultural Research.* New York: Appleton-Century-Crofts.
Lutz, Catherine. 1981. "The Domain of Emotion Words in Ifaluk." *American Ethnologist* 9:113–128.
Mead, Margaret. 1958. Cultural Determinants of Chapter." In A. Roe and G. Simpson, eds., *Culture and Behavior.* New Haven, Conn.: Yale University Press.
Plutchik, Robert. 1962. *The Emotions,* New York: Random House
Rey, Georges. 1980. "Functional and the Emotions." In Amelie Rorty, ed., *Explaining Emotions.* Berkeley: University of California Press.
Sears, Robert R. 1955. "Transcultural Variables and Conceptual Equivalence." In Bert Kaplan, ed., *Studying Personality Cross-Culturally.* Evanston, Ill.: Row, Peterson.
Solomon, Robert C. 1976. *Passions.* New York: Doubleday-Anchor.
Solomon, Robert C. 1978. "Emotions and Anthropology." *Inquiry* 21:181–199.

7

On Emotions as Judgments (1988)

Philosophers have often contrasted "reason and the passions," typically championing the former against the latter. Descartes and his compatriot Melebranch, for example, treated emotions as "animal spirits," distinctively inferior parts of the psyche. Leibniz thought of emotions as "confused perceptions" and Kant rather famously dismissed what he called "pathological love" (i.e., love as an emotion) from the love more properly commanded by the Scriptures and practical reason. Emotions in this tradition are typically characterized as unlearned, "natural," involuntary and non-rational, if not irrational, forms of (more or less) physical excitement. They are quite opposed to the distinctly human (but also "godlike") virtues of calm contemplation, thinking, reason, and judgement.

More than occasionally, one finds one of the enlightenment philosophers defending the passions against the excessive claims of rationality. David Hume, most notably, insisted that "reason is and ought to be the slave of the passions." Nevertheless, he agreed with a long line of philosophers in setting them off against one another and separating emotion from rationality. It is worth noting that such philosophers as Hume not uncommonly employ an emotionally emaciated concept of reason in their analyses, together with a cognitively rich if somewhat convoluted concept of emotion. Indeed, it is this inequitable divorce between emotion and reason that motivates the rather odd problems shared by but separating Hume and Kant—how passionless reason can move us and how non-rational passions can be moral and justifiable. What does not get questioned is the critical distinction between reason and passion, judgment and emotion. So too, into this century, William James famously defended a quite visceral conception of emotions as felt physiological disturbances, quite distinct from cognition. Today, philosopher Robert Kraut and psychologist Robert Zajonc maintains this traditional separation of emotions and cognition.

And yet, there is another tradition in philosophical analysis, not nearly so well known nor so widely accepted. Over 2500 years ago, Aristotle provided (in his *Rhetoric*, but not consistently elsewhere) a detailed analysis of anger in which judgments play a crucial role. Anger, he argued, was the perception of an offense (real or merely perceived), a kind of recognition coupled with a desire for action (namely, revenge). Moreover, the perception and the desire were not effects of emotion but its constituents. It would be *irrational* for a man *not* to get angry in certain circumstances, Aristotle insists. (The fellow would even be a "dolt," he adds.) Reason here is not distinct from passion but a part and a parcel or it, just as passion is part of—and not an intrusion into—the rational life.

Seneca the Stoic argued a more elaborate general thesis about the nature of emotions, following his forerunner Chryssipis. On the Stoic analysis, too, emotions are judgments, ways of perceiving and understanding the world. Unlike Aristotle, however, Seneca saw these emotional judgments as essentially irrational—misinformed or in any case mistaken attitudes, distorted by desire, which philosophical reason, properly applied, would correct. Nevertheless, the distinction between passion and reason, emotion and judgment, now becomes an internal matter within the realm of judgments. Some emotions are rational; others are not. Some judgments are emotional; others are not. The ideal becomes *apatheia*, that Nirvana-like calm that is the hallmark of wisdom. But *apatheia*, we might note, need not be free of all emotion, just those which are "disturbing." Many years later, the Dutch philosopher Spinoza argued a similarly stoic thesis; for him, too, emotions are essentially "thoughts" moved by desire, though they are not necessarily unreasonable. Against James in this century, John Dewey defended a largely cognitive theory of emotion.

In the past twenty years or so, there has been a virtual triumph of the cognitivist theory, in the number of its defenders if not by virtue of any final arguments or agreement. In both philosophy and psychology the idea that an emotion necessarily requires cognitive ingredients, if it does not wholly consist of cognitions, has attracted many, many advocates. There is by no means agreement about the precise nature of these cognitions, whether they are peculiar to emotions or no different as such from other cognitions, whether they consist of beliefs, or thoughts, or judgments, whether they alone constitute an emotion or whether other factors, in particular "feelings," are also required. But the idea that emotions are cognitions is at least an idea that has gained the upper hand in the debate, an idea that has to be refuted rather than fight for recognition. Indeed, one philosophical reviewer has referred to the cognitive theory as the "new view" of emotions, in contrast to the older view of James and his many historical predecessors.

Today, most philosophers and a large number of psychologists have come to accept the idea that emotions are constituted, at least in part, by judgments and beliefs or, more vaguely, by "cognitive elements." But there is a nagging suspicion—or perhaps a dogmatic insistence—that this cannot be all that there is to emotion. After all, the common argument goes, one can make judgments without being emotional, even, it can be plausibly argued, that these judgments are presuppositions or preconditions or causes of the emotion rather than its constituents, thus leaving open the question what other ingredients might be essential to the constitution of emotion—whatever judgments might be necessary as well. One ingredient that is often mentioned in the analysis of emotion is some version of "arousal"—but it is ambiguous whether this is supposed to refer to physiological excitation or the presence of *desires*. The connection between emotion and excitation has often been overemphasized and misunderstood; following David Hume, I would argue that there are calm emotions as well as violent passions, and "arousal" in any case must have psychological components as well as physiological symptoms. I want to follow the Stoics and Spinoza in arguing that emotions are judgments, much more akin to thoughts than to physiological or physical commotion. And what is most important about "arousal," I want to suggest, is not physiological change as such, but rather the intimate connection between the judgments that make up emotion and desire. "Arousal" sometimes means "excited," but it also means, "interested" and "engaged." Emotions, I suggest, are self-interested, desire-defined judgments.

Against this strong cognitivist thesis and any others like it, there is now-standard objection, though it is rarely spelled out in sufficient detail. Here is one typically blunt statement of the standard objection (there are many others) by Jerome Shaffer, from his recent essay, "An Assessment of Emotion":

> Perhaps it is this superfluity of the physiological/sensational component that has led some philosophers to identify emotion with judgments, appraisals, and evaluations. But the identification will not work. One can hold precisely those beliefs and desires in a dispassionate and unemotional way. So getting emotionally worked up must involve more than just beliefs and desires. (Myers and Irani, eds., *Emotion: Philosophical Studies* (New York: Haven, 1983) p. 206)

In short, if "having an emotion E" is analyzed in terms of "making judgments A, B, C" (whether these are construed as constitutive of the emotion, as causally necessary preconditions of the emotion or as logical presuppositions of the description), then a counter-example to the pure cognitive thesis would be an example of a person's making judgments A, B, C without having emotion E. For instance, I have argued that anger is, basically, a judgment that one has been offended. Sally, who has a keen ear for the nuances of supposedly polite discourse, judges that she has been offended. Sally can make that judgment, for instance, because she studied conversational implicature at Berkeley, and knows that the perlocutionary force of utterance U, stated in language L and Context C, is that of an offense. But she does not, as we say, "take it personally." In fact, she is both amused (because she had not heard that utterance employed to make that insult before) and grateful (because it is just the example she needs for the paper on perlocutionary force that she is writing).

One way to deal with this objection is to weaken and modify the cognitivist thesis, to admit, in effect, that emotions are not constituted just by judgments but essentially involve some other ingredient(s)—feelings, physiological reactions, strong desires or frustration of desires or "affective tone" of some sort or other. I do not reject this option; my aim has been to relocate emotions in our geography of the mind, to redeem them from the "lower" realms of involuntary, unintelligent response to their proper status among such learned cognitive skills as judgment, belief and perception. Whether or not emotions are "just" judgments, or judgments plus desires or feelings, is not my primary concern. But I think that it is worth pursuing the strong cognitivist thesis as far as it will go, in order to show just how much of our emotional life is essentially cognitive and that judgments provide at least the complete skeleton if not the body of our emotions. My objective here, accordingly, is to spell out what I mean by "judgment" with regard to emotions. In particular, I want to combat the over-intellectualization of the cognitive thesis as well as the standard objection ("one can make those same judgments or hold precisely those beliefs and desires in a dispassionate and unemotional way").

I use the term *judgment* (*Urteil*) much as Kant (rather than Kafka) did—as prereflectively constitutive of experience. It is of the utmost importance not to confine "judgment" to reflective interpretation and the deliberate consideration of alternatives characteristic (one hopes) of a magistrate on the bench. The judgments involved in emotion might much better be compared to such perceptual-evaluative judgments as the judgment one makes when about to take a step on a platform (to give a speech, let us say) that the platform will in fact support one's weight. One does not reflect on this and, unless one has recently had a nasty surprise, one does not even consider the alternatives. And yet, the judgment that the platform will support one's weight is not an evaluation superimposed on an otherwise neutral perception; it defines that perception and gives the experience its essential structure (as opposed, for example, to wondering whether one is going to be humiliated by falling through just after being introduced). Social scientists will no doubt find these claims innocuous, but for philosophers this emphasis on pre-reflective cognition is nothing less than scandalous.

With this in mind, I would like to defend the following theses, in order of increasing difficulty:

(a) Emotional judgments are spontaneous;
(b) Emotional judgments are pre-reflective;
(c) Emotional judgments are evaluative ("appraisals");
(d) Emotional judgments are constitutive;
(e) Emotional judgments are systematic;
(f) Emotional judgments are self-involved;
(g) Emotional judgments are essentially tied to desires;
(h) Emotional judgments are essentially tied to their expression;
(i) Emotional judgments are "dispassionate" only in pathological circumstances (the standard objection as pathology);
(j) Emotional judgments are particular acts of judgment, not propositional contents;
(k) Emotional judgments are sustaining rather than simply initiating, structural rather than disruptive.

All of these theses, however, should be understood in a qualified way (or, perhaps an "existentially quantified" way, "some" rather than "all" in the impoverished language of quantificational logic). In attacking the distinction between emotion and cognition, I have no desire to replace this counter-productive duality with others. So I will not insist that *all* emotional judgments are spontaneous but rather take this claim to point out a kind of paradigm case. Some of our emotions are not at all spontaneous but the result of considerable deliberation and planning. So, too, I will not attempt to establish any sharp distinction between emotional and "dispassionate" judgments. Contrary to the position I am attacking—in which emotions represent sudden intrusions into life—I believe that virtually all of our experience is to some degree "affective," and even our most dispassionate and reasoned judgments (which are not to be confused with mere matters of indifference) can be understood only within some larger emotional context.

(a) *Emotional judgments are "spontaneous."* That is, they are typically not deliberative. They are not usually preceded by planning or by an explicit intention to have that emotion; indeed, they sometimes seem to "strike us by surprise." But this familiar bit of phenomenology does not say much of anything about the voluntariness of emotions. (Saint Augustine: "Voluntas est quippe in omnibus . . ."—"For what are desire and joy but the will saying yes to the things we want, and what are fear and sorrow but the will saying no to things we don't want?") It is often argued that emotions are involuntary on the basis that they are not deliberative, a fallacy that even Nietzsche displays when he famously suggests that "a thought comes when *it* will, not when I will." The appearance of planning is not necessary for voluntariness, nor, of course, does planning guarantee voluntariness. "Spontaneity" is a way of capturing one familiar phenomenological fact about emotions: it certainly does not weigh against the thesis that emotions are judgments.

It is too often supposed that judgments are not spontaneous, but rather deliberative, on the basis of a narrow paradigm: the case of a philosopher or a magistrate carefully deliberating "what is the case." But, first of all, most of our judgments are not so philosophically or magisterially detached. Most of our judgments are in the midst of and an essential part of our engagements. Choosing a beer at the bar is an act of judgment, but it would be unusual if not neurotic to make that choice only after protracted deliberation. One makes the judgment with a gesture, perhaps by pointing or reaching (in a self-serve bar, presumably.) So, too, moral philosophers often make it seem as if the function of an ethical judgment is to "pass judgment" rather than to choose a course of action. (See e.g., Edmond Pincoffs, "Quandary Ethics," (1971). Aristotle was quite clear that his notion of moral judgment (*phronesis*) had to do with acting rather than theorizing, and the judgments that most of us make in ethics are not deliberated at all—though they are surely not therefore irrational. Judgment in ethics is usually just doing what we are supposed to do, whether it is spontaneous refusal to accept an unethical invitation or an unthinking gesture of support or charity to a stranger. Our thinking usually comes afterward Outside of ethics, too, many judgments other than emotional judgments share this feature of spontaneity. Aesthetic judgments often seem to "strike us" (or rather, the work in question "strikes us" in certain way); nevertheless, we clearly "make" them, are responsible for them, and they are the product of perhaps a lifetime of education (or lack of it) and exposure. So too, an emotion, though spontaneous, may be the product of a lifetime of cultivation; the momentary passivity of "falling in love" may have been years in the preparation (sort of liking falling in one's own trap, according to Jean Paul Sartre), and that burst of anger ("I have no idea where that came from?") may have been silently rehearsed for weeks. Most of the moment to moment judgments we make in such mundane activities as walking and reaching for something are similarly spontaneous, though based on years of practice and coordination, and we might note that even most illustrious of all philosophical paradigms of judgment—Kant's famous system of judgments in the first *Critique*—are clearly spontaneous in that we apply them long before we can articulate them; indeed, it is the hard part of Kant's task to argue against his empiricist associates that we do indeed *make* such judgments, contrary to the appearance of spontaneity.

The spontaneity of emotions is not to be confused with the "emergency" paradigm that is so often invoked in discussion of emotion—the bear in the woods or the snake in the kitchen or the unexpected furtive glance from across the classroom. Sometimes an emotional judgment is clearly spontaneous because the situation that evokes it arises suddenly and without warning. It does not follow that the spontaneity of emotions means that emotions are more reactions to the unexpected, much less involuntary reactions or—as Lyons (1980) has written—"abnormal physiological states." Spontaneous judgments, with or without modest physiological accompaniment, are the moment to moment normalcy of our waking life. Emotional judgments are not only not abnormal; they are a paradigm of judgment.

Let us say here, however, that spontaneity is something less than a necessary feature of emotional judgments. We sometimes "work ourselves into" an emotional state through deliberation and rehearsal, and the resultant emotion is something of an achievement. We have all watched ourselves work ourselves into a rage, by repeating over and over the theme and variations on an accusation which might otherwise be ignored. And readers of Stendhal and Harlequin Romances often get to enjoy a hundred pages or more of what we might call romantic lubrication, the result of which, with feigned spontaneity, is love. Emotional judgments are typically spontaneous, but they are by no means necessarily so.

(b) *Emotional judgments are pre-reflective*. This is to say not only that they are not the subject of (attempts at) self-understanding but, as I suggested above, that they are typically inarticulate as well. This leaves ample room for misinterpretation, misleading interpretation, self-deception and—with the addition of a questionable metaphysics—repression. One might say, along these lines, that emotional judgments tend to be "preconscious" in the sense that Freud used that term in his early work. Since the articulation of the judgment is not available, the description of the "object" of judgment may not be either, thus leaving open not only whether or not one is angry but also, if so, what one might be angry *about*. One's willingness or inability to admit that he or she is angry quite naturally blocks his or her ability to recognize the object of one's anger, that *is* as the object of anger.

The prejudice in favor of articulated and reflective judgment can be met with many of the same counter-examples that I cited in rejecting the paradigm of deliberate judgment, since articulation and deliberation quite naturally go hand in hand. Philosophical articulation has to be juxtaposed with what Hume called our "natural disposition" to judge the world in our everyday actions. The judgment that the law of gravity applies is not the same in making a philosophical pronouncement as in putting a filled-to-the-brim coffee cup down on the table. The judgment that it is wrong to cheat is quite different for the philosopher of sport and for the defensive tackle who carefully puts his toe right to the line. So, too, in aesthetics, one often judges a painting to be pleasant before one has even articulated a barely adequate "I like that." An accomplished critic may judge a work to "not work" before he or she has even a sentence to describe that judgment in a more articulate way. In this sense—but *only* in this sense—A. J. Ayer is saying something not entirely false when he insists (1946) that judgments in aesthetics and ethics are more akin to "Hooray!" than to the elaborated detailed ethical formulations of the philosophers. The connection between guilt and shame and moral self-blame—is intimate and important, for reasons that should be evident in much of the history of ethics. However much philosophers may emphasize the importance of moral principles and their reasons, our ethics consist much more of those human sentiments such as compassion and pride whose proper articulation—as Hume discovered in his *Treatise*—may by no means be obvious.

Emotional judgments are pre-reflective and inarticulate in much the same sense that kinesthetic and perceptual judgments are pre-reflective and inarticulate. Leaving aside certain notorious epistemological difficulties, "I am walking very slowly," "the chair seems to be unstable," and "my arm feels heavy" are all judgments that are readily made pre-reflectivily, prior to the articulation. Of course, one might well articulate the judgment "my arm feels heavy"; what is important is that one can and sometimes does make that judgment without articulation; indeed it is the rare case in which one does not make that judgment before articulation, perhaps even spending a moment trying to describe what it is that one has already judged to be so odd. So too one makes emotional judgments. One is offended before one realizes that one is offended. One is jealous and has to be convinced that one is indeed jealous. Emotional judgments can, in general, be made without articulation. One cannot so make such judgments as "the Pope is not infallible" and "a unified field theory may well dispense with the law of contraction," but then, these are not to be taken as our paradigm of judgment. We would do better with "the floor feels funny" or, more to the point, "something about him disgusts me."

But again, it is worth pointing out that this lack of articulation is not a necessary condition. We often articulate our emotional judgments and every judgment probably *can* be articulated. Some particularly self-aware and articulate people do so all the time. People who do not do so are considered odd if not unfortunate; "out of touch with one's feelings" is a wholly misleading way of describing this inability or unwillingness to articulate emotional judgments. One might say that the therapeutic point of a philosophy of emotion is precisely to encourage such articulation—and the self-understanding, evaluation, and self-expression that goes along with it. But this is just to say that articulation is not essential to emotional judgments, for an emotion need not diminish, much less disappear, just because we succeed in articulating it.

(c) *Emotional judgments are evaluative* ("appraisals"). This is a point that has long been made by philosophers (e.g., George Pitcher in his 1965 article in *Mind*) and psychologists (Magda Arnold's "appraisal theory"). It explains why ethics and emotion are so closely connected, Kant to the contrary, and it explains not only what is right but what is so utterly trivial about the so-called "emotivist theory of ethics," which insists that ethical judgments are nothing but expressions of emotion. If fact, ethical judgments constitute emotions. Anger is in part a judgment that one has been *wronged*, and jealousy is in part the judgment that someone is threatening what is *rightfully* one's own. To make the triviality obvious; how does it help us to understand the nature of ethical judgment to be told that some moral judgments are the expression of the emotion "moral indignation" when the entire apparatus of morality and a number of specific moral judgments are already essential ingredients of that emotion?

The claim that emotion judgments are evaluative involves a much more sophisticated conception of evaluation than the emotivist's "Hooray!" and the usual "love is admiration" sort of value judgments. Let me mention just two examples: many emotions involve judgments of "status." Resentment and contempt provide a pair of contrasting examples in which the evaluations concern not only disapproval but judgments about inferiority and superiority. Some emotions also involve judgments of responsibility. For example, one difference between shame and embarrassment is an essential judgment of responsibility (guilt in the first case, innocence in the second). Given the nature of such judgments and the considerable number of them that may enter into a single emotion, the traditional language of "positive and negative emotions" and "pro-and con-attitudes" seems utterly simple-minded as well as inadequate.

(*Added, 2001*) I would have taken my claim that emotions are evaluative judgments to be fairly self-explanatory, except for an odd twist of fate. Looking for a category in which to classify my theory, philosophers and, especially, psychologists associated me with the then-current work in "cognitive" psychology. But, at the time, "cognition" and "cognitive theories" were (more or less) distinguished from what were called "appraisals" and "appraisal theories," the latter, but not for the former, being identified in terms of what I would consider evaluations (though again, to be sure, I did not take evaluations and appraisals to be necessarily deliberate or conscious). So under the heading of "cognitive theory" my claim that emotions were judgments was interpreted as the claim that emotions were essentially about *information*, a claim I have always vigorously rejected (which is not to say, of course, that emotions do not involve all sorts of information and information-processing). The evaluative and appraisal dimension was left out of it, reducing my theory of judgment to precisely the kind of "cold-blooded and dispassionate judicial sentence, confined entirely to the intellectual realm" that William James once dismissed as the very opposite of emotion. But, on my view, emotional "judgment" embraces cognition, appraisal, and evaluation, and no one of these can be abstracted out without serious loss. When, several years later, no less an authority than Martha Nussbaum declared (in a footnote) that, surprisingly, no one had recently defended the neo-Stoic claim that emotions are evaluative judgments (which she then went on to do admirably in her own *Upheavals of Thought* (2001), I saw that some essential clarification and public relations was long overdue.

(d) *Emotional judgments are constitutive*. Following J. L. Austin (1962) on language, we can point out that some judgments—like some speech acts—are descriptive ("the cat is on the mat") but others are not. Austin sometimes speaks of "performatives" in this regard, for example, "I do" in a marriage ceremony or "I hereby name this dog 'Beefeater.'" Judgments, whether articulated or expressed or not, may also be more than descriptive. They "set up" (literally, "con/stet") a situation or what I call a "scenario." A person may or may not in fact have made some particular gesture with a hostile intent, but in anger that gesture is interpreted as offensive and the entire situation is converted—as in a theatrical performance—into a scenario defined by the offense. It is, as I have argued elsewhere, (Solomon, 1976; following Lewis Carroll) a courtroom scenario, in which one is judge, jury, prosecutor and, sometimes, executioner. So, too, the French Romantic novelist (Stendhal, 1836) writes of love: "it does not find but *creates* equals."

Constitutive judgments are often misunderstood as "distortions" or, in the notorious case of romantic love, as "blind." This is probably why Leibniz thought of emotions as "confused perceptions." But consider the familiar "blindness" of love: the person one loves may or may not *in fact* be "the most wonderful person in the world," but so far as the emotion is concerned, the objective facts (if such there are) are not in question. One might say that emotional judgments are "subjective," in the cautious sense that their significance is determined more by the way an "object" is experienced than by the nature of the thing itself. But this is emphatically not to say that an emotional judgment cannot be wrong, unreasonable, or mistaken. An emotion can be "refuted" by the facts. An interpretation can be recognized to be trivial, far-fetched, vulgar, inconsistent, or pathological. (What goes on when this does not happen—in certain "intractable" emotions—is an important but subsequent question.) Emotional judgments are "about" the facts in much the same way that a magistrate's verdict is about the evidence in the case. Emotional judgments are evaluative interpretations that dictate a mode of experience, a scenario in which things are viewed and thought of in a certain way, on a phenomenological stage in which action is appropriate or compulsory.

(e) *Emotional judgments are systematic judgments*, not a single, isolated act of judgment. Emotional judgments involve an entire system of judgments, beliefs, and desires and one cannot make sense of an isolated judgment. The intelligibility of judgments depends on the context, on the history of the situation (and situations like it). It does not follow, however, that the context of an emotion is to be understood solely by reference to the circumstances. What goes on in imagination and memory may provide much more of the context than one's surroundings, even in the most carefully controlled situation. Where an emotional reaction comes "out of the blue," one can be sure that there is an imaginary or remembered context that is a preoccupation, perhaps all but obliterating awareness of the present environment. Ronald de Sousa (1983) recently resurrected an old observation of C. D. Broad's, that "appropriateness is the truth of emotions." But appropriateness only makes sense when there is a context and a background against which to be appropriate (or inappropriate), and we might add that the appropriateness of the emotion is not at all the same as the "appropriateness" of the emotion label, a second order judgment *about* emotions which is (more or less) articulate and reflective (Schachter and Singer, 1962).

It is often convenient and sometimes sufficient to characterize an emotion in terms of a single judgment—particularly when distinguishing two emotions (shame and embarrassment, jealousy and envy). One might say, for example, that shame involves acceptance of responsibility, whereas embarrassment does not, or that jealousy embodies some claim to a right that envy clearly lacks. But it would be a serious mistake to think that the analysis of an emotion therefore consists—as in the quaint offerings of some of the great philosophers—of a one-line description. To say that emotion is a *system* of judgments is to say that anger is not just a judgment of offense but a network of interlocking judgments concerning one's status and relationship with the offending party, the gravity and the mitigating circumstances of the offense and the urgency of revenge. Love is not just the admiration of the other's virtues but a system of judgments about shared identities and interests, personal looks, charms, status and mutual concerns as well as a multitude of mostly absurd myths and metaphors that have infiltrated that system of judgments that we call "love." And the difference between envy and jealousy is not a single pair of judgments (e.g., a sense of entitlement to the coveted object); it too is a systematic difference, a difference in ways of seeing the world which might be illuminated but by no means wholly described by a single pair of differing judgments.

In the *Passions*, I distinguish a dozen or so judgment types that enter into emotions and form a multidimensional matrix within which our many emotions are differentiated and—just as important—interrelated. (See appendix, p. 114) To focus on a single judgmental difference between two emotions may be useful and adequate for certain purposes, but it gives a false impression of the complexities of emotion.

Just as it may serve the purposes of illustration and illumination to say that anger is a judgment of offense, to distinguish anger from mere irritation or frustration, for example, or to underscore the claim that an emotion is not merely a feeling or a physiological reaction, so it is often instructive to pick out the dominant—or some overlooked but essential—judgmental component of an emotion. It is striking to learn, for instance, that one crucial ingredient in envy may be a judgment of one's own lack of self-worth. It seems to be edifying to hear (whether or not it is true) that love is an emotion with cosmic pretensions. But such abbreviated judgments do not capture the totality of emotion, and it is only to be expected that one might make just those abbreviated judgments, without the rest of the system of judgments, and not have the emotion in question, just as an undergraduate can learn the right formulation of the special theory of relativity without knowing the theory.

The system of judgments that make up an emotion does not consist exclusively of peculiarly emotional judgments. Just as the judgments that are typical of most emotions can be embedded in a context which is (relatively) unemotional, so judgments that would seem to have nothing to do with emotion may be thoroughly embedded in an emotional context and so themselves become emotional. Consider an angry microbiologist's judgments, which might seem to be wholly concerned with microbiology and methodology ("your criticism of my experiment is invalid!"). It is not clear that such judgments should be treated only as the causal background of the anger rather than as part of it. Such judgments alone are not an emotion, but what makes them of particular significance to emotion is the context of other judgments, which we might summarize as the judgment that this is a matter of urgent personal importance. But judging it is a matter of urgent personal importance alone is not enough to constitute an emotion either; an emotion also needs its specific content (often summed up as the idea that emotions are "intentional") such as that provided by the judgment that Jones is offensive, or by the judgment that the criticism of the experiment is invalid. We should not assume that the judgment that the criticism of the experiment is invalid. We should not assume that the judgments constituting an emotion must all have some characteristic content or in themselves be particularly emotional. An emotion is the entire system of judgments, and the judgments that constitute the emotion are emotional by virtue of their place in that system.

The standard objection—that one can make the same judgments without emotion—is more of a strategic maneuver than an argument. It is typically short and to the point. It shifts the burden to the strong cognitivist and then says, in effect, "whatever analysis of whatever emotion you give me in terms of judgments, I will respond that one could make those judgments and not have that emotion." It is not surprising that a one-line analysis of an emotion in terms of a single judgment is always subject to such an objection, but it does not follow that the whole system of judgments is vulnerable to the same objection. Of course, it is incumbent upon the cognitive theorist to spell out in detail an adequate portrait of the various emotions, for it is this elaborate project—rather than the summary declaration of the cognitive position—that will make the case for cognitivism and render implausible the objection, "but couldn't you have all of that and still not have the emotion?" Unfortunately, there is also a very general problem of philosophical analysis here: the possibility of any adequate analysis of any concept in terms of necessary and sufficient conditions. Despite many decades of effort, there may be no such airtight analyses in philosophy; counter examples may be inevitable—by way of showing the limitations of an analysis rather than deflating or refuting it altogether, and the business of the philosopher might be no more than to map out in detail a chart of the terrain. Furthermore, given the holism that lies behind much of my argument, it may be that all of the conditions and preconditions of even the simplest emotion would be as bewildering as the multitude of conditions Stephen Schiffer has catalogued concerning speech acts—leaving the impression that it is impossible for any ordinary human being to produce even the most ordinary, colloquial utterance (*Meaning*, Cambridge University Press, 1973). This is not the place to discuss these problematic metaphilosophical theses, but if an adequate analysis—that is, one that does not admit of any counter-examples, no matter how ingenious—may not be possible in any case, then the a prioristic strategy of the standard objection is hardly a boon to our understanding of emotions. The effort needs to be made to spell out the system of judgments that constitute a single emotion, Chisholming down the analysis to meet counter examples. But this is very different from greeting the unsympathetic and non-specific rebuttal. "Ah, but I can make those judgments too without having the emotion." There will come a point in a thorough analysis where the rebuttal makes no sense; to make that holistic set of judgments *is* to have the emotion.

(*f*) *Emotional judgments are self-involved.* To be emotional is to be self-involved. It is to have a stake not only in the outcome but also in the validity of the judgment itself. One can, of course, make judgments about one's self and not be at all emotional. The most dramatic and possibly pathological cases involve self-ascription of dark Freudian motives such as the urge to murder, but from a purely "objective" if not "scientific" point of view. What is more difficult is to decide whether one can be emotional and not make judgments about one's self. In many emotions—in shame, embarrassment, and most cases of pride, for example—judgments about one's self are evident. In others—moral indignation, for instance—this self-involvement is not as clear. But often an emotion whose "object" would seem to be another may be better analyzed as an emotion that is also about oneself. A classic example, discussed by Hume, is the case of pride in another's accomplishments ("I'm so proud of you"). It can be argued, as Hume does, that there must be some sort of self-identity in order for there to be such an emotion. We can disagree with Hume when he insists that the "object" of love is another person; love is an emotional relationship in which one's self is essentially involved. So too, it might be argued that when one feels loss at another's death, it is one's own loss that is the object of grief, but the problem with such arguments is that Butlerian objections are soon forthcoming. In our emotions as in our ethics; self-concern is not everything; we can be moved by matters that are not in themselves our own. Nevertheless, it is *we* who are so moved, and it is thus the moving rather than the matter that must define our emotional self-involvements.

One might summarize the nature of emotional judgments in a familiar phrase—"taking it personally"—in the sense that one might instruct a friend not to do it when insulted by a street corner drunk or when not invited to a socially significant reception. Taking something personally means experiencing it as particularly important to oneself, as personally "meaningful," perhaps concerning a matter in which we have deep personal "investments." One might also say that emotional judgments, because they are taken personally, tend to have a particular "intensity"—in a sense that must be explained, and that they tend to be "urgent" judgments, in contrast to the relaxed and deliberative judgments that one might make, for example, in deciding where to have dinner on the following Friday night (Solomon, 1976).

A judgment which is taken personally must involve the self, but it is essential to emphasize that the self need not be—in the usual sense—the *object* of the emotion, that is, what the emotion is *about*. What the angry microbiologist gets upset about—the putative object of his emotion—is the doubt cast on the validity of his experimental methods, but what so upsets and involves him is its reflection on his abilities, his professional status and respectability, his self-esteem. It is also essential to point out that to say that an emotional judgment is of particular importance to the person who "takes it personally" is not the same as to say that he or she will insist that the matter itself is of considerable importance, for we are quite familiar with the experience in which we find ourselves peeved, annoyed, or even very disturbed about an issue which we (reflectively) judge to be trivial or of no significance. Again, what one is upset about, and what concerns the emotional judgment, may not be the object of the judgment as such. On the other hand, one can always judge a matter to be important—even important to oneself—in a dispassionate and detached manner. Many Americans judge the threat of nuclear holocaust to be the most terrible threat imaginable, and to be very real. It may be pathological, but most of them make this judgment—which they readily admit is the most important possible concern—with complete detachment, as if it were an evaluation of the odds on a certain horse race to take place tomorrow in New Delhi. That something is important to one does not entail a reflective judgment that it is important, nor does reflective judgment always translate into an emotional judgment.

One key measure of emotionality, and so, too, a mark of emotional judgments, is what is usually called "intensity." But it is important, if we are to make sense of this notion in a cognitive theory, to distinguish between a judgment as a propositional content (in which case the notion of intensity does not apply) and the *making* of a judgment, in which case the notion of intensity clearly applies but it is not entirely clear in what sense it does this. Andrew Ortony (1988) has developed a range of "intensity variables" (in an essentially information-processing model of emotions) to specify certain classes of emotion, and in such a model intensity would seem to be itself a set of judgments, one of the system of judgments that make up the emotion.

This explains how intensity can be fitted into a cognitive theory, but it does seem to violate one commonsense notion about intensity, that intensity does not so much specify the kind of emotion (say anger versus envy) but rather applies in different degrees to an emotion (e.g., being a little miffed versus very angry). Some emotion sets may be distinguished by virtue of intensity alone (e.g., fury might be so distinguished from anger), but there is a sense in which a single emotion may be more or less intense that still needs to be captured. I want to suggest that this sense might be indicated, again, by our hardworking phrase "taking it personally." One can take a matter more or less personally, and intensity is a function of this—not another judgment in addition to those that compose the emotion, but a feature of the emotional judgment itself.

What does not work as an analysis of "intensity" is the usual suggestion that an intense emotion is one that is accompanied by (or is) a strong feeling. One can (when "upset") experience extremely strong physiological reactions concerning utterly trivial matters, and one can be extremely angry or in love and "feel" very little. Intensity, too, must be a matter of judgment—the (perceived) importance of what's at stake, the strength of one's convictions, the extent of one's involvement. One might say that an emotional judgment must have *some* intensity, but if this is not to be ad hoc or trivial, it must specify some *measure* of intensity. Intensity of feeling will not do. The melodramatics of behavioral expression (temper tantrums, plaintive love songs) are unreliable and certainly not essential indications of intensity. And any analysis of the intensity of emotion must also account for what Hume called "the calm passions," either by denying that they are emotions (most implausible) or by providing a measure of intensity that is applicable to, say, a lifelong passion for justice or science or art. This measure, which we have been summarizing in the vernacular as "taking it personally," can be further specified in more precise terms as a measure of *desire*. This is not to say, however, that the intensity of emotion is strictly a function of the intensity of certain desires, nor is it always obvious which desires are essentially involved. A man who is very angry about losing his hat may care very little about the hat, but a great deal about his sense of power, appearance, or ownership. So, too, a jealous husband.

(g) *Emotional judgments are essentially tied to desires.* The judgments that make up an emotion have specifiable links with desires. It is not enough to say that emotions are composed of judgments that are *caused* by desires (as argued recently in *The Journal of Philosophy* by Jenefer Robinson [vol. 80 (1983)]). The desire to be with Joe is not the cause of one's love for Joe (to use one of her examples); it is rather part of the emotion's essence, the motive definitive of—not just behind—the peculiar scenario which we call "love." It "fits" the scenario in a quasi-conceptually necessary way. Given Aristotle's description of anger as a perceived offense demanding punishment, for example, one can see that the urge to vengeance is something more than a cause or an effect (and something less than entailment—the awkward analysis suggested by the logical behaviorists). Judgments in emotion are judgments which have a quasi-conceptual connection with desires. (David Lewis calls such connections "loosely analytic.") Accordingly, the analysis of an emotion yields a more or less precisely circumscribed set of desires. Desire by itself is not an emotion, although it readily functions as a cause and a stimulus to emotion. The desire to punish could not be a component desire of grief, though of course one could have the urge for revenge along with grief. In general, one might analyze the various emotions as judgmental structures enclosing a core desire which is both their motivation and their "conatus." But judgments and desires are not separate "components" of emotion (as, for example, John Searle argues throughout his book *Intentionality*). Many judgments have desires built right into them, for example, the judgment that something is desirable. (A reinterpretation of Mill's infamous argument lurks here.) The judgments that typically constitute the emotions—for example, judgments that something is offensive, desirable, tragic, lucky, degrading, or an admirable achievement—have desires as their logical presuppositions. It is in this sense that the judgments which make up an emotion are to be characterized in part by desires, *as part of,* not in addition to, the strong cognitivist thesis.

One (but not "the") difference between anger and merely knowing that one has been offended is the fact that anger includes the desire for revenge—as Aristotle stated so boldly. The statement seems bold and the ethics of anger behind it seems shocking because Aristotle, unlike a modern gentleman, did not see anger itself as offensive or irrational. Indeed, he even says (in the *Nicomachean Ethics*, bk. IV, chap. 5) that a man who does not get angry when anger is appropriate is a "dolt." Nevertheless, the connection between anger and the desire for revenge is (necessarily) very much intact in us, and while we might fudge elaborately and imaginatively in its expression, the logic of anger and what James called "the urge to vigorous action" are very much of a piece. Indeed, one of the problems with James's noncognitivist theory is precisely that it does not and cannot explain the all-important connection between emotion and intentional action, no matter how vigorously James insists on it.

The essential place of desire in emotion explains quite readily how it is that emotions and their behavioral expression have a conceptual rather than merely causal linkage. It is not, as Ryle (1949) sometimes suggested, that the emotion is defined in terms of behavior. It is rather that an emotion is in part defined by a desire (or set of desires) which in turn circumscribes a set of behaviors (in the obvious sense that the desire described by the phrase "wanting to caress Mary" involves more than a simply causal connection to the act of caressing Mary).

Recognizing the seemingly essential role of desires in emotion, Robinson accepts something like the strong cognitivist analysis with the provision that the judgments that are essential to emotion are themselves "determined" by desires. Robinson takes desires to be causal antecedents of emotion. This does not mean, I hasten to add, that the description and analysis of an emotion need not essentially make mention of desires. Desires are necessarily causal antecedents, and the causal connections themselves must be mentioned as conceptually essential to the concept of emotion. If I may use one of her sex-neutral examples, my fear of bees is caused by my having an intense desire to avoid them. The desire is not itself necessarily part of the emotion, but the fact that the emotion is caused by this desire is necessary for it to be fear. This mode of necessity is not unfamiliar: a father is the cause of the existence of his son, but the son is his father's son only insofar as his father is the cause. So too, one might say that an emotion is caused by desires that are distinct from it but, nevertheless, the relationship between them is an essential one.

I do not think that this is quite right, though it is a vast improvement over the "emotions are desires" thesis and much better than the view that an emotion is (contingently) caused by desires. But I think that fear is a poor example here, for fear is, of all the emotions, that emotion most like a desire. Indeed, one is hard put to suggest any other ingredient in many cases of fear than the desire to avoid, coupled, of course, with some sort of judgment or belief to the effect that "this is the sort of thing to be avoided." One might well construct a kind of practical syllogism here, the conclusion being a kind of desire, the whole argument consisting of both general and particular judgments as well as the desire, constituting the emotion. This could not be taken very seriously had not Donald Davidson (1976) argued a similar thesis—without the desire—some years ago by way of an analysis of Hume's theory of pride. Fear is not so much caused by a desire as it is itself a negative desire, circumscribed by certain judgments about the world.

For more complex emotions, Robinson's analysis has more plausibility, in part because of the difficulty in deciding what is, and what is not, an essential part of an enormously difficult phenomenon. In jealousy, for example, the set of component judgments may include the whole of ethics—questions of rights, the nature of relationships, the legitimacy of "possessiveness" and the attitudes of the community (is one a martyr, a victim, or a "cuckold," for example)—as well as more personal judgments concerning the likelihood of loss, the possibility of betrayal and one's own lovability and abilities. Not implausibly, one might suggest that what motivates this complex emotion and sets all this conceptual apparatus in place is the comparatively simple desire to hold on to what one has, coupled with the fear (that is, the negative desire) of losing it (him/her). Are these desires the causes of or an essential part of the emotion? The answer would seem to be both. To be sure, those desires must precede the jealousy, or the jealousy would be incomprehensible. But there is no reason—apart from defending certain theories—why one would insist on separating these relatively crude desires and the very complex network of judgments (and other emotions) of which they are a part.

One way to think about the role of desire in emotion, and as a measure of how and in what sense we "take things personally," is to think in terms of the familiar "investment" metaphor. The investment metaphor is a financially sound and less ontologically suspect version of Freud's famous "economic model" of mind. The commodity in question, of course, is the self, and investing is thus the Wall Street version of "getting oneself involved" or, by the Bourse, to be "engaged." I have sometimes argued (1976) that emotions could be defined in terms of self-esteem, a thesis which I now think confuses an emotion's essential self-involvement with a particular aim of some emotions. It is one thing to be engaged; it is something else to aspire to increase self-esteem, though in many emotions, e.g., anger, the two are intimately related. I would still argue, as a (more or less) empirical thesis, that many emotions have as their objective (not necessarily their object) the protection or increase of self-esteem (cf. Nietzsche's *Wille Ze Macht*, 1967), but I would separate this from my analysis of the essential nature of emotions themselves. There are, however, a great many (more or less) empirical but still philosophically fascinating theses about the evolutionary function of emotions, the aims of emotions (e.g., getting angry in order to . . .), and the causal conditions of emotion (e.g., whether low or high self-esteem) people are more likely to fall in love (Reik, 1944 versus Rubin, 1973).

(h) *Emotional judgments are tied to their expression in action in a non-causal way*. Jennifer Church has argued that emotions should be construed as "internalized actions," a thesis not incompatible with the cognitivist thesis as I want to develop it here. Emotions are intimately tied to their expression, and the expression of an emotion is not just an effect of the emotion (see, e.g., Jerome Neu, *A Tear Is an Intellectual Thing*, 1985). The system of judgments that make up an emotion does not just constitute a point of view, an observational framework, or weltanschauung; they also constitute a *scenario*, a behavioral stage setting in which the judgments dictate a set of behaviors, including, of course, verbal behavior. Ron de Sousa has offered the suggestive notion of a "paradigm scenario" to explain the nature of emotion; a paradigm scenario is that original situation in which emotional responses are learned. So, too, situational scenarios, not abstract propositions, form the content of most emotions. The judgments that makeup an emotion are not just the components of a syllogism (as in Davidson's reconstruction of Hume's analysis of pride) but—to use a consciously Sartrian expression—an *engagement*. William James had it right when he insisted on "the urge to vigorous action," not as effect but as essence of emotion. (Like Hume, James overplayed the sensational element, at the detriment of the more insightful aspects of his analysis.) The judgments that make up emotion are not made in the merely observational mode. They are as a rule expressed in actions, even if those actions are usually truncated or displaced forms of full-blown, direct expressions (e.g., Wittgenstein's example of the angry man who smacks his cane against a tree). Some emotions (grief and embarrassment, for example) manifest themselves in seemingly pointless action, but they are still action—related in an important sense. Emotions sometimes constitute dramatic breakdowns in organized behavior, but (1) we hesitate to call the resulting awkwardness an "expression" of the emotion though we recognize this as an effect of the emotion, and (2) such breakdowns occur most often when the circumstances are unforeseen, when there is no practiced repertoire of expression. A man who is jilted by his lover for the first time will very likely find himself virtually paralyzed, or at best, able to produce a few childish expletives! A man who has had experience in such matters may, despite his despair, be able to bring off a quite polished performance.

The expressions of emotion are not independent of emotion but built into the system of judgments that constitute the emotion. Aristotle caught this in his insistence (in the *Rhetoric*) that anger includes—rather than causes—the desire for revenge. Now this might seem to support the anticognitivist argument, but only if one maintains—unreasonably, I think—that the intentions embodied in action are not cognitive because they are not "purely" cognitive, or that the desires embedded in emotion can be sharply distinguished and separated from judgment. This is emphatically not to say that desire, too, is a species of judgment, or to deny that one can have the same desires in another context. It is to say that the context of an emotion is not just a cognitive context, but an active context in which we are engaged in a world that we care about. To insist on a concept of cognition (or judgment) that is essentially divorced from all such care and concerns is not only to adopt a wholly demeaning conception of emotion; it is also to accept a wholly useless concept of cognition and judgment.

(i) *Emotional judgments are "dispassionate" only in pathological circumstances* (the standard objection as pathology) The standard objection takes for granted the notion of dispassionate judgment and then challenges the cognitivist thesis to explain how a judgment—which is essentially dispassionate—can constitute an emotion. But this challenge can be turned around. Perhaps the meanest counterargument against the judgments-without-emotion objection is one that I can honestly attribute to (blame on) Michael Stocker. The argument begins by noticing how odd it would be if a person were to make the system of judgments which compose an emotion without having the emotion—for example, the set of judgments appropriate (for most of us non–Davy Crockett types) as a large brown bear comes charging at us in the woods. Of course, we can all imagine a peculiar phenomenological circumstance in which one might dispassionately judge that "the fellow wearing the red shirt—namely me—is about to be mauled and caused considerable pain." But outside of philosophy seminars, such dispassion is better recognized as dissociation, a pathological condition. It is worth noting that the phenomenon of dissociation is what led Freud to distinguish "idea and affect," in order to explain how, for example, a patient could describe the most gruesome scene of murder and incest with the calm befitting a discussion about the weather. Which is to say that the content of a judgment is not wholly separable from the act and its context (which Husserl often emphasized) and, moreover, that the judgments that make up the emotion cannot be separated from the emotion except in the most unusual pathological cases. But then it is the pathology, and not the normal case, that needs to be explained.

One might object that though the circumstances of terror can rarely be conceived without terror, the circumstances of long-term love or quiet pride can certainly be conceived of without passion. But what this shows—and can be shown on other grounds besides—is that many emotions do not depend on a specific, momentary context but involve complex sequences of judgments that may evolve over a period of days, weeks, or years. Not all passion is like explosive anger; indeed, the still popular distinction between occurrent and standing emotions depends upon this false paradigm, and makes little sense without it. Hume had it right when he distinguished the violent versus the calm passions, by which he surely did not mean to eliminate the calm passions as passions. It is true that, over a long period of time, one finds oneself making more or less dispassionately a judgment that one remembers making rhapsodically, hysterically, only a few years before. But it is cynical, or least, to say that such relatively dispassionate judgments—in long-term love, notably—indicate that there is no longer any emotion, now just opinion ("yes, you are indeed beautiful"). Again, it is the total context that counts, and the excitement that accompanies or fails to accompany a momentary judgment is not all there is to say about our emotional involvements in the world.

(j) *Emotional judgments are particular acts of judgment, not propositional contents;* The standard objection almost always seems to focus on the propositional *content* of the judgment: Sally judges *that* Jones has offended her. But the content of a judgment is not the whole of judgment. There is also the act of judging, and very different acts may be "directed toward" one and the same proposition. It has become routine in discussions of intentional states to make a distinction between asserting or doubting and *what* it is that is asserted or doubted, for example, or between the act of perceiving and what it is that is perceived. So, too, we can distinguish between Sally's making the judgments that constitute her getting angry and the proposition in the unemotional context of a Gricean investigation, but this is not the same as making the judgment that would be involved in her getting angry. She does not, as we say, "take it personally." She is rather amused and grateful, entertained by as she entertains the proposition in question. But though she judges that there has been an offense she does not get angry. That is, she is not offended. The fact that she can assert that an offense (against her) has been committed without being offended does not show that she can make the judgments claimed to be essentially involved in the emotion of anger and not be angry. It only shows what we already knew, that it is possible to assert or otherwise entertain propositions that are normally emotional without emotion.

It is worth noting that the distinction between propositional content and the entire act (and various "levels" of acts) of judgment, so long employed so skillfully in discussing the utterance which constitutes the offense, tends to be wholly ignored in the standard objection. To counter that Sally can judge that she has been offended without being angry is no objection to the cognitivist analysis of anger as (in part) judging that one has been offended. Moreover, the judgment that she has been offended is no simple matter. There is the offender, Jones and his remark. There is what he says, but there is also how he meant it. He asserted a certain proposition, presumably, but then he also intended for it to be taken in a certain way, as an offense, or, perhaps, as a compliment. He might have said something offensive without meaning it as an offense, or he might have said something inoffensive with the intention of offending. So, too, we can distinguish between what Sally understands about Jones and his remark and "how she takes it." Recognizing Jones's intention is not the whole story, for she might know that Jones is trying to be offensive and not be offended (indeed, perhaps just because she knows how hard he is trying to be offensive). Or she may know that he is not trying to be offensive but is offended anyway. In her judgment, as in Jones's remark, we can distinguish between the proposition asserted and the holistic mental act(s) involved in the making of that judgment—what the offense means to her. It is one thing that she understands the meaning of the utterance, that is, the sentence in its context. She understands that the sentence was intended as offensive to her. But it is something more—considerably more—for her to also *be offended*. In Gricean circumstances she dispassionately judges that someone has said something (intentionally) offensive to her. When she gets angry, on the other hand, she gets offended. The propositions may be the same but the judgments are importantly different.

This is not to say, of course, that the propositional content of a judgment has nothing to do with a judgment's being a component of an emotion. The proposition that Jones offended Sally is not merely an incidental ingredient in Sally's anger, but neither is it entirely clear that such propositions are explicit in every judgment constitutive of an emotion. For example, the explicit propositional content of our angry microbiologist's judgments might be concerned wholly with microbiology and methodology; "your criticism of the experiment is invalid!" Such judgments alone could not constitute an emotion, but combined with other judgments (e.g., that this is a matter is of urgent personal gravity) they certainly could be components of emotion, and it is the way in which such judgments are made—indicated by the tautness of the voice, the clenched fist on the lectern—that make them part of emotion. But I say "indicated," for such noncognitive features of judgment making are expressions of, not identical to, the emotional act judgment. It is the making of the judgment itself, not the accompanying bodily expression or the content of the judgment, that is accusatory, malevolent, vindictive. The propositional content of a judgment is germane and often essential to the emotion it (in part) constitutes, of course, but at some point our attention must be shifted from the propositional content to the whole act of judgment. Although the judgment that one has been offended is essential to anger, it should not be thought that what distinguishes passionate from dispassionate judgment is just the assertion of that particular proposition.

The key claim in the standard objection is that one can make "the same judgment" without having the appropriate emotion. But, given what I have said above, it is not the case that judgments expressing the same proposition are thereby *the same* in the required sense Sally sometimes judges dispassionately that she has been offended and at other times she is deeply hurt. Sometimes she simply judges that Jones has offended her; sometimes she makes that judgement and is therein offended and angry. In both cases, the judgment can be summarized "Jones offended me (Sally)" but these are not "the same judgment," whether or not they involve the same proposition. Having an emotion is not just affirming the truth of a certain proposition. To object that the making of certain judgments is possible without having the respective emotion is to confuse the narrowly epistemic act of affirming the propositional content of a judgment with the many other ways in which judgments can be "made" which are essential to having an emotion.

(k) *Emotional judgments are sustaining rather than simply initiating, structural rather than disruptive.* The aim of a cognitive theory of emotions is not to reduce the drama of emotion to cool, calm belief but to break down the insidious distinctions that render emotions stupid and degrading, disruptive and disturbing. Part of the problem is the kind of limited examples philosophers often choose as instances of emotion; Shaffer, for instance, takes suddenly running across a log in the middle of the highway as a paradigm case. I would say that the resulting startle reaction is not an emotion at all, but the more general point is that, so long as examples of emotion tend to be cases of sudden shock or disclosure, the unintelligent, unprepared, dysfunctional, and merely physiological aspects of emotion will always loom large, and the cognitive aspects of emotion will be comparatively inconspicuous. When on the other hand, one starts with the grander passions as examples—Hume's sense of justice, the revolutionary's passion, the lover's life-long devotion—one gets a very different picture of emotions. And these, not being startled at the inopportune log in the road or the unwelcome sight of the bear, is where a more positive view of emotions, and a more cognitive view, is most plausible. We readily dismiss the three-day flush of an adolescent as "not really love" and we recognize that a similar flush lasting several decades would be both an odd symptom of love and extremely unhealthy. A lover of many years has many *reasons* for love, and it surely makes no sense to suggest that such love is devoid of such judgments as respect and regard and a wide variety of judgments that are aesthetic and ethical as well as personal. The virtues (and vices) of emotion have to do with their endurance—even their intractability—not sudden excitement and fleeting irrelevance.

This emphasis on the durability of emotion raises a problem, however, for the analysis of emotion in terms of judgment. I have not said anything in this essay to indicate why judgments should be favored among the variety of "cognitive elements," instead of beliefs or thoughts, for example. Beliefs (unlike judgments and thoughts) lack the requisite experimental component, although it still may be true to say that emotions presuppose certain beliefs. Thoughts (unlike beliefs) seem too episodic to account for emotions, even if, to be sure, every emotion is exemplified by characteristic thoughts, appropriate to the circumstances. Judgments seem to have the requisite place in experience (leaving aside the question of unconscious judgments), though we should certainly not say that what we experience in emotion is a system of judgments; it is rather the world as it is constituted through those judgments. The problem is that judgments, like thoughts and unlike beliefs, seem to be too momentary to account for long-term emotion, and although a judgment might initiate an emotion, it would seem strange to say that the emotion involves making that judgment continuously. One solution would be to say that an emotion is initiated by a judgment (or a system of judgments) but then carried on by (a system of) beliefs, but this then fails to explain the experiential content of the ongoing emotion. A very different solution is to suggest that emotions—like God's universe according to some theologians—require not just creation but an ongoing effort. Thus one should think of judgment not as a momentary phenomenon at all, but as a continuous activity. Making an ethical judgment, for instance, does not consist just of the moment of deliberation and decision, and it is not just the event of pronouncement. It is a vision of wrong- (or right-) doing that is constantly (or inconstantly) renewed—which need not involve renewed deliberation or decision. So, too, the judgment(s) one makes in emotion—that Jones is offensive or that one's lover is wonderful—are continually renewed, and one might speculate that the frequency and difficulty of renewal has much to do with the intensity and violence of the emotion. But in any case, the primary point is that emotions should not be construed as merely momentary intrusions into an otherwise orderly life but rather as dynamic structures of our experience that must be continually reanimated. Understanding emotions as judgments allows us to understand why this should be so and, a not undesirable benefit, helps us appreciate our active participation—as opposed to passivity—in our emotional lives.

Emotions are judgments, but not judgments in the sense that they are detached and disinterested momentary reflections about a world that does not deeply concern us. Rather, they are judgments which cannot be understood apart from the systematic connections with action and desire and a holistic view of our experience over time. Arguing that emotions are strongly cognitive does not make them philosophically less exciting. They can be just as subject to illuminating conceptual analysis as other more established topics in ethics and the philosophy of mind.

Appendix

Key Judgment Categories

Judgment Type	Examples
Direction (intentionality)	
Other directed (self-implicit)	fear, resentment, faith
Inner directed (other possibly implicit)	shame, embarrassment
Bi-polar	love, hate, pity, anger
Object (incl. self)	
Person	jealousy, resentment
Agent	anger, shame
Open	fear, sadness
Criteria for Judgment	
Moral (objective)	indignation, guilt
Intersubjective	embarrassment, vanity
Personal (subjective)	jealousy, sadness, fear
Status	
Other superior	adoration, resentment
Equal	love, hate, anger, pity
Other inferior	loathing, contempt, cherish
Evaluations	
Positive	envy, pride, admiration
Negative	pity, shame, loathing
Scope of Evaluation	
Holistic	guilt, self-love
Particular	shame, regret, pride
Responsibility	
Self to blame	shame, guilt, remorse
Self to praise	pride
Other to blame	anger
Other to praise	admiration
Exoneration	embarrassment, pity
Intentions	
Benevolence	love, worship, pity
Malevolence	anger, envy, resentment
Other intentions	fear (to flee), shame (to hide), grateful (to thank), guilt (to punish self)
Defensiveness	
Defensive	resentment, envy
Trust	love, hate
Indifference	distain, respect
Distance	
Intimacy	love, hate
"At arm's length"	anger, jealousy, pity
Impersonal	resentment, envy, scorn

8

Back to Basics: On the Very Idea of "Basic Emotions"
(1993, rev. 2001)

A few years ago, an enormous battle was raging, just across campus, so to speak, in the department of psychology. The issue was "basic emotions," that is, to use but one of several metaphors, those emotions which were to be recognized as the "atoms" in our emotional chemistry. Symptomatically, the battle seemed not to have been noticed at all by philosophers, even including philosophers of mind and philosophers especially interested in the emotions. Such is the absence of communication and mutual interest between our artificially separated fields. But it was, at its core, a philosophical battle, and its implications are enormous for our understanding of the emotions.

Emotions, long dismissed as irrational distractions, explanations for incontinence, or simply footnotes in the topic of motivation, are no longer confined to the margins of philosophy and the social sciences. There are extensive and successful research programs and increasingly sophisticated debates in philosophy, psychology, sociology, and anthropology, not to mention literary, music, and art theory and criticism. As research on emotions comes into its own as an established discipline, there is a strong temptation to "get to the bottom" of things, to identify the basic building blocks of emotion, *the basic emotions*. As so often happens, the social sciences look to physics and chemistry to show the way. Philosophy, which shares its origins with the physical sciences (in the cosmologies of the ancient Greeks), tends to share the fascination with "ontology," the identification of the most basic elements and the connections between them. In physics, this search was defined in modern times by particle physics, first in atomic theory and, more recently, in quantum theory. In chemistry the basic ontology of the natural elements has long been settled (though the list of created elements may be incomplete). The elements fall into elegant groups in a "periodic chart" according to their atomic number (discovered by Julius Meyer and Dmitri Mendeleev in 1869). In the study of emotions, the analogues of atoms and quarks are supposed to be found in these so-called basic emotions. A basic emotion, if I may define the notion without prejudice, is a fundamental, nonreducible unit of emotional life. (Can a periodic chart of the emotions be far away?)[1]

It is a plausible argument that this fundamental unit of emotional life is to be found in biology. Philosophers such as René Descartes and David Hume, under the swat of the science of their day, sought these fundamental units in the "animal spirits" that pulsed with the blood through the body. Before them, medieval philosophers and physicians looked for them in the "bodily humours." William James, at the turn of the twentieth century, located the source of the basic emotions in the viscera, although he found the individuation of particular emotions something of a problem. Today, many researchers have updated James's theory by taking as "basic" those emotions with "hardwired" expressions and more or less specific neurological processes. Much of the research has followed Paul Ekman (who in turn took his cue from Darwin) in identifying the basic emotions with those which display more or less fixed, more or less automatic, universal, and "hardwired" manifestations, including neuro-muscular-hormonal changes, characteristic facial expressions, and associated feelings. Ekman (following a suggestion from Sylvan Tompkins) called these "affect programs," and now the term is often used more or less synonymously with basic emotions. At any rate, it is widely supposed that the basic emotions are characterized, first of all, in terms of their associated affect programs.

But this is not the only conception of basic emotions. Talk of "basic" or "primitive" emotions preceded current emotions research by several centuries. Descartes, Hobbes, and Spinoza, for example, all specified some small set of emotions that were the "building blocks" or bases for all of the others. The building block metaphor has a long history, going back to the earliest days of science, when the first Greek and Babylonian cosmologists suggested that the basic elements of the universe were earth, air, fire, and water (or, alternatively, the hot, the cold, the dry, and the wet). Even then, the temptation was to reduce the list still further to pick out just one of these (Thales, water; Anaximenes, air; Heraclitus, fire) as more basic than the others. One could argue that this urge for simplicity and reduction ("nothing-but"ery) goes back as far as Western thought itself.

Descartes enumerated "six simple and primitive passions" (wonder, love, hatred, desire, joy, and sadness) and noted that "all the others are composed of some of these six or are species of them."[2] Hobbes similarly distinguished the "simple passions called appetite, desire, love, aversion, hate, joy, and grief," and then suggested that more complex emotions are formed by the *succession* of these or the addition of an "opinion" (for example, "of attaining" in hope).[3] For Spinoza, too, there are three "primitive or primary" emotions—desire, pleasure, and pain. Love, then, is pleasure accompanied by the idea of an external cause.[4] Hatred is pain, similarly accompanied, and so on. Spinoza analyzes three dozen emotions each as a pleasure, pain, or desire arising from or accompanied by some idea (for example, in fear and hope and inconstant pain/pleasure accompanied by some uncertainty about the future). It's not exactly atomic theory (preceding Dalton by almost two centuries) but, as Spinoza intended, it pretends to the precision of the hard sciences. In the eighteenth century a great many philosophers (including Hume, Rousseau, and Adam Smith) wrote essays and treatises on human nature, identifying the basic elements of the mind and the basic emotions (their favorites were *sympathy* and *self-love*) that were the foundation for all of the more complex and sophisticated human sentiments and emotions. Hume was explicit and straightforward in admitting that it was Newton's physics which he emulated in his development of a model of mind.

Some researchers, particularly philosophers wedded to the "analytic" tradition of conceptual analysis (those whom Paul Griffiths dubiously calls "propositional attitude theorists") have suggested that the distinctions we make between emotion types as well as the notion of basic emotions is a matter of how we use language. Thus Errol Bedford, in a seminal article in the 1950s, argued that the difference between shame and embarrassment was a difference in how we identified the circumstances in which a person had an emotion. The difference was not between the emotions themselves (construed as some sort of feeling) but a distinction between the different kinds of behavior and circumstances in which the emotion was ascribed. Following Wittgenstein, philosophers who wrote about emotions place a heavy emphasis on the interplay between language and the world. Which emotions are "basic" depends on the "language games" we play and the "forms of life" in which those emotions play their role. Andrew Ortony, a Bedford student who turned to psychology and cognitive science, thus suggested that there are no basic emotions (in his 1988 book with Clore and Collins) and, with Turner, followed that up with an outright attack on the notion in 1990. In 1988, he allowed that "some emotions are more basic than others because we can give a very specific meaning to [this claim], namely that some emotions have less complex specifications and eliciting conditions than others." In 1990 that concession is gone. What are "basic" may be subemotional components, but not emotions.

Other researchers, too, have focused on the vocabulary and taxonomy of emotions, "the emotion lexicon," as a way of approaching the question of basic emotions.[5] How does language reveal the composition and order of our emotional repertoire? Our emotion vocabulary is not arbitrary. It captures something significant (even if not essential) about our emotional experience. So perhaps the way our language of emotion is structured and organized determines what is more "basic" about emotions and what is not. The words we use for emotions should not be confused with the emotions, but there is no way we can "get at" our emotions apart from the language we use to identify and discriminate them. So the idea that some emotions are "affect programs" is but one among several explanations as to which emotions are more "basic" than others.

In this chapter, I would like to take on the question of "basic emotions," first from the recent debate in psychology, then from the much longer-running literature on emotions in philosophy. I would like to explore the matter from a number of different angles, for instance, from the claims that there are basic emotions (and try to see what they might be) and that there are no basic emotions (and see what that leaves us with). I also want to ask whether the current emphasis on basic emotions is directing our attention in an overly narrow way, or perhaps in the wrong direction altogether. The question is not only whether there are any such basic building blocks of emotion but also whether the search for them distorts rather than furthers our understanding of emotions. The search for simples is bound to obscure all sorts of complexities. My aim is to combat what I see as a debilitating reductionism in emotion theory and to defend the view that emotions provide a particularly rich field of complex phenomena in which chemical and building-block models are simplistic, inappropriate, and utterly misleading.

The Discovery of the Face in Philosophy

The debate over basic emotions emerged most recently in psychology in an arena virtually untouched by philosophers of emotions: the face. To say what is obvious, we express our emotions in our faces. What is not so obvious is whether all people express the same emotions with the same facial expressions. Darwin famously claimed that emotion expressions are universal (and so, in some sense, were the experiences that they expressed), and he argued this on the basis of shared features with animals. But Edgar Rice Burroughs of *Tarzan* fame suggested a race of people who "reversed" all of the usual emotional expressions, smiling in anger, frowning in joy. It is a subject that is fraught with the temptation to a priori reasoning on the basis of what is familiar to us. And then we remember the exotic films we have seen in which we simply assumed that the tears and smiles are everywhere the same. But to what extent are facial expressions of emotion biologically determined, and to what extent are they learned, perhaps even taught, within a culture? Insofar as they are biologically determined, in what sense does this render them "basic"? And insofar as they are culturally learned, to what extent does this preclude their being universal—or expressing (possibly in different ways) the same (universal) emotions? And to what extent are the facial expressions of emotion truly indicative of *the emotion*? We cannot simply dismiss Burroughs's fantasy a priori.

Many years ago, Paul Ekman set out to empirically disprove Darwin and show that facial expressions were cultural, not biological.[6] Much to his credit, Ekman's own research proved him wrong and he is now the most fervent advocate of biologically based universal facial expressions. Those emotions which manifest such biologically based universal facial expressions are the basic emotions. But even so, there is good reason to suppose that we have never met a raw, unembellished, basic emotion, one not "covered over" with the trappings of culture and experience, and constrained and complicated by the "display rules" of society. Fear and anger are supposed basic emotions, but surely what one fears and what makes one angry, as well as the display rules for expressing those emotions, depends on the society and the situation. Thus in some societies the facial expression for anger might be a stone face, while in others it might be a grimace or even a malevolent smile.

I also want to scrutinize what Peter Goldie calls the "avocado pear" model of emotions, that is, the idea that emotions have a basic (neurologically hardwired) core with a softer, more pliable covering provided by culture and individual experience. Our brains developed as the *product* of our particular circumstances, which includes (in a gross fashion) our cultural and social arrangements, so those cultural and social arrangements are not just an overlay or embellishment of our neurology. This need not be understood as Lamarckian. It does not mean that acquired facial expressions have become genetically inheritable. But the gross biohistorical fact that we live in societies and are highly interdependent creatures is not merely an afterthought of evolution. Our "hardwired" facial expressions are not simply a product of our neurology.

All of which is further complicated by "display rules." Many cultures have very different display rules regarding fear and anger for men and women, and this difference in display rules in turn determines a stark difference in their emotions. Many cultures have very different display rules depending on one's age and social status. Our emotions are not just "given"; they are subject to reflection. Some emotions are "hypercognated," to borrow a term from Robert Levi, and this in turn affects their expression. So how much of emotional expression is a product of affect programs and how much is an affect of habit, learning, reflection, and culture? Which leads to more questions: To what extent are the expressions of emotion voluntary, to what extent not? To what extent can they be willfully controlled or masked? And, perhaps most essential, what is the connection between the expression and the emotion? If one is the manifestation of the other, what is this *other*—a neurological state or process? A feeling? Some other "inner" state, and "affect"? Or are the expression and the emotion ultimately one and the same with no inner "mental way station"? (The term is Skinner's, but his behaviorist ideas have permeated psychology for many years.)

With the emphasis on the face we step across the imaginary barbed wire that separates so much of philosophy and psychology. Psychologists, desperate for observables and something to measure, tend to lean toward the description of behavior, not necessarily denying "inner" experience but minimizing both its role and its significance. Philosophers, still wedded (even despite themselves) to the Cartesian tradition, tend to argue over whether an emotion is a feeling or a set of beliefs or judgments or evaluations, all "inner" phenomena. They do not deny the fact that emotions are "expressed" outwardly in behavior, including in the face, but this is treated as an inessential and uninteresting matter. Even the questions, so essential to James, of whether the feelings of emotion are learned or innate and how they are based on physiological, if not also neurological, processes, hardly get raised. Both the psychologists and the philosophers give an appreciative but merely passing nod to the neurologists, who with their long-term promissory notes offer to tell us—*someday*—what an emotion "really" is. But, for the time being, the standoff continues between those who want to talk about the "outer" and minimize the "inner" and those who want to talk about the "inner" and marginalize the "outer" aspects of emotion.

But the face is not merely "outer," and it occupies a philosophically awkward position in the mind-body debate. It is neither physiology nor behavior in the usual sense, that is, as full-blown intention action. Facial expressions are both involuntary (or, at least, "spontaneous") and voluntary (or else all actors would have to wear masks). They are not merely manifestations or consequences of emotion, which leads philosophers like Maurice Merleau-Ponty to insist that we *directly perceive* the emotion (and not just the expression of emotion) *in the expression*. The face is our primary means of "display" toward other beings. A smile indicates safety and acceptance; a frown or a scowl, danger or disapproval. We display facial expressions from (and possibly before) birth, whether they represent frustration, fear, or gastrointestinal gas. It is all but obvious that some facial expressions, and in any case the neural and muscular capacity for facial expressions, are inborn or "hardwired." Thus an evolutionary hypothesis presents itself to supplement the neurological hypothesis: emotions and their expressions evolved as an efficient way of communication with our fellow beings.

As our primary means of communcation—before speech, before overt action of any kind, and as an inborn feature of our psychological repertoire—emotional expression would seem to be about as "basic" as any aspect of human psychology. (Jean-Jacques Rousseau believed that the origins of language were to be found in the need to express our emotions.) If there are facial expressions that are universal, that can be found and recognized in every culture in the world, and if there are some emotional expressions that are invariant while others vary from culture to culture, then it at least looks as if we have our theoretical finger on what is basic in our emotional life: those emotions—indicated by those emotional expressions—which display this invariant universality. Those would be, on the facial expressionist account, the basic emotions. (The further argument often goes, "If it is universal and invariant, then it must be neurologically hardwired," but this fallacy is not necessary to the basic emotions thesis and need not detain us here.)

Paul Ekman deserves enormous credit for developing this set of ideas and a remarkable research program to see it through. The basic scheme is multidimensional, but it significantly limits or minimizes all of those features of emotion which most philosophers would be keen to emphasize (thoughts, appraisals, feelings, beliefs, and desires). Ekman's model is threefold: the facial expression, the (unspecified) neurological process that directly brings it about, and the evolutionary process that explains the neurology.[7] But neither neurology nor evolution is the domain of the psychologist, much less the ordinary philosopher. The former is still largely unknown, and the latter is dangerously speculative. The face, by contrast, is immediately accessible and observable, and so it becomes the primary unit of study.

Ekman mastered the study of the face not only by identifying every complex of muscle movements that make up each and every fixed emotional expression, but also by learning how to initiate every such movement in his own face, "at will." By cataloging the range of emotional expressions and specifying exactly what muscle movements make up each expression, Ekman and his many associates have developed an anatomical–physiological language for identifying emotional expressions that is not question-begging, that is, it does not require us to identify the expression of happiness as "looking happy" or the expression of sadness as "looking sad." They then launched a global search for universals in facial recognition, and seemed to find them. (Their techniques need not occupy us here. The primary method was the identification of photographs of people with various facial expressions. The validity of this method has been in hot dispute in the psychological literature.)[8]

Ekman hypothesized that a small set (originally six, perhaps eight or nine) of invariable emotional expressions represented a corresponding small set of basic emotions, which were neurologically based and had evolved over time because of their Darwinian adaptiveness. Basic emotions are those emotions which are found and recognized (via their facial expressions) everywhere, whose evolutionary value can be hypothesized to have been crucial both for individual and group survival. Insofar as it is the expression of emotion rather than "the emotion itself" that is highlighted, the group communication aspect of expression will naturally seem more important then the "felt" aspect of emotion. The baby cries to display its discomfort, but what it actually feels is of no obvious evolutionary significance.

There have been many arguments against Ekman's theory, such as debating whether universal *recognition* of facial expressions allows the inference to there *being* universal facial expressions. But what concerns me here is Ekman's concept of basic emotions and which emotions seem to be basic in his threefold sense (universal facial expression, neurologically hardwired, and of evolutionary significance). Ekman himself has gone back and forth on a couple of candidates for basic emotions, notably disgust and the startle response. Are these emotions, or are they *too* hardwired to count as emotions?[9] Surprisingly few of the psychological arguments take as their main target what would attract the attention of most philosophers, namely, the identity of *the emotion itself*, which seems to waver phantomlike into and out of focus between facial expression, neurology, and evolution. Ekman himself has by no means been consistent in this, sometimes seeming to insist that the emotion *is* its expression (along with its neurological substratum), but he nevertheless has no hesitation about appealing to "the subjective evidence of how it feels."[10]

Gone, happily, are those hidebound behaviorists who insist, absurdly, that such feelings are nonexistent or irrelevant to emotion, but what remains at issue is the centrality of felt or conscious states (allowing for multiple ambiguity in both expressions). But the mainstream of philosophical tradition would insist that an emotion *is* the felt or conscious state, and even William James, despite his emphasis on physiology, famously insisted that emotions are sensations (caused by physiological disturbances). But in his *Principles* and elsewhere, he also suggested that conscious phenomena were "epiphenomena," nomological danglers with at best a marginal role in the emotional process. James may have said (the most quoted phrase in the emotions literature) that *"our feeling of [bodily changes] as they occur IS the emotion,"* but it is noteworthy that he limits himself to emotions with a distinct bodily expression and then goes on to cite the very strong connection between emotion and expression: "A woman is sad because she weeps," not the other way around. That is certainly giving the facial expression (if we consider weeping as facial expression) top billing and the feeling of sadness at best a supporting (or an "epiphenomenal") role.

But what are the grounds for inferring from the sameness of expressions to the sameness of emotions? What grounds are there for thinking that these expressions are expressions *of* anything at all? And when does invariance or universality imply a neurological basis? Alternatively, the invariance might be due to "the human condition," some contingent similarity among cultures, or simply the shape and musculature of the human face. We have all speculated on the origin and efficacy of certain facial expressions, such as the tensing of the jaw in anger as a vestigial preparation to bite someone, the widening of the eyes in fear as a means of enhancing one's attention, the smile as (a) a means of getting more air in certain excited states or (b) a vestigial display of submission before superiors, the laugh as a "roar of glory" (Hobbes). But whatever such explanations may offer, they seem to reinforce the highly *contingent* nature of the connection between emotions and their facial expressions. Edgar Rice Burroughs's imaginary creatures may be implausible, but they do tap into a deep vein of skepticism about the supposedly necessary connection between emotion and expression.

Dialectic and Debate in Psychology

Psychology, compared to philosophy, tends to be a gentle field, defined by mutual support (every journal article begins with a generous list of credits, whereas philosophy articles tend to begin by specifying the target) and a hesitancy to criticize, much less to openly attack the foundations of a whole field of research, the blood sport of the philosophers. The basic emotion debate, accordingly, has been shocking in its ferocity. The most cutting arguments and attacks have come from two sources. There were the attacks on Ekman's methodology, not just the details and the findings but the very notion of cross-cultural research he employs, and the denial, on empirical grounds, that the supposedly universal facial expressions he cites are in any sense universal.[11] And then there were the more philosophical (conceptual) attacks from within psychology and cognitive science which argued that the very notion of a "basic emotion" is deeply problematic.

This culminated in 1990 in an issue of *Psychological Review*, where Andrew Ortony and T. J. Turner challenged Paul Ekman, Carroll Izard, and Jaak Panksepp, all avid defenders of the idea of basic emotions, who responded with equal vehemence (1992). Ekman, Izard, and Panksepp produced not only different lists of basic emotions but also employed differing criteria according to which emotions are basic. For Ekman, basic emotions are essentially "hardwired" products of evolution and manifest themselves, first and foremost, in characteristic, invariant, universal facial expressions. For Izard, they are also products of evolution and "precognitive" (by his definition), and involve characteristic, invariant, universal facial expressions as well as, he suggests (without elaboration), characteristic feeling states. Panksepp, by contrast, bases his claims concerning basic emotions strictly on recent findings in neuropsychology. Basic emotions are those which have "prewired" connections in the brain. Ortony and Turner, in response, played the various criteria and differing lists of basic emotions off against one another and concluded not only that there was little agreement between them but also that the search itself was confused.

In their enumeration of competing lists, Ortony and Turner include, for example, Watson's (1930) minimal list of three (fear, love, and rage), Izard's (1971) list of ten (anger, contempt, disgust, distress, fear, guilt, interest, joy, shame and surprise), Ekman's (1982) list of six (anger, disgust, fear, joy, sadness, and surprise), Panksepp's (1982) list of four (expectancy, fear, rage, and panic), Kempers's (1987) list of four (fear, anger, depression, and satisfaction), Oatley's (1987) list of five (happiness, sadness, anxiety, anger, and disgust), and Frijda's (1986) list of six (desire, happiness, interest, surprise, wonder, sorrow). (They do not include the lists from early modern philosophers—Descartes and Spinoza, for instance—but the similarities and overlaps should be obvious.) Ortony and Turner rightly raise the question of whether some of the inclusions (e.g., interest, surprise) are emotions, much less basic emotions, but mainly they raise the question of whether the rampant disagreement about the number and identity of the basic emotions and the "disorder" of the various lists signals some basic confusion in the search for basic emotions in the first place.

In response to this charge, Ekman replies that there is much more agreement in these lists than Ortony and Turner are willing to grant. Fear and anger, for example, appear on virtually every list. (In Oatley, fear appears as anxiety, and in several lists anger appears as rage.) But the variation in lists reflects the variety of criteria employed to define basic emotions, and the variation in numbers may reflect only a transitory period in the research, not its futility. Ekman is surely right that the current disagreement by itself does not reflect negatively on the project of identifying basic emotions, any more than early disagreements about which substances were chemical "elements" should have cast suspicion on chemistry or current disagreements about the number and nature of fundamental particles in physics should cast suspicion on particle physics. So, too, the disagreement over the criteria for "basicity" can also be viewed as the usual healthy dialectic of a discipline trying to reconcile differing points of view. Thus the "disorderly" nature of the debate does not lie in the lists nor does it lie in the variety of criteria proposed, which can easily enough be argued to complement and reinforce one another.

I would argue that the notion of "basic emotions" is neither meaningless nor so straightforward as its critics and defenders respectively argue, but it is historical and culturally situated and serves very different purposes in different contexts, including different research contexts. It is a serious mistake, I think, to overinterpret the evidence of neurobiology and studies of facial expression to claim that they reflect something about the essential nature of emotions. The discussion of basic emotions has been going on for several thousand years. It did not begin in this century with Watson, Izard, Ekman, and Panksepp. It is a subject with a rich history, and it is not one that can be readily understood within the confines of a technical debate in *Psychological Review*. The quest for basic emotions must be situated in a larger sociohistorical context involving not only the scientific context (which includes, among other things, the new and promising techniques in brain biology) but cultural and moral contexts as well. Science does not take place in a vacuum, and the newfound interest in the emotions transcends the emotions' often minimal place in science and goes straight to the heart of the recognition that emotions define human nature, human culture, and human morality.

Although the very mention of a "larger sociohistorical context" tends to make scientists understandably nervous, none of this is to deny for a moment the importance of the current research. The precision with which Ekman and Izard and others have described and measured facial expressions, and the results they have achieved, has surely changed the face (so to speak) of emotions research. The importance of the brain research carried out by Damasio, LeDoux, Panksepp, and others will surely define much of our discussion in the new millennium. But to ignore the larger context that gives this research meaning is one of the liabilities of "science," which too readily identifies itself only by reference to its carefully controlled, "value-free" studies. The real power of Ortony and Turner's critique of basic emotions is, I believe, the fact that they challenge this narrowness and thus open the way to a more critical examination of much of the recent research into emotion.

In a Different Voice: "Basic Emotions" as a Moral Category

Aristotle had a keen interest in the emotions, but he spent relatively little time listing or analyzing them, despite his proclivity for taxonomies. Nevertheless, he sort of offers us a list of basic emotions, even if it is rather casual. In the *Rhetoric*, Aristotle defines emotion "as that which leads one's condition to become so transformed that his judgment is affected, and which is accompanied by pleasure and pain," adding, "Examples of emotion include anger, fear, pity, and the like, as well as the opposites of these." (He does not tell us what else might be "like" or what those "opposites" might be.) In the context of his various writings, it is clear that anger, in particular, in one of the most "basic" emotions. (Others are fear and pity.) He defines anger (also in the *Rhetoric*) as "a distressed desire for conspicuous vengeance in return for a conspicuous and unjustifiable contempt of one's person or friends." He then adds that "anger is always directed towards someone in particular, e.g., Cleon, and not towards all of humanity." He mentions, if only in passing, the physical discomfort that virtually always accompanies such emotion.

Aristotle had little to say about emotion as "feeling" and nothing about facial expressions. He knew nothing of neurology, much less the anatomy and physiology of the brain. (At most, Aristotle notes in *De Anima* that "the conditions of the soul are connected with the body," p. 403.) So, in the modern sense, he knew nothing of basic emotions at all. Nevertheless, it is clear that Aristotle thought certain emotions were much more important than others. They were "basic" in terms of their significance in human life and, in particular, in terms of ethics. Aristotle considered himself a "scientist," to be sure, but what he had in mind by that already honorific term was quite different from the purely empirical, value-neutral discipline pursued by contemporary social scientists. A scientist is one who looks carefully and thoroughly, and recognizes the place of things in the grand scheme of the universe.

Anger was of interest to Aristotle, in particular, because it plays a central role in the nature of "man" as a rational and social animal. Anger is not irrational or antisocial, as is often thought today. It is a natural reaction to an *offense*. It is a moral force, which can be cultivated, controlled, and provoked by reason and rhetoric. Whether a person gets angry, and when and how, is of enormous importance to his or her family, friends, and fellow citizens. Aristotle famously insists that only fools don't get angry, and while overly angry people may be "unbearable," the total absence of anger (when there are slights and offenses) is a vice rather than a virtue. If the cause of anger is a slight or offense (perhaps an instance of "scorn, spite, or insolence"), then it is *right*, even *obligatory*, to get angry (on the *right* occasion, for the *right* reasons, to the *appropriate* degree). Anger is a telltale mark of one's moral character, and so it is a basic emotion, according to Aristotle, because it is so familiar, so natural, so important in our daily lives. So, too, fear is the essential ingredient in courage (as overcoming fear), and pity is "basic" in considerations of tragedy, and not just in the theater.

I want to hold up Aristotle as a model here because I think that his interests shed a very different light on what is going on in the search for basic emotions. Aristotle's ethical concerns were clearly employed several centuries later when Pope Gregory and then Aquinas put together the various lists that constitute the familiar theological psychology of the Christian Church, including the list of "seven deadly sins—anger, envy, sloth, gluttony, lust, pride, and avarice. Anger, envy, and pride are clearly emotions; gluttony, lust, and avarice might rather be thought of as excesses of desire. sloth, always the odd one, is a deficiency (not laziness, as we tend to think, but a deficiency of spiritual interest). The (more or less) corresponding virtues—prudence, fortitude, temperance, justice, faith, hope, and charity, plus love, of course—are also emotions or related to emotions (reading "charity" as "pity" or "compassion" rather than simply the act or habit of giving, and prudence, as Aristotle and Aquinas conceived of it, as having just the right amount of fear). The virtues (and vices) are classified according to their role in human morals, not according to their physiology or autonomic expressions. To be sure, there may have been a quasi-physiological theory explaining the (physical) origins of such emotions (the four "humors," for instance), and the overt expressions of the emotions was of considerable importance for their moral consequences. (Thus faith was judged on the basis of one's behavior, not just inner feeling.) But the classification itself was according to ethics, not medicine. (In fact, the language of medicine itself tended to be, until very recently, steeped in the concepts of morals.)

So, too, looking at a very different tradition, Buddhist psychology classifies what we would call "emotions" into at least two groupings, the *klesas* (or agitations)—ignorance, desire, hatred, fear, and pride, and the *rasas* (love, humor, courage, disgust, anger, astonishment, terror, and pity). Again, we recognize the ethical and social basis for the division, and the ethical and social importance of each of those "emotions." The *klesas* are disruptive, while the *rasas* are essential to the moral life. Again, we find an elaborate physiological "chakra" theory to support and explain the distinctions, but, again, the physiology serves the ethics, not the other way around.

It is in this context, too, that I want to try to understand the search for basic emotions in modern philosophy and, eventually, in psychology. Two thousand years after Aristotle, Descartes defined "the passions" in general as "the perceptions, feelings or emotions of the soul which we relate specifically to it, and which are caused, maintained, and fortified by some movement of the [animal] spirits." ("Emotions," in his terminology, referred to particularly disturbing passions.) Descartes, like Aristotle, may have been a serious scientist, but he was also a Christian and the heir of the Scholastics. His list of basic emotions was much more precise than Aristotle's, but a glance shows quite clearly that what his six "primitive passions" have in common involves no obvious physiological manifestations. Wonder, love, hatred, desire, joy, and sadness are central concerns of ethics. We might take note that neither anger nor fear appears on the list. These he lists among the "perceptions which we relate to our soul," sensations that are "excited by the objects that move our nerves and sometimes by other causes" (*Passions of the Soul*, art. XXV). In other words, the basic emotions are *more morally significant* to the soul than fear and anger.

Descartes is usually characterized as presenting a distinctively physicalist model of the emotions, his title *Passions of the Soul* notwithstanding. His problem was how to define and differentiate the different emotions, given his well-known theory about the agitation of "animal spirits" in the blood and the mind and body "meeting" in the pineal gland. But the distinctions between the six basic emotions were defined by their psychological and not by their physiological features, in terms of perceptions, desires, and beliefs. Thus the emotion of hatred, for example, "ultimately arises from the perception of an object's potential harmfulness and involves a desire to avoid it." Though he may have been fascinated by the physiology, Descartes (like Aristotle) was ultimately wedded to a value-oriented, wisdom-minded analysis of emotion. His six basic emotions are thus not merely disruptive agitations of the animal spirits, of interest only to physiologists. They are essential ingredients (or obstacles) in the good life.

Spinoza and Hume, too, were both interested in emotions as part of their overall interest in ethics. In his book *The Ethics,* Spinoza clearly pulls away from Descartes in classifying the emotions as "thoughts" (by which he means something far more specific than Descartes's use of *cogitationes*) and quite explicitly—following the Stoics—contains his discussion of the emotions within his search for wisdom. Spinoza, too, had a physiological theory "behind" his theory of emotions, and this emerged, in particular, in his distinction between the positive (innervating) and negative (enervating) emotions, signified by pleasure and pain. He also provided us with a taxonomy of emotions with desire, pleasure, and pain as the basic emotions. Most emotions are passive reactions to our unwarranted expectations of the world. They leave us hurt, frustrated, and enervated. The active emotions, by contrast, emanate from our own true natures and heighten our sense of activity and awareness.

Pleasure and pain, benefits and harms also play a central role in Hume's theory of the passions, which in turn plays the central role in his ethical theory as expounded in his *Treatise of Human Nature.* All passions, says Hume, are sensations of a certain kind ("secondary or reflective impressions"), and while these may be distinguished by any number of ideas that are their causes and causal consequences (e.g., the idea of "self" in pride), the emotions themselves are really of only two kinds, pleasant and painful. Love is a paradigm of the pleasant emotions; hatred, of the painful. These move us to act in various good and evil ways, and, in this regard, Hume famously tells us, "reason is and ought to be the slave of the passions." It is not reason that moves us. (It just tells us the best way to do what we want to do.) It is passion that moves us, and the most important thing about the passions is *what* they move us to do. Thus compassion (or "sympathy") is among the most important of our "natural" (i.e., basic) emotions, for it moves us to act for the benefit of others as well as for ourselves. (Adam Smith shared this view with his friend Hume, and this forms the basis of his *Theory of the Moral Sentiments.*) Hume's understanding of the passions (emotions) was not based on physiology or science alone (though Hume, too, endorsed the theory of animal spirits) but rested on a much broader conception of the role of emotion in human life and well-being.

It was about this time (the early nineteenth century) that the increasingly secular hand of modern science began to infiltrate philosophy and the dream of modern scientific psychology started to take hold. Thomas Brown introduced the term "emotion" (which he borrowed from Descartes and Hume) to characterize the large class of "feeling" phenomena that we now classify using that label.[12] He rejected both "passion" and "affect" because of their long history in religious debates and their theological baggage. Hume, of course, was also strictly secular in his thinking. He had modeled his theory of the mind after his hero, Isaac Newton. Thomas Hobbes had years before defended a materialist model of mind in which the passions were analyzed in terms of "matter in motion," but both Newton and arguably Hobbes were religious men, for whom physics and the physical world were never wholly divorced from their overriding concerns for religion and the moral world order. Hume rejected religion but held onto the importance of morals. But by the beginning of the nineteenth century the study of emotions had become a supposedly straightforward secular, scientific, and "value-neutral" activity.

This is a point worth making repeatedly, I think, because the study of emotions is so often viewed as a scientific and value-free activity, as if it had no other history. But I want to argue that the current search for basic emotions is illustrative of this narrowing of scope, and as such represents something of a *detour* in our quest for emotional understanding. That, in itself, is no criticism, of course. It could be, as modernists are prone to say, that the scientific impetus of philosophy was stunted or distorted by the continuing intrusion of moral and religious prejudices. But my argument is that, a few mixed metaphors aside, it has been by no means clear what the aim of the current concern about basic emotions is, if not an extension of that ancient moral and religious debate, a debate about *human nature*. The ferocity of the debate in normally staid social science circles surely suggests that something more is at stake than the number and identity of a few psychological building blocks or affect programs.

Philosophers from Aristotle and Aquinas to Hume were all interested in human nature. That was the heart of their ethics, whether by way of natural law theory or by way of proving how sinful we are or, in the sixteenth to eighteenth centuries, by way of explaining the utter selfishness or inner goodness of the species. Most philosophers and theologians assumed that the psychological features they observed in themselves and their countrymen were universal, although they occasionally remarked on some foreign (and largely unknown) people across the seas who lacked such features and were, accordingly, thought to be something less than human. What was "basic" about some of the emotions was the fact that they were essential to being a complete human being. Anger indicated an acceptable sense of propriety and limits. Faith and hope were exemplary of a certain kind of life. Love—in its proper place, of course—was soothing and essential to the harmony and continuation of the species. An emotion was basic if it played such an important role in everyday life, if it was basic to our essential character and the communal goals of human beings.

It does not follow that the emotions are irreducibly cultural, depending on the values and goals of a particular society. It might well be that the basic emotions, so construed, are those which are essential to the human condition and thus pancultural. Martha Nussbaum writes about "nonrelative virtues" with this in mind.[13] It might well be the case that such universal emotions also have a basis in evolution and neurology, but this certainly does not follow necessarily. There may well have been convergent or parallel paths of evolution. The human condition and evolutionary contingency probably intersected at many points in our development as a species. And our brains may have developed as the *product* of our particular circumstances (which is why Goldie rejects the "avocado-pear" interpretation of neurology and enculuration). In such discussions of basic emotions, there need be little mention of feeling as such and minimal attention to the particular facial expressions that are so characteristic of emotions. Were Aristotle and Descartes blind or oblivious to the obvious? Or did they see that whatever an emotion may be, it was not to be characterized by phenomena so "superficial" as mere feelings and facial expressions? Did their ignorance of neurology and evolution incapacitate their studies of emotions? Or did they just have different interests and, consequently, a different reason for thinking about basic emotions? I have suggested that the answer is that they had different interests and different reasons for thinking about basic emotions. But with this difference in interests the conception of basic emotions itself becomes very different as well. Aristotle and Descartes would be surprised to hear that facial expressions are even part of an emotion, much less, as some contemporary theorists argue, definitive of the emotion itself.

But could not one argue that what Ekman, Izard, and Panksepp are doing, carefully, scientifically, is just what Aristotle, Descartes, and the others *ought* to have done—indeed, *would* have done if they *could* have, if they knew more neurology and had more rigorous means of measurement? Perhaps. But my intention here is to open up the discussion, to remind us that the interest in basic emotions precedes scientific psychology by many, many centuries, and to recapture the larger context in which this has been true.

The Problem of Reductionism

What is a basic emotion? Ortony and Turner distinguish two approaches to this now "ubiquitous" and controversial notion: (1) a psychological building-block theory, a "combinatorial model" in which "basic" elements combine to form more complex, compound emotions, and (2) a biological thesis, that some (but not all) emotions have a biological basis and an "evolutionary origin." These are not always distinct theses, however, and more and more neurology-minded psychologists are promoting biological elements as building blocks or, at any rate, cornerstones of more complex and sophisticated emotions.

I have already pointed out that this "building block" metaphor has a long history, dating from the earliest days of science. Democritus, a contemporary of Socrates, defended the first "atomic" theory, and it was this sort of theory that would prevail in the new chemistry of the seventeenth and eighteenth centuries. Boyle and Newton also presumed some such theory, and it came fully of age with John Dalton in the early nineteenth century. Democritus had suggested an atomic model of psychology as well, and the modern philosophers Descartes, Spinoza, Hobbes, and Hume pounced on the idea. For much of modern times, chemistry and the atomic model have provided the metaphors of the mind, and the philosophers (and poets) who talked of emotions typically talked in terms of the latest theories in the physical sciences. The great German poet Johann Goethe, for example, employed such a metaphor in the title of his "Elective Affinities."

But such a model also encourages and promotes *reductionism* ("nothing-but"ery). Thus the continuing effort to define emotions as purely physiological even while describing them phenomenologically. William James, on the usual reading, is the classic case in point. Descartes illustrates the awkward relation between the "neurological affect program" type of reductionism and the "phenomenological building block" model. His theory may be physiological, but his attempt to distinguish and explain the emotions is thoroughly psychological. So, too, Hobbes employed the materialist metaphor of "motions that move us" to behave in various ways, but he quickly retreated to a psychological account of the particular emotions. For Spinoza, too, an emotion is a "modification of the body," but it is also (and more decisively) "the idea of such modifications."

About the same time that Niels Bohr was thinking up his theory of atomic structure as a way of ordering the elements, Freud defended the idea of a "scientific psychology" and suggested the possibility of reducing all questions about "the psychic apparatus" to questions about the anatomy and physiology of the brain. But like his philosophical predecessors he found it necessary to supplement his biological speculations with psychological hypotheses, and so he proposed several lists of basic emotions or psychic forces using the explicit analogy of Newton.[14] Freud famously kept changing his mind about the basic elements, but like Heraclitus, he believed that the character of the mind is defined by its conflicts, between lust and propriety, between reality and fantasy, between id and ego, between self and others, between the thirst for life and the desire for death. Freud often employed transformational as well as combinatorial analyses, for instance, in his famous hypothesis that depression is "really" anger turned inward or (my favorite) "love is nothing but lust plus the ordeal of civility." But the overall idea was to "reduce" the list of basic drives and emotions to as short a list as possible, ideally, to two.

Just before Freud and strongly influencing him, the philosophers Arthur Schopenhauer and Friedrich Nietzsche tried to defend the notions of "instinct" and "drive" in the psychology of the emotions as biologically basic emotions that provided the impetus and the unavoidable template for all of the others. Ideally, all of these would be reduced to just one. Neither Schopenhauer nor Nietzsche was very helpful in identifying these basic drives, but they both showed every evidence of attempting a radical reduction. Schopenhauer remained for the most part at the very general level of "the Will" (or sometimes, the Will to Life), while Nietzsche specified the identity of the most basic drive only vaguely (if dramatically) as "the Will to Power." But their shared idea, anticipating Ortony's second "biological" thesis, was that the basic emotions are singular, primitive, and unconscious biological drives and all other psychic phenomena are mere "superstructures," constructions (or rationalizations) based upon them.[15] The idea is to reduce the seemingly open-ended enumeration of emotions to a manageable core and to explain, if not reduce, all of the more complex emotions to variations or embellishments of the basic emotions. Thus the precise nature and number of the basic emotions and the mechanism for combining them is secondary to the quest for simplicity.

But what's wrong with reductionism? Isn't this the ambition of all science, to reduce complexities to simples, to explain biological processes in terms of biochemical reactions and chemical reactions in terms of more basic physical principles? Biochemists still dream of putting biologists out of a job. The study of life is reduced to the study of the nonliving. Physicists still dream of putting biochemists out of a job, and sociobiologists brag about eliminating the need for philosophers and sociologists.[16] Thus the study of human morality and justice is reduced to the study of the evolutionary mechanisms of what is dubiously called "altruism." In emotions research, the temptation is to reduce the study of emotions to something else, the study of brain processes, or the study of facial expressions, which is a way station on the way to a neurological theory. Life is complex and messy, and reductionism removes those complexities.

Well, yes, but science is also the appreciation of those complexities. Molecular genetics is fascinating because it explains the basis of heredity, which in turn provides the explanation for evolution, which in turn provides an account of the enormous variety of life forms. But it was a fascination with this enormous variety of life forms that moved Darwin in the first place. There is no disputing the enormous strides that have been made in research on emotions because of the reductionist impulse, but what got most of us interested in emotions in the first place was the enormous complexity and variety of emotions. I do not want to decry reductionism as such (there is too much of that mindless reflex in some of the "cultural theory" literature), but I want to "save the appearances," that is, the richness and subtlety of the subject matter itself. The problem with reductionism is that it tends to focus too avidly on the reduction and lose sight of the manifold that is reduced.

There is a further reason for resisting reductionism, closer to the core of the subject. I have argued that every emotion can be viewed from different perspectives and has different *aspects* (I do not endorse the popular "components" analysis, which seems to me overly mechanical and reductionist). I take it that every emotion has five such aspects: (1) behavioral expressions, including elaborate plans for action and verbal behavior); (2) physiological (hormonal, neurological, neuromuscular); (3) phenomenological (including sensations and ways of construing the objects of emotion); (4) cognitive (appraisals, perceptions, thoughts, and reflections *about* one's emotions); and (5) the social context (the immediacy of interpersonal interactions, pervasive cultural considerations). These aspects are systematically interwoven and they should not be construed (as they often are) as competing conceptions or as components of emotion. Philosophers tend to pay primary attention to the phenomenological and cognitive aspects of emotion; neuroscientists and biologically inclined psychologists tend to pay more attention to the physiological. But an emotion is a *holistic* phenomenon, and any exclusive emphasis on one aspect or another tends to distort the phenomena under investigation. This is what reductionism tends to do, cognitive reductionism as well as biological reductionism.

This last comment is worth repeating because even if one rejects the idea that some emotions are basic, the temptation to reductionism is very strong. For example, one can readily imagine a theorist (not me) who holds that emotions are cognitions and that cognitions are judgments which can be broken down into logically simple components. These various judgments could then combine to form increasingly complex emotions. Judgments, on such a theory, would be the quarks of psychology, combining to form elemental atoms or basic emotions, which in turn could combine to form more complex emotions. I do not hold such a theory (as will become evident), but I think it is important to note that it is not the biology-minded search for basic emotions alone which represents the craving for reductionism in emotions psychology.

One source of the urge to reductionism has to do with the sheer number of emotions (or, hedging our bets, emotion names). It is also the absence of any single criterion that defines what is and what is not an emotion. (Given the recent history of the category "emotion," it is not hard to understand why this should be so.) This has proven to be enormously frustrating to emotions researchers, who would like some clear and concise definition of their subject matter. Thus Paul Griffiths, in his polemic *What Emotions Really Are*, lets loose and proclaims that there is no one process underlying all of the things that are called emotions, and so no proper category of "emotions."[17] It is a "folk" concept (like Aristotle's category of "superlunary objects") that has been superseded by science. Just as our knowledge of astronomy has shown that Aristotle's category was an arbitrary grouping of objects, so current neurology has shown that our concept of emotion is an arbitrary grouping. But the truth is that Griffiths gives us only two different categories of emotion, affect programs and "higher cognitive" emotions (plus a problematic third category of illusory emotions). This undercuts his polemic considerably (one would have expected much more), and then it is affect programs—basic emotions—that draw most of his attention and emerge as *real* emotions (as opposed to all of those ephemeral superstructures).[18] Thus the bewildering complex of social, cultural, and creative emotions is reduced to a few simple biological forms.

The claim that some emotions have a biological basis and are thus "basic" can be taken in several ways, not all of which are compatible or equally defensible. If one simply argues that some (but not all) emotions have a biological basis, this claim is too weak. *All* emotions have a biological basis, as do all other "mental" phenomena, including the most abstract thoughts on mathematical or mystical matters. On the other hand, if the argument is that some emotions have an *entirely* biological basis such that sociocultural context and cognition of any kind are at best secondary if not irrelevant, then the thesis is exclusive in just the sense that I criticized above. Even strong advocates of the "affect program" understanding of basic emotions (including Griffiths) allow that there are emotions that cannot be understood this way and must, rather, be understood in terms of sociology and culture. But even the most basic emotions as affect programs must be understood in terms of sociology and culture. An affect program may be a "proto-emotion" (to employ a useful term from Jon Elster), but it is not yet an emotion. An affect program may emerge as an emotion, but by itself it is just a physiological reaction, like the "startle" reaction—which I would deny is an emotion at all.[19]

Thus one might be tempted to say that every emotion has *some* basic neurological core plus some cognition (or appraisal, etc.). But this is to succumb to what Peter Goldie calls the "avocado-pear" model of emotion, "an inner core of 'hard-wired' reaction, and an outer element which is open to cultural influence" (Goldie, p. 6). The inner core is the basic emotion. But tempting as it is, the model does not stand up to scrutiny. Goldie argues, and I follow him here, that any adequate account of the evolution of our emotions must take account of what he calls *developmental openness* or *plasticity*. He uses our ability to learn language as an example, and then follows by citing Simon Blackburn's conception of "plastic second-order dispositions to form different affective responses of different kinds in various social environments" (Goldie, p. 99; Blackburn, p. 147). I confess to accepting some form of the "avocado-pear" model myself in trying to untangle the confusion of the univeral-culturally specific debate about cross-cultural comparison of emotions. But Goldie turned me around, if only by bringing the absurdity of the metaphor to my attention. To twist around a question from William James, "Once you subtract cognition and culture from an emotion, what is left?" The answer is *nothing*, or at any rate nothing that would be identifiable as an emotion.

Let us remind ourselves what fascinated most of us about the emotions in the first place: the convolutions of love; the dialectic of anger, resentment, and revenge; the agonies of humiliation, embarrassment, and shame; the long-term passions of an Othello or an Iago; *not* the tenth of a second startle reaction or the spontaneity of disgust. And if one wants to refer to any of those as a "basic emotion," it is clear that we are now talking in a very different sense of that term than are the affect program theorists.

Jaak Panksepp holds a reasonable line on the role of neurology in emotions. He claims, "There appear to be a limited number of executive neural systems in the brain that instigate and orchestrate the various facets of a coherent set of emotive response," including behavior and psychology as well as neurophysiology as an integral part of "emotive response." The premise of his argument is that it is "not just response components but integrative systems that mediate primal affective states that characterize the basic emotions." In other words, basic emotions are anything but "simple," and as systems, not isolated processes, they allow for all of the flexibility and malleability that we would want, leaving room for cognitive and cultural conditioning and learning. Which is to suggest that, in a fundamental way, there may be no basic emotions.

Against Reductionism: Life Without Basic Emotions

In an early effort to combat reductionism, I developed a "structuralist" or matrix theory of emotions. That theory, which first appeared in *The Passions* (1976, 1993), tried to maintain that our emotions are, in an important sense, all on a par. I suppose I could have called it an "egalitarian" theory of emotions, but I am sure that would have been misinterpreted. Anger and fear are just two emotions among hundreds or possibly thousands of others. They may in fact be wired into our nervous system more directly and demonstrably than, say, jealousy, pride, or righteous indignation, but I did not take this to be a defining feature of their identity. All emotions have a neurological basis, but the identity of particular emotions lies elsewhere, in their phenomenological structures. The emotions differ, to be sure, but they are not compounds or molecules concocted out of one another. So, I argued, no emotion deserves to be elevated over others as more "basic."

In "folk psychology" (which has taken an undeserved amount of abuse lately) "folks" have been distinguishing emotions for thousands of years, often in much more fine-grained ways than are available in scientific psychology. Whereas psychologists talk rather clumsily about "anger" and "rage," for instance, we readily distinguish between resentment, contempt, pique, displeasure, irritation, moral and righteous indignation, wrath, hatred, being in a bad mood, sulking, bitterness, rancor, acrimony, outrage, fury, raving, fretting, frustration—as well as all of those metaphors, fuming, foaming, simmering, stewing, boiling over, bristling, bursting, being hotheaded, becoming incensed, "crabby," blowing one's top, and flying off the handle. To be sure, those metaphorical descriptions of emotion experience (fuming, foaming, simmering, stewing, etc.) need to be literally unpacked in terms of phenomenology, and many of the emotions mentioned are not even plausibly basic emotions, but that, of course, is just the point. The distinctions being made here refer not to an emotion's physiological origins but to its content, context, and structure. And on the basis of content, context, and structure an enormous number of subtle and sophisticated distinctions can be made that could not possibly be captured in the reductionist perspectives which would rather talk about a limited number of affect programs.

Thus in *The Passions* I defended the idea of an enormous, multidimensional matrix of judgments within which we distinguish an indefinitely large number of emotions. It was, in this sense, a structuralist account. The dimensions in the matrix include such matters as object orientation (self, other, the relation between them), a number of different evaluations and appraisals (not just "positive" and "negative" but also all sorts of judgments of responsibility and status), matters of scope and focus, strategic questions of trust and defensiveness, estimations of the other's intentions, associated desires, plans of action, and prognoses of consequences (see Appendix, Ch. 7).[20] An emotion is not a discrete entity but a node in a nexus. For example, a node of negatively evaluated other-directed attributions of blame yields anger, while a node of negatively evaluated attribution of blame that is self-directed yields shame. A node of self-directed negatively evaluated "in an awkward situation" without any attribution of blame yields embarrassment. A node of positively evaluated relationship-directed attributions of affection and shared identity yields love, while a node of negatively evaluated relationship-directed attributions of hostility and opposition yield hatred. A node of positively evaluated relationship-directed attributions of affection and shared identity, at a distance, yields admiration, and so on.

This is, needless to say, greatly oversimplified. All of the above-named emotions involve several other dimensions not mentioned. In the book, I suggested a list of some dozen or so more or less distinct dimensions, many of them judgment types, some of them concerning desires and action tendencies. A bit of crude math suggests that the matrix thus yields a thousand or more possibilities, many of them unrealized in any given culture and its emotional repertoire. A slight shift in the matrix might yield a very different emotion, for instance, frustration or resentment as opposed to anger, guilt or embarrassment as opposed to shame, love as opposed to hate. These are not distinctions that can be made in a situational vacuum. Electrical stimulation of the brain or the stimulation of an affect program (even fear or anger) without a context can only be described as a particular emotion ("fear" or "anger") insofar as it can be located in the matrix. Shame and embarrassment, as rightly described by Bedford in the 1960s (though in an overly behaviorist way), depend on the social circumstances in which these emotions are ascribed.[21] Attributions of responsibility are essential in the ascription of certain emotions; however, this is a function not just of third person-ascription but of first-person experience of emotions as well. Thus Ortony (et al.) develop a similar if simpler matrix of emotion types depending on whether the emotion concerns an event, and agent, or an object, and on such matters as desired or expected consequences.[22]

I have not even mentioned the fascinating complications that enter into this picture with cross-cultural comparisons and considerations of differences in emotion vocabulary as well as cultural differences. On this structuralist account, there is no reason to suppose that either (a) emotion terms in different languages and cultures are fully translatable or (b) emotions in different languages and cultures are *not* translatable, and therefore incommensurable. When researchers assume that emotions are discrete psychological entities, they feel pressured to opt for one of the other of these equally unpalatable alternatives. On the neurological affect program account, of course, the question of cross-cultural comparison never arises, since assuming that we all have basically the same brains, what would be the point of comparison? I take Peter Singer very seriously when he writes (with regard to animal suffering), "It is surely unreasonable to suppose that nervous systems that are virtually identical physiologically have a common origin and common evolutionary function, and result in similar forms of behavior in similar circumstances should actually operate in an entirely different manner on the level of subjective feelings." But it does not follow, when we are talking about sophisticated emotions rather than pain and suffering (Singer's concern), that the "subjective feelings" will be much alike, even when we find "similar forms of behavior in similar circumstances."

In *The Passions*, I argued against the idea of basic emotions on the grounds that one could carve up or select from the matrix in any number of ways, and there was nothing privileged about any one set of judgments (desires, etc.) rather than any other. I now think that this response was too "even-handed," although I haven't changed my mind about the nonexistence of basic emotions *in that sense*. There is nothing privileged about any emotion or set of emotions. To be sure, some emotions are more tightly "wired" neurologically than others. Others are more prone to voluntary control. Some are more socially connected and some are more appropriate to isolated individuals. But they are all just nodes in the nexus. But as Lévi-Strauss and the structuralist anthropologists found when they developed these ideas with relation to myth and other cultural constructions (the raw and the cooked, the civilized and the savage), the actual constellation of myth components is by no means arbitrary. A constellation may even come to seem necessary as some emotions prove to be central and even essential to a culture's way of life.

But in the abstract, that is, apart from any concrete social situation or culture, a constellation of emotions may indeed seem arbitrary, just as it is arbitrary which phonemes and which words a cultures employs to refer to which entities. (Thus the thesis that there are nothing but "differences" invented by Saussure, popularized by Derrida.) In actual practice, however, there is no arbitrariness. From the matrix each culture has "selected" a particular emotional repertoire. Anger will be basic to a society that puts a premium on responsibility (blame in particular), fear will be basic to a society that faces dangers it cannot cope with, and faith will be basic to certain sorts of religious societies. There is nothing more basic about the emotions in a culture's repertoire except, perhaps, its overall way of life and circumstances, and the language that goes along with (and in part determines) that way of life and circumstances.

I do not mean to suggest that a person or a society actually "chooses" his or her or its emotional repertoire from a large set of logical (or psychological) possibilities. A person simply "grows up" into a particular emotional life and range of emotions, sometimes expanding (or altering) the repertoire by joining a different group (say, a group of artists, self-styled aristocrats, or Bohemians) or by moving to another culture. (Batya Mesquita has a fascinating story about what it was like to move from her home in Amsterdam to America, and how she learned to accommodate herself to the "happiness culture."[23]) The matrix model provides us with a sense of the general topography, the range of possibilities, of emotion. We can envision combinations of judgments and feelings that are not part of our culture (e.g., the Ifaluk emotion of *fago* or the Japanese emotion of *amae*). But the matrix model becomes inadequate when it comes to understanding the emotional life of any particular culture (which is why structuralism gave way so readily to post-structuralism). In the matrix, no emotion is more basic than any other, but within a particular culture, there will always be emotions that are more central, more "basic," than others.

Basic Emotions as Simplicity versus Complexity

It is sometimes said—but, I suspect, much more often thought—that the distinction between basic and nonbasic emotions is in fact a crude distinction based on the structural complexity of emotion. Or else, why is fear a basic emotion while jealousy is not? Fear is a relatively simple emotion, almost no more than a negative desire. Thus an affect program might well account for all of the immediate reactions of fear, leaving aside the complicated behavior that might follow fear or the complications of long-term fear. Jealousy, by contrast, involves not just a single "object" but a complex dynamic involving one's engagement with both another person and a rival (in romantic jealousy, for instance). There is no way that an affect program could possibly account for such interpersonal dynamics. Fear has often been described as a "component" of jealousy, and indeed, fear and jealousy share something in common—the awareness that one is or might be in danger. But this constitutes all of the fear but only one small part of the jealousy. Thus fear is said to be basic and jealousy is not.

But insofar as the distinction between basic and nonbasic emotions is said to be a matter of complexity, we run into trouble, and again the source of the trouble has long been the subject of concern in physics.[24] Wherein lies the difference between simplicity and complexity? Descartes initiated one part of the contemporary problem when he invented analytic geometry. Given any pattern of dots (for example, the platting of data points on a graph), it is possible to derive at least one equation (in fact, indefinitely many equations) that describe the various lines that connect the dots. Between any two equations, one can readily discern which is simpler and which is complex, and so one can, presumably, determine which of many possible equations is the simplest for any given pattern of dots. And given any pair of patterns, one can, presumably, discern which is the simpler and which is more complex, by comparing the (simplest) equations that describe the two connecting lines. Thus primitive fear might be described as a straight line between self and object, while jealousy would seem to allow for any number of convoluted scenarios suitable for a yearlong soap opera.

But, now, suppose one is confronted with three different patterns: one an Italian tablecloth design of regular dots and squares, one a picture of a gallery of swirls and nebulae, and the third a collection of random dots. Eliminating the first, most viewers are quick to say that the random dots form the more complex of the two remaining designs. But the mathematics of randomness is in fact much simpler than the mathematics of swirls and nebulae. So, too, compare two portraits, one of a human face (with an ambiguous expression) and one a photograph of an uninterrupted field of wheat with shadows that might be interpreted as a face. Which is more complex?

Mathematics won't help us here. What constitutes complexity and simplicity is a "subjective" matter, which means that it is the observer who determines, in part, what constitutes simplicity and complexity. But can we trust subjectivity in such matters? Don't emotions that seem simple to some people seem complicated to others (such as when the emotion in question is someone else's as opposed to one's own)?

A seemingly simple example of fear, but where the object of fear is something monstrous, such as a spouse turned into a vampire (an old favorite of horror movie buffs) may well seem far less simple than a "simple" case of jealousy (boy meets girl, girl meets another boy, first boy gets jealous). What constitutes simplicity, accordingly, is by no means a matter of the structure of the emotions alone. It has to do with a great many nuances of context, expectations, and complexities, some of which might be built into the matrix of emotions itself. For instance, the vampire example might be a combination of the fearful judgment typical of fear and a number of other, more unusual judgments (sometimes described as the "limnal") that are more typical of horror. When theorists talk about the basic emotions, I fear, what they are often after are the crudest, least nuanced, least subtle and least sophisticated emotions. Thus the identity of such emotions with affect programs is a matter of some convenience but also considerable embarrassment. It makes the emotions look stupid and reinforces the old stereotypes of emotions as mindless, disruptive reactions that get in the way of human flourishing.

Basic Emotions as Basic *to* a Society

The seeming universality of some emotions has always been one of the main supports of the claim that there are basic emotions. A basic emotion (as an affect program) is universal; emotions that involve cognition and complex appraisals, by contrast, might be "socially constructed." There is some ambiguity which way the argument goes—is an emotion basic because it is found to be universal, or is an emotion necessarily universal because it is basic? Emotions that involve cognition and complex appraisals might be socially constructed but nevertheless be found to be universal. I have little doubt that affect programs as currently defined are universal, but this tells us very little about whether emotions are universal or not. Is jealousy universal? This seems to be an interesting question even if there is no affect program for jealousy. (David Buss, for example, has pushed an evolutionary account of jealousy without invoking affect programs.[25])

Is anger a universal emotion? It will not help to be told that everyone is "wired" to respond to an intrusion by "lashing out" in some primitive way. This is quite compatible with anger being quite absent from a society, for example, as reported by the anthropologist Jean Briggs in her *Never in Anger*, an account of the emotional lives of the Utku people of the Northwest Territories in Canada. It is not the universality of anger as an immediate and programmed reaction that interests us but anger, including protracted anger, as it fits into a way of life.

This is not the place to address this fascinating question—which emotions are universal? Rather, I want to address a very different question, namely, What if basic emotions are those *considered to be important in some particular society*? But "important" here does not necessarily mean, as many commentators have taken it to mean, most *common*. The most common emotions may be deemed of no interest or importance at all, for example, mere irritation or frustration. They may be so common that it is only their absence, not their presence, that is worthy of comment, which is not to say that, were such emotions suddenly to disappear from the face of society, that they would be missed. One can easily imagine a generally grouchy or vindictive society, "cured" by a rash of clear, sunny days or some psychogenic chemical dumped into the water supply, feeling no sense of loss whatever. Such emotions would not be deemed basic.

Nor need "important" mean *most valued*.[26] An emotion could be of great importance in a society because it is greatly feared. Thus anger (*riri*) among the Tahitians is an emotion rarely felt or displayed, but it is the topic of much talk and worry. It is, in the terms of the distinguished psychoanalyst-turned-anthropologist Robert Levi, "hypercognized." Anger is often talked about, greatly feared, and rarely experienced. It is, one might therefore argue, a basic emotion, even if it is rarely displayed and negatively valued. It does not matter whether the emotion or its expression is hardwired or universal. After all, why would the Tahitians care whether anger is so viewed, for example, on the streets of New York (except by way of warning, perhaps, a kind of emotional travel advisory)?

One must also carefully distinguish what people say they value from what they in fact (as demonstrated by their behavior) value. Americans generally condemn anger as a "negative" emotion, but a short drive on any American highway makes it amply clear that anger is as basic to American culture as an emotion can be. So, too, Americans generally accept an ideology that places little emphasis on trust, especially trust in government and large institutions. But even a casual study of American political and social behavior shows that this supposed lack of trust is far more imagined than real.[27] By contrast, I think it is safe to say that Americans tend to be obsessed with the idea of (romantic) love, but their actual attitudes toward this emotion are far more nuanced and complex (as evidenced by almost any randomly selected country music song).

I do not doubt that some emotions, as well as some facial expressions, are universal in the sense suggested by Ekman and others. But whether these should be called "basic" emotions is nevertheless open to question, and not just as a matter of terminology. Insofar as "basic" means "fundamental" (as significance) and not just "foundational" (in the building block sense), it might well be the case that those emotions as defined by (and limited to) affect programs are too limited, too stereotyped, too uncomprehending, too socially insensitive to count as basic emotion.

Rejecting the affect program interpretation of basic emotions and my overly egalitarian matrix theory as well, what remains? One might make the argument that fear and anger are universal insofar as human vulnerability and the possibility of frustration are ubiquitous, in other words, inescapable aspects of "the human condition." If this were so, it would tend to follow that fear and anger are basic emotions in virtually every human society, not because they involve affect programs but because they are fundamental in understanding and appreciating behavior in that (as in every other) society. By contrast, jealousy, shame, and embarrassment would seem to depend on more specific cultural contexts and conditions. It does not follow that they are not universal, but in those specific cultural contexts and under those conditions they will almost certainly be considered basic emotions. There has been a good deal of argument about this, but I do not see how such debates could possibly be settled by neurology or, for that matter, by abstract arguments about the human condition.

How is it possible that fear and anger might not be basic emotions? If they are unimportant (in a particular culture), they would not be basic—whether or not they are initiated by affect programs. In a warrior society, fear is not a basic emotion. That is not to say that no one ever feels it. It is rather to say that to experience fear is a disgrace, that most people do not feel it or (if they do) they refuse to acknowledge or express it, which is not to say that they "repress" it. The true warrior has through skill and training all but eliminated this emotion from his or her repertoire. So, too, with anger. When Jean Briggs argued that the Utku Inuits (or Eskimos) never got angry, she was not claiming that the affect program of anger never got triggered.[28] In two-year-olds, as in two-year-olds everywhere, that affect program was on ample display. But in mature adults it played no socially acceptable role, and the word for "anger" in that society, telling enough, translates literally as "childish." Psychoanalytically inclined anthropologists insisted that the Utku repressed their anger, but Briggs's descriptions make that implausible. It was not that the Utku *never* got angry. It was just that the affect program in question played no important role in their culture.

Could envy, even if it is not associated with any affect program, be a basic emotion? I think that the answer is yes, if it plays a dominant role in a culture. It is, unfortunately, not difficult to find such cultures. Colin Turnbull famously describes the Ik of Africa such that characterization in terms of universal envy is unavoidable.[29] Closer to home, Helmut Schoeck lauds the importance of envy in his book on that subject, leaving no doubt that envy is, and ought to be, a basic emotion of consumer capitalist society.[30] Is envy part of human nature? I doubt it, but I think the remaining socialists among us face a real challenge if envy is to be eliminated from society. It is not human neurology that needs to be manipulated but the structures of society, its competitiveness, its acquisitiveness, its "winner take all" psychology.[31] I am not even sure that this would be an entirely good thing, but not because it would deprive us of one of our essential human characteristics. Envy is not part of human nature and it is no affect program, but it is (in some societies) a basic emotion nonetheless.

Consider jealousy again. Jealousy, in adults, is a sophisticated emotion that involves judgments of "possession" (variously construed), judgments of warrant, a judgment of threat (which is why so many theorists have insisted that fear is a "component" of jealousy), a certain hostility toward the other person who threatens to take the object away from you (which is why many theorists have suggested that anger is also a "component" of jealousy), and, perhaps, hostility toward the valued person or object, as in the standard love triangle. It has also been suggested that jealousy involves a fourth party, namely, the abstract "other" who looks on and judges (consider the humiliation of being cuckolded). Thus the most vehement jealousy is not born out of love but out of pride. On the other hand, it is clear that there are what seem to be examples of jealousy among two-year-olds, for instance, between one child and another regarding a toy, and among animals, for instance, between one cat and another regarding affection from their "owner." But in none of these cases has it been suggested that jealousy is an affect program, even by those who would insist that jealousy is universal and therefore a basic emotion.

But what is it for jealousy to be a basic emotion (in some society)? I think the answer is similar to, but more complex than, our response regarding envy. Thinking about sexual jealousy, for instance, we would expect that in a society in which romantic competition, possessiveness, and sexual exclusivity dominate, jealousy will be a permanent possibility. But in the 1970s, there was a popular argument (which I endorsed) to the effect that jealousy was a retrograde and eliminable emotion. Jerry Neu argued against me, citing the evidence of two-year-olds, but I see Neu's battling two-year-olds just as I see the Utku two-year-olds. They are too young to fully participate in the emotional practices of their culture. What they exhibit (like the cats) is what we might call "proto-jealousy," which, brought to consciousness and filtered through the social fabric of appropriate cognitions, becomes a full-blooded adult emotion. In a society like ours, jealousy will indeed turn out to be a basic emotion, but because of the emphasis on possession that dominates our society. If, by contrast, the society were to look a lot more like Margaret Mead's Samoa, I think that jealousy, while occurring occasionally, would not be a basic emotion but rather some sort of eccentric (or even neurotic) exception.

Conclusion: Back to Basics

There are many questions that can be asked about emotions. Some of them have to do with the causal substrata of emotion. The most promising research on this front comes out of neurology and psychopharmacology, and the question of which emotions involve affect programs is a lively part of that perspective. While I think such matters have only limited value in the analysis of emotions in general, I expect this interesting research to continue to emerge.

A second set of questions has to do with the phenomenological "feel" of emotions.

A basic emotion would then be one that is prominent in experience or *"eidetic"* in the sense that Husserl used that term. Thus the phenomenologist Max Scheler defended the idea of an "emotional a priori," emotions that were necessary to our distinctively human emotional life. Sympathy was his chosen candidate (thus joining other prominent moralists). By contrast, Husserl's most famous pupil, Martin Heidegger, suggested that anxiety or angst would be the best candidate as the basic emotion of human life. According to Heidegger, angst permeates our every experience and defines our very being-in-the-world. But this, too, is an approach with limitations. What seems basic or "a priori" from the first-person standpoint might nevertheless be revealed as culturally specific. I think it would be an enormous mistake to abandon the phenomenological perspective, but I hope it is evident that it cannot stand alone.

Thus the third set of questions comes out of the social sciences, that is, sociology, anthropology, and social psychology. As I have described the basic emotions issue, it turns out to be neither neurological nor phenomenological but emphatically social (which is not to deny the relevance of either neurology or phenomenology). But whereas the social sciences insist on remaining "value-free," I think that they are at their best when they admit their submergence in the values of society and embrace a "critical theory" which both describes and prescribes problems and solutions, respectively.[32] Thus the question is whether anger, envy, or jealousy is part of the basic structure of society, not whether it is triggered by a more or less definitive neurological program or whether it permeates our experience in some necessary way (although, to be sure, it is hard to imagine an emotion that is part of the basic structure of society which will not *also* permeate our experience in a definitive way). This does not mean that an emotion cannot occupy a basic place in the structure of *every* society, but this is something that must be shown and not merely presumed.

The quest for basic emotions can be traced to one of the oldest Western aspirations and one that still resides at the very core of science, the quest for an ontological theory that requires only a few basic elements. In terms of scientific theory, this remains an apt goal. But in the richness of our moral life, we should resist this reductive impulse. It leads to a "dumbing down" of life and the vulgarization of our emotional experience. This does not mean that we should give up the fascinating research that is revealing to us the complex and subtle workings of the human brain, not does it mean that we should give up our quest for basic emotions. But the quest for basic emotions should be understood and pursued in such a way as to capture the richness and variety of human experience and not by way of reducing our emotional lives to the preset workings of a limited number of affect programs.

# 9

The Politics of Emotion (1998)

What is an emotion? William James asked that question in the title of one of his most famous psychological essays, in 1884.[1] James offered several different answers to that question, even in that same essay, but the one that every student of emotions knows is summarized in his heavily italicized statement *"our feeling of [bodily changes] as they occur IS the emotion."* Ever since (and long before, of course), the idea that the core of emotion is some sort of physiological "arousal" has governed a good deal of psychological and, until recently, philosophical theorizing about emotion. An emotion, in short, is a physiological disturbance, caused by some untoward or disturbing perception (thought or memory), that is *felt* in some more or less distinctive way. Thus the focus on emotion is aimed at the individual organism, its physiology and feelings. Today, of course, it is the neurophysiology of emotion that is attracting a good deal of attention, but the basic model of emotion as "arousal" remains the same.

What is an emotion? That same question was also asked, rather casually, by Aristotle, some twenty-three hundred years earlier. Aristotle mentioned feelings, physical agitation, and arousal only in passing when he defined anger, as a paradigm of emotion, as "a distressed desire for conspicuous vengeance in return for a conspicuous and unjustifiable contempt/slight of one's person or friends."[2] What should strike us first and foremost about this characterization of emotion is the fact that it seems to have much more to say about ethics, politics, and social relationships than it does about anything that most psychologists would recognize as "emotions." The key terms "vengeance," "contempt," "person or friends," as well as the twice-repeated word "conspicuous"—suggest that the nature of anger is essentially entangled in questions of perceived status, questions of offense and appropriate retaliation, and interpersonal relationships. Indeed, Aristotle goes on to insist that only fools don't get angry, and that while overly angry people may be "unbearable," the absence of anger (aimed at the right offenses) is a vice rather than a virtue. It is a "contempt/slight" that causes the anger (perhaps an instance of "scorn, spite, or insolence"), and because of this, it is *right*, even *obligatory*, to be angry (on the *right* occasion, for the *right* reasons, to the *appropriate* degree). Anger, and other emotions, are *political* in nature. They have a great deal to do with relationships between people living together in society.

Between the two of them, James and Aristotle establish a certain dialectic in emotion research. On the one hand, an emotion is a relatively primitive mental state or process, some combination of physiology and feeling. Like most "mental" phenomena, an emotion is a feature of the individual organism, something "inner" or—if "inner experience" is to be eschewed as too "unscientific" (James himself often denied "the existence of consciousness")—then something literally inside the skull, that is, in the brain. In psychology, because of methodological suspicion of private experience and because the science of neurology is still in development, the study of emotions is tentatively reduced to or focused on the superficialities of behavior—expressions on the face, short-term behavioral sequences, or the not always so credible self-reports of nineteen-year-old psychology hopefuls. On the other hand, there is what I have called the "political" approach to emotions. It takes as the framework for describing emotions neither the mind nor the body but the social situation, in all of its elaborate ethical and interpersonal complexity.

Beyond the Cartesian Tradition

Part of what I find so appealing about the "political" approach to emotions is the way it escapes or bypasses what is now generally called the "Cartesian" tradition in mind–body research. That tradition, well summarized in the recent debates between Dan Dennett, John Searle, David Chalmers, and many others, focuses on the "question of consciousness"—obviously a central concern for James as well—and slips back and forth, in tellingly technical language, between (more or less) commonsense dualism and reductive materialism.[3] Aristotle, of course, was burdened with no such concerns, enjoying the twin benefits of his innocence of both Cartesian dualism (and any such notion as "consciousness") and the reductive obsessions of modern science. The emotions, in particular, play an awkward—some would say unintelligible—role in the Cartesian picture, as an unwieldy causal complex of physiological processes, on the one hand, and personal experiences (or "feelings"), on the other. Descartes, who was as sophisticated as anyone in the physiology of his day, spent considerable time (in his *Passions of the Soul*) worrying about how the "animal spirits" in the blood affect the appropriate changes in the soul.[4]

On the "mental" side of the causal relation, however, Descartes's language changes abruptly. Hatred, for example, "ultimately arises from the perception of an object's potential harmfulness and involves a desire to avoid it"[5] Though he may have been fascinated by the physiology, Descartes (like Aristotle) was ultimately interested in a value-oriented, wisdom-minded analysis of emotion, how emotions fit into and define a good life. Nevertheless, the tradition that bears his Latinate name has tended to give scant attention to the political dimension of emotion and excessive attention to the emotions as feelings or "affects." There is some awestruck and occasionally apocalyptic admiration for the possibilities of neurological research, but Cartesian dualism has pretty much delimited a phenomenon defined on the one side by a neurology that is still very speculative and on the other side by a set of experiences—variously described as rich and meaningful or as primitive and inchoate—that each person allegedly has as his or her own private domain.

My own work, which is usually labeled (not by me) a "cognitive" account of emotions, has tended to remain within the same Cartesian tradition.[6] You may take this as a confession. My largely "phenomenological" approach emphasizes the role of "judgment" in emotions, following (among others) Aristotle, the ancient Stoics, and, more recently, Jean-Paul Sartre. To be sure, I have often emphasized the interpersonal and ethical nature of those judgments—as in judgments of affinity, intimacy, and responsibility—but insofar as I have continued to treat emotions as personal experiences, I have found that I tend to neglect several important dimensions of emotion. I have come to especially appreciate this since the 1990s in my interdisciplinary work with social scientists and psychobiologists. Neurology and the connection between brain processes and emotion are still beyond my ken, but I paid inadequate attention to more readily accessible aspects of emotion, such as the role of facial expressions and cultural "display rules" in emotion, despite their prominence in psychology and anthropology, respectively. Indeed, to this day, philosophers in general seem not to have discovered the significance of the face in emotion theory, despite the fact that this has all but ruled the work of the psychologists across the hall for more than twenty years. The reason, of course, is Cartesianism. The face is but superficial body. It is, at best, *expression*. But that, supposedly, tells us very little about that *of which* it is an expression, namely, the emotion. And the emotion, on the Cartesian account, is necessarily something "inner," not in the face or the expression but in the private experience of the subject.

Here we might again return to James, who had his own confusion about where to identify the emotion. Like Hume before him, James nominally identified the emotion as such as a sensation (or a set of sensations, an "impression") that he distinguished from the causes and the expressions of emotion. As a physician, James was naturally struck by the importance of the bodily responses, and he was keenly aware of the complex relations between an emotion and its bodily expressions, so much so that he famously urged that the latter were the cause of the former (although he sometimes conflated the behavioral with the physiological) and suggested, anticipating today's Hallmark greeting cards, that putting on a happy face will indeed result in feeling happy as well. Nevertheless, the official Jamesian doctrine, which resembled the doctrines of so many philosophers before him, was that the emotion IS the feeling, the distinctive set of sensations. An adequate integration of the "felt" and the physical aspects of emotion continued to evade him.

The Cartesian view of emotions has taken many different forms. Many philosophers and psychologists have thought that the definitive feature of those sensations which made up emotions was the fact that they were either pleasurable or painful. David Hume, for instance, distinguished love and hate, pride and humility, in this way. Spinoza sometimes made similar suggestions, and Spinoza's best twentieth-century incarnation, in the person of Dutch psychologist Nico Frijda, has argued the same.[7] Others, notably the Stoics and later Spinoza, suggested that the emotions were not so much feelings as "judgments" or "thoughts" about the world and oneself. I locate myself in this tradition. Nico Frijda, leaning toward behavioral (but not behaviorist) analysis, insisted that they were proto-actions, intentions, action tendencies. Outright behaviorists suggested, with varying degrees of implausibility, that emotions were *nothing but* behavior and dispositions to behave in certain ways, thus remaining Cartesians but simply denying "the ghost in the machine." More often than not, however, they hung onto some vestige of the mental, for instance, Ryle's infamous "twinges and itches" and Wittgenstein's "wheel that plays no part in the mechanism."[8] Others suggested that emotions were complexes of beliefs and desires—the rather simpleminded model of "folk psychology" that now reigns supreme in some cognitive science circles. But what all of these views have in common is their shared acceptance (or, in the case of behaviorism, a defiant rejection) of an emotion as an "inner" psychological state. The differences between these views are significant, of course, and I have spent much of my career defending one of them over the others. But I now see the challenge in a very different way, one that provides a Hegelian *aufhebung* to the "emotions are judgments" view and relocates it in non–Cartesian space.

One of the philosophers who best pursued a nondualistic alternative to the understanding of emotion was James's pragmatist colleague John Dewey. He insisted on a holistic, all-embracing view of emotion. Another is Martin Heidegger, whose obscurity on other matters did not seem to cloud his view of "moods" (*Stimmung*, but which, in his treatment, clearly includes many emotions), and Sartre, who despite his seemingly Cartesian ontology defended a view of emotions (and consciousness in general) as thoroughly political.[9] Other such views can be found scattered through the history of philosophy and psychology (before those fields were so unfortunately wrenched apart by university administrators and mutually jealous colleagues). But the prototype of the political approach still seems to me to be Aristotle. What all of *these* views have in common is a perspective on emotions as primarily situated in human relationships and inextricable from ethics.[10] The problem, as I now see it, is to retain the personal and experiential ("phenomenological") grasp of emotions but situate the emotions in a larger social context, treating them not only as the result of, but also as constituted in relations with, other people.[11]

The Purpose(s) of Emotions

One of the more exciting theses about emotion to (re)emerge in the twentieth century is the insistence that emotions are purposive. They have what Jean-Paul Sartre called *finalité*.[12] That is to say, they are not only functional and occasionally advantageous, and they are not just the fortuitous residue of fickle evolution; they are *in themselves* strategic and political. To put it differently and somewhat controversially, emotions do not just "happen" to us, as the whole language of "passion" and "being struck by" would suggest. They are, with some contentious stretching of the term, activities that we "do," stratagems that work for us, both individually and collectively. Or, to put it yet another way, there is a sense in which the emotions can be said to be rational (or irrational) despite the fact that "rationality" is often restricted to those contexts involving articulate thought and calculation. (Vengeance born of anger is exemplary here.) But rationality is often used in an "instrumental" way as well, to refer to the choice of means employed to reach some end. Insofar as emotions are purposive, they have ends. It is not just a matter of their happening (and how to get rid of or enjoy them). There are also questions about what will *satisfy* them. As strategies, emotions seek their own satisfaction, in anger, through vengeance, in hatred, through vanquishing, in love, through "possessing." This is not to say that all emotions can be satisfied or have conditions of satisfaction. (Grief, for example, is an emotion with no such conditions, except *per impossible*, the resurrection of the lost loved one.) Nevertheless, even such emotions may have a purpose or purposes, for example, to mend a suddenly broken life, not only for the individual but for the group together.

No doubt much of this can be explained via both biological and cultural evolution, but that is not the critical point. Of course, one can readily surmise, the energizing supplied by both anger and fear prepares an organism for extraordinary bursts of aggression or retreat, as the case may be. Such an account of emotions requires nothing whatever by way of self-awareness or voluntariness. In evolutionary theory, an individual or a species need not "figure out" its adaptive advantages. It simply lucks into them. It turns out that frogs and butterflies which resemble poisonous members of their classes have a competitive advantage. They are not so often eaten. It turns out that certain male birds with more tail plumage are more likely to attract a mate and thus have a reproductive advantage. So, too, it will turn out that creatures with a certain temperament, who react emotionally and express certain emotions in appropriate situations, may have a competitive or reproductive advantage. A dog that growls and attacks may be better suited to survive in certain environments. Dogs that run, hide, or cuddle may have competitive or reproductive advantages in other environments. (Dog breeders thus supplement Nature with marketing considerations.) I take it that none of this, as such, is all that controversial.

But most of what passes for evolutionary explanations of emotion in both psychology and philosophy these days are no more enlightening than Molière's famous explanation of the powers of a sleeping potion. To show that something serves a purpose or a function says no more and no less about the evolutionary process than the crudest creationist or contingency theories. Evolution is the new magic wand, which with a wave changes something inexplicable into something only seemingly explained. As Nietzsche famously noted, we always prefer bad explanations to no explanation at all.

But evolutionary theory is only background and does not play the central role in what I am arguing here. Emotions, according to the evolutionary hypothesis, turn out to be strategic or functional because they happen to contribute to "fitness," with all of the ambiguities and objections that term has inspired in the past century or so. A person (or creature) who has an emotion, according to the evolutionary line, does not have it because he, she, or it has a purpose (or because anyone, including "Nature," has a purpose) but because it has proved to be useful and alternative strategies have proved to be fatal. In such cases, the emotional responses themselves may be (what used to be called) "instinctual" or, in current computer-based jargon, "hardwired." An overly simple example (because it isn't really an emotion) would be the "startle reaction." Much more complicated are various forms of maternal affection and protectiveness, territorial jealousy, fear at the sight of certain shapes or in the presence of certain smells. But what I am arguing is that however biologically based our emotions may be, whether "hardwired" or not—indeed, whether voluntary of not—our understanding of emotion gains a great deal when we shift from thinking about emotions and emotional responses as mere products and think of them instead as strategies for dealing with others and strategies for dealing with ourselves.

The idea that emotions are purposive and functional can be found in ancient and medieval philosophy, and, of course, some of the world's great philosophers and religions have endorsed love and compassion in particular as divine strategies. But the thesis emerges with particular power not only in evolutionary accounts of emotion and their development but also, more controversially, in the anti–Jamesian theories of William James's contemporary and fellow pragmatist John Dewey and, more recently and more radically, in the writings of the French existentialist Jean-Paul Sartre. Sartre famously tells us that emotions are "magical transformations of the world," by which he means that emotions are intentional and strategic ways of coping with "difficult" situations. We choose them, and we choose them for a purpose.

This Sartrean view of the strategic nature of emotions will, no doubt, strain the credulity of most contemporary emotion theorists, although similar if more modest evolutionary-functionalist theses have been argued by many psychological investigators. Perhaps I could blunt some doubts by noting that there is nothing in this voluntaristic thesis which requires emotional strategies to be recognized, articulated, or even articulatable as such. In other words, they do not have to be conscious, in the usual sense of that term, and the "choices" we make need not be explicit, deliberative choices. Nevertheless, an emotion may be a strategy, a way of coping, and, in particular, a way of coping with other people. Especially when that way of coping involves power, I believe that we are justified in calling it "politics," the politics of emotion. But this ambitious phrase admits of quite a few very different interpretations.

The Deweyan-Sartrean view takes on a good deal more ontological baggage than the traditional Cartesian model of emotions. Essential to this view is the idea that emotions are *intentional*, which means that they are directed toward objects (real or imaginary) in the world. They therefore involve concepts and cognition, including recognition. Of course, they also involve neurology and physiology, and there may therefore be an instinctual or hardwired biological basis for intentional states. (William James certainly suggests that this is so.) But what this notion of "intentionality" tends to do is to break down the Cartesian barrier between experience and the world, between the "inner" and the "outer." Of course, the objects of emotion are not always real. (They may be merely imagined, or remembered, or, in extreme cases, hallucinated.) In which case we might continue to talk about the whole process remaining "inside" the subject. But in the more usual case, in which Harry loves Sally, in which Fred hates spinach, in which Woody is jealous of Alan, the intentionality of emotion is clearly directed at something real and in the world. There is an enormous philosophical literature about how to deal with these issues, whether the case of the "nonexistent object" is to be given priority or rather treated as some sort of odd exception. But these intrigues need not slow us down here. The point is that an emotion is not merely a "feeling," as, say, pain is a feeling. It is also an outlook, an attitude, a reaching out to the world.

As such a reaching out, it has aims and values (not just "appraisals," as some of the prominent psychological literature would suggest. Appraisal is much too "observational" to be strategic.) We perceive things, people, and events—and have emotions directed toward them—that embody attitudes of approval and disapproval, desires and repulsion, and goals of much more intricate sorts. Whatever else they may be, emotions are intimately and not merely contingently tied to behavior. (Which is why they were, for so many years, coupled as a poor cousin to "motivation" in psychology textbooks. No one knew where else to put them.) Strict behaviorists, of course, would simply say that an emotion IS the behavior, but here the conceptual tie is too tight, even with the usual qualifications.[13] Others (Nico Frijda, for instance) would more judiciously insist only that an emotion is a set of action tendencies.[14] But it is in the conceptual connection to behavior—which is to say, clumsily, that the emotion and its expression are one thing and not two—that the "politics" of emotion becomes particularly prominent.

If emotion were simply an impersonal judgment, or an "appraisal" and strictly "inner," like a spectator sitting passively, hundreds of yards from the field of play, the idea of emotional strategies and politics would make, at most, minimal sense. But emotions are tied to action, whether it is in the "cool" and protracted strategies of revenge that sometimes flow from anger or the spontaneous and momentary expression of delight or surprise on someone's face. However, it is the controlled, unexpressed, hidden emotion that requires special explanation, not the connection between emotions and their expression. When an employee gets angry with her boss, or when a mature, respectful child gets angry with a teacher or a parent, it is not the absence of expression that is notable but the restraint, the distortion of expression, which is almost always evident to those who know what to look for. Nevertheless, there are many emotions in which their expressions are of no significance, not because the expressions are controlled but because they occur in a situation in which there is no one to notice or be affected by them. We often have emotions when we are all alone. Accordingly it is important to note that there is an "internal" politics of emotions, so long as we do not take this in a Cartesian way. A subject may adopt an emotional strategy quite independently of any bit of behavior, display, or expression of emotion, and in the absence of any other person or creature who might be influenced, affected, or even amused. Nevertheless, the emotion, and not just its expression, takes place in a public, not a mysterious Cartesian, space. The emotion is "in the world," not in the mind, the psyche, or the soul.

The Politics of Emotion

The "politics" of the emotions might be divided into four different realms, each of which I will discuss briefly. There is first of all a general thesis about the ontology—or, better, the conceptual geography—of emotions, what they are, "where" they are to be located, and in terms in which they should be discussed. Second, there is the most obvious sense in which emotions are political, that is, they are about power, persuasion, manipulation, intimidation. Anger is the most familiar example here, but love, jealousy, shame, resentment, envy, sadness, and even despair deserve recognition as well. Third, there is what we might call the internal politics of emotion, the ways in which we position and (one might even say) manipulate ourselves in relation to the world, quite apart from the effects of our emotions or expressions on other people. In fact, when I first started seeing the importance of emotional strategies, given my (unacknowledged) Cartesian stance, it was such internal politics that initially intrigued me.[15] Again, getting angry is a paradigm example. One gets angry to "save face," not only in other people's eyes (the overtly public politics of anger) but in one's own eyes as well. Finally, the politics of emotion extend to the "meta" realm of emotion: "labeling," emotion recognition, emotion reportage, emotion description, and theorizing about emotion. It should not be thought that this "level" of emotional politics is easily separated or, sometimes, even distinguished from the other levels of politics in emotion and emotional expression.

The Ontology of Emotion

Ontology refers us to the basic nature of things, their place in the universe and how they relate to other things. The ontology of psychology or of psychological phenomena has long been trapped in the Cartesian picture, which, crudely, means that "mental" states, processes, or acts had to be treated *either* as odd manifestations or misleading descriptions of material states, processes, and behavior (Watson and

Skinner in psychology, Gilbert Ryle in philosophy) or as extremely odd nonmaterial entities, what Ryle famously mocked as "the ghost in the machine." But Descartes himself was keenly aware that the emotions, in particular, straddled this ontological abyss, composed, he said, of both kinds of "substances" (material and immaterial), agitations of the animal spirits (material) on the one hand and defined by beliefs and desires (immaterial "thoughts") on the other. Behaviorism, whatever its obvious absurdities, had the good sense to reject this impossible dichotomy and point out, with various levels of sophistication, that almost everything we know and just about everything we wanted to say about emotion depended on behavior (including verbal behavior, notably first-person reports). What was left over, of course, was that nagging "first-person case," the subjective "feel" of emotions, but a variety of deft and sometimes daft strokes whittled away at the prominence of this residue.

Without denying subjectivity, it could nevertheless be plausibly maintained that much of what philosophers had formerly described as "inner" could just as plausibly be redescribed as "outer," for example, in the expressions of the face, in tendencies to particular actions or action types (aggression, possession, caring for, withdrawing), in the verbal descriptions and evaluations that were employed to express the emotion. Sadness, for example, could be understood only minimally in terms of the "twinges" and sense of "deflation" that characterized the distinctive "feeling' of sadness. The bulk of this basic emotion could be better understood through an analysis of appraisals and evaluations of loss. So, too, the difference between embarrassment and shame could be understood not so much in terms of any particular differences in feeling or sensation (are there any?), but rather in terms of the differences in attribution of these emotions in decidedly distinctive contexts.[16] Describing an emotion as shame implies an accusation of blame, whereas describing an emotion as embarrassment implies no such accusation. Thus, in the wake of Wittgenstein, Ryle, and their psychological counterparts, the mysterious "mental" elements came to play a minimal role in the discussion of emotion.

Talk of evaluations and judgments can be neutral with regard to the Cartesian dichotomy. To be sure, a judgment may be made *by* a particular person, the subject, but nothing much follows about the subjectivity (in the crucial sense of first-person privacy) of judging. A judgment or an evaluation is *about the world*. It is made or can be articulated in a public language in terms of (more or less) shared concepts and standards. To be sure, again, a person can keep a judgment to herself, but the judgment is, nevertheless, about the world and analyzable in perfectly public terms. So, too, these judgments or evaluations can themselves be judged to be judicious, faulty, biased or foolish. Thus, "the conceptual geography of emotion" would suggest that the realm of emotion is neither the mind nor the world but both together, the world as experienced, the world as phenomenon.

Phenomenology, adequately described, is the natural medium for emotion description. Any description of the body, the brain, the circumstances, or behavior is bound to be incomplete or missing the point (the point of view, that is). Any description of merely "inner" sensation is bound to be pathetic. One can misdescribe the phenomenology as "the peculiarity of the first-person case"—and raise the puzzle of how we recognize our own emotions and what they "feel like" as opposed to how we recognize and understand other people's emotions. But the question of "where" emotions are to be located—in the material or the strange immaterial world—no longer serves any purpose. Emotions are, in every important sense, "out there," in the world. Or, rather, there is no "out there" because there is no contrasting "in there," unless, perhaps, one wishes to speak rather peculiarly indeed about processes "in" the brain. This is not what is commonly called "materialism," which disappears along with the odd view—held only by philosophers, neurologists, and some social scientists—that emotions are "all in the brain." Nor is it in any way to deny the "existence of consciousness," whatever that odd phrase is supposed to mean. It is just to say that emotions are vital experiences had by conscious social creatures (even if the very limited role of the social is a constant awareness of predators and the occasional awareness of an available mate). Emotions involve any number of interrelated aspects of such creatures' sensibilities, social relationships, self-awareness, shared and individual outlooks on the world, their physiology, their various expressions in speech and behavior. Such complex creatures should not be split up into a simplistic and arbitrary ontology of bodies and minds.

Emotions, Power, and Persuasion

On this view, the most obvious sense in which emotions are political is that we use our emotions to move other people, or other creatures. Our dogs respond rather quickly to a shout or a scowl, even if it is disciplinary and feigned rather than genuine emotion. This, of course, raises a crucial point about the politics of emotion: that it is the convincing expression of emotion, rather than what one might call the emotion itself, which is doing the work. But, in our account of the conceptual geography of emotions, I tried to cast some doubt on the distinction between emotion and expression, and argue—as William James did—that a "convincing" display of emotion either presupposes or tends to create the very emotion being displayed. Could one gain the same ends by pretending, by acting *as if* he or she has the emotion in question without, in fact, having it at all? In theory, perhaps, but I think that the practical answer is that few of us are such accomplished actors that we could bring off such a performance, so that actually having the emotion seems necessary. But if this is so, then it seems to follow that one has the emotion precisely in order to bring about the desired results. Whether or not this is so (and certainly the range of cases is far richer than James's simple formula would suggest), it is clear that emotions are not just self-contained and not usually self-contained, but are more or less continuous with their expression. This means that the lines between authenticity, self-deception, and bad faith get enormously complicated here, but I want to remark, rather baldly, on just one piece of this intricately human puzzle. And that is, to have an emotion for a purpose does not entail "not really having" the emotion. That thesis, of course, would undermine everything else I've said here. Nico Frijda puts the thesis rather innocently but, I think, correctly when he says, "Emotions—their kind, their intensity, their manifestations—are not only determined by significant eliciting events, but, in addition, are influenced to an important extent, by the anticipated desirable effects they exert upon others." Emotions, in other words, are strategies, and there is little reason to doubt that our emotional expressions evolved, in part, because of their effectiveness in communicating our emotions to others.

Sometimes our emotions and emotional displays involve solicitude, a cry for help, an expression of need. Expressions of submissiveness, shrieks of terror, a baby's cries of distress are all directed (which is not to say, consciously or intentionally) to getting the attention and directing the actions of others. Because they work so well, they can also be learned, cultivated, practiced, and thus employed in an intentional (which is not to say "feigned") way. A young female soon learns to win favors by being submissive, which involves feeling submissive, and so she learns to feel submissive. A clever young monkey learns to scatter the troop, at least once, and get the food for himself, by overreacting to a sign of merely modest danger. Babies, children, and even adults learn to cry to win the sympathies of others, and, again, they are not "faking it" but rather just being particularly alert about finding things to cry about. (A young woman on *Seinfeld* bursts into genuine tears when her hot dog slips out of its bun, but later shows no sign of sadness at all when her grandmother dies. She may be despicable, but she is not a fraud.)

Many emotions are about power, persuasion, manipulation, and intimidation. We use anger, for example, not only to pump up the energy and boldness needed for a confrontation but to intimidate the opposition as well. One of the more unpleasant members of my academic department had the habit of highlighting every meeting in which there was a controversial issue by standing up (he was very tall), leaning menacingly over the conference table, and shouting quite threateningly at whoever was opposing his position. Since most of the controversial issues discussed were also quite trivial, the opposition virtually always gave in, and he had his way. What was telling was that these cheap victories rarely had any correlation to the merits of the case, and, more telling still, there was no reason whatever to suppose that his angry displays would ever lead to actual violence. (In fact, the fellow was a coward who would most probably back away from any real fight.) But, for most of us, our fear and foreboding of anger is so visceral that the mere display of anger leads us to act *as if* there is a real threat of harm behind it, even if we know there isn't.

So, too, of the seductive emotions. How many of us have been taken in by appeals that, we knew at the time, were insincere, misleading, or disasters-in-waiting? Advertising and salesmanship depend on such vulnerabilities. Our responses to emotions, as well as the emotions and the expressions themselves, are also inbred, habituated, cultivated, and, possibly, sometimes "hardwired." It is no surprise, then, that emotions have this obvious political element, that their existence is not a neutral social or psychological fact but a political force, moving us and influencing our actions in any number of ways.

When we begin to discuss the many aspects of the display and expression of emotion, the power of such strategies should be obvious. Paul Ekman and Carroll Izard have maintained for years that the facial expressions they have classified have an evolutionary basis, and they take this to mean not only that they happened to appear in evolutionary history but also that they in fact served some social, and therefore reproductive, advantage. But what is true in the evolutionary story must surely be true in the more ordinary social story. Bad-tempered people tend to get their way by being intimidating. (They could possibly get their way by just pretending to be angry, but, their thespian talents aside, actually getting angry would seem to give them a double advantage, for reasons suggested above.) To what extent this is true of other emotions will involve emotion-by-emotion analysis. A case can surely be made for love, generally considered. Shame and guilt would suggest an advantage for the group but, perhaps not directly for the individual. Grief and sadness invite speculation. (There is certainly manipulative grief, and tears by way of a plea.) Pity and gratitude would be fascinating cases to explore. (Nietzsche has done so polemically, and at some length.[17]) But what all such analyses would be looking for would be the ways in which expression and display constitute a strategic advantage over other people (whether intentional or not).

The Internal Politics of Emotion

The internal politics of emotion are the ways in which we position and (one might even say) manipulate ourselves in relation to the world, quite apart from the effects of our emotions or expressions on other people. When Nico Frijda writes that emotion politics is "displaying or even experiencing a given emotion because of its desired effects in the power,"[18] there is an important ambiguity embodied in that word "experiencing." What we experience certainly influences or even determines our attitudes and our behavior, which in turn influence, move, or coerce other people. But we can sometimes see a truncated version of the process in which the effects are unexpressed or unrecognized, in which they are even intended to remain so. Anger is a hostile emotion that adopts a familiar stance in the world, if only in one's own perspective. But that perspective has a purpose, whether or not it has expression or results in action, even if the subject goes off by himself and avoids all possible detection or prompting to action. It is a judgmental stance, one that resembles a courtroom scenario. It is a scenario that has been succinctly captured by Lewis Carroll in *Alice in Wonderland* (in "The Mouse's Tale"). It goes, "I'll be judge, I'll be jury, Said cunning old fury." The strategic advantage, I think, should be obvious. Emerging from a situation in which one has been hurt, offended, or humiliated, one positions oneself as nevertheless superior, even as righteous. It is a powerful psychological position. It is emotional politics at its most profound and subtle, whether or not effective in the world.

A similar example is developed at length by Nietzsche, in his *Genealogy of Morals*, where he suggests that resentment, by its very nature, is an emotion that evades direct expression and confrontation but prefers to alter the world as perceived to suit its own particular vulnerabilities and weaknesses. Thus one might talk about these "internal politics" as the "strategic rearrangement of one's own attitudes," or what Sartre more poetically called "magical transformations of the world." This internal politics of emotion fits in very well with what I have often referred to as the judgmental role of emotion, following certain Stoics, who argued a similar thesis two thousand years ago. The question, for the Stoics, was not how our emotional behavior affected the world (negatively or negligible, most of them argued), but rather how our emotional judgments affected our own outlook on the world and, consequently, our chances for happiness. A somewhat more public version of the same idea has been nicely characterized, in his *Rationality of Emotion*, by Ronald De Sousa, who introduced the notion of "paradigm scenarios," in which one learns not only the "appropriateness" of certain emotions and emotional behaviors but also their power and significance. What one learns, presumably, is not only the effect of one's emotional responses on others (and their approval or disapproval and responses in return) but also the way an emotion makes one "feel," where the "feeling" in question is by no means to be confused with the sensations caused by the concurrent physiology or that inchoate sense of "affect" which is so often alluded to by authors who lack the facility to pin the "felt" emotion down.[19] One could (and De Sousa encourages this) provide an evolutionary background story for such scenarios. But for my purposes here, it is important to insist that these scenarios are not, and need not be, as such, public or physically situated. No doubt they originally always are public and physically situated. But once one has "internalized" the paradigm of an emotion, one can, as it were, play it back privately, rehearse and instantiate a strategy as if it were public, and, in so doing, achieve a sort of competitive advantage, even if only in one's own eyes.

The Politics of Emotion Language and Theory

Thus far, I have been talking about the politics of emotion strictly in terms of the strategies of and in emotion. But this is only part of the story. We do not just have emotions. We know that we have them. We label them, talk about them, devise theories about them, and, not incidentally, make a good living off of those theories. Here is a second level of competitive advantage, if you will, not in the emotions but in the "metalevel" in which it is talk about the emotions that comes into play. I suggest that, because we so easily tend to think of language as something over and above the emotions, a facility or faculty quite separate from the "having" of an emotion, we do not tend to take emotion talk as part of the same set of phenomena. But the truth is, our language, our concepts, and our conceptions of emotions are intimately linked with, pervade, and define the emotions themselves. (This is not for a moment to deny that animals and preverbal infants have emotions. It is only to deny that adult humans, who do have such a language, are capable of clearly separating their emotions from their talk and thinking about them.)

There are several dimensions of this "meta" reflection on emotions. The simplest has to do with the nature of emotions' names, that is, what we *call* them, or what psychologists refer to as "labeling." Whether a person labels her hostile feelings "hatred," "anger," or "resentment," for example, makes quite a difference in how she will express, evaluate, think about, and talk about her emotion. More complicated is the way we talk about and sometimes mythologize emotions. Love in America would be an apt illustration. It is a highly mythologized, one might say "hypercognated," emotion, so much so that cynics have often suggested that "love" is *only* a word, a confusion of fantasies, not a genuine emotion.[20] Finally, and most sophisticated of all, is the way we, as philosophers and psychologists, conceptualize and theorize about emotions. The target of my arguments for almost twenty-five years now has been the still strong tendency to "primitivize" emotions, by way of denying, I suggest, our responsibility for them. To say that we "choose" our emotions is, I admit, something of a stretch. But as a self-fulfilling prophecy, as a way of taking control and becoming increasingly aware of the emotional choices we do make, I would suggest that it is an invaluable piece of existentialist wisdom. The primary alternative, thinking of emotions as physiological disruptions and psychic "forces" beyond our control, is also a self-fulfilling prophecy, an invitation to think of ourselves as victims and make excuses for our own behavior. Thus the politics of emotions becomes part and parcel of the politics of personal responsibility and the self-cultivation of the virtues.

Does it matter whether we call [it] "anger" or "ire" or "riri" or "childishness"— or even "fury" or "outrage" or "moral indignation"? (What are the differences here?) Jean Briggs has famously told us that in Utku the naming of (what we call) anger "childishness" serves to demean the emotion even as it is identified.[21] Similarly, Robert Levi has shown us how *riri* in Tahitian demonizes the emotion even before it is described. "Ire" (directly from the Latin) has a nobility about it that anger doesn't have.[22] So, too, "fury" suggests violence, "outrage" indicates violation, and "moral indignation" suggests righteousness. (Mere "irritation" or being "pissed off" is dismissive, by contrast.) "Rage," I would suggest, refers to something much more (or much less) than anger, a totalizing neurological response that is, comparatively, out of control and involuntary. There is more in a name, dear Juliet, than that which arbitrarily names that which smells so sweet. And when the "subject" supplies that name to his or her own emotion (as Schachter and Singer have shown), it is the emotion itself, and not merely its name, that alters.

The politics of emotion language is by no means limited to the naming of emotion. Consider, for example, the general dismissal of emotion in such terms as "sentimentality" and, simply, "getting emotional." Once upon a time, it used to be that "sentimentality" suggested the superior sensibility of aristocrats, no more. Today, it tends to refer to bad art, cheap morals, and a distinctive defect of character. "Emotional" and "sentimental" are employed as put-downs, for example, in a long-standing (and still not extinct) dismissal of women and "effeminate" men from positions of responsibility.[23]

Finally, there is the politics of our theories, including the now controversial depiction of what is misleadingly called "folk-psychological" theories. A good deal of commonsense theory (and the language of emotions) implies what I have called "the hydraulic theory," the dismissive view that emotions are "nothing but" physiological "pressure," as drawn, for example, by Freud in his "boiler system" model of the "psychic apparatus," in the early decades of his career. My objection here is not only theoretical but also existential or ethical. The politics of the hydraulic model (and a good deal of folk psychology) is a politics of irresponsibility. Our emotions are an 'it' not part of the 'I.' So, too, those ancient theories which make out love and anger to be a breed of madness, rather than strategies. Here is where Sartre comes charging in with his "existential" theory: no, the emotions do not "take us over" or "sweep us away." They are strategies, and we *choose* them. Personal responsibility is an important piece of the emotions story, and any theory that does not face up to this is itself political (or should we say politically irresponsible?).

The Startle Response and the Primitivization of Emotion

Finally, I want to discuss one of the most straightforward examples of what I called the "primitivization" of the emotions in the recent philosophical literature, Jenefer Robinson's defense of the "startle response" as a paradigm of emotion.[24] Robinson rightly suggests that this example provides a striking contrast to the "judgmental view" of emotions as cognitive, defended by many philosophers but (she says, incorrectly) not by many psychologists. Being startled is, one might say, a "pure" and "primitive" emotion, without the cause or accompaniment of belief, thought, or judgment and certainly not constituted by them. Being startled is an immediate and involuntary physiological response. Robinson suggests that philosophers pay more attention to the psychological research on emotion and, in particular, physiologically "hardwired" "emotional" responses. Indeed, she is right that philosophers (with some obvious exceptions) have paid too little attention to the sometimes fascinating work going on in psychology and, especially, neurology (though it must be said that the neglect has mostly been mutual). But the startle response is, I want to argue, much too primitive to count as an emotion—even given the messiness and open-endedness of that category, and certainly too primitive and unpromising to serve as a paradigm of emotion or a "basic" emotion.[25]

The range of emotions, if one were to (mistakenly) consider them along the line of a single dimension, extends from almost straightforward physiological reactions (disgust, elation) to extremely sophisticated, fully cognitive responses (indignation, humiliation, certain forms of romantic love and devotion). But even disgust presupposes some (disgusting) perception, and although elation certainly need not be accompanied by the articulated thought or belief that "all is well" (or something like that), it would be difficult to defend the attribution of "elation" without some such evaluative judgment. So, too, even the most extreme "judgmentalist" will agree that indignation, humiliation, love, and devotion involve some possibly intense, probably involuntary, neurologically based response, although the causal story in such cases promises to be both bidirectional and extremely complex. I, too, will ignore the longer-standing emotions, such as lasting love, enduring anger, envy and resentment, lifelong guilt or shame in my response to Robinson, although it seems to me to be an enormous (if long-standing) mistake to not treat these emotions at all, or to think of them as merely dispositions or derivative of more "episodic" responses. Indeed, I would argue that it is the more durable emotions, "the passions," that ought to serve as our paradigm, in part because it is so obviously they, and not the sudden movements of the moment, that carry political weight and significance.

The idea that some version of "surprise" is a basic emotion isn't new, of course. Descartes lists wonder ("a sudden surprise of the soul") as one of six "primitive passions" (*Passions de l'âme*, LXIX), but it is clear from the convoluted description which follows that it is not being startled that he has in mind (". . . which causes it to apply itself to consider with attention the objects which seem to it rare and extraordinary. It is thus primarily caused by the impression we have in the brain which represents the object as rare . . ."). One could helpfully distinguish here between surprise, astonishment, shock—as in "I was shocked to find . . . ," not physiological shock, which is very different—being "stunned," and being startled (and, perhaps, being merely unprepared). The difference between shock and startle and the difference between shock and its pathological namesake (a collapse of circulatory function) are particularly revealing. Startle is, as Robinson argues, an autonomic reflex. (Even one-celled organisms can be argued to display it, for example, when poked.) Shock is a sudden emotional disturbance, but it is not caused only by some sudden event; it also has that event or some complex surrounding that event) as its object. It therefore presents itself as a candidate for emotionhood.

The relationship between shock and the sudden pathological malfunction of circulation is worth noting. Of course, one can lead to the other; the shock of being arrested for a serious crime or seeing the body of one's mangled loved one dangling from the fence will likely cause physiological shock as well. Physiological shock, like some other medical conditions, can be caused not only by physical but also by psychological trauma, by extremely intense emotion as well as physical damage (e.g., extensive loss of blood). Jean-Paul Sartre probably overstates the case when he suggests that a young woman who is shocked by her companions' comments faints as a strategic response, but some relationship between emotion and the "magical transformation" of the body is not unfamiliar in medical circles.[26] But this relationship between emotion and physiology pervades the study of emotions. For example, extreme anger can give way to rage, a physiological reaction. (Neurological experiments with cats have demonstrated that this response can be triggered by stimulating a specific part of the brain.) So, too, extreme fear gives way to panic, arguably another "primitive" physiological response defined by limited cognition or judgment. I have been arguing that there is no clear dividing line between psychology and physiology in emotion, but the attribution of emotion as opposed to "mere reflex" would seem to be precisely the presence of some "cognition," some "directedness towards an object," as opposed to the physiological response alone, as in the startle reaction.[27]

It is worth noting that at least one of the psychologists to whom Robinson appeals most often in her argument, Paul Ekman, has himself given up the view that the startle response counts as an emotion. He has instead moved to "surprise" as a basic emotion, where this is understood not merely as "being startled" but as "being surprised by."[28] The startle response as such is impossible to stimulate or inhibit. Indeed, it is only in the most generous sense a "response" at all; rather, it is a reflex. This is particularly significant because Ekman's theory of emotion leans very heavily on a particular kind of "hardwired" physiological response, namely, facial expressions. Of course, what is particularly interesting here is the fact that such expressions can be either voluntary or involuntary. For an expression to be "hardwired," in other words, means that it is not therefore fully determined by physiology. Ekman, who provides one of the main psychological supports for Robinson's thesis, has abandoned it himself under scrutiny from his psychology colleagues. (One might note that even Robert Zajonc, the harshest critic of "cognitive" theories in psychology, speaks unflinchingly of "motor systems" as "representational" and as "encoded." And Joseph LeDoux, to whose neurological views Robinson appeals, insists on the significance of interactions between the subcortical parts of the brain essential to emotion and the neocortex and hippocampus, suggesting that cognition is not irrelevant even in the most primitive emotion.)

Why not include startle, as Robinson argues, at the "extreme" and "primitive" end of the emotion spectrum? One could, of course, raise the question of whether the "spectrum" model makes much sense for what is in fact an extremely complex and by no means obviously related set of psychological phenomena. (Erotic love certainly involves an enormous number of autonomic [enduring] physiological responses. It also involves historically and culturally bound concepts of considerable complexity.) One could also challenge the notion of an emotion as a "response." So, too, Robinson: "According to my model, my response is a bodily response which makes this event salient to me and registers it as significant to my goals and values" (pp. 18–19). But doesn't the event have to be perceived as "salient" in order to provoke any such bodily response? My primary concern, however, is not how we circumscribe or carve up the territory we too casually identify as "the emotions," but the purpose at which such "primitivism" moves are aimed. This is a particularly tantalizing question in Robinson's case, for she has written some sensible and sensitive essays on the role of emotion in the arts. Nevertheless, I suspect that the "primitivism" move is more often than not a preliminary to a debunking, the suggestion that emotions as such are too conceptually uninteresting for philosophers to talk about.

Let me offer a brief example of such debunking. It is "An Assessment of Emotion" by Jerome Shaffer.[29] In that "assessment," Shaffer begins with a most unflattering example of "undergoing an emotion": "I am driving around a curve and see a log across the road. I take it that bodily harm is likely and I don't want that. I turn pale, my heart beats faster, I feel my stomach tighten. I slam on the brakes. . . ." (202). Not surprisingly, Shaffer uses this and similar examples of emotion to conclude that emotions are not very pleasant or valuable experiences and, accordingly, are "neither necessary nor in general desirable for the main concerns of life" (220).

This is not merely a matter of being "startled." Indeed, I suspect that it falls into the category of an unwelcome surprise. But should we characterize (much less define) surprise by this "turning pale, heart beats faster, stomach tightens"? Consider the very different analysis that would accompany taking as our lead example, say, experiencing a powerful sense that justice has not been done, or the possibly decades long experience of being passionately in love. (Shaffer's analysis of love as an emotion in the same essay reduces love to "butterflies in the stomach" and other such "waves, currents, surges or suffusions," concluding that love, too, is an emotion of little value. This is hardly the passion that moved Tristan and Isolde.) Furthermore, we can readily agree that coming across a log in the road is an undesirable experience without concluding that the surprise itself is an undesirable experience. Indeed, in safer surroundings, millions of people have been known to stand in line in order to pay up to six dollars each to have the wits satisfyingly shocked out of them not only by misplaced logs but also by killer sharks, madmen, monsters, and chainsaw murderers.

Emotions are still on the defense in philosophy. (Indeed, they have come into prominence in psychology only since the 1990s.) For that reason, one might well agree with Robinson that emotions have a "primitive" component and, in a few cases, are extremely "primitive" themselves, but still have good reason to insist on focusing on just those emotions which are comparatively sophisticated and have the sorts of conceptual components which are the familiar subject matter of philosophical analysis: an interest in symbolic logic or scientific curiosity, being awestruck by the beauty of a golden eagle, being warily suspicious of an insurance salesman, being embarrassed about wedding publicity, falling in love, having a keen sense of justice, becoming indignant or jealous, joyful or even depressed. One need not deny physiology to engage in philosophy, but neither should we allow the facts of physiology to eclipse significant philosophical investigations.

Conclusion

There is one further form of politics in the study of emotion that ought to be mentioned, and that is the academic politics of departments and professional prestige. We redefine emotions to suit our methods. Philosophers, not surprisingly, tend to view emotions through the frame of conceptual analysis, as the phenomenology of experience, as "cognitive science." Neurologists tend to view emotions as first of all neurological. Behavioral psychologists naturally tend to view emotion by way of expression, and so on. There is nothing wrong with this, as such, but we all too easily let our politics get in the way of joint efforts and mutual understanding. Philosophers are particularly skilled at dismissing as conceptual confusion or nonsense the most devoted efforts of the social scientists, without applying the "Principle of Charity" to seek out what they might be saying that philosophers have systematically ignored or overlooked. In return, predictably, the social scientists lampoon "armchair philosophers" without bothering to see what serious suggestions might be sitting there.

So here, to end, I want to turn again to John Dewey's thoughtful commentary on James, in which he insists on a holistic, all-embracing view of emotion. Emotions have a multiplicity of dimensions and aspects and, consequently, a multiplicity of lines of investigation. But let's not be like those legendary blind Persians, each dogmatic about his own particular part of the elephant. If we are aware of the politics that pervade and surround not only emotion but also our treatments of emotion, we can work together and answer some of the hardest questions, namely, how these different approaches fit together. There may be no single objective standpoint. Indeed, there may be no objective viewpoint at all. The ultimate "truth" about human emotion may be that we never get outside ourselves, and so there will always be political interests and power relationships both in emotion and in the study of emotions. But the fact that emotions are political may be precisely the reason why the emotions remain of such enduring interest to us, not as a test case for Cartesian dualism but as an imminently practical matter regarding our getting along in the world.

10

Against Valence ("Positive" and "Negative" Emotions) (2001)

> By *emotion* I mean the modifications of the body, whereby the active power of the body is increased or diminished. . . .
> I therefore recognize only three primitive or primary emotions, namely, pleasure, pain, and desire.
> Benedict Spinoza
>
> Emotions give evidence of dispositions in the individual that allow events to be appraised as pleasant or unpleasant—that is, to elicit positive or negative affect.
> Nico Frijda

The opposition between positive and negative emotions goes back almost as far as the concept of emotion (or "passions"), and it was, under the rubric of virtue and vice, the hallmark of medieval theories of emotion. The distinction finds a comfortable home in common parlance, but it also widely found in professional social science research publications. (The index entries for "negative affect" and "positive affect" in Ekman's and Davidson's highly respected *The Nature of Emotion* [1994] outnumber virtually all others except "Fear," "Sadness," "Temperament," and, of course, "Emotion." Sometimes "positive affect" and "negative affect" serve as key theoretical structures (e.g., Watson and Clark, in Ekman and Davidson, pp. 90f.), although most of the time the polarity is not required to bear quite so much theoretical weight. It nevertheless enters into even the most sophisticated discussions in casual but telling ways. And it enters into virtually every theory of emotion in at least an indirect way, in the concept of *valence*, borrowed from the natural sciences (from Lewin, 1935).

> From a global perspective, it seems that past research on emotion converges on only two generalizations. One is that emotion consists of arousal and appraisal. The other, emerging from the scaling literature, is that dimensional characterization of emotions is likely to include at least the two dimensions of *activation* and *valence*. . . . [But] the valence dimension [is] the dimension of appraisal. (Andrew G. Ortony, G. Clore, and A. Collins, *The Cognitive Structure of Emotions* [New York: Cambridge University Press, 1988], p. 6)

In this chapter I want to scrutinize the notion of valence and with it another, the notion of emotional "opposites." The most obvious and familiar example of such opposite emotions is the pair *love* and *hate*.

Love is an emotion of the soul caused by the movement of the animal spirits which incites it to join itself willingly to the objects which appear to it to be agreeable. And hatred is an emotion caused by the spirits which incite the soul to desire to be separated from the objects which presents which present themselves to it as hurtful. (René Descartes *Passions of the Soul*, art. LXXIX)

Love is nothing else but *pleasure accompanied by the idea of an external cause.* Hate is nothing else but *pain accompanied by the idea of an external cause.* (Benedict Spinoza, *Ethics*, book III)

I want to challenge the notions of valence and of emotional "opposites," both in their commonsense use and in their frequent employment in serious emotions research. My argument is not that there is no such thing as valence or no such polarity or opposition, but rather there are many such polarities and oppositions. I summarize some (but by no means all) of them in the following chart.

"Positive"	"Negative"
good	bad
pleasure	pain
right	wrong
virtue	vice
innervating	enervating
healthy	unhealthy
calm, comfort	"upset"
conducive to happiness	conducive to unhappiness
approach	avoidance
approval	disapproval
positive attitude to object	negative attitude to object
positive attitude to self	negative attitude to self
positive attitude to relationship	negative attitude to relationship
high status (object)	low status (object)
high status (self)	low status (self)
responsibility (praise other)	responsibility (blame other)
responsibility (praise self)	responsibility (blame self)

The Ethical Origins of Valence

The positive-negative polarity and the conception of emotional opposites have their origins in ethics, not in the scientific study of emotions. Although "valence" is a term borrowed from physics and chemistry, perhaps to disguise the unscientific origins of the idea, the positive-negative polarity and the notion of opposites comes out of the medieval Church, which in turn traces its psychology back to Aristotle. In his *Rhetoric* as in his *Ethics*, Aristotle talks loosely of emotions "and their opposites," and pairs every virtue with two correlative vices, one of excess and one of deficiency.

In the medieval Christian catalogs of virtue and vices, notably in Pope Gregory's infamous official list, seven cardinal and theological virtues were contrasted with seven "deadly" (mortal) sins (although the match between individual virtues and vices was by no means clear). Aquinas updated Aristotle to meet the new demands. Today, this medieval thinking survives but in scientific guise. The model is not ethics but chemistry, from which earlier generations derived their conception of basic emotions (Descartes, "primitive"; Spinoza, "primitive or primary") as well as the notion of positive and negative emotions, which (like ions and radicals in chemistry) had net charges—valence—and, accordingly, "opposites" as well.

But positive and negative valence have been, and still are, invoked in the psychological literature with different ends in mind. For example, those polarities which have to do with health are (obviously) featured more prominently in the medical literature, while those which have to do with virtue and vice are more likely to appear in ethics and moral philosophy. The polarities and contrasts themselves are not at all the same, however. Insofar as there is a meaningful correlation between the two (for instance, envy and resentment are both vices and bad for your health), the connection is clearly empirical and not merely dictated by the "negative" status of those emotions. So, too, whether an emotion is positive or negative in ethics depends on the ethics and the culture. Pride is a "deadly" sin in Christian ethics. It is one of the virtues in Greek ethics. Anger is another "deadly" sin in christian ethics, but Aristotle proclaims in his *Ethics* that a man who does not get angry (at the right person, at the right time, in the right way) is a "dolt." What counts as positive or negative from an ethical point of view depends on one's ethics.

In a moral context, of course, the evaluations built into "positive" and "negative" have everything to do with good and bad, with right and wrong, with virtue and vice. But good and bad, right and wrong, and virtue and vice do not share the same moral scale, and huge turf wars in moral philosophy have led their dramatic separation. To summarize this complex literature very simply, good and bad have to do with the satisfaction of needs and desires, right and wrong have to do with obeying certain impersonal (universal) rules or principles, and virtue and vice are attributes of personal character. (I will not here introduce or discuss the contentious polarity of good and *evil*.) So talking about good and bad, right and wrong, and virtue and vice is to talk about three quite distinct matters (though usually correlated in their results). A "positive" emotion, on one interpretation, has to do with satisfaction. (Thus love is a positive emotion because it makes us happy and satisfies an enormous number of personal and social expectations) On another interpretation, a "positive" emotion is one that motivates us to obey the rules. (Thus love and respect make it more likely that we will act morally, while anger and hate make it more likely that we will act immorally.) A "positive" emotion, on the third interpretation, is one that exemplifies the virtues. (Thus love can be interpreted as a manifestation of a giving personality, while envy and resentment manifest a petty and vicious personality.)

Given the ethical origins of these notions, the most obvious interpretation of the positive and negative emotions polarity is the mundane but relatively nonmoral contrast between good and bad. There are good emotions and there are bad emotions. But this is highly ambiguous. "Good" and "bad" can refer to the various consequences of emotion—whether it leads to health or illness, happiness or unhappiness, or (being more broadly considerate) whether it results in good or bad consequences for all concerned. It can also refer to the causes, context, and circumstances of the emotion, which are all too often confused with the emotion itself. For example, fear is typically considered a negative emotion, that is, a bad emotion, on the grounds that the circumstances provoking fear tend to be threatening to one's well-being. (Indeed, many theorists would take this to be a matter of definition.) But it does not follow from the fact that the circumstances which provoke fear might be bad for us, that the emotion of fear is bad for us. People seek out fear if it is safely contained. They court danger and place themselves in vicarious if not precarious situations.

Thus Aristotle had to face up to the question of why people would willingly go out of their way to feel fear and disgust (another "negative" emotion) by going to the theater and viewing a horrible tragedy (a question typically addressed today by reference to horror movies).[1] Part of Aristotle's answer was that the feeling in such contexts was a cathartic experience that was very good for us. Leaving aside the epistemic complexities of the theater (having to do with the nature of fiction and "acting" and "the willing suspension of disbelief"), we can say that the circumstances provoking emotion may be bad but the emotion itself may not be. And, more generally, an emotion may have moral or immoral consequences; it may be satisfying or frustrating; it may be provoked by desirable or by undesirable circumstances; it may be socially accepted or discouraged or culturally praised or condemned; and these lead to very different kinds of conclusions about the value of the emotion.

How Good Is It for You? "Positive-Negative" Emotions and Health

It has often been held, by the medieval physiologists, for instance, that a good emotion—whether or not it is also a virtue—is one that is conducive to health, and a bad emotion—whether or not it is also a vice—is one that leads to illness. A more specific and more immediate version of the same polarity has to do with stimulation and depression, as innervating and enervating, respectively. It was the great Dutch philosopher Spinoza who suggested that all "passions" could be diagnosed in one of two ways, as innervating or as enervating, as stimulating us to activity and engagement or as "draining" us of interest in the world. Depression ("melancholy") would be the most obvious example of the latter, and joy ("bliss") of the former. But it is doubtful that the entire range of emotions could be so classified, and even Spinoza's own examples (e.g., hatred) bypass his innervating-enervating polarity.

A good commonsense interpretation of this health- and energy-oriented understanding of positive and negative emotions that enters into a good deal of social science as well as clinical research is the idea that negative emotions make us "upset," while the positive emotions do not. (Since the focus typically remains on the negative emotions, the positive counterpart has not been a lively topic of debate. It is sometimes said to be joy, but more often it is simply a state of calm or comfort.) But "upset" is, again, highly ambiguous. Does it refer merely to the state of being agitated or excited, in which case it might include joy and the fevers of intoxicating love as well as anxiety and irritation? How is upset different from arousal, which is a neutral but typical (some would say universal) ingredient in emotion? Does "upset" refer to the having of the emotion or to the circumstances or the objects of emotion, which are "upsetting"? (In this case it would seem that upset is a matter of appraisal, not a matter of mere agitation or arousal.) How much evaluative baggage is thus loaded into the idea of an emotion being upsetting? Love upsets the irresponsible routines of the libertine. Anger upsets the congenial relationship an employee has with her overbearing and harrassing boss. Does ethnic hatred in an Albanian or a Palestinian count as "upset," given that hatred is the cultural norm? Is being upset just being uncomfortable because of a change in one's circumstances, in which case it could be argued that it is part and parcel of every emotion? (Ben-Zeev, 2000). Once again, the complexity of emotion is being reduced to a simplistic and superficial feature of some emotions in some contexts.

By contrast, the modern emphasis on the healthy or unhealthy aspects of emotion (culminating in the diagnosis of "type A" personalities and their lethal liabilities) seems to load the "positive-negative" polarity in emotion research with a lot more than it can handle. The correlation of good and bad health (not to mention specific illnesses) with particular emotions would require a much finer-grained analysis than either available or plausible. To be sure, there probably are such correlations, but as we find them, they will be too subtle or complex to maintain any simple polarity of positive and negative emotions. The much-explored subject of stress, for instance, yields the conclusion that there is "good" as well as "bad" stress, and the consequences for health are very different. But what is good and what is bad stress? Part of the answer seems to be that good stress is healthy and bad stress can make us ill.[2] Another part of the answer is that what differentiates them is the fact that good stress is the result of positive emotions and bad stress is the result of negative emotions, which puts us back exactly where we started.

One way to understand Spinoza's suggestion that all "passions" can be diagnosed as innervating or as enervating, as stimulating or as "draining," is by way of the more utilitarian conception of happiness or well-being. In short, positive emotions make us well and happy; negative emotions make us ill and unhappy. Pride makes us well and happy. Shame makes us ill and unhappy. But this again is to introduce a subjective relativism that is quite out of place in the social sciences and in ethics as well. What emotions might make a person well or happy or ill and unhappy is a very individual matter, depending on context and his or her upbringing and history and culture and religion and all sorts of things. For the oppressed and embittered, resentment, especially in suitable company, can be a delight. (Contrary to folk wisdom, it is not misery that loves company, but resentment.) For the freethinking libertine, love can be the most miserable of emotions.

Most emotions, however, make us neither well and happy nor ill and unhappy. They may or may not be conducive to or components of our wellness or illness, happiness or unhappiness, but their standing as emotions is rarely related to this. Like standards of health, the tendency to lead to happiness is considered an external, as opposed to an internal or intrinsic, feature of emotions. Whatever it is that we use to classify positive and negative emotions, it can be argued (below) to be an intrinsic feature of the emotion rather than just a matter of its consequences in our lives and the world.

Positive-Negative, Pleasure and Pain

The suggestion that good and bad (positive-negative) refer to what is good or bad *for us* tends to limit its focus to the consequences and circumstances of an emotion. Thus Frijda writes, "Valence: Events, objects, and situations may possess positive or negative valence; that is, they may possess intrinsic attractiveness or aversiveness. The adjective *intrinsic* serves to distinguished these features from derived attractiveness or aversiveness"(Frijda 1994, p. 207). In other words, good and bad (positive-negative) emotions have to do with the goodness or badness of the emotion as such. Where would such values be found in emotions? The historical favorite is the suggestion (defended by many of the great theorists of the seventeenth and eighteenth centuries, Spinoza and David Hume in particular) that the goodness or badness of the emotion is to be found in the intrinsic sensations (or "impressions") of pleasure and pain. Thus Frijda (1986) insists that there are just two experiential emotional qualia, pleasure and pain, and Mowrer (1960) at least seems to take the pleasure-pain polarity as primary or basic emotions. But the contrast between pleasure and pain, which is often taken as the template for the positive-negative polarity, is itself a long-standing philosophical problem.

To anticipate the second target of this chapter, the notion of emotion "opposites," the question is whether pleasure and pain from a true polarity, and in what sense pleasure and pain can be compared as well as contrasted. The technical notion of "valence" makes it quite evident that pleasure and pain are intended as quantifiable features of an emotion, very much along the lines of the old "happiness calculus" invented by Jeremy Bentham and the English Utilitarians.[3] Pleasure is positive and pain is negative; both come in degrees or quantities ("hedons"); and pleasures and pains can be juxtaposed and compared on a single measuring scale. Bentham ingeniously laid out a list of dimensions of pleasure and pain—such as intensity, duration, certainty, proximity, fecundity, and purity—and insisted that the number of people whose interests are involved be included, but the result was a single value on a single scale with the most ("highest") pleasure at the top end and pure pain at the bottom. (The obvious analogy is a thermometer, with the highest temperature at the top and lowest at the bottom.)

Thus, according to the standard Utilitarian calculations, the short-term pain of going to the dentist could be weighed against the longer-term pleasure of having healthy teeth (or, if you prefer, against the longer-term and much more severe pain that is sure to follow the neglect of one's teeth). Presumably the interests of the dentist would be accounted for as well, and also one's partner (or whoever would be at the brunt of one's complaining). An emotion, getting angry, for example, might be pleasurable in the short run but (given the consequences of expressing anger) painful in the long run. One might seriously question whether the short run and the long run are psychologically comparable, and this in itself is a hotly debated issue in value theory and social choice theory. But this is the least of our troubles. What is much more pressing is the question of in what sense pleasures and pains are comparable *at all*.

Consider the "positive" end of the supposed hedonic scale. Bentham's erstwhile pupil John Stuart Mill not only talked about "happiness" as opposed to mere pleasure, but he also insisted that pleasures were *qualitatively* as well as quantitatively different. So much, then for the single scale, the "happiness calculus." The pleasure of doing philosophy and the pleasures of bowling are different *kinds* of pleasures and so cannot be quantitatively compared. (Mill rather cheats at this juncture and says that they *can* be compared, but only by a person who has experienced them both, thus begging his own insightful question.)[4] Moreover, is pleasure the same as enjoyment, and doesn't *what* we enjoy determine the quality of the enjoyment? A young boy who enjoys ripping the wings off flies can hardly be praised for his pleasures, and a young Socrates brooding over the meaning of the life is neither to be faulted nor to be pitied for causing himself so much pain. There is something delicious about the emotions that constitute vengefulness, but that hardly makes them positive emotions. There is undeniable joy in schadenfreude, but that does not mean that schadenfreude is a "positive" emotion, however pleasant it may be.

Consider, then, the bottom end of the supposed pleasure-pain happiness meter. Is physical pain comparable to mental anguish and suffering? To be sure, a person might be willing to tolerate so much physical pain to avoid just so much suffering (say, humiliation), but it is by no means evident that the two are being weighed or compared, much less quantified. I might prefer going to the dentist for root-canal work to attending a departmental meeting, but it does not follow that I literally believe that one will be more painful than the other. Pain, strictly speaking, is a more or less specific, physically localizable sensation. (This is not to deny that the localization may be precise or diffuse, and there may be no identifiable physical cause of the pain.) In this strict sense, no emotion is painful. In the strict sense, pleasures and pains cannot be compared. Physical pain is not in any sense a "negative pleasure," and there are no physical pleasures (no, not even the pleasure of orgasm or drug-induced ecstasy) to compare with physical pain. There is the pleasure of a sweet taste, or a good tune, or a soft caress, but these sensations are not comparable (in part because they are so dependent on context and circumstances) to physical pains, even if they are localizable sensations.

Suffering, by contrast, is not a sensation (although, to be sure, it may involve all sorts of sensations, particularly those which are cataloged as "affective feelings"). Suffering involves context, meaning, and interpretation. One can (and usually does) suffer without suffering actual pain. Thus, strictly speaking, pain and suffering are not two of a kind, and therefore not items on the same scale.

But matters are still more complicated. Can a physical pain be measured merely by its intensity as a sensation, or must it, too, be measured by reference to its meaning? A pain in the chest, for example, "hurts" much more if it is believed to be a symptom of a heart attack than if it is thought to be only indigestion or a bruised rib. Thus even physical pain is not simply pain "in itself." It depends on its context, its meaning, it interpretation. There is, perhaps, a level of sheer physical *agony* that is devoid of context and interpretation, but this is not the sort of pain that can plausibly be attributed to any emotional experience, no matter how "painful." Thus it makes sense (as above) to say that we "suffer pain," and this means that pain, too, is subject to interpretation. But suffering an emotion is not to be literally construed as pain.

So are different kinds of suffering, and suffering and pleasure, comparable in the way that "violence" suggests they should be? That depends. The suffering involved in a protracted illness may be compared to the suffering involved in a protracted misfortune, being unemployed, for instance, but that is because the two states have so much in common. So, too, the suffering involved in a protracted illness might readily be compared to grief, with which it also has much in common. But the suffering involved in a protracted illness is not so easily compared to the suffering involved in jealousy or envy or guilt or shame, or the suffering of humiliation, or the suffering of frustration or failure. So we might say that different sufferings can be compared, but only insofar as they have many features in common. There is no one kind of experience called suffering.

Can enjoyment and suffering be comparable in the same sense? I believe so, for instance, if we are comparing two sensations (a sweet taste and a disgusting taste) or two similar experiences (bicycling through France in the Tour de France in first place versus bicycling through France in the Tour de France in last place), or two kindred emotions (not love and hate, perhaps, but pride and shame, or pride and envy). But as for lining up all emotions on a scale from joy at the top to utter humiliation or the profoundest grief at the bottom, that just doesn't make sense. If there is no one kind of phenomenon called suffering, there is certainly no common measure between all of the different kinds of suffering in emotion and all of the different joys and comforts of emotion.

Against the view that all positive and negative emotions come down to the polarity of pleasure and pain, I want to argue that pleasure and pain do not form a polarity and are in no singular sense "opposites." Nor does the rich texture of most emotions allow us to assign a single "valence" on the basis of pleasures and pains, even "all things considered." Anger can be very pleasurable, especially if it is righteous. Anger can be very painful, if it concerns an offense from a loved one. Anger can be very fulfilling on the one hand and nevertheless very painful at the same time, such as when one is winning a heated argument with a spouse or a friend. Love is among the most pleasant of emotions, but it can also be the most painful. It is an essential datum in the study of emotions, this phenomenon of "mixed feelings," but this does not just mean one emotion coupled with another. Within an emotion there can be a number of different "valences," even in terms of the no longer simple dichotomy of pleasure and pain. So, are anger and love "positive" on the basis of pleasure and pain alone? I think there is no simple set of answers, and the question ultimately doesn't make sense.

Approach-Avoidance and Positive and Negative "Appraisals"

The "valence" of an emotion is not to be determined on a single scale of pleasures and pains, and the idea that a positive emotion is an intrinsically good emotion (and a negative emotion an intrinsically bad one (is shot through with ambiguities. With all of this in mind, it is understandable that many theorists, and not just the behaviorists, shifted the analysis of valence and negative affect to behavioral criteria, namely, the classic polarity of "approach-avoidance." This goes back at least to Descartes (quoted above on love and hatred), but it is a part and parcel of many current theories, particularly those with an emphasis on action readiness. But this seemingly straightforward criterion is also shot through with ambiguities. Love and hatred may have a sort of prima facie plausibility in this regard, but it doesn't take much of a literary imagination to realize that love does not always lead to approach; indeed, when combined with shyness or insecurity, love may be the explanation for avoidance. So, too, hatred does not straightforwardly suggest either approach or avoidance, although it does strongly suggest confrontation and "not letting the other out of one's sight." There might be any number of explanations for approach or avoidance. The various emotions, even those that do have some tendency to approach or avoidance, rarely involve anything so simple and straightforward. We are not talking about tropisms here, nor are we discussing the behavior of hamsters in heat.

Many emotions allow for no such simple behavioral measure. In anger, for instance, it depends heavily on the context, on the size and status of one's opponent, on the probable consequences, on the audience, on one's ideology and beliefs about anger and offense, and on what (if anything) is to be done about the offense in question. Of course, one might insist that we should not look at the complex and heavily embellished sorts of anger that all all of this implies, but rather at the "affect program" that is basic to anger. But even at this primitive level—insofar as one can isolate any such response—it is by no means clear that approach or avoidance is an essential part of the program. The anger affect program does indeed ready one for action, but what that action might be, again, depends on context and circumstances. Neither approach nor avoidance is essential or even typical of anger.

In fear, perhaps, the case is clarified. Fear dictates flight. But, even so, it is context that determines whether or not and in what way flight is possible. Fear can also cause paralysis (although Jaak Panksepp would insist that this is *panic* instead[5]) and fear can lead to aggression (for example, in a trapped or cornered animal). But in any case, to characterize the behavioral manifestations of approach and avoidance in terms of "positive" and "negative" seems to add evaluation of the behavior; it is not simply to describe the behavior. Flight is neither more nor less "positive" than fight, although in a larger context (say, a moral or a macho context, respectively) one may certainly think it so.

Many emotions evade the approach-avoidance polarity altogether, or seem to fit it only under special circumstances. Grief may motivate withdrawal from certain situations but attractions toward others. Joy does not seem to signify either approach or avoidance, nor does jealously, envy, or guilt. Shame would seem to, dictate avoidance behavior (hiding one's face in one's hands and all that), but shame also has built into it belonging and attachment to the group in which one has been shamed. One might rightly complain that the behavior motivated by an emotion is neither definitive of nor part of the emotion, even if it is part of that emotion's expression. (Whether the expression is part of the emotion as such is a question I will not take up here.) But in a gross sense, the emotion is one thing and the behavior that follows another. (Thus Peter Goldie distinguishes between the expression of emotion and behavior "out of" the emotion.)[6] Even those who put "action readiness" at the core of their theory (Nico Frijda, most notably) do not insist on the old behaviorist connection between particular emotions and behavior. And many emotions are called positive and negative in the absence of any behavior.

The Importance of Appraisal and Approval

What is essential to emotions—all emotions—and underlies and explains whatever behavior follows emotion is *appraisal*. After a number of much-celebrated debates and refinements, appraisal has once again emerged as the sine qua non of emotion. Thus Ortony, Clore, and Collins again:

> From a global perspective, it seems that past research on emotion converges on only two generalizations. One is that emotion consists of arousal and appraisal.
> . . . A corollary of our view that emotions are valenced affective reactions is

that some putative emotion can occur in the absence of a valenced reaction, it cannot be a genuine emotion. *The Cognitive Structure of Emotions* (pp. 6, 29)

But it is not as if each emotion involves just one appraisal or a single form of appraisal. Anger, for instance, involves not only a hostile or negative appraisal of another person and/or his or her behavior but also an appraisal of oneself, for instance, whether one is worthy of getting angry or not and how deeply one has been "wounded." One appraises how grievous the the offense is and whether or not one is in a position to blame the other person. Anger involves an appraisal of the offending action and of the relationship and of one's standing before the other. It involves appraisals of responsibility and, to an extent, of what I will call "status." One does not get angry at someone much more powerful (God or one's CEO, for instance) or someone much weaker than oneself (for instance, a child). And these are not just "display rules" or metareflections on the appropriateness of anger. They are the rules, one might say, of getting angry, which involve all sorts of appraisals. There are also appraisals of the consequence that depend on whether the emotion is expressed and how it is expressed, and have to do with the short-term and long-term happiness of both people, the future of the relationship, the mental and physical health of both parties, and the impact on other people. To collapse all of these into a single evaluative category, positive or negative appraisal is to put it simply, simple-minded.

The meta-appraisal or reflective evaluation *of* emotions is very different from the appraisals that constitute emotions, and even insofar as moral appraisals figure *in* emotions (for instance, offense in anger, achievement in pride), this is clearly insufficient to distinguish two different groups or "kinds" of emotion, "positive" and "negative." Some emotions involve moral appraisals, for example (moral indignation is an obvious one; shame and guilt are two others). But many do not. (Embarrassment does not involve any such notion of blame, nor does envy or grief, nor need anger at a merely personal offense or slight.) And of those that do involve a considerable number of such appraisals, some may be "positive" or "negative" but many are not so easily classified (appraisals of responsibility, for instance, in pride, shame, anger, and resentment). I will deal with these complexities in due course.

To be sure, we might say that a positive emotion is one which involves appraisals of approval and a negative emotion is one that involves appraisals of disapproval or, if there is more than one appraisal, the preponderance of approvals. So love, to take the obvious example, involves appraisals of approval, and hate, to take the other obvious example, involves appraisals of disapproval. But though this is obviously true and it is certainly the way that the positive-negative polarity is used in everyday "folk psychology," it is again simpleminded. As I will argue at greater length shortly, love and hate involve many appraisals, and it is only by way of an undiscriminating gloss or through a severely selective editing that we can summarize all of these appraisals as "positive" or "negative." But if we were to take anger as our example, by contrast, the different dimensions of these appraisals would utterly shatter such an undiscriminating or selective summary. Anger involves a negative appraisal of another person (or people) and/or his, her, or their behavior, to be sure, but this is just a small part of the story.

Recent research in appraisal theory has made it very clear that multidimensional appraisals, rather than a single appraisal, are necessary to adequately characterize emotion, and multidimensional appraisal already undermines any simpleminded sense of "valence." But the sense of multidimensionality that I want to explore here is a bit different from that recently developed, for instance, by Klaus Scherer and others (Scherer, 1999). There is a matrix of many dimensions of appraisal that make up (in part) the cognitive content of the emotion. The simple distinction between approval and disapproval plays a role here, but the multidimensionality of appraisal that I want to examine immediately breaks this into several distinct aspects. To begin with, there is approval or a "positive" attitude toward the *object* of emotion (assuming, for the moment, that this is unique and ambiguous). Disapproval is a "negative" attitude toward the object of emotion. But, then again, there is in most emotions approval or disapproval and a "positive" or "negative" attitude toward the *self*, even where the self is not the object of emotion (for instance, in anger rather than shame, in admiration rather than pride). And furthermore there is in most social or interpersonal emotions approval or disapproval and a "positive" or "negative" attitude toward the *relationship*, where the relationship is something more than the people in that relationship. Thus marriage and love are both more than just two people together, and even anger is more than just one person angry *at* another. The object of love, despite the romantic schmaltz and cynical witticisms, is neither the dearly beloved nor the narcissistic self (*amour de soi*), but the relationship and what two people (lover and beloved) become within it.

In anger, one takes a hostile view of the other person, and this hostility is based on an offense or a "slight" (in Aristotle's terms). But the object of anger is by no means simple or singular. One is angry *at* another person (or, perhaps, a group of people or an institution), but one is also angry at a person (etc.) *for* something he or she has done and *out of concern for* the relationship between you (even that relationship is limited to just this one transaction). One may be angry at the person *as such*, and such anger will "spill over" and involve every aspect of the person. More often one is angry at the person only insofar as he or she plays a certain role or stands in a certain position. Thus an employee can be angry about what her boss has done but limit the anger to that person's action and the person *as boss*, and leave untouched the same person as friend. Indeed, she might even complain (in retrospect) to her friend about her boss's behavior ("I was so angry at you when . . .").

Behind such anger is almost always some concern for the self, for the self as offended, and to say that an offense is the object of anger is to say that it is both the other person's behavior and its significance for you that is your concern. Thus even when (as in anger) the primary object is the other, the self enters in as well. And so does the relationship. One is concerned not just about the significance of the offense regarding oneself but also about the significance of the offense regarding the relationship. Does this offense constitute betrayal, a breach of trust, a loss of respect, a new tone of envy, or resentment? Is its significance limited or pervasive? And even in a very limited relationship—one driver yelling at another at a jammed-up intersection—the object of the anger is not only the other driver but the significance of the encounter for both oneself and (I'm being cautious here) one's relationship to other drivers and perhaps to other people in general as well. Road rage is rarely aimed at just this one particular driver. It is typically aimed at virtually everyone driving in that particular vicinity. (I sometimes find myself getting irrationally angry at the driver in front of me, who is just as caught up in traffic as I am.)

The disapproval or negative appraisal that is so evident in anger also depends on the nature and severity of the offense. It may be merely irritating or annoying. It may be significantly more deeply personal, signifying fury or outrage. Or it may be rage, which is typically irrational, when it is not about any particular object at all. Or it may constitute a violation of principle, thus nudging anger into the richer moral territory of moral indignation. Thus what is mistakenly called the "level" or the "degree" of anger becomes part of the appraisal process. It is a mistake to call them "levels" or "degrees," because they are not just points on a single dimension. They are different *kinds* of anger, with different parameters. So, too, the so-called *intensity* (or "heat") of anger is not merely the degree of arousal (another obvious thermometer metaphor). It also has much to do with the severity of the offense, and the kind of violation it is (how personal, or moral). Thus the object of the emotion may better be described as "an offense to my dignity" or "a violation of my conception of the moral order" rather than "he called me a jerk" or "he lied to me." (The scholastic notion of "the formal object" of emotion was an attempt to capture this more general formulation of the objection of emotion.)[7]

In short, the complexity of the object of emotion requires not a single but multiple appraisals, often of very different kinds. One might well summarize these in those cases where these appraisals are all favorable or unfavorable, as in love and hate, most plausibly, but even here, I would want to urge real caution. It hatred a global condemnation of the other, or is it (even essentially) mixed with a grudging respect and admiration (which is what distinguishes hate from utter contempt and revulsion)? But such cases are relatively rare among the emotions. Anger, although it may be among the "basic" emotions, is such a complex of appraisals that no summary will do. So, too, among the more complex social emotions sexual jealousy, for example, which is mixed with love for one's beloved and grudging respect for one's rival; which is loaded with self-condemnation but respect for the group and its (now violated) rules; guilt is even more self-condemning, but in the light of some judge (God, one's parents) who is held in awe. And if we are to condemn some types of emotion (anger, envy, pride) as "sins" or "vices" and call them "negative," let us be very clear that we are passing judgment on a complex in the light of complex considerations, and not just analyzing the emotion itself. The seven "deadly" (mortal) sins are such only because of their place within the theological framework in which they are being judged and cataloged. Pope Gregory laid down the law for generations of Christians, but he did not undertake an adequate analysis of the emotions he condemned.

Nonvalenced Appraisals

Appraisals are typically couched in "positive" or "negative" (approval-disapproval, good-bad) terms, but this is just what I am arguing against. Approval doesn't have to be so one-dimensional or "valenced." It can involve more sophisticated concepts than good or bad, approval and disapproval. (Imagine going to an opera or an art museum, and being told that your only critical response can be a "boo" or a "bravo!") Thus two other sources of appraisals of great significance in the analysis of emotion are judgments of what I call *status* and *responsibility*. In the classical "valence" and "appraisal" models, these really do not count as appraisals at all. But all the worse for the classical notions of "valence" and "appraisal."

Status is essentially a comparative measure, and in most emotions it is rather immediately the relative status of oneself and the other. (There are judgments of status in self-directed emotions, for instance, guilt, but the complications here go far beyond the bounds of this essay. But see Pat Greenspan's *Practical Guilt* for a very useful analysis, although she does not use this terminology.)[8] Thus an emotion might be deemed "positive" because it gives high status to the object or "negative" because it gives low status to the object, or it might be deemed "positive" because it gives high status to the self or "negative" because it gives low status to the self. In contempt, for example, one "looks down" on the other. In admiration, one "looks up." In love (and, I would suggest, in hatred) there is a strong tendency to equality. (Stendhal: "Where love does not find equals, it creates them.")

What this means, in terms of overall valence, has much the same to do as multiple appraisals of approval and disapproval. In most emotions, they will differ. In contempt, one ranks oneself high but the other low. So is contempt a "negative" emotion? Only if one focuses exclusively on the judgment of the other. Are admiration and awe positive emotions because they rank the other so high? Or are they negative emotions insofar as they put oneself in the lower position? (In this light, envy is deemed a negative emotion not only because of its ill effects on both society and one's mental health but also because it focuses on one's comparative inferiority by virtue of the object envied.) I hope that it is by now evident that these are useless questions and the result of trying to treat an impressively complex and multidimensional phenomenon as something simple and one-dimensional.

Finally, judgments of responsibility are key ingredients in any number of emotions, both self-directed and other-directed, both in terms of blame and praise and, just as important, "not-to-blame." Thus embarrassment, to illustrate this last judgment, is an emotion that has innocence ("not-to-blame") built right into it, as opposed to shame and guilt, which blame the self. Anger blames others, while pride praises the self. Again, one has to look at the variable contexts in which all of this takes place. Anthropologists long distinguished shame and guilt societies, based on the very different social codes and religious teachings of the respective societies. But the upshot is that though an emotion might be deemed "positive" insofar as it involves praise and "negative" because it involves blame, this is to isolate but one of several dimensions. Indeed, Aristotle (and many different ethical traditions) have cited shame as a "positive" emotion, a "quasi virtue," insofar as a person *without* shame is a very bad person. And pride, although it is full of praise for the self, has often been condemned, and not only by Christianity. (Buddhists in general have no better opinion of this self-praising emotion.)

The analysis of emotion in terms of "valence," while it recognizes something essential about emotions (that is, that they involve appraisals and evaluations of the world and are relevant to a life well or ill lived), is an idea that we should abandon and leave behind. It serves no purpose but confusion, and perpetrates the worst old stereotypes about emotion, that it is a simple hedonic phenomenon unworthy of serious research and analysis.

"Emotional Opposites"

One of the more celebrated campaigns of the postmodern "deconstructionist" movement is its rejection, or rather its ridicule, of "oppositional" thinking, thinking in terms of polarities: good-bad, white-black, male-female, up-down, and God knows what else. The thinking goes back at least to Nietzsche (who engaged in a good deal of oppositional thinking himself), but the idea has a good deal of merit in combating the dogmatic moralizing of the "seven sin" crowd and some of the lazy thinking that goes on in the social sciences. Thinking and talking in terms of positive and negative emotions, I have argued, is an example of such lazy thinking in the name of an easy organizational principle. The insistence on oppositional thinking is of the same genre. In discussions of love, for example, it is an old debate (going back to Plato) whether "opposites attract" or whether "like loves like," reducing the multiplicity of features and interactions that bring two people together to a supposedly single dimension of similarity or difference.

In discussions of emotion, similarly, there seems to be a strong and long-lasting temptation (dating back to the Middle Ages if not to Aristotle) to think of emotions in terms of opposite pairs, the polarity of love and hate being the prime example. But even there, it might be argued that the opposite of love is indifference, or resentment, or possessiveness. Once that discussion starts, it seems to be interminable—and interesting, because there is no single "opposite" to love, any more that there is a single opposite to *red*. Are we talking about primary colors (blue, yellow) or light spectrum colors (blue, green)? And why not count other colors as well: yellow and green (traffic lights), the complementary color (also green) a fashion alternative (purple), or a litmus test (purple again)? Black and white is the perennial favorite of the oppositional crowd, but why not black and any color—black and orange (popular at Princeton), or black and blue? Anyway, you get the idea. The very notion of an "opposite" depends on a context and a preset contrast. There are emotional opposites, of course, and love-hate suggests to us an obvious context, given all of the novels that plot the (not always straightforward) transformation from one to the other. But let's not conclude too quickly that love and hate are always opposites, much less that all emotions form oppositional pairs, like the men and women at a (heterosexual) folk dance.

The reason for rejecting the notion of emotional opposites doesn't depend on ridicule. It follows from the analysis of emotion and emotion concepts. If an emotion is multidimensional, then it immediately follows that the notion of "opposites" is confused. Opposites depend on polarity, and polarity is just what is not available in even the simplest emotions. (What is the opposite of fear? Is it courage? Is it recklessness? Is it indifference? Is it panic? Or rage?) Take shame. If we were to focus on the self-blame aspect of shame, the opposite of shame would be without-blame, or embarrassment. Or, perhaps, if we were to focus on the blame aspect of shame, then its opposite would be pride. If we were to focus on the cultural framework of shame-blame, the opposite of shame would be guilt, a different kind of self-blame. Or if we were to look at the other-directness of shame, its opposite would be anger. Then, again, if we were to focus on both the blame aspect and the self-blame aspect of shame, the opposite of shame would be admiration. At which point, the game of opposites has obviously become quite pointless.

Conclusion

In this chapter, I have argued against the facile use of "positive" and "negative" characterization of emotion as simpleminded and detrimental to serious research on the emotions. In particular, such thinking blocks our appreciation of the subtlety and complexity of emotions (Ben-Zeev, 2000). It also leads us to misleading "oppositional" thinking that belies the complex relationships among emotions. Emotion research can do perfectly well without such distinctions, and making it a point to do so will encourage us to be much more attentive to the rich phenomena that brought us to emotions research in the first place.

11

Thoughts and Feelings: What Is a "Cognitive Theory" of the Emotions, and Does It Neglect Affectivity? (2001)

I have been arguing, for almost thirty years now, that emotions have been unduly neglected in philosophy. Back in the 1970s, it was an argument that attracted little sympathy. Now, the philosophy of emotions is a major research area. I have also been arguing that emotions are ripe for philosophical analysis, a view that, as evidenced by the Manchester 2001 conference and a large number of excellent publications, has now become mainstream. My own analysis of emotion, first published in 1973, challenged the sharp divide between emotions and rationality; insisted that we reject the established notion that the emotions are involuntary; and argued, in a brief slogan, that "emotions are judgments." Since then, although the specific term "judgment" has come under considerable fire and my voluntarist thesis continues to attract incredulousness, the general approach I took to emotions has been widely accepted in both philosophy and the social sciences. When Paul Griffiths took on what he misleadingly characterized as "propositional attitude" theories of emotion as the enemy of all that was true and scientifically beautiful, I knew that we had made it.[1] Such ferocious abuse was surely a sign that our view of emotion had shifted, in Kuhnian terms, from being revolutionary to becoming the "normal" paradigm. The current counterrevolution of affect programs and neuroreductionism says a lot about who we are and how far we have come. Progress in philosophy, I hate to say, is moved more by this drama of one outrageous thesis attacking another—once called "dialectic"—than by cautious, careful, "normal" argument.

The view that I represent is now generally referred to as the "cognitive theory of emotions," a borrowing from psychology and "cognitive science." The cognitive theory has become the touchstone of all philosophical theorizing about emotion, for or against. But what, exactly, is a "cognitive" theory of emotions? The label "cognitive theory" is not mine, and I fought it for years, not because it was wrong but because "cognition" is so variously or ill defined. In this chapter, I would like to take on "cognition" directly and try to say what I think it is and what it isn't, with particular reference to emotion. But to begin with, I want to reject, or at any rate call into question, the very *dimensions* of the emotional phenomena that are now under investigation. In recent work by Joe LeDoux, Jaak Panksepp, and Antonio Damasio, for example, an emotion is sometimes presented as if it is more or less over and done with in 120 milliseconds, the rest being mere aftermath and cerebral embellishment. An emotion, so understood, is a preconscious, precognitive, more or less automatic excitation of an affect program. Now, I do not deny for a moment the fascinating work that these researchers have done and are doing, but I am interested, to put it polemically, in processes that last more than five minutes and have the potential to last five hours or five days (or five weeks, months, even years). I am interested, in other words, not in those brief "irruptive" reactions but in the long-term narratives of Othello, Iago, Lily Bart, and those of my less drama-ridden but nevertheless very emotional friends. I am interested in the meanings of life, not short-term neurological arousal.

Those bold and intriguing discoveries in the neurobiology of emotion have stimulated a mantra of sorts, "emotion *before* cognition," which rather leaves the cognitive theory, so to speak, with its pants down. (A fair turnaround, one might argue, from my old slogan, "emotions are judgments," i.e., judgments before Jamesian feelings.) But the very statement of the new mantra provokes a cognitivist rejoinder: surely the very fact of a *response* indicates some form of recognition, and (just to say the obvious) recognition is a form of cognition. What gets thrown into question, therefore, is not the intimate connection between emotion and cognition but the nature of cognition itself. Cognition is not to be understood only as conscious and articulate. There are primitive preconceptual forms of cognition, "a cognitive neuroscience of emotion."[2] These are not the forms of cognition or emotion that primarily interest me, perhaps, but they are extremely important in understanding not only the very brief phenomena studied by the neuroscientists but also the long-term emotional psychodramas that do interest me. Whatever else I may have meant or implied by my slogan "emotions are judgments," I was not thinking of necessarily conscious and self-conscious, reflective, articulate judgments.

In this chapter, I want to scrutinize and clarify the cognitive theory as I understand it, and I would also like to look once again at the role of feelings or "affect" in emotions and, finally, at my claim that emotions are, at least sometimes, "chosen" and voluntary.

Emotions as "Thoughts" and Other Things

"Cognition" is a not very informative technical term. It demands a translation into the vernacular. (If the charge against me is that I am struck in what is now called "folk psychology," I can live with that. Jerry Fodor may overstate the case when he insists that "folk psychology is the only game in town," but it is certainly the Mother of All Games in Town.) The number of candidates that have been put forward to front the cognitive theory is impressive. Many authors, Jeffrey Murphy and Kendall Walton, for example, suggest *beliefs*. Jerome Neu, one of the prominent voices in the philosophy of emotions for more than twenty years, suggests that the cognitive elements which matter most are *thoughts*, a view that (at least nominally) goes back to Descartes and Spinoza (Neu, 1977). Several philosophers (including myself) defend the theory that emotions are *evaluative judgments*, a view that can be traced back to the Stoics. Cheshire Calhoun has suggested "seeing as," and Robert Roberts has offered us "construal" as alternative, more perceptual ways of understanding cognition in emotion (Calhoun, 1984; Roberts, 1988). Other theorists, especially in psychology and cognitive science, play it safe with "cognitive elements" or "cognitive structures" (e.g., Ortony, Clore, and Collins, 1988; Gordon, 1986). Some psychologists split on the question of whether "appraisals" are "cognitions," sometimes leading to a narrowed and critically vulnerable conception of both.[3]

Many philosophers prefer the technical term "intentionality," although interpretations of this technical concept are often even less helpful than "cognition" (Kenny, 1963). Pat Greenspan has played it coy with "belief warrant" while rejecting the "cognitive" theory in its more committal forms (Greenspan, 1988). Michael Stocker is more directly combative when he rejects all of this in the defense of "affect" and "affective states," although I have always suspected, and will again here, that Stocker's "affect" sneaks in a lot of what others portray as cognition (Stocker, 1996). Ronald De Sousa suggest "paradigm scenarios," an intriguing and more contextual and behavioral conception that is intended (among other things) to undermine the cognitive theory (De Sousa, 1987).

Sometimes the interpretation is absurdly more than the concept will bear, for example, in the overly committed conceptions of "cognition" as *knowledge* (and therefore in some sense veridical). But it should be obvious that the cognitive constituents of emotion can be wrong or mistaken. As my favorite philosophical author, Nietzsche, writes, "The falseness of a judgment is not necessarily an objection to [it]. The question is to what extent it is life-promoting, life-promoting, life-preserving . . . ."[4] Whether or not the falseness of a cognition is an objection to an emotion (sometimes it is, sometimes it ain't), it is amply clear that whether or not it is an emotion or not is independent of its truth.

So, too, "cognition" is interpreted in an overly narrow cognitive science framework as "information." But while every emotion may presume information (for instance, in the recognition of its object), no amount of information (including information about one's own physiological and mental states) is sufficient to constitute an emotion. Appraisal and evaluation, or what Ortony et al. call "valenced reactions," are necessary in emotion, even on the most basic neurological level, and belief too readily slides into the exclusively factual and epistemic if not into mere information. But an emotion is always value- or valence-laden (Damasio, 1994). Emotion does not point merely to information processing, and it cannot be captured in any list of beliefs or in terms of passionless states of knowledge.

By the same reasoning, I think the common linkage between emotion and belief is misleading. Beliefs and emotions are related in many important ways: belief as precondition or presupposition of emotion, and belief as brought about by emotion (say, by way of wishful thinking or rationalization). But belief isn't the right sort of psychological entity to *constitute* emotion. Belief are necessarily dispositions, but an emotion is, at least in part, an *experience*. A belief as such is not ever experienced. Beliefs are propositional attitudes, while many emotions are not (which is what's wrong with Griffiths's characterization). If Fred loves Mary and hates spinach, the objects of his emotions are Mary and spinach, respectively, not propositions. If Fred believes that spinach is good for you (and that, perhaps, is *why* he loves it), the object of his belief (but not his emotion) is the proposition that spinach is good for you.

Furthermore, there is considerable confusion concerning the "level of awareness" of congnition, with neurological ("hardwired") response at one end of the spectrum and consciousness as recognition, as self-consciousness, as reflection, as articulation, and as deliberation at the other. The ambiguity of the word "consciousness," referring as it does both to unreflective awareness (the emotional experience) and to reflective self-consciousness (our recognition that we have such-and-such emotion), is the source of many problems, though I would argue that it is also the simpleminded dualism. based on the metaphor of "reflection" (that is, mental activity versus the *observation* of that activity) that is at fault here. In the sense of consciousness as awareness, every emotion is (necessarily) conscious. In the sense of consciousness as articulate and self-conscious reflection, an emotion can become conscious only if one has (at the minimum) a language with which to "label" it and articulate its constituent judgments.

Thus I would challenge Jerome Neu's Blake-inspired title, *A Tear Is an Intellectual Thing*, on the grounds that it is not the *intellect* which is typically engaged in emotion. But it is often charged (from the other side) that cognitive theory—which is conflated with the view that emotions are products of the intellect—*excludes affect*. But the fact that many if not most emotions are nonreflective has no bearing on the question of whether affect (so called) might be an essential part of the cognitive aspect of emotional experience. Thus what continues to exercise me is the ambiguity and confusion sown by both the overly vague notion of a "cognitive" theory of emotion and the accusation (for instance, by Michael Stocker and more recently by Peter Goldie) that such theories are pathologically dissociative insofar as they deny or neglect affective feelings. I want to argue that a cognitive theory can include affect, or much of what is intended by that misleading term.

In his early work, and I see little evidence of radical change since, Jerome Neu took the defining element of emotion to be very Spinozistic notion of a "thought." He makes it quite clear that one cannot have an emotion (or a particular kind of emotion) without certain types of thoughts. Emotions, simply stated, *are* thoughts, or dispositions to have thoughts, or defined by thoughts. (I am not considering here the very general Cartesian sense of *cogitationes* that would include virtually and mental process, state, or event, making the claim that emotions are thoughts utterly uninformative.) At the very least, Neu is correct when he says that thoughts are indicative of emotions and are typically produced during emotions.

I think that the notion of a "thought" is too specific and involves too much intellect to provide a general account of the emotions. To be sure, a person with an emotion will have thoughts appropriate to the emotion and to the context shaped and constrained by his or her language and culture. In the case of adult human emotions, I think that this may necessarily be so. One can paraphrase James (in an anti–Jamesian way: *What would anger be, stripped of thoughts—the thoughts of the offense, perhaps of the leer on the face of the perpetrator, thoughts of retaliation, thoughts about one's now-threatened states in the eyes of the world—but a mere agitation and physiological disorder, a mindless tendency to vigorous action?* But this raises a problem with regard to animals and infants. I suppose that my dogs have the thought of food when I open the refrigerator and babies in some sense think of their mother when they hear her voice across the room, but such thoughts are sufficiently tied to perception (or the immediate stimulus) that they might better be classified as associations rather than thoughts. But, in any case, it is as an analysis of adult human emotion that the thesis that emotion is cognition (i.e., thought) becomes plausible.

But if belief is too dispositional to capture the essence of emotion, thoughts are too episodic for emotions, which often turn out to be enduring processes rather than mere episodes. Thus a thought may punctuate and manifest an emotion, but it is in itself not a process. *Thinking*, of course, is a process, but thinking is clearly too cerebral, too explicit, to characterize most emotions. A thought is a momentary appearance. It is a more or less articulate formation, and it is more or less independent of perception. Most thoughts involve words and the use of language, whether or not the thought is explicitly couched in words. Thus my thought of Paris (a postcard view of the Seine, looking toward Notre Dame) is a visual image, but it's being a thought *of Paris* requires a complex act of recognition on my part. Thus I would say that dogs and babies have emotions, but they do not have thoughts.

Philosophers since Gottlob Frege have confused the matter by taking "the thought" to be the proposition expressed by the thought, but the proposition alone (a logical construction) is never tantamount to a thought in the psychological sense, as an episodic phenomenon. Much less is a proposition (or a set of propositions) ever tantamount to an emotion. Thus the absurdity of Donald Davidson's much heralded analysis of emotion (following Hume's example of pride) in terms of a syllogism of propositions in logical sequence.[5] Philosophers also confuse the matter by conflating thoughts and thinking (Davidson, again), but although both might be involved in emotion (some emotions certainly "get us thinking"), it is *having* them without necessarily thinking that is most pronounced both as symptom and as constituent of emotion. When I have recurrent thoughts of violence or recurrent sexual fantasies, a plausible hypothesis is that I have the appropriate (or, rather, inappropriate) emotion. But insofar as thought is an aspect of emotion (rather than just a symptom or sign), it cannot merely be a proposition (or a set of propositions), and it must not be tied too tightly to the activity of thinking. (I would argue that it is also important not to insist that thinking *cannot* be an aspect of emotion, but only an antecedent or consequence of emotion. Sometimes, the manifestation of emotion seems to consist of nothing but a feverish process of thinking.)

One feature of thoughts of particular interest to me that more or less follows from the distinction between thought and thinking is the fact that thoughts do not always appear by way of organized activity (like thinking), but appear in at least three ways, which I would summarize as "conjured up" (when, for example, I think my way through a problem or try to remember the answer to a query), "invited" (as when I work on a problem, give up on it for the evening, and the answer "comes to me" in the middle of the night), and "uninvited" (as when a thought "pops" into my head, unwanted and unanticipated). These three different manifestations of thought are particularly relevant to the question of whether and in what sense one can choose one's emotions, for it is true both that one can (through thinking) choose one's thoughts and that thoughts can come unbidden. Insofar as thoughts are essential aspects of emotion, one might note that thoughts are sometimes straightforwardly voluntary and even "willed," but thoughts also display considerable degrees of involuntariness, as when they "pop" into my head (or, as Nietzsche wrote, "A thought comes when it will, not when I will").

Peter Goldie makes the interesting argument that while thoughts are voluntary, our imagination often "runs away with us." This depends on the nature of the distinction between thought and imagination. If a "thought" is something abstract and merely conceptual (such as the *idea* that someone could possibly run off with my wife), while an image is by its very nature something fully fleshed and robust (such as an exquisitely detailed scenario in which my wife is having sex with another man), then Goldie's claim is surely correct. But why should we restrict ourselves to such an emaciated sense of "thought" or such an overly provocative sense of imagination? I think that Goldie is thinking primarily of thoughts "conjured up" as opposed to thoughts merely invited or uninvited. I would say that both our thoughts and our imaginations are sometimes willful, sometimes obsessive and beyond our control. Either way, willful or obsessive, thoughts are usually evidence that we have an emotion (whether or not we acknowledge it or know what it is) and it is suggestive of at least one sense in which our emotions are not in our control.

In distinguishing reflection from recognition, I am *not* denying that one can have a thought without recognizing it as a thought. That is surely too strong a demand. Nor am I denying that we have thoughts which are not necessarily "put into words" (for instance, my thought of that delicious dinner at the Grand Vefour in Paris six months ago). But for me to have such a thought to a large part depends on my ability to identify (or "label") my mostly visual and inadequately gustatory memory as "dinner, Paris, last year." And I was capable of having that thought at all only because I have this still ill-understood linguistic file-retrieval device called memory. Of course, a memory (as a thought) might spontaneously "pop" into my head, and I may not be able to identify it. (At my age, this is becoming more often the case.) But my emotion (of nostalgia) presumes both that I recognize my memory as the memory it is and my emotion as emerging from that memory. Of course, my memory may not be exactly right and it may be rather vague, but it is hard to imagine an emotion based on memory if it does not have built into it some representation of the past.

Our immediate emotional responses often seem devoid of thoughts, although, to be sure, immediate emotional responses necessarily involve cognitions, if only the immediate *recognition* of a situation or a face as threatening or harmful, for instance. There is room for rampant confusion here, thinking that the cognition involved in emotion is the *reflective* recognition *that* one has an emotion rather than the recognition constitutive of the emotional response. Joseph LeDoux has been quite wrongly interpreted as conflating constitutive cognition with reflective cognition in his argument that immediate emotion response precedes cognition by a significant amount of time (several seconds). But the argument does have merit regarding the thesis I am examining here, that thoughts are essential to (or themselves constitute) emotions. Thoughts are present in many emotions, but thoughts represent one form of cognition, a particularly sophisticated one, that is not necessarily omnipresent in all adult human emotions (and it is dubious indeed in animal and infant emotions). Thoughts are articulate (to varying degrees) and episodic (expressing an underlying disposition to have such thoughts, to be sure), but they are by no means adequate to explain the range of emotional phenomena.

Beyond Belief

"Belief" has now become a catch-all term in cognitive science that specifies very little even while it suggests something very specific. (Thus emotion theorists in the late 1980s, such as Ronnie De Sousa and Robert Gordon, spent considerable time arguing that emotion cannot be captured by any combination of beliefs and desires, but inevitably found that they were trying to get hold of conceptual jellyfish.) Belief is too loosely tied to perception to account for those cases where one has an emotion immediately upon a situation, and it is to tightly tied to the logic of propositions to explain, for example, how it is that we can often hold conflicting (but not literally contradictory) emotions at the same time (what Pat Greenspan raises as "the problem of mixed emotions").

Belief is typically described as a state, and though emotions may be states (that is, if they are of considerable duration and one ignores the dynamic engagement that goes on in emotion), it is surely inadequate to suggest that all emotions are states. Beliefs are often taken to be only "cognitive preconditions" of emotion, not constitutive of emotion, because emotions are dynamic and often in flux while belief, as a holding onto a proposition, is a steady state. One either believes a proposition or not (although one might misleadingly express doubt or skepticism by saying that he or she "sort of" believes that p). Of course, one can "come to believe," often instantly (in the case of perception, for instance). But we should critically ask in what sense "seeing is believing," rather than, for example, seeing is sufficient evidence for believing, seeing leads to believing, seeing is required for believing. The perception is not itself the belief, but perception and perceptual judgment are one and the same. Furthermore, beliefs are not experiences, though to be sure they shape and explain experiences. In Neu's vocabulary, they are always explanatory (they must always be postulated to explain behavior and utterance in the third-person case) rather than phenomenological. Belief may be perfectly appropriate in *explaining* emotion, but it is inappropriate in the *analysis* of emotion.

These doubts about "belief" explain the appeal of "perception" as the "cognitive element" most appropriate to the analysis of emotion. Ronnie De Sousa makes this case, as did John Dewey years ago, and I think that perception does indeed capture the heart of one kind of emotional experience, that which I would call "immediate" (though without bringing in the heavy philosophical baggage that term conjures up in the history of epistemology). That is, those examples in which I have an emotional reaction to a situation unfolding right in front of my eyes, that is, the sorts of examples employed (for obvious reasons) by William James in his classic analysis of emotion. Pointing out the close link between emotion and perception seems to me a plausible way of proceeding. Indeed, one of its virtues is that it blocks the insidious distinction (still favored by some positivistic psychologists) that perception is one thing, and appraisal, evaluation, interpretation, and emotional response are all something else. Again, I prefer the concept of judgment precisely because it maintains these close ties to perception but at the same time is fully conceivable apart from perception.

But when the trigger of an emotional response is a thought or a memory, the perception model looses its appeal. In general, when the object of emotion is something not immediately present, it makes little sense to say that the emotion is essentially a kind of perception. Thus my hesitation with such notions as "construal" or "seeing as." Cheshire Calhoun defended "seeing as" in criticizing my theory many years ago (in a book we coedited).[6] As I have been revising my own "judgment" theory over the years, I have come more and more to construe "judgment" as "construal," though I still think that "judgment" has a number of advantages, not least of which is that it is pointedly less concerned with perception and other "immediate" circumstances. "Seeing as," to be sure, is also tied to vision and thus to perception, although (of course) it can be treated as a metonym (as Husserl, for instance, used the term) and extended not only to all of the senses but to all cognitive processing as well. But many of our emotions concern merely imaginary, distant, or abstract (but not therefore impersonal) concerns, and the "seeing as" metonym is seriously stretched."Construal" is less problematic in the regard, but it nevertheless suggests an overly reflective sense of interpretation. So, too, I resist the familiar psychological category of "appraisal," although emotions are shot through with as well as based on all sorts of appraisals and evaluations. (Lazarus, 1994; Scherer, 1999). Insofar as "appraisal" is more or less synonymous with "cognition" and "judgment," of course, appraisal theory more or less dovetails with my own. And as opposed to "cognition," "appraisal" has the virtue of making the evaluative nature of emotional judgment explicit. But I think that there are no overpowering arguments in favor of one or another in this family of quasi-perceptual and appraisal concepts. What is important, I think, is to avoid the twin pitfalls of taking an emotion to be overly intellectual and taking an emotion to be overly stupid in nature, to maintain the critical features of intentionality and evaluation, and to emphasize the active contribution of the subject in judging, construing, interpreting, or appraising the object of emotion rather than taking the emotion as something that just *happens* to the subject.

Which brings me to Ronnie De Sousa's very fruitful idea of a "paradigm scenario." In his book *The Rationality of Emotion* De Sousa does not take this as a specification of cognition so much as an alternative to cognition. I have openly expressed my intrigue and admiration regarding this notion of a "paradigm scenario." Part of what is so exciting about it is that (unlike virtually all of the cognitive theories I have mentioned so far) it has an explicitly developmental and evolutionary bent. It takes a bold step in the direction of speculating how it is that we come to have the cognitions (or whatever) which constitute emotions, namely, by being taught to respond in certain ways (or taught what responses are appropriate) in specific situations. It thus has the virtue of being quite particularist, as opposed to those overly ambitious cognitive theories that try to draft broad generalizations which govern or constitute emotions. I would note that De Sousa has always been deeply involved in the theater (and is pretty theatrical himself), and his theatrical shifting from emotion content to emotion context and behavioral training has always seemed to me a huge step forward in emotions research. It goes much farther than superficially similar theories of "action readiness" in that it postulates not only an ingredient in emotion and emotional experience but the *dynamic* of emotion as well. In what follows, I will find two more virtues in De Sousa's theory: its explicit bringing in the body in a behavioral (not physiological) mode and its explicitly social nature, where other people are not just objects of our emotions or those who (in some sense) share our emotions but also, in a critical sense, are co-conspirators in the cultivation of our emotions.

Emotions as Judgments

Back there in ancient history, in "Emotions and Choice" (1973) and *The Passions* (1976), I suggested "judgment" to capture many of these insights. If Neu had the camaraderie of the neo-Stoical Spinoza, I could claim a linkage with the original Stoics, although I obviously rejected their conclusion that emotions as judgments are as such irrational. Briefly put, I take judgment in a way that is not episodic (although, to be sure, one can make a judgment at a particular moment). It is not necessarily articulate or, for that matter, conscious. (Neu clearly follows Freud in maintaining that thoughts, too, can be unconscious.) I take it as uncontroversial that animals make all sorts of judgments (e.g., whether something is worth eating, or worth chasing, or worth courting), but none of these are articulated or "spelled out," nor are they subject to reflection. We make nonreflective, nondeliberative, inarticulate judgments, for instance, kinesthetic judgments, all the time.

The ambiguity of the word "consciousness," referring as it does both to unreflective awareness (the emotional experience) and to reflective self-consciousness (our recognition that we have such-and-such emotion), is the source of many problems.[7] In the first sense, every emotion is (necessarily) conscious. In the second sense, an emotion can become conscious only if one has a language with which to "label" it and articulate its constituent judgments. An example of unconscious, nondeliberative, inarticulate judgment is kinesthetic judgment. Kinesthetic judgments are usually or at least often inarticulate and not deliberative, but they can become conscious in the sense of becoming both articulate and deliberate. We judge that the size of the next step on the stairway will be identical to the several we have already descended and move our bodies accordingly, our minds entirely on the conversation we are having with our companion. Walking down a set of uneven or crumbling steps, or descending the stairway after an accident, we become acutely aware of the nature of these judgments. Having once tripped and hurt ourselves, we might make such judgments quite consciously and deliberately, even reminding ourselves articulately ("now lower your left foot slowly") as we go. But usually such kinesthetic judgments are, and remain, quite unconscious. Michael Stocker has a poignant story about his falling on the ice, thus making both his fear and his bodily awareness painfully conscious. But the example only illuminates the fact that such judgments are not usually conscious at all.[8]

Judgments, unlike thoughts, are geared to perception and may apply directly to the situation we are in, but we can also make all sorts of judgments in the utter absence of any object of perception. Thus while I find the language of "thought" just too intellectual, too sophisticated, and too demanding in terms of linguistic ability, articulation, and reflection, to apply to all emotions, judgment seems to me to have the range and flexibility to apply to everything from animal and infant emotion to the most sophisticated and complex adult human emotions such as jealousy, resentment, and moral indignation. In other words, I find the following to be essential features of emotions and judgment: They are episodic but possibly long-term as well. They must span the bridge between conscious and nonconscious awareness. They must accept as their "objects" both propositions and perceptions. They must be appropriate both in the presence of their objects and in their absence. They must involve appraisals and evaluations without necessarily involving (or excluding) reflective appraisals and evaluation They must stimulate thoughts and encourage beliefs (as well as being founded on beliefs) without themselves being nothing more than a thought or a belief. And (of considerable importance to me) they must artfully bridge the categories of the voluntary and the involuntary.

Thus emotions are like judgment. And emotions necessarily involve judgments. Does this entitle me to say that emotions *are* judgments? Well, not by logic alone, needless to say. But as a heuristic analysis and a way of understanding the peculiarities of emotion, I think so. But, of course, an emotion is not a single judgment. (In many traditional philosophical analyses, in Hobbes, Descartes, and Spinoza, the complex character of an emotion is reduced to a single one-liner, e.g., "Love is an emotion of the soul caused by the spirits which incites the soul to desire to be separated from the objects which present as harmful." [Descartes, *Passions of the Soul*, art. LXXIX]; "Hatred is pain, accompanied by the idea of an external cause" [Spinoza, *Ethics*, bk. III, def. VII]). An emotion is rather a complex of judgments and, sometimes, quite sophisticated judgments, such as judgments of responsibility (in shame, anger, and embarrassment) or judgments of comparative status (as in contempt and resentment).

Emotions as judgments are not necessarily (or usually) conscious or deliberative or even articulate but we certainly can articulate, attend to, and deliberate regarding our emotions and emotion judgments, and we do so whenever we think our way into an emotion, "work ourselves up" to anger, or jealously, or love. The judgments of love, for instance, are very much geared to the perceptions we have of our beloved, but they are also tied to all sorts of random thoughts, daydreaming, hints, and associations with the beloved, with all sorts of memories and intentions and imaginings. A judgment may be made at a certain time, in a certain place ("I loved you the first time I ever saw you"), but one continues to make, sustain, reinforce, and augment such judgments over an open-ended amount of time.

I am willing to admit that different cognitive candidates may work better or worse for different emotions, and here I see further reason to heed and embellish the warning that Amélie Rorty and Paul Griffiths (for very different reasons) have issued, that "emotion" is not an adequate category for across-the-board analysis. Different emotions employ different kinds of cognition. This is the virtue, perhaps, of such noncommittal notions as "cognitive elements" or "cognitive structures." They are elastic enough to cover just about anything vaguely conceptual, evaluative, or perceptual. But while these seem to me to be useful conceptual tools for working out the general framework of cognitive theory (Ortony et al., 1988), they clearly lack the phenomenological specificity that I am calling for here. Judgment seems to me to be, all in all, the most versatile candidate in the cognitive analysis of emotion. But by embracing (without distinction) the whole host of cognitive candidates, it is left open whether some emotions might be better analyzed in terms of perception, others in terms of thoughts or judgments, other in terms of construals. The real work will have to be with regard to particular emotions, and often with specific regard for the particular instance of a particular sort of emotion.

What Is Affect? Emotions, Feelings, and the Body

Michael Stocker and more recently, Peter Goldie, have accused the cognitive theory of neglecting feelings, or "affect." I admit that in *The Passions* I was dismissive of the "feeling theory" that then seemed to rule what passing interest there was in the emotions (particularly in the work of William James and his successors). I argued that whatever else it might be, an emotion was no mere feeling (interpreting this, as James did, as a bodily set of sensations). But what has increasingly concerned me ever since and brought me back to James is the role of the body in emotion, and not only the brain. In my original theory, it was by no means clear that the body had *any* essential role in emotion. I presumed, of course, that all emotional experience had as its causal substratum various processes in the brain, but this had little to do with the nature of emotion as such, as experienced. But as for the various physiological disturbances and disruptions that serve such a central purpose in James's analysis that the *"sensation IS the emotion"* (with all of the oomph that italics and caps can capture) and in later accounts of emotion as "arousal," I was as dismissive as could be, relegating all such phenomena to the causal margins of emotion, as merely accompaniments or secondary effects.

What has led me to this increasing concern about both the role of the body and the nature and role of feelings in emotion is in fact just the suspicion that my own cognitive theory had been cut too "thin," that in the pursuit of an alternative to the feeling theory I had veered too far in the other direction. I am now coming to appreciate that accounting for the feelings (not just sensations) in emotion is not a secondary concern and not independent of appreciating the essential role of the body in emotional experience. By this I do not mean anything having to do with neurology or the tricky mind-body relationship linked with Descartes and Cartesianism, but rather the concern about the kinds of *bodily experience* that typify emotion and the bodily manifestations of emotion in immediate expression. In retrospect, I am astounded that facial expression is hardly mentioned in *The Passions* (although, to be sure, my interest increased enormously when I met Paul Ekman some years later.) These are not mere incidentals, and understanding them will provide a concrete and phenomenologically rich account of emotional feelings in place of the fuzzy and ultimately contentless notion of affect.

The role of physiology in feeling is not straightforward. On the one hand, many physiological changes (including autonomic nervous system responses) have clearly experiential consequences, for instance flushing and the quickening of the heartbeat. Many others (including most neurological responses) do not. James was rather indiscriminate in his specification of bodily and "visceral" disturbances, but then he clearly referred to just those bodily processes (not necessarily disturbances) which had clear experiential or phenomenological effects. He did indeed capture something of what goes on in the *feeling* of emotion, although he shortchanged the nature of the emotion itself. I now agree that feelings have been "left out" of the cognitive account, but I also believe that "cognition" or "judgment" properly construed captures that missing ingredient. The analogy with kinesthetic judgments suggests the possibility of bringing feelings of the body into the analysis of emotion in a straightforward way.

What are the feelings in emotion (though, to be sure, an emotion may last much longer than any given feelings, and feelings may outlast an emotion by several minutes or more)? The working of the autonomic nervous system (quickened pulse, galvanic skin response, the release of hormones, sweating) have obvious phenomenological manifestations (feeling excited, "tingly," flushed). Moreover, the whole range of bodily preparations and postures, many but not all of them within the realm of the voluntary, have phenomenological manifestations. Here, too, the well-cataloged realm of facial expression in emotion plays an important role. So do other forms of emotional expression. The category of "action readiness" defined by Nico Frijda and others seems to me to be particularly significant here, not in terms of dispositional analysis of emotional behavior but rather as an account of emotion feelings. Anger involves taking up a defensive posture. Some of the distinctive sensations of getting angry are the often subtle and usually not noticed tensing of the various muscles of the body, particularly those involved in physical aggression. All of these are obviously akin to kinesthetic feelings, the feelings through which we navigate and "keep in touch with" our bodies. But these are not just feelings, nor just sensations or perceptions of going-on processes in the body. They are also *activities*, the activities of preparation and expression. The feelings of our "making a face" in anger or disgust constitute an important element in our experiences of those emotions.

The voluntary status of these various emotion preparations and expressions is intriguing. Many gestures are obviously voluntary, and the feelings that go along with them are the feelings of activity and not passivity. Many bodily preparations, even those which are not autonomic nervous system responses, are not voluntary and our feelings are more of "what's happening" than of "I'm doing this." Facial expressions are an especially intriguing category in this regard. Paul Ekman and others have analyzed what most of us have recognized, and that is the difference between (for example) smiles that are genuine (that is, to a certain extent involuntary) and smiles that are "forced" (that is, voluntary but to some extent incompetent). Action readiness includes both autonomic (involuntary) and quite conscious and reflective posturing, for example, adopting a face and stance fit for the occasion: a darkened frown and threatening gesture in anger, a "shamefaced" expression and a gesture of withdrawal or hiding in shame, a sentimental or even teary-eyed smile and a tender gesture in love. And each of these has its phenomenological manifestations, its characteristic sensations or feelings that are part and parcel of emotional experience (whether noticed or recognized as such or not).

To put my current thinking in a nutshell, I think that a great deal of what is unhelpfully called "affect" and "affectivity" and is supposedly missing from cognitive accounts can be identified with the body, or what I will call (no doubt to howls of indignation) *the judgments of the body*. George Downing has put the matter quite beautifully in some of his recent work.[9] He writes of "bodily micro-practices" and suggests that emotions are to a very large extent constituted by these. This could, of course, be taken as just another attempt at behavioral reductionism, but Downing also insists that an emotion is essentially an experience. He is, in addition, quite happy to insist that cognitions (judgments) are also an essential part of any emotional experience. But he adds, and I have come to agree, that a good deal of cognition is radically prelinguistic (very misleading called "precognitive") in nature. Building on the work of Hubert Dreyfus and suggestions in Heidegger and Bourdieu, Downing insists that a good deal of emotional experience and even emotional knowledge can be identified in the development of these bodily micro-practices.

Does it make sense to call these judgments? I am sure the answer is yes, and I would defend this in two steps. First, I have already insisted that judgments are not necessarily articulate or conscious, and so the sorts of discriminations we make and the construals we perform are sometimes (often) made without our awareness of, much less reflection on, our doing so. Second, a relatively small store of human knowledge is of the form "knowing that." Philosophers of course, are naturally concerned with such knowledge, and that leads them not unnaturally to the prejudice that only such knowledge, propositional knowledge, is important. Not that they deny the need for all sorts of nonverbal skills of the "knowing how" variety, but these are hardly the stuff of philosophical analysis—first, perhaps, because there may be nothing distinctively human about them (animals display such nonverbal skills at least as impressively as humans), and second, it is well known that "knowing how" cannot be reduced to any number of "knowing that" propositions. But it is a distortion of cognition and consciousness to suggest that "knowing that" propositional knowledge is in any way primary or independent of "knowing how." The thesis here obviously takes us back to Heidegger and Merleau-Ponty (and, to a lesser extent, to Heidegger's onetime disciple Gilbert Ryle). But since I have already insisted that emotional judgments are not necessarily propositional, the way is open to make the further claim that they are not necessarily "knowing that" cognitions either.

It goes without saying that many of our most "knowing" responses to the world and the ways in which we bring meaning to our world have much more to do with the habits and practices we perform than with the ways in which we think about and describe the world. Feelings of comfort (and discomfort) have a great deal to do with doing the familiar and finding ourselves acting in familiar ways with familiar responses. These feelings of comfort and discomfort range from felt satisfaction, frustration, and low-level anxiety to exuberant joy, full-blown anxiety, rage, and panic. Anger often involves feelings of discomfort, but to be anger (and not just frustration or irritation) the emotion must be further directed by way of some sort of blame, which in turn involves feelings of aggression and hostility, which may themselves be readily traced (as James did) to specific modes of arousal in the body (tensing of muscles, etc.). Shame is at least in part a feeling of discomfort with other people, a feeling of rejection, as love is (in part) a feeling of unusual comfort with another. One might object that there is nothing *distinctively* bodily about any of this, and I would agree. But this only to say that the Cartesian distinction of mind and body serves us ill in such cases, that it is only as an embodied and mobile social being that we have any but the most primitive cognitions about the world to begin with. And more to the point, it is in light of such preverbal and also active and engaged judgments that we have any emotions at all. We then embellish and enrich these through language, both by increasing (exponentially) the range of descriptions and behaviors and situations in which we become engaged (adding morality, aesthetics, and politics) and by increasing (logarithmically) the kinds of reactions we can have.

Thus the judgments that I claim are constitutive of emotion may be nonpropositional and bodily as well as propositional and articulate, and they may further become reflective and self-conscious. What is cognition? I would still insist that it is basically judgment, both reflective and prereflective, both knowing how (as skills and practices) and knowing that (as propositional knowledge). A cognitive theory of emotion thus embodies what is often referred to as "affect" and "feeling" without dismissing these as unanalyzable. But they are not analyzable in the mode of conceptual analysis. That is what is right about Griffiths's otherwise wild charges. But neither are the feelings in question simply manifestations of the biological substratum, as James and Griffiths (at least sometimes) suggest. There are feelings, "affects" if you like, critical to emotion. But they are not distinct from cognition or judgment, and they are not mere "readouts" of processes going on in the body. They are judgments *of* the body, and this is the "missing" element in the cognitive theory of emotions.

On Emotions and Choice

It was the great liberal political philosopher John Rawls who made me a radical. It was more than twenty-five years ago, when I was just starting to think my way through *The Passions*, that Rawls and I were having lunch while we were both visiting the University of Michigan. I explained my blooming thesis to him, and he asked, rather matter-of-factly, "But surely when you say we choose our emotions you are saying something more than the fact that we choose what to do to bring about a certain emotion?" This was John Rawls, whose Great Book had just been published, and I was not about to say, "Oh, well, yes, only that." Thus began a twenty-year stint of dramatic overstatement, to the effect of "*we choose our emotions*."

There are two immediate obstacles to any such claim that emotions are matters of choice. The first is the obvious fact that emotions *seem* to happen to us, quite apart from our preferences or intentions. The phenomenological point is reinforced by a semantic-syntactic observation, that the language of the passions (starting with the word "passion") is riddled with passivity—"being struck by" and so on. (Though this set of observations should be balanced with another, that we sometimes feel guilty or glad about feeling what we feel, and that we often assess our emotions as warranted or not, wise or foolish, appropriate or inappropriate.)

The second is the enormous range of emotions and emotional experiences, from being startled to carefully plotting one's revenge, from inexplicable panic upon seeing a little spider to a well-warranted fear of being audited by the Internal Revenue Service, from falling "desperately" in love to carefully cultivating a lifelong loving relationship, from "finding oneself" in a rage to righteous and well-considered indignation and a hatred of injustice. And it is not merely the difference between emotions that is at stake here but (as several of the listed examples indicate) a difference in kinds of emotional experience in the same sort of emotion (fear, anger, love). The enormous range of emotions suggests that no single claim about choice will suit all emotions.

The voluntariness of emotions is obviously a contentious thesis that will require far more careful explication and defense than I can give it here. Let me limit myself to a few well-chosen arguments.

First of all, I certainly did not mean that emotions were *deliberate* actions, the results of overt plans or strategies. We do not think our way into most emotions. Nor do emotions fit the philosophical paradigm of intentional action, that is, actions which are preceded by intentions—combinations of explicit beliefs and desires and "knowing what one is going to do." Insofar as the emotions can be defended in terms of a kind of activity or action, it is not fully conscious, intentional action that should be our paradigm. But between intentional and full-blown deliberate action and straightforward passivity—getting hit with a brick, suffering a heart attack or a seizure, for example—there is an enormous range of behaviors and "undergoings" that might nevertheless be considered within the realm of the voluntary and as matters of responsibility.

Second, I was not claiming that having an emotion is or can be what Arthur Danto once called a "basic action" (namely, an action one performs *without performing any other action*, such as wiggling one's little finger). One cannot "simply" decide to have an emotion. One can, however, decide to do any number of things—enter into a situation, not take one's medication, think about a situation in a different way, "set oneself up" for a fall—that will bring about the emotion. Or one might *act as if* one has an emotion, act angrily, for instance, from which genuine anger may follow. There is William James's always helpful advice: "Smooth the brow, brighten the eye, contract the dorsal rather than the ventral aspect of the frame, and speak in a major key, pass the genial complaint, and your heart must be frigid indeed if it does not gradually thaw."[10] But this does not mean that we simply "manipulate" or "engineer" our emotions, as if *we* perform actions that affect or bring *them* about. Following Danto, one might say that virtually all human actions—writing a letter, shooting a rifle, signaling a left turn, working one's way through law school—involve doing something by doing something else, and this does not mean that the latter action *causes* the former. The one act (or course of action) *constitutes* the other.

Third, although it is certainly true that most of our emotions are not premeditated or deliberate, it is not as if *all* emotions are devoid of premeditation and deliberation. We often pursue love—the having of the emotion and not just the beloved, and we "work ourselves into a rage," at least sometimes with obvious objectives in mind (e.g., intimidating the other person). Even where an emotion is premeditated and deliberate, however, we may not experience the emotion as a choice among options. We may not think to ourselves, "I could get angry now, or I could just resign myself to the fact that I'm a loser, or I could just forget it." Given the situation, I simply choose to get angry. Nevertheless, I think that the notion of "choice," like the notion of "action," is instructive here. It suggests a very different kind of framework for the study of emotion, one in which choice, intention, purpose, and responsibility play important, if not central, roles at least some, if not most, of the time. If we think of ourselves as authors of our emotions, we will reflect in such a way as to affect and possibly alter them. It would be nonsense to insist that, regarding our emotional lives, we are "the masters of our fate,"[11] but nevertheless we are the oarsman, and that is enough to hold that we are responsible for our emotions.

12

On the Passivity of the Passions (2001)

> The existentialist does not believe in the power of passion. He will never regard a grand passion as a destructive torrent upon which a man is swept into uncertain actions as by fate, and which, therefore is an excuse for them.
>
> Jean-Paul Sartre

How much control do we have over our emotions? Does it make any sense to say that we *choose* our emotions? Psychologists talk about "emotion regulation," leaving it open to what extent and in what ways the languages of control or of choice might apply. Philosophers have long taken the position, in part because of their celebration of reason, that we can control (but not choose) our emotions only by constraining them, or by controlling their expression. But is the question of control and constraint perhaps the wrong question? Or a much too limited question? Is controlling an emotion something like controlling a wild animal within? (Horace: "Anger is like riding a wild horse.") Is it like controlling one's blood pressure, or one's cholesterol level, something that (certain Yogis excepted) we can do only indirectly? Or is it rather like a boss controlling his or her employees by way of various threats and incentives, the "boss" being reason? (Plato's model in *The Republic*.) Or is controlling an emotion like controlling one's thoughts, one's speech, one's arguments, putting them into shape, choosing one's mode of expression as well as one's timing? (The difference between spontaneously "blurting" out a comment and giving a considered response may be applicable here.) Or is it like coordinating one's actions through practice, like riding a bike, which may be "mindless" (that is, wholly unreflective and unselfconscious) but is nevertheless wholly voluntary and both very much within one's control and a matter of continuous choice?

The question of responsibility (for one's emotions) has been largely neglected in both philosophy and the social sciences. I have tried to move such matters to center stage. In my first (and I admit very polemical) book on emotions, *The Passions*, I argued outright that emotions should be construed as "actions," as "doings," as matters of "choice." There, and in subsequent books and essays, I suggested that such emotions as love and anger might sometimes be better understood in terms of the choices we make rather than in terms of visceral reactions, metaphorical or neurological "chemistry," or passively undergone feelings. Critics and commentators have correctly noted that I was (and still am) influenced by the philosophical psychology of the French "existentialist" Jean-Paul Sartre. They also noted that about the same time Roy Schafer was pursuing much the same line of argument for the disciplines of psychiatry and psychoanalysis. My own aim, following Sartre, was to reinforce the role of *responsibility* with regard to our emotions. As my work developed, this became part of a larger Aristotelian conception of ethics centering on the cultivation of good character, including the "right" emotions. What has remained more or less constant is my insistence that more attention be paid to the various roles of choice with respect to our emotions. [The next several paragraphs repeat chapter 11.]

There are two immediate obstacles to the argument that emotions are akin to actions and even matters of choice. The first is the obvious fact that emotions *seem* to happen to us, quite apart from our preferences or intentions. This phenomenological point is reinforced by a semantic-syntactic observation, that the language of the passions (starting with the word "passion") is riddled with passivity, "being struck by" and so on. (This set of observations should be balanced with another, however, that we sometimes feel guilty or even proud about feeling what we feel, and we often assess our emotions as warranted or not, wise or foolish, appropriate or inappropriate). The second is the enormous range of emotions and emotional experiences, from being startled to carefully plotting one's revenge, from inexplicable panic upon seeing a small spider to a well-warranted fear of becoming the victim of some distracted telephone-talking, behemoth-wielding SUV driver, from falling "desperately" in love to conscientiously cultivating a lifelong loving relationship, from "finding oneself" in a rage to righteous and well-considered indignation and a hatred of injustice. And it is not merely the difference between different emotions that is at stake here but (as several of the listed examples indicate) a difference in kinds of emotional experience in the same sort of emotion (fear, anger, love).

The enormous range of emotions suggests that no single claim or analysis will suit all emotions, or *emotion as such*. But each and every emotion also has different *aspects* (although I do not endorse the popular "components" analysis, which seems to me overly mechanical). I have suggested that every emotion has five such aspects: (a) behavioral (including everything from facial expressions and verbal expressions—"Damn!" and "I love you"—to elaborate plans for action, including elaborate verbal behavior): (b) physiological (hormonal, neurological, neuromuscular): (c) phenomenological (everything from "physical" sensations to ways of construing the "objects" of one's emotions and "metaemotions"); (d) cognitive (including appraisals, perceptions, thoughts, and reflections *about* one's emotions, all of this tightly tied to the phenomenological); and (e) the social context (from the immediacy of interpersonal interactions to pervasive culture considerations). These aspects are often interwoven (e.g., behavioral and physiological, phenomenological, cognitive, and cultural), and they should not be construed (as they often are) as competing conceptions or "components" of emotion. As a philosopher, I have always paid the most attention to the phenomenological and cognitive (and belatedly the cultural) aspects of emotion, but I now think that it was a (heuristically fruitful) mistake to elevate the cognitive aspects of emotion at the expense of the others. But the different aspects of emotion require very different sorts of arguments regarding the voluntary-involuntary, active-passive status of emotions.

Moreover, there is a broad range of claims regarding such status that might be made regarding emotions, from the relatively innocent view that one can always do something not only to control but also to "set up" (or prevent) particular emotions (indeed, Paul Ekman agrees with this modest view), to the mild (but still controversial) insistence that we are responsible for our emotions (*whether or not* we can control or choose them), to the aggressive view that emotions are active and do not just 'happen" to us, to the very strong claim that an emotion is a matter of choice. And since different aspects (and different aspects of those aspects) invite very different considerations, any discussion of the passivity of emotions is no simple matter and yields no single conclusion. We sometimes hold people responsible for what they think. We usually hold them responsible for what they do. Some expressions of emotion are voluntary, but not all are. But in what sense are we responsible for what we believe, think, judge, appraise? And does it make any sense at all to say that we are responsible for what happens in our brains (leaving aside the willful intake of mind-altering substances) or that we are responsible for we feel? What does happen when we choose or force ourselves to have an emotion (like Arlie Hochschild's airline stewardesses), and is the resultant emotion therefore "inauthentic"? Or is it rather only the "setup" of an emotion for which we can (sometimes) be held responsible, knowingly getting ourselves into a situation (e.g., a confrontation with one's ex-wife's new boyfriend) in which we will almost certainly be "moved" by one or another emotion?

I now see that my early emphasis on action and choice was misleading, but not because I so flagrantly flew in the face of what seems obvious to us, the passivity of the passions. Rather, I ignored or gerrymandered the many differences and distinctions alluded to above and tried to defend a thesis about emotions *simpliciter*. But it will not do simply to separate the different emotions (that is, different kinds of emotions) into groups, for instance, "basic emotions" or "affect programs" on the one hand and "higher cognitive emotions" on the other, and make separate arguments for each. Fear and anger, two "basic" emotions on almost every researcher's list, have many different manifestations. Contrast sophisticated fear (say, of being audited by the tax authorities) with sheer panic. Or, righteous and well-thought-out anger and indignation, on the one hand, with "blind" rage on the other. I have no qualms about saying that there is something involuntary, something that "overwhelms us," in the cases of panic and rage (which is not to say that there is *no* sense in which we are responsible for them). On the other hand, sophisticated fear and righteous and well-thought-out anger are shot through with judgments, choices, and plans for behavior that are clearly matters of choice and responsibility (as evidenced by the fact that, in righteous anger, for instance, we happily *take* responsibility for our emotion). And in the realm of "higher cognitive emotions," it is not necessarily the case that cognition implies responsibility. Those emotions, too, have to be examined case by case.

(For instance, in what sense is a person responsible for his or her own embarrassment, or shame, or guilt? Surely it depends on the case and the context.)

Nevertheless, as a general strategy, I would like to push the idea that we choose and are responsible for our emotions as hard as I can, if only because the opposite idea, that our passions render us passive, has such a grip on both our ordinary thinking and the rich literature on the emotions. In general, I think that questions of agency and responsibility regarding the physiological aspects of most emotions are out of order (aside from questions about medication and, much more subtly, the ways our cultivation of emotional habits have measurable effects on our physiology). But where behavior is concerned, even such "programmed" movements as facial expressions are at least subject to question. Our facial expressions may sometimes "betray" our emotions, but we also quite conscientiously "express" our emotions with our faces. A wince or a frown may be beyond our control, but a hearty handshake or a caress is surely within the realm of appropriate and inappropriate behavior. And when our focus turns to the phenomenological and cognitive, at least when we are talking about such matters as ways of seeing the world and thoughts and judgments, the questions of choice and responsibility are always looming.

In Sartre's essay of 1938 and in my 1976 book, our shared target was William James (along with the many discussions and analyses that followed his classic arguments in "What Is an Emotion?" and *Principles of Psychology*). Sartre's and my emphasis on action and choice was in direct opposition to the "passivity" of James's account, especially its emphasis on visceral disturbance and bodily sensations. (This explains, I hope, my somewhat rabid separation of physiological and "feeling" aspects of emotion from what I took to be the essence of emotions, evaluative judgments or what more generally today is referred to as "cognition." I wanted to highlight the more intelligent and active aspects of emotion, whereas James sought to emphasize the more physical and reactive aspects of emotion.) What has always centrally concerned me is what Sartre captured in his famous concept of "bad faith" (*mauvaise foi*), that is, our tendency to deny responsibility by making excuses for ourselves. One of the most prevalent modes of bad faith is our blaming our behavior on our emotions and so excusing ourselves from any responsibility. ("I didn't mean it, I was angry at the time," "I'm sorry I was so foolish. I was hopelessly in love"). It is in response to this pervasive form of bad faith that I wage my various arguments against the "passivity of the passions" and in favor of a framework which highlights our responsibility for our emotions as well as our expressive behavior.

Clearing the Ground

The idea that our passions render us passive, often taken to be a defining characteristic of emotions, tends to assume that emotions are all more or less the same and treats them as an undifferentiated block phenomenon. Thus Peters and Mace, years ago, and Robert Gordon, more recently, have argued that emotions are of a single kind, a kind that can be summed up in terms of "the category of passivity"[1] Even Paul Griffiths, who most vehemently denies that emotions form a "natural kind," nevertheless does not flinch from describing all emotions as "irruptive."[2] So, too, Jon Elster in a recent book asks "Actions or Passions?" and comes down solidly on the side of "the traditional view," "that emotions are involuntary, suffered in a passive mode."[3] This treatment of emotions as essentially passive has led to a number of overblown and mistaken interpretations of even my strong claim that emotions are voluntary and involve choices.

First of all, I certainly did not mean that emotions are *deliberate* actions, the results of overt plans or strategies. We do not think our way into most emotions. Nor do emotions fit the philosophical paradigm of intentional action, that is, actions which are preceded by intentions—combinations of explicit beliefs and desires and "knowing what one is going to do." Insofar as the emotions can be defended in terms of a kind of activity or action, it is not fully conscious, intentional action that should be our paradigm. But the realm of semiconscious, inattentive, quasi-intentional, habitual, spontaneous, and even "automatic" activity and action have received little attention in philosophy, despite the efforts of such seminal figures as William James and Maurice Merleau-Ponty. But between intentional and full-blown deliberate action and straightforward passivity—getting hit with a brick, suffering a heart attack or a seizure, there is an enormous range of behaviors and "undergoings" that might nevertheless be considered within the realm of activity and action and (more generally) as matters of responsibility.

Second, I was not claiming that having an emotion is or can be what Arthur Danto once called a "basic action" (namely, an action one performs *without performing any other action*, such as wiggling one's little finger). One cannot "simply" decide to have an emotion. One can, however, decide to do any number of things—enter into a situation, not take one's medication, think about a situation in a different way, "set oneself up" for a fall—that will bring about the emotion. Or one might *act as if* one has an emotion, act angrily, for instance, from which genuine anger may follow. There is William James's always helpful advice: "Smooth the brow, brighten the eye, contract the dorsal rather than the ventral aspect of the frame, and speak in a major key, pass the genial compliment, and your heart must be frigid indeed if it does not gradually thaw." But this does not mean that we simply "manipulate" or "engineer" our emotions, as if *we* perform actions which affect or bring *them* about. Following Danto, one might say that virtually all human actions—writing a letter, shooting a rifle, signaling a left turn, working one's way through law school—involve doing something by doing something else, and this does not mean that the latter action *causes* the former. The one act (or course of action) *constitutes* the other. Thus (as Paul Ekman has argued, in pursuit of a very different kind of theory), one's intentional smoothing of the brow is already constitutive of the ensuing kindly emotion.

Third, although it is certainly true that most of our emotions are not premeditated or deliberate, it is not as if *all* emotions are devoid of premeditation and deliberation. As I shall argue in what follows, we often pursue love—the having of the emotion and not just the beloved—and we "work ourselves into a rage" at least sometimes with obvious objectives in mind (e.g., intimidating the other person). It is simply not true that intending (even announcing) that one is going to have a certain emotion means that the emotion (when realized) is insincere or in any sense not "genuine." Nor in so intending (or announcing) does one merely *predict* one's emotional state. *Rather*, the intention (and perhaps the announcement) help bring the emotion about, and whether or not that emotion is genuine or sincere is a complex and subtle matter which is by no means reducible to the simple formula "If it is by choice, then it cannot be genuine." (This argument is often conflated with an argument about the expression of emotion, namely, that insofar as the expression—for instance, a smile—is "faked," then not only does it not express the emotion but it is also not a genuine smile. The evidence and argument here are complex and by no means conclusive. There is a difference between the genuine [Duchenne] smile and the faked smile, but it does not follow that the faked smile cannot express a genuine emotion. And with other facial expressions the distinction is by no means so clear. For instance, a frown seems to be just a frown, whether it expresses an emotion or not.)

Even where an emotion is premeditated and deliberate, however, we may not experience the emotion as a choice among options. We may not think to ourselves, "I could get angry now, I could just resign myself to the fact that I'm a loser, *or* I could just forget about it." Given the situation, I simply get angry. Nevertheless, I think that the notion of "choice," like the notion of "action," is instructive in such contexts. It suggests a very different kind of framework for the study of emotion, one in which choice, intention, purpose, and responsibility play important if not central roles at least some of the time. And when we look for moments in the process of having an emotion where choice, intention, purpose, and responsibility might be playing a relevant role, we may very well be surprised by how much we can find.

The "Passivity" Paradigm of Emotion: Emotions as Emergencies

It is often supposed that our emotions are to be construed primarily in terms of "ways of being acted upon."[4] They are, after all, called "passions" for just that reason. But while our emotions are often reactions to events or things that happen to us, it does not follow that the emotion itself is something that happens to us. We talk of anger "overwhelming us" and of love "sweeping us away," but as colorful and common as this Sturm und Drang language of emotion may be, it remains on the level of picturesque speech. It should be viewed suspiciously. Are we really the victims of an internal emotional tempest? Or are we instead not only the subject but in some sense the *agent* of our emotions as well? This is not to say, again, that we usually deliberate and choose our immediate emotional responses. But the question of agency here is a subtle matter, and it is by no means resolved by way of the simpleminded disjunction, that *either* an emotion is a full-blown deliberate intentional action or it is something that happens to us or victimizes us "from the inside," so to speak. Agency involves many different kinds of responses that are something less than "willful."

There is a vital if obvious distinction to be made from the outset here between the situation that evokes emotion and the emotion itself. I acknowledged that we do not (usually) deliberate and choose our immediate emotional responses, and it does (usually) seem as if our emotions arise unbidden, "spontaneously," in the face of some unexpected or (in James's phrase) "disturbing" situation. *But it is the situation and the circumstances that suddenly confront us, not the emotion.* I am driving along a mountain pass and I suddenly see a rock slide in front of me.[5] The rock slide is unexpected and does indeed "happen to me," but my emotional response is quite a different matter. Depending on my driving skills, my self-confidence, and my previous experience (not to mention my temperament, tendency to panic, etc.), both my emotional response and my actions (which cannot be easily separated) are just that, *my responses*. They may be spontaneous, unthinking, and, if I am practiced in the art of driving in dangerous conditions, habitual. My response need not be fully conscious. It certainly need not be articulated or explicitly "thought" at the time. There is no room for deliberation. What I do and feel no doubt depends on my history of habits and kindred experiences, but it is the situation, *not my emotion*, that suddenly confronts me. My response, whatever else it may be, is a *response*, an action of sorts, not a reflex. I am not its recipient or its victim. I am the *agent* of my emotion, and as Aristotle argued in his *Ethics*, twenty-five hundred years ago, we are responsible for *even those actions which are involuntary* if we can be held responsible for the *cultivation* of the relevant habits, perhaps from childhood.

But the example I have chosen—the most plausible kind of example for those who wish to view emotions as "happening to us"—is by no means the only or the most plausible paradigm of emotion. Rock slides happen suddenly, and our response (if we have time for a response at all) must be quick as well. But many of our emotions are not suddenly provoked, nor are they provoked by sudden circumstances. To say the obvious, our emotions do not always depend on the immediate situation. Often the evoking situation or incident is emblematic or symbolic of a much more general, perhaps repetitive, set of events, as when a colleague's sarcastic comments finally provide "the last straw" and I get furious. Thus Gordon reminds us that emotions and actions share "an ontogenesis in propositional attitudes" ["by way of beliefs and attitudes"] rather than in "brute causes exclusively."[6] The case of the rock slide may seem to be an example of emotion with a "brute cause," but even this is mediated by a complex cluster of perceptions, beliefs, memories, experience, and skills as well as desires (e.g., the desire not to be crushed by a rock).

Sometimes *no* situation or incident confronts us. Thinking back to my colleague's behavior over the past few months, I "work myself into" a rage. Or thinking back to my junior high school sweetheart, I find myself "falling in love all over again" or, at any rate, enjoying an interesting combination of nostalgia and arousal mixed, perhaps with a tinge of regret. Starting from nothing, or perhaps from the most fleeting association or fantasy, we "work ourselves into" a passion. Anger and jealousy are most familiar in this regard. We quite intentionally seek out evidence, review the situation, build a case, even provoke the very behavior that concerns us (perhaps as a kind of "test"). One might still hesitate to call such a carefully cultivated emotional response "deliberate." One might insist that what we cultivate is the "setup" and not the emotion (which predictably follows), but this says something about the subtlety and complexity of our emotional lives. What is caused? What is constitutive? It certainly does not suggest that our emotional lives are "out of our hands." Falling in love is not (as the metaphor suggests) a sudden "fall" but a slow campaign, looking for, finding, and to some extent creating ever new charms and virtues in the beloved (what Stendhal famously calls "crystallization"). It is not a matter of "falling" but of making incremental decisions and commitments and occasional major ones (saying "I love you" for the first time), nurturing both the beloved's good feelings and (more to the point) one's own. Even grief, which of all emotions would seem to be the most obvious candidate for an emotion that simply befalls us, turns out to be a (more or less) cultivated response to tragedy. As the grief goes on, we get to make many choices that will affect—directly or indirectly—the trajectory of both the grief and our lives.

The rock slide example would suggest that our emotions are by their very nature "short-lived." One might say: I see the rock slide, I have a quick (but at the time imperceptible) emotional reaction, and I make the skilled move necessary to come to a safe and nonskid stop. Or we might say: I see the rock slide, I make a well-practiced stop, and *then* (in safety) experience (that is, *notice*) my emotional reaction. Having an emotion is to have an experience, but it is not necessarily to notice that one is having an experience, much less to identify it, "label" it, or think about it. It is a matter of some phenomenological delicacy in what sense I had the emotion before I noticed it, in the midst of my feverish response. To be sure, I had a reaction, but whether this was emotional is a matter of some controversy. But now, in the safety of the aftermath, I feel my heart beating furiously as sweat pours down my brow. Morbid thoughts race through my mind, and this continues for several minutes until I "compose" myself and I can drive on. But, again, the example is by no means typical or paradigmatic of emotion. Nico Frijda and I have both argued for years that restricting emotions to short-term responses is arbitrary and limiting (not to mention a grotesque violation of common usage). A stipulative definition of emotions as momentary and short-lived may be highly convenient to theorists who wish to utilize episodic measures or techniques (changes caused by the autonomic nervous system, MRI phenomena, spontaneous facial expressions, immediate retrospective reports). But I see no justification for shutting the door to all of the other emotions that do not fit this artificial paradigm. Not all emotions involve what is commonly referred to as *arousal*. Long-term love, "simmering" resentment, and "cold," vengeful anger seem to me to be cases in which the presumption that all emotions are episodic is extremely doubtful. (Jon Elster here talks about "short-lived" versus "durable" emotions. Peter Goldie offers a useful set of distinctions between an emotion "episode," an emotional experience, and an emotion. An emotional episode may by definition be relatively short-lived, but an emotional experience and certainly an emotion need not be that at all.)[7]

Many emotions are enduring processes. Some emotions—and not merely emotional dispositions—last a very long time. On the basis of the insistence that emotions are short-term physiological responses, I have often heard love eliminated as "not really an emotion." It is only a long-term disposition to have (other) emotions. This, I suggest, is nonsense. Love involves many dispositions, including a disposition to feel protective or jealous as well as a disposition to experience moments of passionate affection, but it is not itself a disposition. It is a protracted process. So, too, long-term anger and indignation and simmering resentment and envy are said not to be emotions because of their duration and the fact that they do not continuously display the physiological arousal in question. But this is outrageous to common sense and trivializes the role of emotions in human psychology, motivation, and life. I do not deny that many emotions do occur as short-term responses, but it is arbitrary and ad hoc to limit the range of emotions to just those short-term phenomena. Many emotions, especially the more morally interesting ones, are processes, not mere dispositions or episodes. And they are processes within which we make various choices and thus have considerable control.

Thus I distinguish what has often been conflated, the sometimes sudden and urgent circumstances under which we often have emotions, on the one hand, and the nature of the emotional response itself. To be sure, in cases where the circumstances constitute a sudden emergency, our emotional response will also be sudden and urgent. (Indeed, it would be hard to explain the evolutionary development of emotions without some such notion of a capacity for immediate response.) But suddenness and urgency are compatible with skill and spontaneity, and the fact that we find ourselves in an emergency situation does not mean that our emotional response is similarly imposed upon us. One might make some exception for the extremes of emotional response, such as panic and rage, where the response is indeed more hardwired and more a matter of neurology than of psychology, but it is certainly not the case that all emotions should be so understood (indeed, not even such "basic" emotions as fear and anger).

Finally, the emergency paradigm suggests that the emotions necessarily happen first, and experience and reflection only afterward, a thesis that has been reinforced by some powerful but misleading neurological arguments.[8] But we often *produce* an emotional state in ourselves through deliberation and reflection, starting from nothing (or nothing emotional). In this sense, in particular, we can be said to "choose" our emotions. We "work ourselves into" an emotional state, building a case for getting angry at someone who, we come to realize, has offended us. We nurture grief (even if we begin by not feeling any) by forcing ourselves to remember the person who has just died and the many ways in which he or she affected us over the years. (This is a particularly important technique at funerals, and it is helped along, of course, by the funeral "service.") In any case, it is simply false that we should generally construe our emotions in terms of "ways of being acted upon." Our emotions do not render us passive but the very opposite; they are sometimes the engines of our behavior and the actively chosen motivation of meaningful action.

The Question of Agency

Agency is a subtle and tricky notion, and going considerably beyond what I am willing to argue in this essay, I think that the heavily existentialist notion of choice too readily suggests a problematic conception of freedom and responsibility. It is a conception typically associated with "Cartesianism" but that is expressed most exquisitely in the philosophy of Immanuel Kant. It is the idea that free choice entails a form of metaphysical "subject" or "agent" by way of the "Will." I have never quite understood what this Will is supposed to be, unless it is just an archaic reference to agency and voluntary action. (Arthur Schopenhauer simply uses "Will" to refer to the whole of our "inner experience," although he adds to this an outrageous metaphysical thesis about its true nature.) Insofar as the Will is supposed to be some distinctive "faculty" of the mind, there are many reasons to reject it, and insofar as the Will (or "volition") is limited to those rather distinctive experiences we understand in terms of "willpower," the notion is much too bound up with reflection and deliberate effort to make much sense in this context. (One can imagine someone deliberately determined to fall in love with someone he finds not at all attractive, say, in a badly arranged marriage, but this is hardly what anyone would mean by choosing emotions.)

The conceptions of freedom and responsibility that presume such metaphysical notions of the subject and the Will have often come under fire in philosophy, and they are routinely dismissed—with good reason—by social scientists. But there is another conception of freedom and responsibility, one that I associate with the German philosophers Hegel and Nietzsche as well as with the ancients and certain modern "pagans" (e.g., David Hume and Harry Frankfurt). That is a conception of freedom and responsibility which is tied not to some mysterious notion of agency but to the "fit" between an action (or an emotion) and the rest of a person's character, circumstances, and culture, including his or her reflections on these. It is a conception of freedom and responsibility that makes sense in terms of the narrative of one's life. The troublesome idea that an action or a decision must in some sense be a "cause of itself" (and not wholly caused by antecedent conditions, etc.) need not play a role in this conception of agency as fit. An act (or an emotion) that fits and makes sense in one's life story can be said to be free (and one is thus responsible) even if the act (or emotion) in question is inattentive, only quasi-intentional, habitual, spontaneous, or even "automatic." One might insist that this still involves a conception of agency, but there is nothing mysterious about it. Nor, contrary to my earlier polemic, is "choice" necessarily the best way to capture this sense of agency. As Ronnie De Sousa has written (following Oxford philosopher C. D. Broad), "*appropriateness* is the truth of emotions." What characterizes freedom and responsibility with regard to emotions, one might say, is the appropriateness of the emotion not only to the immediate circumstances but to one's whole life and character.

On almost any account of freedom and responsibility, I am the undisputed agent of my coolly calculated, long-planned, and clearly intended actions, the conscious products of my beliefs, desires, and intentions, for which I have at the ready any number of more or less convincing reasons. But even here, philosophers have often noted that I am perhaps an agent in only a limited sense and with limited responsibility. For instance, I may deliberately decide to write a check to my favorite charity, but my pen may not work, my hand may cramp, my account may be overdrawn, the check may be lost in the mail, the charity may have gone out of business, and so on. Thus some philosophers have said that my agency is no more than my volition or act of will, that is, my *attempt* to act. All the rest, the consequences, are (so to speak) out of my hands. Or it has been suggested (and long before Freud) that even my most coolly calculated and deliberate actions may in fact be motivated by forces beyond my ken—from my unconscious, my social upbringing, and desires and motives unacknowledged—and to that extent not be *my* actions or the product of my agency. On such a view, the conscious beliefs, desires, and intentions that are my reasons are not the *real* beliefs, desires, intentions, or reasons behind the action, and thus the action is not really mine either.[9] I find both of these worries ultimately unconvincing, but I think they both lead to some valuable questions about the nature of agency. Even agency of the seemingly most straightforward variety is subject to scrutiny and suspicion, and when the action in question is not a matter of planning, nor deliberate, nor even voluntary or clearly intentional, then the question of agency (and consequently of choice) becomes much more subtle and discerning.

Take for example, matters of habit, actions that are carried out unthinkingly, as a matter of "second nature" (such as Aristotle described the proper expression of the virtues). I shake the outstretched hand that greets me without thinking about it, more or less automatically, because this is what I do, what I have always done, what I have always been taught to do. In fact, my mind may be entirely elsewhere, noting (with fascination) the dancing elephant motif on my acquaintance's tie, or worrying (with alarm) whether or not I remember his name. Nevertheless, even in the absence of all deliberation there is little doubt that the act of "mindlessly" shaking his hand is *mine* (and not just in the minimal sense that it is *my* hand which does the shaking[10]). So, too, I thoughtlessly scratch the fresh, itchy scab, utterly mindless of the nurse's explicit warnings, making it bleed profusely. Doing so is my responsibility (or irresponsibility), no question about it. But at least the itch provides a clear-cut reason for scratching, and thus the action was intentional even if thoughtless. The issue becomes much more complicated with *unintended* actions, such as mistakes and forgetting and Freudian slips. Nevertheless, we no longer hesitate to attribute agency to such acts. Indeed, that was the whole point of Freud's radical and enduring insight.

Do such considerations apply to strictly "mental" acts, that is, thoughts, desires, and emotions which may have only minimal expression in behavior? Some thoughts are carefully and conscientiously cultivated, as when we "think our way through" a problem. On some occasions, it may make sense to say that the thoughts are "invited," for instance, when we have been mulling over a philosophical puzzle, given up on it for the day, and find that the answer "comes to us" in the middle of dinner or the middle of the night. But thoughts also come to us unbidden, even unwanted, and it is such cases that support Nietzsche's famous observation that "a thought comes when *it* will, not when I will." Nevertheless, I have always thought that Nietzsche's observation served mainly to throw the whole idea of agency open for closer examination (not, as it is often interpreted, as a rejection of the notion of agency as such). The fact is that most of us take full responsibility for our thoughts, no matter how unbidden, so long as they fit into our personal agendas, particularly if it is an original or particularly brilliant thought. But also, more generally, we accept responsibility and take it as "our own" if it fits a problem we are working on or an issue in which we are engaged. This might suggest to some that (as Nietzsche is said to argue) there is no need for such concepts of "agency" at all, but I think it rather relocates the question. It suggests that our sense of agency is far more expansive than the limited realm of "the will," that is, what we conscientiously *try* to do, and so is our sense of responsibility.

Our emotions are a lot like thoughts, and not only in the sense that emotions typically involve thoughts. Jerome Neu, following Spinoza, suggests that emotions simply are thoughts.[11] When we find ourselves having certain thoughts, for instance, momentary homicidal or sexual fantasies, even in the absence of any other evident signs of emotion, that is some reason to accept the attribution of the relevant emotions (fury and eros, respectively). If the thought is sufficiently horrifying, we may well dismiss it as nothing but fleeting and insignificant, but if it comes back, again and again, mere dismissal is no longer plausible. Thoughts, whatever else they are, are telltale symptoms of emotion. Freud may have been wrong when he early on insisted that all such thoughts are manifestations of a wish, but he was surely right that they are typically manifestations of *some* desire or emotion.

Are thoughts a kind of action? Well, not if we insist that actions must be overt, of course, but the legacy of talk about "mental acts" should not be easily dismissed. When thoughts are products of thinking, they would certainly count as such acts and we are held responsible for having them. Invited thoughts, not quite so clear. If I spend an hour thinking about the problem of free will and I spontaneously have the thought that this is all a waste of time, it seems to me that I am responsible for having that thought. I "invited" it by thus spending my time. When a thought is uninvited, by contrast, it would certainly seem to come when "it will." But if I spend an hour thinking nasty thoughts and then a particularly nasty thought occurs to me, it is difficult to deny that I am responsible for having such a thought. Thus it is not always easy to tell when a thought is invited in the course of thinking. (One might suggest that *all* thoughts are invited, that thinking is nothing but the invitation to have thoughts, but then who is doing the inviting?)

I might say "Think about Amsterdam" or "Think about what you are doing" and one can, to be sure, "conjure up" appropriate thoughts (in the first instance) or force oneself to pay attention (in the second), so thoughts certainly can be voluntary (perhaps they are even "basic actions"). But more often the appearance of a thought is (as Nietzsche noted) ambiguous between conjured up and invited, and in the process of thinking it is by no means clear which thoughts are invited and which are not. As Freud pointed out so powerfully, what counts is the *meaning* we attribute to our thoughts, whether they fit into our chain or pattern of reasoning or not. During a metaphysics lecture, thoughts of sex are probably (but certainly not always) uninvited and distracting. During a romantic conversation or a Freud lecture, they tend to be invited if not conjured up. But how we think of our thoughts has a lot to do with the context in which they occur, and whether that occurrence is deemed an action or an "appearance" is also subject to ample interpretation, depending on (among other things) whether we want to take credit for a thought or not.

These complex observations apply to emotions, at least insofar as emotions involve (and are not just indicated) by thoughts. Depending on the circumstances and the acceptability, as well as the frequency and vivacity, of the thought, we take it to indicate an emotion. Depending on the intensity as well as the circumstances and the acceptability of the emotion, we tend to "own" the emotion or not, embrace it as an aspect of the ego, or confront it as the unwanted product of the unscrupulous id. In many cases, I would argue that the matter of acknowledging agency with regard to our emotions rests with how we think of the emotion in question, whether we (and others) think of it as part of ourselves or not, whether it fits into our emotional narratives. A sudden burst of anger, utterly out of character, will very likely be greeted with "I wonder where that came from." An equally sudden burst, following a long history of similar bursts in similar circumstances, raises no such questions. This is not to suggest that all emotions which fit are also flattering or acceptable, of course. A person who recognizes his or her envious or resentful nature will grudgingly accept envy or resentment as his or her own, and acknowledge the larger narrative in which the unflattering emotion plays a part.

In his account of the passivity of the passions, Peter Goldie makes the interesting observation that while thoughts remain more or less within our control, it is imagination which "runs away from us." I have not yet ascertained, in my own experience, whether this is true or not, in part because I am not so sure about the distinction between thought and imagination. If "thought" means (as most philosophers seems to mean) something abstract and merely conceptual (such as the *idea* of an offense), while an image is by its very nature something fully fleshed and robust (such as an exquisitely detailed replay or projection of the very scene in which I am both offended and humiliated), Goldie's claim is surely right, but why in the world should we restrict ourselves to such an emaciated sense of "thought" or such a provocative sense of an image? Does imagination here include the bodily feelings that Goldie argues to be essential to emotion? (To be sure, remembering a humiliating incident may well produce uncomfortably familiar shivers.) Does thought necessarily exclude such feelings? To what extent is Goldie thinking only of voluntary thoughts, thoughts conjured up as opposed to thoughts invited and uninvited? Nevertheless, it is true that both our thoughts and our images sometimes become obsessive. This is both evidence that we have a strong emotion (whether or not we acknowledge it or know what it is) and suggestive of a sense in which our emotions are *not* in our control. But Goldie's observation that thoughts are often within our control, that we can choose to think (or not to think) of some upsetting subject matter, also suggests just the opposite: that one key ingredient in adult human emotion (leaving aside the question of whether infants and some animals have thoughts in the requisite sense) is indeed something we can choose to do something about. Whether or not there is a viable distinction to be made here between thoughts and images, it would seem that here is an aspect of emotion which is indeed at least sometimes within our control.

Such talk about emotional thoughts needs to be further qualified. I am talking about thoughts *in* the emotion, thoughts that are constitutive of the emotion (whether or not we want to join Neu in insisting that the thoughts *are* the emotion.) But we also have thoughts *about* our emotion. Thus one might suggest that we exemplify agency and responsibility not in having emotions but in our *thinking about* our emotions (and consequently what we do about them). Perhaps this could be described as a matter of *taking* responsibility rather than *being* responsible for one's emotions, for one can clearly take responsibility for a situation that is no way one's own doing. That would give us one way to talk about responsibility for emotions without invoking anything like the notion of choice (of emotions). It is therefore important for me to insist that I am talking mainly about the thoughts *constitutive of* the emotion (and thus *being* responsible for one's emotion) and not just *taking* responsibility in thinking about one's emotion. Nevertheless, the most obvious source of freedom and choice regarding our emotions is to be found in reflection, our thoughts about and our taking responsibility for our emotions. The reflective recognition that we *can* change or intensify our emotions is the royal road to having choice with respect to our emotions.

Philosophers will recognize that I am here opening the door to a large and valuable literature, recently initiated by Harry Frankfurt of Princeton University, regarding what he calls "second-order desires," that is, the desire to act upon one or another (first-order) desire.[12] In the context of adult human emotion, we might say that regarding most emotions there will be second-order desires and emotions. These depend, of course, on the context, on one's self-conception, on the perceived consequences, and so on. One might have a second-order desire, for example, whether to intensify or suppress one's anger, or to continue or bring some sort of closure to one's grief. Then it would be a second-order choice whether or not to further or to suppress the anger or the grief. Such second-order desires and choices may involve many instrumental steps, or they may involve what Sartre called "magical" thinking, an abrupt change in the way we perceive and construe the relevant situation. Our desires and emotions about our emotions (being ashamed of getting angry or embarrassed about falling in love), coupled with the freedom to "distance" ourselves from our own feelings, provide choices and make us responsible for our emotions. Indeed, that is what "emotional intelligence," as popularly promulgated, is all about.[13] And in that great majority of emotions in which there is sufficient time to reflect and reconsider what one is feeling and doing, such second-order desires, emotions, and choices, and not the initial (first-order) emotions, will often turn out to be definitive.

One of the more frequent points of criticism against Frankfurt's theory is his hierarchy of desires, as if one set of desires is clearly *about* the other. But the life of desire—as of emotion—is by no means so neat or structured. Our desires concerning who we would like to be, for example, are typically of a piece with our emotions. This is especially true of the emotions of self-regard (pride, shame, embarrassment) and those which involve judgments about our status with regard to others (such as anger, envy, and resentment). Frankfurt says that an act is "free" (and we are responsible) if it conforms to our second-order desires. I would say that an emotion is "our own," and thus a matter of agency, insofar as it fits into the larger pattern of our desires and emotions, regardless of whether or not some of these stand in a clearly hierarchical relation to (or are "about") the others.

The reason for this amendment is that I think that the familiar distinction between having an emotion and thinking about the emotion is problematic. Insofar as emotions are cognitive (without making any stronger or more specific claims here), cognitions in and cognitions *concerning* one's emotion tend to be *logically* connected. The thoughts of one's being wronged that are constitutive of anger and one's thoughts *about* one's anger (for example, that it is justified, and it is justified because one has been wronged) tend to be very much of a piece. That is to say that one's reasons for anger, not only in the sense of what one says in explanation or elaboration of anger but also of what one would say to *justify* the anger, are not readily distinguishable from the anger. Thus what one thinks about one's emotion and what one feels and thinks by virtue of having the emotion are not necessarily different thoughts, and what one thinks about his or her emotion may well be not only instrumental but also logically conclusive in changing or reinforcing the thoughts and judgments that are constitutive of the emotion.

Reflection does not simply comment on our emotions like some detached observer watching a game on the distant playing field below, nor does it act like some sort of supercop or charioteer directing our unruly emotions. To *think that* one is in love, or jealous, or angry is not just to recognize one's emotional state. Such thoughts are part and parcel of the emotion. To judge that one has indeed been offended or suffered a loss is not a commentary on emotion but constitutive of it. The fact that animals and infants do not reflect and do not (in this sense) think about or acknowledge their emotions in no way compromises the fact that in adult human emotions our reflective judgments are akin to and logically related to the judgments which constitute our emotions. Thus the agency of our emotions and the agency of our thinking about our emotions often come down to a complex, multidemensional phenomenon, some aspects of which are clearly within our control and some of which are not.[14] Thus to insist that, across the board, we are the agents of and responsible for our emotions is surely wrong. But it is at least as wrong, and far more irresponsible, to insist that, across the board, we are passive with respect to our emotions. But once we come to this more nuanced conclusion, the real work begins. In what ways, and in which emotions, do the notions of agency and responsibility provide the best framework for the understanding of our emotions? And in what ways, and in which emotions, is the category of passivity justifiable without making us irresponsible (as opposed to merely not responsible) and putting us in "bad faith"?

Emotions as Acts of Judgment

I will not here repeat my now-familiar arguments for a "cognitive" theory of emotions in which emotions are primarily constituted by judgments. Suffice it to say that I still hold that emotions are judgments and that *we make* judgments and judgments are acts for which we can be held responsible. But this is not to say (as in many traditional philosophical analyses) that an emotion is a single judgment. An emotion is a complex of judgments. Nor is it to say that emotions as judgments are necessarily conscious or deliberative or even articulate. For instance, kinesthetic and aesthetic judgments (to which many emotional judgments are kindred) are usually or at least often inarticulate and not deliberative. We judge that the size of the next step on the stairway will be identical to the several we have already descended and move our bodies accordingly, our minds entirely on the conversation we are having with our companion. Walking down a set of uneven or crumbling steps, or descending the stairway after an accident, we become acutely aware of the nature of these judgments. Having once tripped and hurt ourselves, we make such judgments quite consciously, even reminding ourselves articulately ("now lower your left foot slowly") as we go.[15] But usually such judgments are and remain quite unconscious. On reflection, we "find ourselves" making or having made such judgments, perhaps with amazement, unable to articulate the nature of those judgments.

So, too, we "find ourselves" liking an abstract painting, or a piece of music, or a view, without being able to say much of anything about why we like it. We need not even acknowledge that we like it, and yet our behavior (pausing before the painting and smiling, swaying to the music, gravitating to the landscape) indicates that we do. Needless to say, this notion of aesthetic judgment is very much at odds with a thesis long popular in aesthetics, the idea that aesthetic appreciation involves "aesthetic distance," "detachment," that "purposiveness without a purpose" insisted upon by such giants in the field as Immanuel Kant and Arthur Schopenhauer. Against this I join Nietzsche, who argued that what makes art so powerful is precisely the deep desires and feelings it expresses and "taps into." So considered, aesthetic appreciation and judgment is the very antithesis of "distance" and "detachment." It is a kind of emotional engagement. Only secondarily do we "distance" ourselves as we try to articulate the experience.

A great deal of aesthetic appreciation and judgment remains unconscious and unanalyzed. An art critic might be trained to identify and skillfully articulate those aspects of the painting which so move her, but for most of us, most of the time, the closest we come to articulation and consciousness is to think, "I like that." So, too, with emotions: we get annoyed without thinking "I am annoyed" and often without being aware what annoys us. We find our beloved charming and lovable without thinking, "She is so charming [or lovable]." If queried, one may be quite unable to say what it is about her that is so charming or lovable. But, of course, we can also become exquisitely articulate about such matters, and thus it would be as much of a mistake to insist that emotions in general are unconscious as it would be to insist that they are always conscious. And this is even before we enter that dangerous territory mapped out by Doctor Freud.

Using kinesthetic and aesthetic judgments as test cases, let me again ask whether it makes sense to say that we are active, that we choose and are responsible for making judgments. That we do "make" them may, of course, be an accident of grammar (just as the passivity patterns in the vernacular may be accidents of grammar, too), but it certainly gives the voluntariness of judgment a prima facie plausibility. But it is also true that, often, we judge unconsciously, without thinking or reflection, and this, it could be argued, suggests that we do not make our judgments voluntarily. We rather "find ourselves" making (or having made) them.

But the fact that a judgment is "unconscious" is no argument against its being voluntary or an aspect of our activity. Our many habitual actions are similarly unconscious. Habitual action is not devoid of intention. Rather, we do not pay attention. Some habits, for instance, drumming on the table with one's fingers, are devoid of any intention other than the minimal or "basic" one, namely, to drum one's fingers. Sometimes they have a minimally ulterior motive, for instance, to release some tension by drumming on the table with one's fingers or to annoy others sitting at the same library study table or to signal one's impatience to underlings. It is an open question (and, I think, a very difficult one) whether such drumming as an expression of restlessness implies an *intention* to express one's restlessness in this way. (Whether or not such expressions of emotion are intentional is a matter we will briefly tackle in the following section.) Other habitual actions are rich with intention and purpose, however, such as one's skillful typing on the keyboard as one tries to express one's thoughts. But the typing itself is (and better be) unconscious in the relevant sense. Unconscious actions are still actions, and unconscious intentional actions are still intentional actions.

Speaking of intentional actions is different from speaking of "choice." Speaking of "choice" is clearly appropriate when an action or a judgment is deliberate, since deliberation quite explicitly is a conscious activity leading to choice. But where an action or a judgment is not deliberate, is "choice" still appropriate? It is often said that "choice" remains appropriate where it is evident that one could choose or have chosen otherwise, even if one did not think of or give any weight to alternative options. There is certainly good reason to consider such a thesis. Such "prereflective" choice is critical for Jean-Paul Sartre, who rejects the idea that we are responsible only for what we think of or reflect upon. He rightly sees that this would let too much bad behavior "off the hook." A person who thoughtlessly performs a vile act or unselfconsciously allows himself to "lose his temper" both can be held responsible for his action or anger and can be said to have chosen it. On these grounds, a great many more of our judgments as well as our actions and habits count as choices, whether or not there is any process of deliberation or conscious awareness of choice and options. We blame a man for making racist judgments (and not only racist pronouncements), whether or not it ever occurred to him that he might not make them. If the language of "choice" is too much here, I am perfectly happy to drop back to "responsibility."

It is not unimportant that we usually *find ourselves* making such judgments (and performing such habitual actions). But it does not follow from this that we do not *do* them, or do them voluntarily. One might say that they are "spontaneous," which is not to say that they just happen, but rather that we do them without preliminary thought or intention. (It is important to distinguish here between there being an intention that precedes action and an action that is intentional, which means that it is performed for some purpose. I would add only that the sorts of judgments and actions we are talking about here might sometimes both lack a prior intention and not be intentional.) Even spontaneously, making judgments is something we do. On reflection, we may come to discover, sometimes to our horror, that we have *already made* this or that judgment and, accordingly, are already in an emotional state. But to find oneself already doing something or in a "state" is not to deny that it is our doing. Spontaneity does not imply passivity.

The misleading talk of passivity follows from the way we talk about both aesthetic and emotional matters. A piece of music is said to "move us," and something "strikes us" as offensive. One's beloved's beauty "astounds" him as she walks in to the room. But the fact that our judgments typically emphasize the "object" side rather than the "act" side of perception does not seem to me to be an argument for passivity. If one sees a situation as threatening or one's beloved as lovely, it obviously makes sense to say of the object (the situation, one's beloved) that it is threatening or lovely. But it does not follow that this feature of the object exists independently of the subject, much less that it victimizes the subject with its power. Talking about how the music affects us, how we feel assaulted by an offense, and how we are dazzled by beauty all makes perfectly good sense so long as we do not conclude that we are merely passive recipients. Whether or not we are responsible for constituting the world, as Kant thought, we are surely *in this sense* responsible for our emotional world. We bring our experience, values, and expectations to it. There is no such thing as a totally naïve perception and no emotion that is not based on perspectival, evaluative construal of the world. This does not mean that talking about the causal powers of objects is wrong, but we should understand that we give as much as we get. (The lengthy literature on moral realism and "quasi realism," with substantial contributions by Simon Blackburn and Michael Smith, presents an elaboration of this view in which moral (emotional) properties are to be understood as *both* features of the world (the object) and projections of the subject. This, of course, has been a central thesis of phenomenology for a century.)

Most of our kinesthetic judgments are sufficiently "automatic" that they might seem to be more bodily mechanism than an activity bound to perception. And in a sense, this may be true. There is what W. B. Cannon famously described as "the wisdom of the body," which current research has only rendered more impressive. It is truly remarkable how the body responds to stress and circumstances, much of it never reaching the level of consciousness, much less full reflection. Some of this, I will argue, is a matter of confusing autonomic bodily responses, bodily expressions of emotion, and action. But much of it reveals an important point, often neglected by philosophers in particular. And that is (as I have argued elsewhere) that judgments should not be construed as "mental acts" alone. One can, and sometimes must, speak of "bodily judgments" (although, to be sure, a creature must have a mind if it is to make sense to speak of "judgment" at all). But it does not follow that if a judgment is bodily and utterly unreflective, it is therefore not done, not voluntary, and not intentional. To suppose so is to put much too much emphasis on the paradigm of reflective judgment and, more often than not, to confuse cultivated (but still unreflective) judgments with mere autonomic bodily responses.

I would hesitate to extend this argument to preprimate animals. Fleas may indeed show remarkable skill in locating and jumping from one warm, furry animal to another, but I do not think that this in any way reflects their skill in judgment. In adult humans, kinesthetic judgments are thoroughly cognitive and for the most part the product of skillful practice. Even seemingly simple movements probably involved years of cultivation, and, again, what becomes evident when we try to unlearn such judgments is how intractable they are and how thoroughly ingrained in our behavior That does not remove them from the realm of activity, nor does it show that we are merely passive in relation to them.

There are cases in which any notion of judgment seems dubious. An example much in the literature for several decades is the supposedly "basic" emotion of surprise. (It is worth noting that surprise is not only a basic emotion in the contemporary literature, e.g., in Paul Ekman's list of 1984. Descartes also listed surprise as one of his six basic emotions back in 1650.) But there is a spectrum of considerable breadth between the "startle reaction," on the "hardwired" end of the emotional spectrum, and a highly cognitive notion of surprise. (Descartes means by "surprise" something more like Aristotle's *wonder*.) Do we make any judgment at all when we are simply startled? I suspect the answer is *no* (though we will surely make any number of judgments immediately afterward). But, then again, there is considerable dispute over whether the startle reaction is an emotion at all, and that question is firmly focused on the question of whether it involves a judgment (or some sort of cognition). Jenefer Robinson has argued, mainly against me, that the startle reaction is not only an emotion; it is a paradigm of emotion.[16] But I would at least argue that, if it is an emotion, it is at most a marginal one and gets included in lists of basic emotions only because of its affiliation with more cognitively informed emotions of surprise and the like. Surprise is not simply a reaction but a judgment (or set of judgments) to the effect that something unexpected has happened. But knowing what is expected and what is not is obviously a matter of considerable cognition, and it is most likely learned and cultivated and arguably cultural as well. (Certainly the *objects* of surprise tend to be culture-specific.) And as we move farther along the cognitive spectrum, we note that being shocked by someone's immoral behavior, for instance, already involves a considerable moral as well as cognitive structure.

In a previous section, I suggested (as a conciliatory gesture) that we might except *panic* and *rage* from our arguments about agency, since these emotions seem to be sufficiently "hardwired" (that is, neurological in their nature) to eliminate the plausibility of any sort of choice or control. But let me put into question even the excepting of panic and rage in this regard. First of all, panic and rage are not devoid of cognition, judgment, or intentional objects. Neurologists sometimes refer to a panic reaction or a rage reaction rather than just panic or rage, suggesting that one can distinguish between neurological syndromes on the one hand and the emotions on the other. Panic and rage, as opposed to neurological syndromes, involve recognition of their object (something fearsome or infuriating, respectively). And that means that they involve judgments, however much "in the grip" of passion those judgments may be. Panic and rage may be remarkable in the limited rationality of the judgments in question as well as in the intensity of the response. But we nevertheless *make* these judgments, and as such the emotion falls within the realm of the voluntary, *even if we cannot act or feel other than we do*.

But, of course, we can. As William James points out, one increases one's panic by giving in to it and fleeing. I think that much of the matter of choice and responsibility in emotion can be understood by analyzing exactly what is meant by such phrases as "giving in to it" and "letting it happen." Of course, much depends on what the "it" is. We may find ourselves facing a hardwired or otherwise preset emotional response, but we virtually always have sufficient reflective ability to consider, if only in an extremely harried and hurried way, "what to make of this." Here is where Harry Frankfurt's notion of second-order desires becomes particularly important, even in the extreme cases of panic and rage. Again, this is what all of the recent hubbub about "emotional intelligence" is all about.[17] Even in panic and rage, where there tends to be no time to reflect or reconsider what one is feeling and doing, such second-order desires may turn out to be powerful influences on the cultivation of alternative emotional habits.

In general, judgments are not "basic actions," that is, they cannot be "simply" made. In this, they are lot like beliefs. They involve evidence, a framework, cross-references, consistency, and coherence requirements. One cannot simply change one's beliefs. One has to seek out new evidence, reconsider old evidence, and rethink in the light of other beliefs. One can also seek out new acquaintances who think in other ways. One can subject oneself to new influences (go to church, take a course, join the army). So, too, to change one's judgments one must look to the evidence, think in terms of other judgments and beliefs, seek out new friends, break with old ones, and subject oneself to new influences. The judgments that constitute an emotion involve an object and a situation, and they have a history. One cannot simply decide to judge that a long-standing offensive situation is no longer offensive (and thus relinquish one's anger). One cannot simply decide to love someone who does not already have lovable or attractive features. One cannot decide not to grieve, when one's whole life has been intimately and happily tied up with a loved one who has just been lost. It has been often argued, by both radical empiricists and metaphysical idealists, that one cannot change a single one of one's beliefs without some (however minimal) adjustment to the whole fabric of one's beliefs. Judgments belong to a context, and in order to change or modify them, one must often change the context or one's position in the context. We change our judgments by undertaking any number of projects, and this is not always a simple matter.

Judgments also involve a history, and this history is, in part, a history of responsibility. If someone is a racist, no matter what his or her upbringing, we hold him responsible for not opening his eyes and opening himself to better influences. If someone has a "bad temper," we hold him responsible not only for not "controlling it" but also for making the frequent accusatory (and often unwarranted) judgments that constitute his anger and for not having cultivated other ways of judging and assessing potentially offensive situations. I am responsible for my judgments, in other words, because I am responsible for cultivating them, criticizing them, and correcting them. Here, it seems, Aristotle strikes a vitally important note. Responsibility doesn't so much reflect whether or not we have a choice at the moment but rather reflects the whole history of our choices and self-cultivation.

Judgment is not the whole of emotion, and I attribute my once seeming to say so to my overzealousness in prosecuting a case. But the other aspects of emotion, even those which are not plausible candidates for choice and responsibility, do not drag the emotions down into the irresponsible swamp of passivity. The distinguished classicist and philosopher Richard Sorabji, who has written extensively on the Stoic view of emotions, suggested to me an interesting account of our current way of talking—and consequently thinking—about the emotions in terms of passivity. The Stoics, who were very keen on the analysis of emotion as judgments and developed some very insightful "therapeutic" views of emotion, introduced a vocabulary (which I have called "hydraulic") in which the emotions are described metaphorically in terms of a "sinking" or "expansion" of the soul, which is experienced (whether or not it originates) in the chest. The metaphors stick (even if the philosophy does not), and we come to describe, and thus to feel, emotions "in" ourselves in these terms. The language grows around the metaphors, and naturally tends to become pervaded with the concept of passivity.[18]

The Stoic view, however, is precisely the opposite: that the emotions are not these "first movements," this swelling and contracting, but the subsequent sequence of judgments. The judgments are, in a way, about the "appropriateness" or rationality of the "first movements," and one gives or withholds "assent" to them. But the "first movements" that we experience are emphatically *not* the emotions. The emotions are our judgments about the warrant of our feelings, which in turn were judgments about our ways of looking at the world (in other words, judgments about our judgments). The Stoics were obsessed with this question of the rationality (or irrationality) of emotions, of course, and their various theories were all attempts to understand and develop a therapy for coping with them. But what required coping were our irrational ways of looking at the world, for which the "first movements" (such as swelling and contracting) were merely symptoms. In other words, what was passive about the passions was nothing more than an indicator about what we ourselves were actively doing, how we were living, and, according to them, how we willfully but mistakenly viewed the world.

Passivity and the Expression of Emotion

The question of the activity versus passivity of the passions is often conflated with the question of the voluntariness of expressions of emotion. This is quite understandable, since many philosophers and psychologists (and by no means all of them "behaviorists") have argued that an essential aspect of emotion is behavioral expression and it is primarily through the expression of emotion that other people can recognize that one has any emotion at all. But here again we tread onto dangerous territory. Some behaviorists would say that an emotion *is* its expression (that is, the complex "multitrack" disposition to behave in various ways), and all the rest is just the myth of the "ghost in the machine."[19] Some would even insist that the *only* way to recognize that one has an emotion *in one's own case* is by way of the expression of emotion.[20] Behaviorism aside, it is clear that behavioral expression is essential to emotion (even if one also insists that experience is essential to emotion). But there are many modes of behavioral expression, and it is by no means obvious that all of them are equally essential or constitutive of emotion. Nor is it obvious that all of them are similarly active or passive or intentional.

Toward the beginning of this chapter, I noted that "both my emotional response and my actions (*which cannot be easily separated*) are just that, my responses." But why cannot my emotional response and my actions be easily separated? Surely an action is one thing, and an emotion is something quite different. An action (leaving aside those pesky "mental acts") is something overt, something observable, in principle, by anyone. An emotion, by contrast, is something "internal," known directly only by the subject through "introspection." This distinction, so described, is fraught with all sorts of philosophical and conceptual difficulties, especially those associated with Cartesian dualism. But even without getting into that hoary pit, it is extremely important, from both sides of the issue, that we not artificially separate an emotion from its expression, as tempting as it may sometimes be to do so. Moreover, there are many different kinds or aspects of emotional expression, and some are more easily distinguished from the emotion than others. To begin with, we might distinguish various sorts of bodily expressions, verbal expressions, facial expressions, various sorts of postures and gestures, full-blown actions and courses of action, and actions performed because of or "out of" emotion. But, as I shall argue, these distinctions should be made with caution and the understanding that an emotion is a dynamic, holistic phenomenon and not easily separated into various parts or components.

There are many psychologists, seizing on one or another of these sorts of expression, who would more or less identify the emotion with its expression, and from the holistic point of view I am arguing, I think that this is a healthy suggestion. Nevertheless, the conception of "expression" is too often limited, for example, to just facial expression or (as in James) to the most primitive unlearned bodily responses. By contrast, so many philosophers (myself once included) have insisted on the "purely mental" status of emotions, emotions as experience, that the obvious connections between emotion and emotional behavior either get lost altogether or are rendered quite mysterious. It is illustrative, for example, that until very recently few philosophers who discussed emotion (even going back to Aristotle) said much of anything about the face and facial expression. They rather referred (as in James) to "the urge to vigorous action." Against this background of neglect, Paul Ekman's strong equating of emotion and facial expression makes a lot of sense, so long, of course, as we do not thereby deny the experiential aspects and other expressions of emotion.

This concern about the connection between emotions and expression is important because the "voluntariness" of emotions can be confused with the voluntariness of certain expressions of the emotions. Or, arguing in the opposite direction, the alleged passivity of the passions is confused with the undeniable passivity with which we suffer certain sorts of bodily reactions. That is why it is important to appreciate both the enormous range of emotional expressions and the intimacy of emotion and expression. To be sure, there are all sorts of circumstances and ways in which we might distinguish emotion and expression, for instance, when the expression (that is, the bodily response, the behavior) occurs quite independently and without any emotion at all. Or when we have a strong emotion but suppress its expression (or, more accurately, suppress certain expressions of it.) But even this is not entirely obvious. An act of revenge may follow the initial anger by many years—indeed, it may follow the *end* of the anger by many years. Nevertheless, it is evident that the act of revenge follows "out of" the anger, however distant it may seem to be. (One might even argue that if one had not gotten angry, the act would not be one of *revenge* at all.)[21] And the fact that we seem able to suppress some but not all of the expressions of emotion would seem to indicate that some link between emotion and expression—though not, perhaps, a link with any *particular* expression—is somehow essential to emotion.

If we restrict our attention for the moment to full-blown action (as opposed to facial expressions, gestures, and more "basic" bodily responses), there is some question of which actions count as expression of emotion and which are related to the emotion in some other way. I get angry, but I decide to suppress my expression. Or I count to ten, and then verbally punch the offender with a quick, wry, cutting comment. Where the expression is delayed, it makes some sense to distinguish one's emotional response from one's subsequent action. Thus Peter Goldie distinguishes "acting out of emotion" from true emotional expression, although his criterion for distinguishing such action from expression of emotion is not the mere fact of delay but rather the "ends-means" nature of such action.[22] An act is an expression of emotion if it just expresses that emotion. An action is "out of" an emotion (that is, one acts out of an emotion) if it has an independent means-to-end structure, as an act of revenge so clearly does. If an action is subsequent to and distinct from the emotion, we might well hesitate to call it an expression of emotion, but I think the distinction here founders.

I say "I love you." I blurt it out in the midst of a passion. And then I say it again the next morning in calm repose because I want to be sure that you know that I love you. Does it make sense to say that the first is an expression of love but the second is not? Need we say that the latter is an "act of love" as opposed to an expression of love? Or a *report* of one's love?[23] Doesn't it make more sense to understand the whole history of my loving behavior as an ongoing expression of my love and, if you like, focus on some acts that are more direct expressions of my emotion, others that are motivated in part by more diverse concerns. Thus my saying "I love you" may sometimes be nothing other than an expression of love. At other times it may also serve as reassurance, and at others it may even serve as a threat, a warning, or a plea.[24] My making breakfast for you on a Sunday morning is almost certainly an expression of love, but that surely does not preclude its also being my way of assuring that you get your proper nutrition for the day, my way of hurrying up your morning so we can leave on our road trip on time, my chalking up "points" in our domestic arrangement to more or less evenly distribute the household duties, and so on. Indeed, it makes sense to say that my just *being* with you, quite apart from the particulars of my behavior, is an expression of my love.[25]

All of these examples of expression are more or less voluntary actions. It does not much matter whether we classify an action as an expression of emotion or as an action "out of" emotion, and it does not much matter whether an action is relatively simple or "basic" (like making a rude gesture) or an elaborate course of action (such as taking on a career in politics to prove your father wrong in his low estimation of you). And I do not see that a radical distinction between verbal expression (from "ooh" to the composition of an ode) and verbal reports or descriptions of emotion makes much difference here either. Insofar as the expression is an action and it is part of (and not only subsequent to) the emotion, the emotion itself is, *to that extent*, clearly in the realm of action and responsibility. But if we are to argue this position, we should also be prepared to confront those less obviously voluntary aspects of expression which might therefore be argued to drag the emotion down into the category of passivity.

To say the obvious, not all expressions of emotion are voluntary actions. I mentioned as different forms or facets of the expression of emotion: Bodily expressions, verbal expressions, facial expressions, various sorts of postures and gestures, as well as full-blown actions, courses of action, and actions performed because of or "out of" emotion. I have already indicated that I think that some of these are quite indistinct, and that any attempt to sharply distinguish the expression from the emotion runs into considerable trouble. Between actions as expressions and those performed because of or "out of" emotion, between spontaneous expressions (blurting out "I love you") and deliberate, reflective actions and gestures (announcing "I love you" after an evening of soul-searching and soft, longing looks), there is considerable overlap and interplay, and it probably is a mistake to try to define any of these (and, consequently, the parameters of proper or genuine expression) in opposition to the others. Nevertheless, philosophers have tended to restrict emotional expression to just these sorts of voluntary actions, and they have almost systematically ignored (William James most obviously excepted) expressions that are not so obviously (and sometimes obviously not) voluntary.

Among these expressions, I would include facial expressions and various sorts of postures and gestures as well as bodily expressions that border or cross over into the involuntary. But it is important not to follow James in conflating these various sorts of expressions, not all of which lead to the same conclusions about either the relationship between emotion and expression or the voluntariness of emotion. What links these sorts of expression together is the fact that they need not be conscious or in any way attended to. They are most often not attended to, and in that sense "unconscious." This is not to say, of course, that they *cannot* be attended to or made conscious, nor is this yet to say anything about their voluntariness or passivity. It has often been observed both by novelists and by psychologists that people are typically unaware of their expressions and equally oblivious to their posture as expressive of emotions. So, too, such expressions as "nervous" fidgeting are only rarely the object of one's self-consciousness. But it is important to note that such behavior is not, strictly speaking, involuntary, since it is the "voluntary" musculature that makes it possible.

One can learn to act out various facial expressions of emotion without having the emotion (Paul Ekman has famously mastered the art of doing so), and of course actors have long mastered the arts of semblance. Whether or not we should say that facial expressions, postures, spontaneous gestures, and fidgeting are themselves voluntary acts, the components that make them up—wrinkling the brow or hanging one's head (in shame), slapping one's forehead in horror or curling one's fingers in a fidget—are all voluntary in an undeniable sense. They involve the voluntary muscles and (with some discipline and practice, perhaps) they can be performed quite voluntarily, even on command.

It is thus a matter of considerable interest that even a master cannot get some of these expressions quite right. The "Duchenne" smile often illustrates the difference between a genuine smile and even a very skillful "faked" one, and (according to one recent medical report) it is not possible to voluntarily "fidget." Fidgeting properly done is necessarily not done "on purpose." But it does not follow that such expressions are involuntary. So, too, the status of facial expressions remains a matter of dispute if the component behaviors are voluntary but the whole expression (or expression "syndrome") is not. Of course, when a person normally expresses an emotion with an appropriate look of horror, or satisfaction, or sadness, he or she does not do so with any kind of forethought or intention. He or she may well not even be aware that an emotion is being expressed. But one can learn to "control" such expressions; indeed, cultures typically have various "display rules" that render the control of expressions as unthinking and automatic as the original "natural" expression. And, to be sure, we do hold people responsible (and strongly encourage them to learn the appropriate skill) when they display an inappropriate expression (or express an inappropriate emotion).[26]

On the other hand, there is no reason to deny full "expression" status to such unintentional and unconscious behavior. Which would seem to make the voluntary status of the expression, and thus of the emotion, problematic. But does the fact that an emotion has unintentional and unconscious aspects render it passive?

More problematic are those expressions focused upon by the psychophysiologists, those manifestations of emotion brought about by the autonomic nervous system (sweating, flushing, increased heartbeat, electrodermal response, and the like). Here, I think, we may properly hesitate to call these "expressions" of emotion, however important they may be as symptoms or signs of emotion. To the extent that an emotion consists of such autonomic nervous system responses *or the sensations caused by them*, we might rightly insist that an emotion—*so considered*—is not all voluntary, but an agentless product of a disturbing perception and the nervous system. Insofar as the focus remains on such "expressions," William James seems to be right. An emotion insofar as it is defined by such expressions is something that happens to us. But James, it has often been pointed out, conflates such physiological responses with other expressions and even with full-blown actions, his famous example of a woman weeping being one of the more interesting ambiguous cases. Weeping is, on the one hand, an autonomic response. But weeping can also be done voluntarily (though again, the question of whether this is genuine weeping is a serious question). Moreover, weeping is or can be intentional, not here in the sense of voluntary but rather in the sense that it is *about* something.[27] Indeed, insofar as autonomic responses are *also* under voluntary control, their status, too, remains problematic. (Breathing is the obvious example, but Yogis have shown the ability to directly "will" heart rate and metabolism as well).

Are such expressions to be counted as an essential aspect of our emotions? In my early work I flat-footedly said "No." I am no longer so sure. Are they components, aspects, manifestations, symptoms of emotions? Surely by themselves (despite some contentious attempts of practitioners to *define* them as emotions) these are not plausibly to count as emotions. But I would suggest a compromise. Such responses should not by themselves be considered as emotions, but should be considered part of or an aspect of emotion only *together with* such essential features as evaluative judgments. (Thus Goldie says, in a nice phrase, they have "borrowed intentionality.") Autonomic responses often accompany emotions and they may well persist after the emotion has ended. Thus I stick by my old example: I am furious because [I believe that] my friend John has stolen my car. I then find out that no one stole my car. I immediately cease to be furious, although the physiological symptoms that accompanied my fury remain for a few more moments. So, too, I see the rock slide, skillfully maneuver around it, and *then* experience the sweating and palpitations. But the fear is gone. Now there are only these irritating symptoms to be gotten over as quickly as possible.

James may have been mistaken when he too tightly identified emotion with autonomic nervous system responses, but he was surely right when he challenged, famously, "What kind of an emotion of fear would be left, if the feelings neither of quickened heartbeats or of shallow breathing (etc.) were present?" And rage, he insisted, is surely not "some cold-blooded and dispassionate judicial sentence, confined entirely to the intellectual realm." But autonomic nervous system responses are not an essential part of every emotion. In short-term rage or fear, it may seem so. But could one plausibly have such responses over a lifetime of anger about one's deprivation as a child or of fear of government authorities? Nor does it make any sense to say that one has such emotions *only* in those episodes in which the autonomic responses are present. But neither should it be concluded (as I once concluded) that such responses are *not* an essential aspect of the emotion. Indeed, the question of whether autonomic responses are an aspect of an emotion seems to me a pointless haggle: Is a symptom part of the disease, or just an indication of it?

I have entered this long digression on the expression of emotion because it is so obvious in the literature that philosophers have tended to overly separate expression and emotion while psychologists (and psychophysiologists) have tended to conflate them. But the argument that emotion and expression are not to be separated has a good deal to be said for it, and insofar as expression is an essential aspect of emotion and the expression can be rightly said to be voluntary behavior (rather than "ways of being acted upon"), the emotion can to that extent be considered voluntary as well. The upshot is that both emotions and their expressions span the entire spectrum from deliberate, intentional actions to "automatic" responses, but we should be careful not to leap to the conclusion that what is not entirely deliberate and intentional is not a matter of agency. We might well refuse to call autonomic system responses "expressions" in the appropriate sense, but it seems obvious that even the most unthinking facial expressions are both bona fide expressions and to *some* extent voluntary.

Thus to the extent that an emotion is its expression, there are very good arguments for denying what has long been called the passivity of the passions. And insofar as we want to distinguish an emotion (as experience) from its expression, it is essential that we do not think of the experience in its stripped-down and utterly minimal form, as just those sensations produced by visceral disturbances. Nor should we think of the expression in its stripped-down and utterly minimal form as mere bodily movement that does not even distinguish it from muscle spasms and reflex arcs. But once we have fleshed out the intimate relation between emotion and expression, it seems that the weight of the argument falls heavily on the side of activity. It is not that we are responsible for *both* the emotion and its expression. It is rather that we are responsible for the emotion *as* expression, for the two can be totally separated only at our peril.

"Emotions and Choice" Revisited

I would like to end this chapter by turning to two distinguished theorists I very much admire who have quite explicitly taken me to task for my early thesis that we "choose" our emotions, Jon Elster and George Downing. They attack me from very different directions. Elster finds my choice thesis implausible and some of it even "reckless," while Downing thinks that I do not go far enough. Examining their arguments, without trying to score points, has helped me enormously to get clear about just what the thesis I have been grappling with all of these years amounts to.

Jon Elster's discussion of "the traditional view" (that "emotions are involuntary, suffered in a passive mode . . . rather than chosen in an active mode") is of a piece with his more general concern about "rationality and the emotions."[28] Elster's book is marvelously rich and insightful, but his defense of the traditional view suggests to me just how much we have invested in the idea that we "suffer" our emotions. This investment provokes resistance to the very idea that emotions involve choice and responsibility, even though (I will suggest) it is a thesis Elster grudgingly comes around to acknowledging.

Elster distinguishes three sets of issues. First, there is the "impact of emotions on the rationality of decision making and belief formation." He agrees with many contemporary theorists, from philosophy to neurobiology, that emotions need not be detrimental to, and may even be necessary for, rational decision-making. Second, there is the question of whether the emotions themselves can be assessed as more or less rational, to which his answer is a clear "yes," although the "trade-off" between emotional rewards and other rewards is complicated by the fact that the emotions often shape the terms of the interaction. Third, there is the question of whether the emotions can be the object of rational choice, that is, "whether people can and do engage in rational deliberation about which emotions to induce in themselves or in other people." Here he demurs, while I, obviously, would give a hearty if qualified "yes." It is a fact that we sometimes feel guilty about our emotions, Elster admits, but he goes on to ask, "Is this guilt itself misguided or irrational?" I agree with Elster's answers to the first two sets of questions, namely, that emotions should not be considered merely interferences or disruptions ("sand in the machinery") of rational choice and, yes, emotions can be assessed as more or less rational. But he calls into question much of what I have been arguing, that we are responsible for our emotions in "an active mode" (whether or not we "choose" them).

I have said that I am willing to back up on "choice," but I do not want to thereby abandon the emotions to the category of passivity. Elster's position on this more general "activity" framework is by no means clear. He argues, for instance (referring back to Aristotle), that it is "implausible to assume that when people feel guilty about their emotions it is because they believe there is something they could have done at some earlier time to develop different emotional dispositions" (p. 307). But neither activity nor responsibility entails "could have done otherwise," and a significant literature has grown up around the problem of addiction (to which Elster has notably contributed) and "agent regret" (Bernard Williams), where not being able to have done otherwise is no obstacle to feelings of guilt or regret. The question is rather whether an emotion is "done" at all.

One source of support for the claim that emotions are active would be the observation that our emotions are (at least sometimes) purposive and functional. This does not just mean that they serve us well (this may be true of any number of features and facts that are not in any sense our doing nor of our choosing) or that through evolution they serve or once served some purpose (as Darwin famously argued). It rather means that they are purposive in the substantial sense that they (try to) accomplish something (or, without the personification, we try to do things by way of them). One might indeed employ the word "strategies" here, so long as one doesn't take strategies to require "calculation." There are strategies that one settles on by way of imitation, strategies that one arrives at through trial and error, and perhaps even strategies based on evolution and instinct. (I cannot think how to explain a good deal of purposive animal behavior without some such hypothesis.) Elster's "alchemies of the mind" shares with my view the idea that emotions serve our purposes and our interests, although he wants to downplay the voluntaristic implications of this as much as I want to build on them. Serving purposes opens up the "why?" questions, such as "What are you getting out of this?" and Elster's wonderful replay of the seventeenth-century French moralists (La Bruyère, La Rochefoucauld, et al.) makes the appropriateness and poignancy of such questions inescapably clear.

One of Elster's key arguments, which he first employed against Roy Shafer, is that people *cannot decide to believe* and *therefore* cannot decide which emotions to have. I think that this argument betrays a good deal about what Elster takes the thesis that he is attacking to be, and in particular, the quite simpleminded notion that we can simply choose our emotions as basic actions. But I have maintained from the beginning that emotions, whatever else they may be, are not basic actions, that one cannot "simply" change one's emotions anymore than one can "simply" decide what to believe. On the other hand, Elster focuses a good part of his argument against me on my 1976 claim that "emotions are subjective strategies for the maximization of personal dignity and self-esteem" (p. 309). I now find this claim overblown (though hardly the "reckless overgeneralization" he suggests). But I would maintain the claim that emotions are often, even typically, subjective strategies. This, I take it, is the significance of Elster's own observations of the "alchemies of the mind," a less voluntaristic way of understanding how emotions serve "some further psychic purpose." (Elster's use of the term "mechanism" to refer to such strategies betrays, I think, the anti-voluntaristic leanings of his inquiry.)

In my book, I give an example of a woman who continues to shop at a store that cheats her because she values the self-righteous satisfaction of her continuing indignation more than her small monetary losses. Elster approves of the example but claims that it undermines my case. He says that she chooses to *get into* the situation because it "predictably—that is, independently of her will—generates the gratifying emotion." Here again I think that his argument betrays a misunderstanding. I could indeed be taken as arguing that people choose situations (rather than the emotions themselves) because of the emotional gratification they provide. That is one way, indeed, in which we choose our emotions. But it is not just the situation as such that is chosen. It is the situation *as conductive to the emotion,* or more to the point, the situation as the *object* of her emotion. Elster himself warns of the tendency of emotions to shape the terms of the interaction. Thus it is the emotion that already shapes her choice of the situation. To choose the "setup" and to choose the emotion are pretty much the same thing, given that one cannot simply choose to have the emotion *de nihilo.*

Elster distinguishes, as Ryle did fifty years ago, between occurrent emotions and emotional dispositions, but also "short-lived" and "durable" emotions. It is not clear to me to what extent these two distinctions are coextensive. I have already raised some serious doubts about the distinction between occurrent emotions and emotional dispositions (consider again a person who is angry all the time, or two people in love), but it does limit the focus of the discussion in an obviously helpful way. Elster is happy to agree that we can and do make resolutions and take steps to cultivate our emotional dispositions, whether or not this is very likely to succeed. The more difficult question for him is whether we can and do choose to have a particular emotion at a (more or less) particular time. Sometimes, as Elster points out, it is obvious that we do make such choices, for example, to render one emotional response more likely than another. In other words, we choose the "setup" of our emotions, to engage or not to engage in those situations which will surely provoke them. (We avoid going to a party, knowing that our ex-wife will be there with her new boyfriend. We spend the night on a lovely moonlit beach, predicting correctly that the romantic scene will evoke romantic feelings.) But, one might object, this is to choose only the "setup," not the emotion itself (Elster, p. 310), and Elster criticizes Schafer, in particular, for conflating the two. But, as I said, the choice of the situation *is* often the choice of one's emotion, and I see no reason to thus dismiss the claim that the emotion itself (in such cases) is chosen.

As for my supposed claim that "*All* emotions *always* exist to promote self-esteem" ("a reckless over-generalization from a few selected cases"), I never said or suggested any such thing. (I hedge my bets much better than that.) but it is hardly "a few" cases, and "not all" does not imply "very few." I admit that "self-esteem" is an overly restrictive way of referring to what might more generally be called "self-regarding" or "self-interested," but even thus expanded, I am willing to confess that the claim is an overgeneralization, and for fairly far-reaching reasons (that I would not have had twenty-five years ago). I am now quite skeptical of theories that postulate "self-interest" as the pervasive motive, and I see no reason not to be skeptical of any such hypothesis in emotion theory as well.

Thus Elster's argument against me as to the importance of self-esteem in emotion is one that I agree with. Self-esteem is too close to egoism, and I started to doubt my hypothesis soon after I published the first version of *The Passions* in 1976. But what I found wrong with that overgeneralization was not just that it was false and it gave much too much credit to psychological egoism, but rather that it betrayed my making the same mistake that I had already criticized in Sartre (in his little 1938 book on emotions). Sartre, I argued, made the mistake of trying to view all emotions as pursuing more or less *the same goal,* albeit with very different strataegies. But what I did not give up, nor does Elster, is the goal orientation of many (but certainly not all) emotions. I continue to think that many emotions embody strategies. I do not think that all do. But I also do not think that strategies necessarily involve calculation. There are strategies that one settles on by way of imitation, trial and error, and so on. The way I would put this issue now, still following Sartre, is to insist that the questions Why are you having this emotion, for what purpose? What are you personally getting out of this? are always intelligible whether or not they are in fact applicable or appropriate or polite.

One thesis that I have never retreated from is the thesis that how we conceive of our emotions is itself a matter of choice, a question of what Richard Rorty calls "optional vocabularies," the vocabulary of "mechanism" being one kind of choice, the vocabulary of "action" and "responsibility" being quite another. To be sure, the term "mechanism" is quite appropriate in writing of those wonderful French moralists of the eighteenth century, whose philosophies were transfixed with that Newtonian metaphor, but what they argue suggests something far more human, and far more rational, than such mechanical imagery would imply.

Admitting that objections to arguments are not yet objections to the conclusion, Elster finally focuses on six arguments directed against the view that we choose our emotions. Some of these reiterate and clarify the points I have been arguing. Others seem to me somewhat desperate.

1) Those who see emotions as actions either have to argue that this view applies to non-human organisms and small children as well as to adult humans or to argue for a radical discontinuity. Both horns of the dilemma are highly unattractive.

To be sure. But what is the dilemma? I certainly want to attribute emotions to animals and infants, but that does not mean that I want to attribute *adult human* emotions to animals and infants. And it is only regarding adult human emotions that I would want to employ the vocabulary of "responsibility" (although I would be extremely hesitant to deny that animals "act"). If this is what is meant by "a radical discontinuity," it seems to be worth objecting that virtually every philosopher who has thought about the issue, including Darwin and animal liberationist Peter Singer, has accepted it. Adult humans have a language with which they can reflect on their emotions. Animals and infants do not.

2) Even in adult humans, there is very strong evidence that [quoting Ekman] "because emotions can occur with rapid onset, through automatic appraisal, with little awareness, and with involuntary response changes in expression and physiology, we often experience emotions as happening to, not chosen by us. One cannot simply elect when to have which emotion."

But of course. That emotions are experienced as happening to, and not as chosen by, us is one of the data that prompt the question of activity/passivity. But it does not follow (and Ekman does not commit himself to concluding) that emotions *therefore* happen to us and are not chosen. The fact that emotions sometimes (but by no means always) occur with rapid onset, the fact that some emotions involve automatic appraisal, the fact that some appraisals involve little reflective awareness, and the fact that emotions often involve involuntary response changes in expression and physiology, do not by any means lead to the conclusion that *no* emotions can be "elected." And as for the "when" and "which," surely we do often decide *which emotion* we will have by going to one film (a comedy) rather than another (a horror film), and we decide *when* by going to the matinee instead of the midnight show. The tricky word, of course, is that seemingly innocent "simply." Can one "*simply* elect when and which emotion"? Surely not. But it does not follow that emotions are not modes of activity rather than passivity.

> 3) If we can choose our emotions without any costs and constraints, why not choose always to be happy?

It is hard to take this argument very seriously. First of all, happiness is not an emotion, and in any case it is not a matter of mere subjectivity. Elster knows his Aristotle well, and he certainly knows that. Why not choose to *feel* happy? Well, many of us do, and we have a pharmacopia of chemicals to help us do so. But more to the point, who ever said that we could choose our emotions "without any costs and constraints"? Choosing to perform any action involves costs and constraints, and every action (including an act of omission) has its consequences. Choosing to be angry has its obvious costs, both medical-physiological and in terms of the various ways that anger shuts off other emotions and avenues of communication with others. It has its constraints not least in the fact that it is only in certain sorts of situations that it is appropriate to get angry. And choosing to feel (not to be) happy has its own costs and constraints as well, for instance, a certain indifference to ambition and success, a certain obliviousness to the needs and desperation of others, and a certain appropriateness to the situation. Isaac Babel famously remained in a miraculously good humor throughout the horrors of the Holocaust. The fact that this was indeed miraculous points to the enormous difficulty of simply choosing to feel happy. (And as for *being* happy, that is something that one chooses, as Aristotle points out, with every action in the course of our lives.)

> 4) If there are costs and constraints where do they come from? Also, would not these costs and constraints precisely reflect the involuntary nature of emotions?

I have trouble reading this argument (and the preceding) as much more than sophistry. (Beware those arguments nestled in the middle of a list of six.) Where do the costs and constraints of and in emotions come from? From the nature of the emotions themselves, from the various ways in which they perceive and construct the world around them, from their situations and objects, from other people who are affected by one's emotions, from the laws of nature and the causal networks within which we have emotions. But does any of this suggest "the involuntary nature of emotions"? Obviously not, any more than the costs of and constraints on any action reflect its involuntary nature. The costs and constraints of my buying myself a rocket launcher do not imply the involuntary nature of my going into the international arms trade.

5) Most emotions are triggered by beliefs, which cannot be chosen.

The idea that emotions are "triggered" is already a concession to "mechanism" that I am not willing to buy. To be sure, emotions are initiated, prompted, provoked, evoked, and caused in any number of different ways, more often than not by causes that themselves are not chosen. An emotion may be provoked by the circumstances, which we had no hand in choosing. An emotion may be brought about with an injection of norepinephrine, despite our objections or possibly without our even knowing about it. It makes no difference, with regard to the question of the voluntariness of emotions, whether their causes, including beliefs, are themselves voluntarily chosen. But can one choose his or her beliefs? Not "simply," to be sure. But one can and does choose to examine further evidence, check the arguments leading up to the belief, test and confirm the belief with experts and interlocutors, talk to other people and get different opinions, and so on. And in what sense would a belief ever be a "trigger"? An event or an incident, perhaps. But belief is in the wrong logical category to serve as a "trigger."

6) Emotions that are not triggered by beliefs, such as panics and phobias, are even less plausibly chosen for the purpose of maximizing self-esteem.

Well, again, I've given up the claim about the centrality of self-esteem, but even in my more reckless days I never claimed that panics and phobias were plausible candidates for maximizing self-esteem. To the contrary, I have always held panic (along with rage) to be exceptional in that, in such cases, there does seem to be a sufficient neurobiological explanation for their occurrence, quite apart from any but the most minimal cognition (including beliefs). (By phobias, I take it that Elster means something more than merely "irrational fears.")

In the end, Elster finds an element of truth in our otherwise "false" thesis: "when an emotion arises from some external stimulus, we can 'let it happen,' amplify it by giving full rein to its expression, or try to limit it, for example, by directing attention elsewhere." (He adds a footnote to Nico Frijda.) But what is the "it"? Is it the full-blown emotion? Or what Elster elsewhere calls a "proto-emotion"? Or is it just those "sinking" or "expansive" feelings described by the Stoics, which in turn provoke our emotions as attempts to understand and deal with them? Is it the situation that we decide to "let happen"? I find myself attracted to someone and I then decide whether or not to follow through in any way. Need love as a choice involve more than this? Do we really have to insist that we choose to find the other attractive as well? Of course, there are such ways of cultivating one's taste, so I wouldn't rule this out. But Elster here is considering only immediate emotional reactions and not the cultivation of sensibility. I find myself in a deeply offensive situation. I can decide to leave, or I can decide to distract myself, or I can decide to stay in the situation and (more or less inevitably) get angry. So what is the "it" that I "let happen"? It seems to me that Elster is endorsing just what I have been arguing: that many of our emotions are pervaded by choices, and through those choices we take responsibility for our emotions.

Finally, Elster refers back to the Jamesian technique of evoking an emotion by "eliciting the verbal and nonverbal behaviors that normally express" it.[29] But then he quotes Arlie Hochschild, who suggests (based on her now famous study of airline stewardesses and how they "manage" emotions) that such self-stimulated emotions are "parasitic on genuine emotion." But this claim is much less damaging than Elster suggests. Of course, one has to have an emotion or at least know what it is before one can "create" it, but why suppose that such created emotions, as opposed to the originals, are not "genuine"? James seems to suggest just the opposite, and here I agree with him. What is a "genuine" versus a "fake" emotion (as opposed to a faked expression)? What Hochschild says does not suggest that the simulated emotions are not genuine, only that the hard work of simulating (stimulating?) them, as opposed to the effortless way in which we naturally find something happy or pleasant, can be exhausting.

Elster concludes that the traditional view is "basically sound." But I think that what he has shown is that emotions are undeniably "in the active mode." He puts considerable emphasis on choosing one's situation and how one perceives a situation with an eye to what emotions this will evoke. But the main theme of Elster's book, very much in accordance with Sartre's and my own work, is the idea that emotions are *strategies*, which need not imply deliberation or, for that matter, even conscious acknowledgment. Elster misrepresents me and misdescribes the phenomenon when he objects that there is no evidence "for the mind's capacity to engage in these strategic calculations."[30] Strategies may be the product of habit or practice. They may even (as in animals) be instinctual. This compromises the strong voluntaristic language of "choice" considerably, to be sure, but the point I want to make, and which Elster fails to appreciate, is that the emotions are not simply "passively undergone." Even if what he calls "proto-emotions" (primitive and apparently unlearned responses in infants, for example) may be passively undergone, both our assessments and the nature of our engagements in a situation are in an important sense our doing and our responsibility, which is precisely what Elster's "alchemies" are all about.

George Downing, as a psychiatrist, is far more sympathetic to the notion of choice.[31] But he thinks I err (as does Sartre) in limiting choice to the *beginning* of an emotion. Downing's primary concern is the understanding of the role of the body in emotion, a much-neglected topic of inquiry. But among the various contributions of the body in emotion, some (e.g., autonomic responses) are clearly involuntary, while others (preparation for action) are more clearly within the realm of the voluntary. Downing's comments on the question of choice in emotion follow from his concern for the (more or less) voluntary aspects of emotion. Like Elster, he begins by noting that the traditional view was that emotions were "passions": "an emotion simply happens, the subject is passive before its onslaught. Choice was viewed as belonging only to subsequent actions." But unlike Elster, Downing finds a good deal of truth in the countervailing view, which he attributes to Sartre, that "we choose our emotions; and we do so for strategic ends, whose exact nature we camouflage from ourselves. Far from 'suffering' an emotion, we implement it."

But as Downing sees it, "the question has been wrongly posed." Up to now, he suggests, the terms of the debate have been "Do we have a choice of an emotion or only *after* an emotion?" Instead, Downing opts for a third alternative, "choice *during* an emotion." Oddly, given the boldness of this assertion, Downing then states his agreement with "persuasive criticisms of the countercurrent position." "In normal instances," he affirms, "it makes no sense to say that we choose to have an emotion. Emotions do *happen to us*. We react; and that reaction . . . is underway, is well in movement, before we really know what is happening. Up to this point the traditional view is quite right. We discover ourselves in the middle of our emotion as if we had been dropped into the sea."[32]

Now first of all, it is not at all clear whether Downing (like Elster) is talking about a full-blown emotion here, or rather something more like the Stoic "first movements." To be sure, the onset of the emotion process is often rapid, far faster than our recognition of what is happening, beginning with "automatic" assessments and provoking physiological response, and only after a few moments allowing for reflective emotional experience, "knowing what is happening." But it is not obvious that discovering that a process is already going on is finding ourselves "in the middle of our emotion," much less floundering as if "we had been dropped into the sea." Moreover, Downing is simply ignoring all of those cases where we do not simply find ourselves in the middle of an emotion process, but quite consciously take steps to initiate such a process.

Nevertheless, he quickly adds, "But does that imply no dimension of choice is involved? Not in the least. Once the first wave of these parallel events [initial appraisal, the autonomic, muscular contractions] has crossed the threshold of consciousness, *then* we can talk, and should, about parameters of agency." For example, we can talk about how a person might "steer" his emotion, or accentuate or attenuate or interrupt it; or interrogate it, or refuse to acknowledge it, etc. There follows "a steady stream of minute potential decision points." But "all of this comes after the emotion's onset, yet during its duration." On reading this, I was tempted to conclude that (with regard to such sudden-onset emotions) we could not be more in agreement.

Nevertheless, the bias in favor of the traditional view keeps its hold. Downing insists, against Sartre, Shafer, and me, that "The idea that we are the authors of our emotions represents a basic misunderstanding of their function." Emotions force us to reevaluate the world, he argues, and they would be of no use as these "delicate instruments" if they were only "the whims of our own choosing." His argument here is strongly reminiscent of Elster's argument that if we choose our emotions, why don't we simply all choose to be happy? And, to be sure, we do not "simply" choose our emotions. They are constrained by the situations in which we find ourselves; by our beliefs, our prior emotional investments, and our personalities; by our interests and our commitments; and by our human natures. It is not only our emotions that force us to reevaluate the world. The world forces us to reevaluate the world by frustrating us, by not meeting our demands and expectations, by presenting us with all sorts of difficulties, not the least of which are tragic loss and impending death. To be sure, we do not choose to have emotions *as such* (although some of the Stoics made noble attempts to choose *not* to). But given that we are emotional creatures and we respond to our circumstances by getting emotional, there seems to be little to Downing's suspicion that thinking of emotions in terms of choice turns out to be a "kind of autistic short-circuiting."

Downing's second argument is this: it is a virtue of choice theory that it tries to explain why we "so often fail to perceive the potential for the exercise of agency," that is, not only why we experience our emotions as happening to us but also why we fail to make the choices during the emotion process that Downing suggests (and which, no doubt, are particularly called for in a psychiatric session). The problem is that we (Sartre and I) pin the entire blame on self-deception. Downing counters that that is but one factor. One "carrying far more weight is the lack, for any given person, of the necessary bodily skills and habits." Here Downing's own analysis has a great deal to offer us. I happily concede the charge that I (and Sartre) overemphasize self-deception. But the point, with regard to choice, is that Downing's emphasis on the development of skills and habits only underscores the importance of actively acquiring and refining such skills as a way of cultivating our emotions.

Downing's third argument also echoes what I have already argued. "The countercurrent view also ignores the fact that the physiological buildup has its own momentum, its own forward flow. . . . One can no more 'will' this collective pressure instantly to disappear than one could stop a heavy moving object in its tracks." I would question Downing's choice of analogies (one *can* stop a heavy moving object in its tracks, if one installs a sufficiently heavy obstacle to block it.) And, again, I would question the presumption that an emotion is (according to me) a basic action, something one can simply "will." So why "will" and why "instantly," as if the few minutes one takes to calm down counts for nothing. But the main point, again, is that the physiological response by itself is not the emotion, and it counts as an aspect of the emotion (or as symptomatic of the emotion) only in the presence of the emotion (the judgments, appraisals, ets.) I readily admit that the physiological responses may outlast the emotion by several minutes, but it does not follow that it is *the emotion* which is out of our control.

But again, Downing's seeming hostility turns to coconspiracy almost immediately. "This is not to say that such physiological responses lie in one realm and choice in another. On the contrary. To the extent these processes are subjectively perceived they can be guided and modulated.[33] He even adds, "Research strongly suggests our autonomic responses are far more subject to voluntary control than one would intuitively think." Downing goes on to make a series of extremely valuable suggestions about how we might use these bodily phenomena to "interrogate" the world around us. With an insightful reference to Heidegger, he suggests that it is through our emotions that we determine the "facts of the matter" in our experience, culminating in the very Heideggerian concern for making sense of my life in the face of (among other things) my impending death. Downing concludes, "We then give choice its due, acknowledging its pervasive presence in emotional experience."[34] I could not agree more.

Conclusion

One can look at emotions from several different perspectives: neurological–physiological, behavioral, social, experiential, practical, moral. I do not think that these are all that distinct, and they are certainly not (or certainly should not be) in competition with one another. But I want to rest my case on practical and moral considerations, and I would urge that these should always be kept in mind. The main consideration is this: how we *think* about our emotions—as something we suffer or as something we "do"—will deeply affect both our behavior and our understanding of our behavior. In other words, theses about emotions tend to be self-confirming. If one thinks of oneself as the victim of irrational forces, one need not examine the reasons and motives for acting as one does. On the other hand, if one thinks of oneself as the author of his or her emotions, one does reflect and resolve in such a way as to affect and possibly alter one's emotions. "Counting to ten" when angry is an overused but always valuable illustration. I would argue that it is not so simple as "one is already angry, but give it a moment to die down," but rather, "Here's the situation. I am getting upset. Now, let's take a moment to examine the circumstances before deciding whether or not it is worth getting angry."

The truth is, we are adults. We must take responsibility for what we do and what we feel. And in our taking responsibility we learn to recognize the responsibilities we have, including responsibility for our own emotions. Arguing as I have amounts to nothing less than insisting that we think of ourselves as adults instead of children, who are indeed the passive victims of their passions. Jerome Bruner, writing about infants back in the 1960s, summarized a great deal of research that has since become familiar: "they [the infants] were much smarter, more cognitively proactive rather than reactive, more attentive to the immediate social world around them, than had been previously suspected." What I am suggesting is that we think no less of ourselves than of those infants, taking what hold we can of our world.

Notes

Chapter 1

1. Perhaps we should distinguish getting into an emotional state and being in one (e.g., getting angry vs. being angry). But nothing turns on this, for being in a state as well as getting into a state, like God's maintenance of the Universe as well as his creation of it, requires devoted activity. Accordingly, I shall be arguing both that we choose an emotion and that we continuously choose our emotions. There is no need to separate these arguments.

2. I take this to be definitive of the difference between "emotion" and "feeling" as I am using those terms here. Emotions are intentional; feelings are not. I do not deny that the everyday use of "feeling" is broader than this and includes both of these concepts. I find this ambiguity less objectionable than others surrounding "sensation" and like terms.

3. There is nothing in my analysis which is not compatible with an all-embracing causal theory. I would agree with writers like A. I. Goldman, who argues that intentional characterizations of actions (in terms of "reasons") also function in causal explanations of a Hempelian variety. I do not wish to argue a similar thesis regarding emotions here, but I want to be careful not to preclude any such theory. Similarly, nothing I have said here bears on the so-called free will problem; I want to show that emotions should be viewed in the same categories as actions, whether or not there are further arguments that might lead us to conclude that not even actions are chosen freely.

4. Freud has a curious way of defending this thesis, which is surely central to much of his theory. Because he attempted to maintain a thesis of the intentionality of the "affects" within a strictly causal model, he obscured the distinction between object and cause. Without crucifying Freud on this point, as Peters, MacIntyre, and others have attempted to do, it is important to see that Freud typically confuses first-person and third-person accounts, and the concept of the "unconscious" as an "assumption" (e.g., see the essay "The Unconscious," *Collected Papers*, Vol. VI) often depends upon the failure of the subject to be capable of applying third-person ascriptions—notably, ascriptions of the cause as opposed to the object of an emotion—to himself. Without in the least detracting from Freud's overall conception of the unconscious, we must insist that the subject is never logically privileged with respect to the causes of his emotions, but that he does have some such authority (without infallible authority) with respect to what he is "affected about."

5. Though perhaps I can simply *express* such a judgment.

6. Aristotle, *Rhetoric*, book II, 1378ff. See also W. W. Fortenbaugh, *Aristotle on Emotion* (London: Duckworth, 1975), chaps. 1, 4; Gorgias, *Hel.*, 10, 14.

7. Aristotle, *Rhetoric*, 1378a30–32.

8. Ibid., 1378a33–34.

9. *De Ira*, esp. vol. II (Oxford: Loeb Classical Library). Seneca argues that the "cause" of emotion is beyond our power, but whether a cause affects us is not.

10. See Fortenbaugh, *Aristotle on Emotion*, pp. 63ff.

11. R. Solomon, *The Passions* (New York: Doubleday-Anchor, 1976).

12. Here I still follow E. Bedford, "Emotions," *Proceedings of the Aristotelian Society*, 57 (1956–1957), 281–304. Where we differ is his (too) strong emphasis on the behavioral expression of emotion.

13. For example, Robert Gordon, "The Aboutness of Emotions," *American Philosophical Quarterly*, 11, 1 (January 1974), 27–36; J. R. S. Wilson, *Emotion and Object* (Cambridge: Cambridge University Press, 1974); and Donald Davidson, "Hume's Cognitive Theory of Pride," *Journal of Philosophy*, LXIII, 19 (November 4, 1976), 744–757.

14. A. Kenny, *Action, Emotion and Will* (London: Routledge and Kegan Paul, 1963).

15. *Philebus* and *Topics* (150b27f.). See Fortenbaugh, *Aristotle on Emotion*, p. 11.

16. Wilson, *Emotion and Object*, rightly accuses Kenny of confusing properties of the emotions themselves here with properties of their description (chap. 3, sec. iii).

17. Gordon, "The Aboutness of Emotions," p. 27.

18. Solomon, *Passions*, chap. 2.

19. I have defended this cryptic suggestion in detail in my "Emotions' Mysterious Objects," *Journal for the Theory of Social Behavior* (1979).

20. Descartes, "The Passions of the Soul," Part First, article XLff. in Haldane and Ross, *The Philosophical Works of Descartes* (Cambridge: Cambridge University Press, 1911).

21. Frithjof Bergmann, review of *The Passions* in *Journal of Philosophy*, LXXV, 5 (May 1978), 208, who insists I either defend *just* my slogan or nothing.

22. Aristotle does this, too, using the idea of the efficient causes of different emotions (e.g., *Rhetoric*, 1382a3–7ff.).

23. Ibid., 1378a30–32. Cf. Hume on pride in his *Treatise of Human Nature*, ed. L. A. Selby-Bigge (Oxford: Oxford University Press, 1951), book II, "Of the Passions," esp pp. 277f.

24. E.g., Bergmann, review of *The Passions*, pp. 204f.

25. Some of the judgments constitutive of an emotion imply their own personal concerns and desires, for example, judgments of praise and blame, inferiority, superiority, trust, intimacy, and power.

26. See Amélie Rorty, "Explaining Emotions," in Rorty, ed., *Emotions* (Berkeley: University of California Press, 1979).

27. See ibid. Also Bergmann, review of *The Passions*.

28. Solomon, *The Passions*, chap. 9, esp. sec. 1.

29. "Emotions and Anthropology," *Inquiry* (1978).

30. Solomon, *Passions*, chap. 9, est. sec. 4, and "The Rationality of Emotions," *Southwestern Journal of Philosophy*, VIII, 2 (December 1977).

31. Bergmann, review of *The Passions*, p. 202.

32. The idea that jealousy involves "rights" has been disputed, notably by Jerome Neu (in Amélie Rorty, ed., *Emotions* [Berkeley: University of California Press, 1979]), chap. 18. But the difference between being merely "hurt" or disappointed, on the one hand, and being jealous, on the other, seems to be a kind of vindictiveness and indignation ("That bastard!") that requires moral claims, not just sense of loss.

33. See Rorty, "Explaining Emotions."

Chapter 2

1. See, for example, Ernst Gellhorn and G. N. Loofbourrow, *Emotions and Emotional Disorders* (New York: Harper & Row, 1963); and Magda Arnold, ed., *The Nature of Emotion* (New York: Acade-

mic Press, 1970), essays nos. 23 and 27, and by the same author, *Emotion and Personality* (New York: Columbia University Press, 1960); D. G. Glass, *Neurophysiology and Emotion* (New York: Sage Foundation, Rockefeller University Press, 1967); and West and Greenblatt, *Explorations in the Physiology of Emotions* (APA Report 12, 1960).

2. There are serious but often unappreciated problems concerning what is to be correlated with what. The old "phrenological" assumption of a one-to-one correlation between a mental process and a brain process has been repudiated by most neurologists. The workings of the "higher" centers of the brain are simply not that simple. (See my "Doubts About the Correlation Thesis," *British Journal for the Philosophy of Science*, March 1975.) But the thesis can surely be restated in some such way that the ever-increasing fund of "correlations" and "localizations" can be given some indisputable role in a psychophysical theory.

3. The extreme of this thesis—the idea that such neurological understanding could *replace* our mentalistic language of the emotions—has been persuasively argued in a now-classic paper by R. Rorty, in S. Hampshire, ed., *The Philosophy of Mind* (New York: Harper & Row, 1966).

4. In Germany it gave may to the more subjective movement of the Gestaltists. See, for example, A. Lehman's early critique of James and Lange, in M. Arnold, ed., *The Nature of Emotion*, pp. 37–42.

5. It is not unusual for the National Science Foundation to provide elaborate funds and equipment for the empirical substantiation of what any philosopher worth his salt could prove to be a conceptual truth in a matter of an hour or so. And philosophers are much less expensive as well.

6. R. S. Lazaras, in M. Arnold, ed., *Nature of Emotion* (London: Penguin, 1962) p. 260.

7. The concept of "feeling" has many different uses, ranging from the "feeling" (i.e., sensation) of cold water running down one's leg to the "feeling" of satisfaction one gains after winning a difficult tennis match, to "feelings" of anxiety and depression and "feeling like" leaving town. And, of course, there is the central synonymy between feelings and emotions (love, hate, jealousy, etc.). As I am employing the term here, a feeling is but a nonlocalizable sensation, as, for example, "feeling nauseous."

Chapter 3

1. "Emotions and Choice," *Review of Metaphysics*, 28, no.1 (1973), and *The Passions*.

2. *"The Emotions," A Sketch of a Theory*, trans. B. Frechtman (Philosophy Library, 1948).

3. One must temper this expectation, as Philip Slater sarcastically points out in a footnote in *Pursuit of Loneliness*, with our unwarranted expectations, which we apply to other people and fictional characters but rarely to ourselves, for absolute consistency and predictability of emotions and behavior (an angry man is always angry; a loving man is always loving, etc.). The logic of emotions typically involves contraries, such as, love and hate, resentment and indignation, worship and spite, which only psychological naiveté will confuse for inconsistencies.

Chapter 4

1. *Treatise of Human Nature*, ed. L. A. Selby-Bigge (Oxford: Oxford University Press, 1951), esp. book II, "Of the Passions," p. 277. All references to this work will be placed in square brackets in the text. Hume also insists that the passions are "secondary impressions," which "proceed from original ones, either immediately or by the interposition of its idea" (Pt. 1, sec. 1). The disjunct, "the interposition of the idea," is an important hint toward intentionality, discussed below.

2. *Les Passions de l'ame* (*The Passions of the Soul*) in Haldane and Ross, trans., *The Philosophical Works of Descartes* (Cambridge: Cambridge University Press, 1911). Descartes' very general definition of "passion" is simply "things which we experience in ourselves"

3. The culminating statement of this tradition is probably William James's classic paper, "What Is an Emotion?" (1884). More recently, see Gilbert Ryle's equally classic *Concept of Mind*, despite the fact that he ultimately dismisses the emotions proper as mere "agitations," breakdowns in our normal behavior patterns, and Errol Bedford, "Emotions," in D. Gustafson, ed., *Essay in Philosophical Psychology* (New York: Doubleday, 1964), in which he, too, attacks the "feeling" view for a more behavioral conception of emotion. For a philosophical survey of the leading position and arguments in this not very fruitful debate, see William Alston's contributions on "Emotion and Feeling," in P. Edwards, ed., *Encyclopedia of Philosophy* (New York: Macmillan, 1967). A survey of the psychological literature occupies the first chapters of David Rapaport's *Emotions and Memory* (New York: International Universities Press, 1971) and, more recently, Magda Arnold's *The Nature of Emotion* (London: Penguin, 1968). (Justice requires at least some mention of Spinoza, the one philosopher to quite clearly develop an intentional theory of the emotions, particularly in part III of his *Ethics*.)

4. Notably, Páll Árdal, *Passion and Value in Hume's Treatise* (Edinburgh, 1966), and Donald Davidson's defense of "Hume's Cognitive Theory of Pride" (*Journal of Philosophy*, LXXIII, no. 19, November 4, 1976): 744–757.

5. It is important not to move with the usual ease from this notion of "intentionality," which designates a property of mental attitudes, to "intensionality," which designates a property of certain types of sentences. I will make no use whatever of this latter notion in this essay.

6. For example, Donald Davidson, whose reinterpretation of Hume is discussed in this essay; but also, at greater length, J. R. S. Wilson, in *Emotion and Object* (Cambridge: Cambridge University Press, 1974) and Robert Gordon, "The Aboutness of Emotions," *American Philosophical Quarterly*, 11, no. 1 (1974), 27–36.

7. See, in this regard, P. L. Gardiner's excellent essay "Hume's Theory of the Passions," in *David Hume: A Symposium* (London: Macmillan, 1963), esp. pp. 38–42. Also, John Passmore, *Hume's Intentions* (Cambridge, 1952) esp. pp. 126–127, and Árdal, op. cit., p. 16.

8. If we were to be more obstinate, we would ask Hume how he can so confidently introduce such a notion when he has flatly rejected it in book I. His answer would be that he had denied the concept of self "only as it regards thought and imagination, not as it regards our passion or the concern we take in ourselves" [*THN* 253]. But when we look to see what the difference might be, there is nothing in Hume's meager ontology to make out that difference. This is discussed at some length by Jerome Neu in his *Emotions, Thought and Therapy* (Berkeley: University of California Press, 1977), and by Annette Baier, in her "Hume's Theory of Pride as a Non-Prepositional Attitude," *Journal of Philosophy*, 22 no. 1 (1979), 27–40.

9. Davidson, op. cit., Baier, op. cit., and K. Donnellan "Hume on the Objects of the Passions," an unpublished reply to Davidson. Also, Árdal, op. cit., p. 22. The conclusion is that Hume wasn't sure what to believe. Davidson distinguishes particular and general pride for Hume, but continues to lean to the latter. Baier flatly rejects the idea that Hume accepts pride "without qualification." But can't we be, in fact, at least on occasion, proud of ourselves, *in general*, whatever the cause?

10. Neu discusses these at length, op. cit., chap. 1.

11. R. Árdal defends this objection, op. cit., p. 23, and in "Another Look at Hume's Account of Moral Evaluation," *Journal of the History of Philosophy*, xv, no. 4 (October 1977).

12. For a slightly different way of arguing this in defense of Hume, see Baier, op. cit., esp. pp. 29f.

13. Davidson, op. cit.

14. Davidson, "Actions, Reasons and Causes," *Journal of Philosophy*, 66 (1963), 685–700.

15. Baier argues precisely that pride is a "nonpropositional attitude," op. cit., pp. 28f.

16. *The Passions* (New York: Doubleday-Anchor, 1976).

17. It is this essential qualification that is ignored, for example, in Frithjof Bergmann's attack on my analysis, *Journal of Philosophy* (April 1978).

18. But cf. Baier, op. cit. See also note 9, above.

19. In phenomenology, this formulation raises hoary and familiar questions. The move I am making here is evidently similar to Husserl's notion of "bracketing" ontological questions in favor of phenomenological description. The difference between us, however, is that I am doing so only *within* the context of a naively accepted ontology, so that questions of "reality" don't even arise. But since he intends to have a "first philosophy," and question the nature of ontology itself, he must deal with these difficult questions of the identity of intentional objects as I need not. I can glibly say, "Sure, the house mentioned in the belief and in the pride are identical, but the way they are experienced, i.e., the intentional objects, are different" is closed to him. Thus it becomes a problem how a thoroughgoing Husserlian phenomenologist can ever establish a sense of objective identity. (I have argued this at length in my "Husserl's Private Language," *Husserl* [The Hague: Nijhoff, 1977].) John Searle has developed a parallel version of this kind of analysis of intentionality in some of his recent not yet published work.

20. It is important to insist myself as "object," not "subject": see Árdal, op. cit., p. 18.

21. In *The Passions*.

22. A. Kenny, *Action, Emotion and Will* (London: Routledge and Kegan Paul, 1963), for example, uses "feeling" in this way, insisting, without explanation of any kind, that some feelings are intentional, others not. He then simply follows the grammar of intensionality—always dangerous—to some very problematic ontological obscurities.

23. Baier, op. cit.

Chapter 5

I am indebted to Lee Bowie and Meredith Michaels, to Izchak Miller, to Amélie Rorty, and to the philosophy departments at the University of Wisconsin (Milwaukee), the University of Auckland, and La Trobe University (Melbourne) for their criticism and discussion of this paper.

1. Hume, *Treatise of Human Nature*, ed. L. A. Selby-Bigge (Oxford: Oxford University Press, 1951), book II, "Of the Passions." All references to Hume will be included in the text, preceded by *THN*.

2. Donald Davidson, "Hume's Cognitive Theory of Pride," *Journal of Philosophy*, LXXIII, no. 19 (November 4, 1976), 744–757. Page numbers parenthesized in the text.

3. I have argued this interpretation of Hume and Davidson's revision of him at length in my "Nothing to be Proud of," at Bowling Green Applied Philosophy Conference, published in *Understanding Human Emotions* (Bowling Green, Ohio: Bowling Green University Press, 1979), pp. 18–35. See also P. L. Gardiner's essay, "Hume's Theory of the Passions," in *David Hume: A Symposium* (London: Macmillan, 1963), esp. pp. 38–42. Against Davidson's analysis, see Annette Baier, "Hume's Theory of Pride as a Non-Propositional Attitude," *Journal of Philosophy*, 22, 1 (1979), 27–40.

4. A merger of the two answers can be identified in Husserl's work, for example. I have argued a general version of this thesis in "Sense and Essence: Frege and Husserl," *International Philosophical Quarterly*, 10, no. 3 (1970).

5. A. Kenny, *Action, Emotion and Will* (London: Routledge and Kegan Paul, 1963).

6. Ibid.

7. Robert Gordon, "The Aboutness of Emotions," *American Philosophical Quarterly*, 11, 1 (1974), 27–36.

8. J. R. S. Wilson, *Emotion and Object* (Cambridge: Cambridge University Press, 1974). Page references in this section parenthesized in the text.

9. D. Davidson, "Causality," *Journal of Philosophy* (1977). It may be argued, however, that causal explanations, too, are context-dependent, that identification of a cause is necessarily bound to a certain theory or paradigm. (David Lewis has argued this, for example.) But the context determining the scope of causal explanation would in this case still be a theory or a paradigm of explanation; the context determining the proper identification of the object of an emotion would be the outlook of the person who has the emotion.

10. It has been argued, by Hegel in 1807, for example, that a scientific explanation is in fact nothing more than a more detailed description of the case. This is probably wrong, but I will not tend to this possible complication here.

11. Again, "viewed" must here be construed rather broadly, more like "perceived" or, perhaps, even including imaginings as casual thinking about the object in question. I take it that Husserl's own use of visual verbs (*sehen*) should be taken in this way as well.

12. I have here ignored that much heralded theory of possible worlds "counterparts," a view argued by David Lewis (and others) such that "the same" person cannot exist in more than one possible world (according to which David Kaplan's "trans-world-heirlines" become distinctively Braniff).

13. Husserl, despite his ontological denials, exemplifies this situation at the very basis of his work. "The things themselves" are treated both as phenomenological evidence and, as Husserl reminds us continuously, the only ontological commitments we can sensibly talk about. The notion remains obscure throughout his works. More striking is the sacred cow of extensionality in analytic circles. So "moonstruck" are so many philosophers that the very idea of objects-as-viewed, and so intensional entities in general, cannot be considered. When it comes to something so simple as describing the experience of emotion, therefore, these philosophers find they are allowed to say virtually nothing. What we get instead is the elaborate evasions we saw in Davidson's account of Hume.

14. Ed Allaire did not contribute to Mary's denuding so far as I know, but did help in conversation with some of the main points of this section.

15. Wilson, op. cit. p. 27.

16. Ibid.

17. Amélie Rorty calls this the "target" of the emotion in her "Explaining Emotions" (*Journal of Philosophy*, 1978; repr. in her book of the same title [Berkeley: University of California Press, 1980], p. 106).

18. Keith Donnellan has defended Hume on this point in an unpublished comment on Davidson's essay.

19. This blurs the usual distinction between emotions and moods. Emotions typically have determinate objects; moods, indeterminate objects. One is always angry about something, but one is typically depressed about everything. But one can be angry about everything ("in an angry mood") and one's depressions are often if not usually more or less focused on some particular aspect or dimension of one's life.

20. See note 10.

21. I have argued this in *The Passions* (New York: Doubleday-Anchor, 1976). What I did not adequately emphasize there is the *product* of judgment, which is a certain kind of perception ("a scenario") and the way in which this perception includes within it many of the properties usually ascribed to "feeling" (such as "affectivity" and "affective tone" and other less than precise or helpful correctives to an overly cognitive view, such as Davidson's).

22. The "possible world" ontology, of course, interprets the ontological commitments of its semantics in a variety of ways, ranging from the modest heuristic interpretation of possible worlds as a model for semantics (Stalnaker) to the extravagant view of all possible worlds as equally real (Lewis). But for our phenomenological purposes, we need not consider these alternatives here.

Chapter 6

This chapter was stimulated by the Social Science Research Council meeting in May 1981 on Concepts of Culture and Its Acquisition. Special thanks to Richard A. Shweder for his helpful criticism and encouragement. A portion of the "methodology" section has been adapted from my "Emotions and Anthropology," *Inquiry*, 21 (1978), 181–199, with the generous permission of the editors.

1. This has often been argued, and I shall not repeat the primary arguments here. See Solomon 1976, chap. 7; 1978.
2. It is worth noting, however, that the criterion used for distinguishing emotion words in Ifaluk was whether or not they were identified as "about our insides," despite the argument that "the Ifaluk see the emotions as evoked in, and inseparable from, social activity" rather than "internal feeling states" (Lutz 1982:114, 124).

Chapter 8

1. There are, of course, already claimants for the Meyer-Mendeleev position in emotions research. Robert Plutchik's color wheel would be one candidate. See his *Emotions: A Psychobioevolutionary Synthesis* (New York: Harper & Row, 1980). Andrew Ortony, G. Clore, and A. Collins, in *The Cognitive Structure of Emotions* (Cambridge: Cambridge University Press, 1988), give us something of the sort (although their chart could be argued to refer more to eliciting conditions than to cognitive structure as such).
2. René Descartes, *The Passions of the Soul*, trans. S. H. Voss (Indianapolis: Hackett, 1989), art. LXIX.
3. Thomas Hobbes, *Leviathan* (Indianapolis: Hackett, 1994), book VI.
4. Baruch Spinoza, *Ethics* (Malibu, Calif.: J. Simon, 1991), book III.
5. Anna Wierzbicka, *Lexography and Conceptual Analysis* (Ann Arbor, Mich.: Karoma, 1985).
6. Darwin has become the locus classicus for all such discussions through his book *The Expression of Emotions in Animals and Men* (1862). Ekman's work was virtually unknown by philosophers until recently, but now he has become *the* psychologist of note. See Jerome Neu, "A Tear Is an Intellectual Thing" in the book of the same title (New York: Oxford University Press, 2000); Paul Griffiths, *What an Emotion Really Is* (Chicago: University of Chicago Press, 1997); and Peter Goldie, *The Emotions* (Oxford: Oxford University Press, 2000).
7. For instance, the idea that "emotions are a product of our evolution" (Paul Ekman, "Are There Basic Emotions? . . ." *Psychological Review*, 99 [1992]: 550), "that emotions can be dealt with by understanding their evolutionary origins and significance" (Andrew Ortony and T. J. Turner, "On 'What's Basic About Basic Emotions?'" *Psychological Review*, 97 [1990]: 315–330), or "that emotions are specific neuropsychological phenomena, shaped by natural selection, . . . that facilitate adaptive responses to a vast array of demands and opportunities in the environment" (C. E. Izard, "Basic Emotions . . . ," *Psychological Review*, 99, no. 3 [1992]: 561), or "evolutionary homology," according to Paul Griffiths (op. cit., pp. 11ff).
8. James Russell, "Is There Universal Recognition of Emotion from Cross-Cultural Studies?" *Psychological Bulletin* 115, (1994) pp. 102–141.
9. For a defense of the most primitive reactions as basic emotions, see Jenefer Robinson, "Startle," *Journal of Philosophy*, 92, no. 2 (1993) pp. 53–74. But also see Edward R. Royzman and John Sabini, "Something It Takes to Be an Emotion: The Interesting Case of Disgust," *Journal for the Study of Social Behavior*, 31, no. 1 (March 2001): 29–60, in which they argue that disgust, because it is so fixed in its response, does not have the flexibility and "intelligence" to count as an emotion.

10. Paul Ekman, "All Emotions Are Basic," in Paul Ekman and Richard J. Davidson, eds., *The Nature of Emotion* (New York: Oxford University Press, 1994).

11. Russell, op.cit.

12. I owe this reading of the history of the term "emotions" to Thomas Dixon, who develops it at length in his unpublished manuscript "The 'Emotions': A Conceptual History."

13. Martha Nussbaum, "Non-Relative Virtues," in Peter French, ed., *Midwest Studies in Philosophy*, vol. 13 (Notre Dame, Ind.: University of Notre Dame Press, 1988).

14. Freud, *Project for a Scientific Psychology* (1895), Standard Edition, vol. 3.

15. Arthur Schopenhauer, *The World as Will and Representation* (New York: Dover, 1969); Friedrich Neitzsche, *On the Genealogy of Morals* (New York: Random House, 1967).

16. Edward O. Wilson, *Sociobiology* (Cambridge, Mass.: Harvard University Press, 1975), chap. 27.

17. But against this, I recommend Louis Charland's "The Natural Kind Status of Emotion," *British Journal for the Philosophy of Science* (2002). Forthcoming.

18. We find Izard, for example, *defining* the very concept of emotion as the most primitive possible phenomenon and thus eliminating pride, envy, and jealousy as emotions. (op. cit., p. 562).

19. Robinson, op. cit.

20. Although *The Passions* is often read as a pure "cognitive" theory, I make it a point throughout to emphasize the importance of context and consequences, including actions motivated by the emotions in question. I think Nico Frijda is surely right in putting action-tendencies at the center of the analysis of emotions, and this is an important corrective to both an overly restrictive cognitive theory and to the emphasis on pure physiology and more or less "automatic" facial expressions. William James famously blurs together physiological (autonomic) reactions, automatic, semi-voluntary and voluntary manifestations ("expressions") of emotion, but it is important not to make the opposite mistake and separate these too thoroughly. An action tendency is, after all, a form of physiological readiness defined by one's recognition (whether conscious or not) of one's situation in the world. Thus my "cognitive" theory is much more than merely cognitive.

21. Errol Bedford, "Emotions," repr. in D. Gustafson, ed., *Essays in Philosophical Psychology* (New York: Doubleday-Anchor, 1963).

22. Ortoney et al., op. cit., p. 19.

23. Batya Mesquita and Hazel Markus, "Culture and Emotion: Models of Agency and Relationship as Sources of Cultural Variation in Emotion." In *Feelings and Emotions: The Amsterdam Symposium* (Cambridge: Cambridge University Press, 2002).

24. Thanks to Harald Atmanspacher (Institut für Grenzgebiete der Psychologie, Freiburg).

25. David Buss, *The Dangerous Emotion* (New York: Free Press, 2000).

26. This theme has been briefly explored by Aaron Ben-Zeev and Keith Oatley in their "The Intentional and Social Nature of Human Emotions: Reconsideration of the Distinction Between Basic and Non-Basic Emotions," *Journal of the Theory of Social Behavior*, vol. 26, 1996.

27. Robert C. Solomon and Fernando Flores, *Building Trust* (New York: Oxford University Press, 2001).

28. Jean Briggs, *Never in Anger* (Cambridge, Mass.: Harvard University Press, 1975).

29. Colin Turnbull, *The Mountain People* (New York: Simon and Schuster, 1972).

30. Helmut Schoeck, *Envy*, trans. Michael Glenny and Betty Ross (New York: Harcourt, Brace and World, 1969).

31. Robert Frank and Philip J. Cook, *The Winner Take All Society* (New York: Free Press, 1995).

32. The name "critical theory" was put forward by Max Horkheimer in his "Traditional and Critical Theory" published in the late 1930s during the horrors of the Nazi takeover of Germany. In that definitive piece, Horkheimer rejects the idea of value-free scientific theory in favor of a theory that admits its submersion in a certain kind of society but insist on criticizing as well as describing its structures.

Chapter 9

This essay was originally written for a conference on emotions organized by Jack Barbalet and Margot Lyons in Canberra, Australia, in July 1997. Since then, a version of it has been published in Peter French et al., eds., *Midwest Studies in Philosophy*, vol. 22 (Notre Dame, Ind.: University of Notre Dame Press, 1998), pp. 1–20. Reprinted with very slight revisions with the permission of the editors of *Midwest Studies* and Notre Dame Press.

1. William James, "What Is an Emotion?," was first published in *Mind* (1884). It is reprinted in Cheshire Calhoun and Robert C. Solomon, eds., *What Is an Emotion?* (New York: Oxford University Press, 1984). See also Phoebe C. Ellsworth on James's theory, "William James and Emotion," *Psychological Review*, 101, no. 2 (1994): and Jack Barbalet, "William James' Theory of Emotion," *Journal for the Theory of Social Behavior* (1999).

2. Jon Solomon did this translation of Aristotle's *Rhetoric 1378–1380* (in Calhoun and Solomon, *op. cit.*). Aristotle's *Rhetoric* is translated in full by George A. Kennedy (New York: Oxford University Press, 1991).

3. Daniel C. Dennett, *Consciousness Explained* (Boston: Little, Brown, 1991); John Searle, *The Rediscovery of the Mind* (Cambridge Mass.: MIT Press, 1992); David Chalmers, *The Conscious Mind* (New York: Oxford University Press, 1996); Searle's review of Chalmers in *The New York Review of Books*, Feb 1997. See also, for a compendium of articles over the past century, William Lyons, *Modern Philosophy of Mind* (London: Penguin, 1996), and my review, *Philosophy East and West* 46, no. 3 (July 1996): 389–399.

4. René Descartes, *The Passions of the Soul*, trans. S. H. Voss (Indianapolis: Hackett, 1989). In fact, one might say (without absurdity) that Descartes was no "Cartesian." See, notably Gordon Baker and Katherine Morris, *Descartes* (Oxford: Oxford University Press, 1996).

5. Descartes, *Passions of the Soul*, para. XXV.

6. Specifically, *The Passions* (New York: Doubleday-Anchor, 1976; rev. ed., Indianapolis: Hackett, 1993); more recently, "On Emotions as Judgments," *American Philosophical Quarterly*, 25, no. 2 (April 1988): 183–191.

7. Nico Frijda, *Emotions* (Cambridge: Cambridge University Press, 1987).

8. Gilbert Ryle, *Concept of Mind* (New York: Barnes and Noble, 1950), esp. chap. 4; Ludwig Wittgenstein, *Philosophical Investigations* (Oxford: Blackwell, 2002).

9. Not so much in his early monograph, *The Emotions*, trans. B. Frechtman (New York: Citadel, 1948), where he characterizes emotions as "magical transformations of the world," a subjective form of "escape behavior," but throughout his monumental *Being and Nothingness*, trans. H. Barnes (New York: Philosophical Library, 1956).

10. There is a bit of perversity that needs a note here. Continental philosophers since Nietzsche, notably Heidegger and, following him, Sartre and Levinas, insist on denying that they are doing "ethics." This is nonsense, a misleading way of indicating their disapproval of what Sartre disdainfully calls "bourgeois ethics," and it is clearly a Kantian model that they have in mind. Levinas, in particular, takes the "priority of the ethical to ontology" as the hallmark of his philosophy.

11. The difference here bears on my disagreements with "social construction theory" (e.g., Rom Harré, James Averill). Part of the disagreement focuses on the existence of some natural rudimentary emotion responses that precede socialization, although, to be sure, such responses are greatly modified and embellished by society. But, more to the point here, it is not so much that the emotions are constructed *by* society as that emotions define, as well as are defined by, the relationships and the societies in which they play an essential role. Love, for example, is not just a "feeling," nor is it biology (or, as Freud put it, "lust plus the ordeal of civility"). It is, to be sure, both of these, and also "socially constructed." But it is not as if the "relationship" is something entirely distinct from the mutual emotions (including, of course, much more than love), nor can the emotions be readily distinguished from the re-

lationship. There are many cases, of course, of "unrequited" love and, needless to say, it makes perfectly good sense to speak of "one person's feeling for another." But the love, to put it crudely, is *in the relationship;* it is not, as some famous poets have tended to suggest, two parallel but wholly distinct sets of inner vibrations in happy harmony.

12. Sartre, *The Emotions.*

13. Ryle, for example, fudges the issue with the idea of "multi-track dispositions," making clear that the number of such hypothetical tracks might be, for any given emotion, indefinitely large (*Concept of Mind*).

14. Frijda, *The Emotions.*

15. Robert C. Solomon, "Emotions and Choice," *Review of Metaphysics,* 28 no. 1 (September 1973).

16. Errol Bedford, "Emotions," *Proceedings of the Aristotelian Society,* 1957 and repr. in D. Gustafson, ed., *Essays in Philosophical Psychology* (New York: Doubleday-Anchor, 1963).

17. Friedrich Nietzsche, *Daybreak,* trans. R. J. Hollingdale (Cambridge: Cambridge University Press, 1982).

18. Nico Frijda, "Emotion, Politics," *International Society for Research on the Emotions Proceedings* (ISRE Publications, 1994) 39–42.

19. Among the more sophisticated such attempts are Robert Kraut, "Love," repr. in G. Myers and K. D. Irani, eds., *Emotion* (New York: Haven Press, 1993), and Michael Stocker, "The Schizophrenia of Modern Ethical Theories," *Journal of Philosophy* 73 (1976) 453–466.

20. Such cynics include François de La Rochefoucauld, Albert Camus, and W. C. Fields.

21. Jean Briggs, *Never in Anger* (Cambridge, Mass.: Harvard University Press, 1970). See Robert C. Solomon, "Getting Angry: The Jamesian Paradigm in Anthropology," in A. Levine and R. Schweder, eds., *Culture Theory* (Cambridge: Cambridge University Press, 1984).

22. Robert Levi, *The Tahitians* (Chicago: University of Chicago Press, 1973).

23. See Robert C. Solomon, "In Defense of Sentimentality," *Philosophy and Literature,* 14 (1990) 304–323.

24. Jenefer Robinson, "Startle," *Journal of Philosophy,* 92, no. 2 (February 1995) 53–74.

25. See chapter 8.

26. Sartre, *The Emotions.*

27. This distinction between response and reflex played a critical role in the discussion of emotion as far back as James and Dewey, at least, and it is the crux of the debate in psychology today, as well. See, for example, Paul E. Griffiths, *What Emotions Really Are* (Chicago: University of Chicago Press, 1997).

28. Paul Ekman, Wallace V. Friesen, Ronald C. Simons, "Is the Startle Reaction an Emotion?" *Journal of Personality and Social Psychology* 49, no. 5 (1985) 1416–1426.

29. Jerome Shaffer, "An Assessment of Emotion, *American Philosophical Quarterly,* 20, no. 2 (April 1983), repr. in Myers and Irani, eds., op. cit., pp. 202–203.

Chapter 10

1. Lee Anna Clark and David Watson, "Distinguishing Functional from Dysfunctional Responses, in Paul Ekman and Richard J. Davidson, eds., *The Nature of Emotion* (New York: Oxford University Press, 1994), pp. 90f., note this as an "exception" to the thesis that positive and negative affect are antithetical, without noticing that this undermines the very thesis they want to defend. On Aristotle, see Amélie Rorty, ed., *Aristotle's Poetics* (Princeton, N.J.:Princeton University Press, 1990), esp. the essay by Alexander Nehamas. For a good discussion of the "paradox" surrounding horror movies, see Noel Carroll, *The Philosophy of Horror* (London: Routledge, 1990).

2. See, e.g., James Pennebaker, *Opening Up* (New York: Guilford Press, 1997); R. Lazaras, *Emotion and Adaptation* (New York: Oxford University Press, 1991).
3. Jeremy Bentham, *An Introduction to the Principles of Morals and Legislation* (New York: Hafner, 1948).
4. John Stuart Mill, *Utilitarianism* (Indianapolis: Hackett, 1979). See Jerome Neu, "Mill's Pig," in his *A Tear Is an Intellectual Thing* (New York: Oxford University Press, 2000).
5. Jack Panksepp. *Affective Neuroscience* (New York: Oxford University Press, 1998).
6. Peter Goldie. *The Emotions.* (New York: Oxford University Press, 2000).
7. The original notion comes from Aristotle. It is elaborated by Anthony Kenny in his classic *Action, Emotion, and Will* (London: Routledge and Kegan Paul, 1963) and in Ronald De Sousa, *The Rationality of Emotion* (Cambridge, Mass.: MIT Press, 1987).
8. Patricia Greenspan, *Practical Guilt* (New York: Oxford University Press, 1995).

Chapter 11

1. Paul Griffiths, *What Emotions Really Are* (Chicago: University of Chicago Press, 1997).
2. Richard Lane and Lynn Nadel, *The Cognitive Neuroscience of Emotion* (New York: Oxford University Press, 1999).
3. Richard Lazarus, J. Averill, and E. Opton, "Towards a Cognitive Theory of Emotion," in Magda B. Arnold, ed., *Feelings and Emotions* (New York: Academic Press, 1970).
4. Friedrich Nietzsche, *Beyond Good and Evil* (New York: Random House, 1967), §4.
5. Donald Davidson "Hume's Cognitive Theory of Pride," *Journal of Philosophy* 73, no.19 (1976):744–757. Davidson's view was taken very seriously by many philosophers who never showed any interest in emotion, much less in any cognitive theory of emotion. But what gets left out of Davidson's reconstruction—as Hume himself clearly recognized—was pride, that is, the emotion. See Annette Baier, "Davidson on Hume on Pride," ibid. pp. 758ff.
6. Cheshire Calhoun and Robert C. Solomon, eds., *What Is an Emotion?* (New York: Oxford University Press, 1984).
7. Since writing this chapter, I have had the benefit of reading Tony Marcel and John Lambie, "Emotion Experience," and Nico Frijda's comment on the same, both of which face this problem of "consciousness" head-on. Marcel and Lambie's piece is forthcoming in the *Psychological Review*. Frijda's essay will be part of his forthcoming book.
8. Michael Stocker, *Valuing Emotions* (Cambridge: Cambridge University Press, 1999).
9. George Downing, "Emotions Theory Revisited," in *Heidegger, Coping, and Cognitive Science: A Festschrift for Hubert Dreyfus*, vol. 2 (Cambridge, Mass.: MIT Press, 2001), pp. 245–270.
10. William James, "What Is an Emotion?" in Calhoun and Solomon, p. 136.
11. The line is from William Henley's "Invictus," which has been forever tarnished by mass murderer Timothy McVeigh, who quoted it immediately before his execution (June 2001).

Chapter 12

1. "Judg[e]ments being disturbed, clouded or warped by emotion, of people not being in control of their emotions." R. S. Peters and C. A. Mace "Emotions and the Category of Passivity" *Proceedings of the Aristotelian Society*, 62 (1961–1962): 117–142, see 119; Robert Gordon, *The Structure of Emotions* (New York: Cambridge University Press, 1987), pp. 110–127.

2. Paul Griffiths, *What Emotions Really Are* (Chicago: University of Chicago Press, 1997).

3. Jon Elster, *Alchemies of the Mind* (Cambridge: Cambridge University Press, 2000) p. 306.

4. Robert Gordon in his *Structure of Emotions* (op. cit.) and more recently in *The Cambridge Dictionary*, 2nd ed. (1999), p. 223.

5. As the genealogy of examples has become a certain concern in emotions research, let me note that this particular example is borrowed from Jerome Shaffer's article "An Assessment of Emotions," in K. D. Irani and G. E. Myers, eds., *Emotion* (New York: Haven, 1983), which I first used myself in my article "Beyond Reason: The Place of Emotions in Philosophy," in J. Ogilvy, ed., *Revisioning Philosophy* (Albany: SUNY Press, 1992), pp. 19–48.

6. Robert Gordon, "The Passivity of Emotions," *Philosophical Review*, 95, no. 3, July 1986: 372. See also his *The Structure of Emotions*.

7. Goldie is by no means consistent in his use of these terms. The distinction between an emotional episode and an emotion is clear enough (although some emotions are sufficiently short-term to be nothing but episodes), but he seems to use "emotional experience" sometimes to refer to the one and sometimes to the other.

8. Joseph LeDoux, in particular, has made much of the argument that the emotion response, indicated and measured in neurological terms, happens much more quickly than cognition, by which he means the reflective recognition *of* the emotion. But as I have already argued, having an emotion and (reflectively) experiencing an emotion are quite different, if not always distinct, and even the most primitive neurological emotional response involves some kind of *recognition* (a form, obviously, of cognition) as a initial stimulus. (We are not just talking about poking and prodding neurons here.)

9. R. S. Peters thus distinguishes, vaguely to my mind, between "*his* reason" and *the* reason explanations" of an action in *The Concept of Motivation* (London: Routledge and Kegan Paul, 1963).

10. Indeed, having my hand grabbed and shaken, without my participation, is a very different and very upsetting experience. What is at stake here is what Wittgenstein famously queried as "the difference between my raising my arm and my arm going up." But for our purposes here, it is sufficiently evident that we are discussing the former and not the latter, shaking the other person's hand and not simply having one's own hand shaken.

11. Jerome Neu, *Emotion, Thought, and Therapy* (Berkeley: University of California Press, 1977) and *A Tear Is an Intellectual Thing* (New York: Oxford University Press, 2000).

12. Harry Frankfurt, "Freedom of the Will and Second Order Desires," in *The Importance of What We Care About* (New York: Cambridge University Press, 1988).

13. Daniel Goleman, *Emotional Intelligence* (New York: Bantam, 1995), with proper credit to Peter Salovey, who initiated the concept of "emotional intelligence."

14. I have not even raised the question, also initiated by Nietzsche and now pursued by a great many postmodernists and contemporary psychiatrists, about the possibility of a "fragmented self" and the questions this raises about agency (or agencies).

15. Cf, Michael Stocker's poignant account of how he felt walking on ice, having once slipped and seriously hurt himself. *Valuing Emotions* (Cambridge: Cambridge University Press, 1999).

16. Jenefer Robinson, "Startle," *Journal of Philosophy*, 92, no. 2 (February 1995).

17. In Goleman's *Emotional Intelligence*, a good deal of the discussion concerns the ability to control one's emotions by way of thinking through consequences. I would object that this is only part (and by no means the more impressive part) of what this rich terms suggests.

18. Peters and Mace, op. cit.

19. Gilbert Ryle, *The Concept of Mind* (New York: Barnes and Noble, 1950).

20. This is an argument often attributed to Ludwig Wittgenstein (in his *Philosophical Investigations*), for example, by Norman D. Malcolm in his influential essay "The Private Language Argument," in D. Gustafson, ed., *Essays in Philosophical Psychology* (New York: Doubleday-Anchor, 1963). The

idea was that the criteria for recognizing an emotion were necessarily public and behavioral, and that what looked like recognition of one's own emotion ("in one's own case") turned out to be not a report but merely another expression, so adamant were the Wittgensteinians that there could be no reference to "private" mental states.

21. Jeffrey Murphy has some excellent arguments on the logical relation between vengeance and vindictiveness. See his *Mercy and Forgiveness* (New York: Cambridge University Press, 1988), written with Jean Hampton.

22. In short, expressions of emotion have no better explanation than the fact that they just are expressions of that emotion. Actions, by contrast, have a belief–desire or ends–means structure that puts them firmly in the field of intentional action. I find this distinction illusory, first, because it presumes to recognize when an action has or does not have "ulterior" motives and, second, because habitual and practiced actions may be purposive even if they themselves have no purpose "in mind" (e.g., scowling as an expression of anger and intimidating those around you; saying "I love you").

23. This, I take it, is what Wittgenstein's much-muddled insistence about first-person mental reports is about. His concern is to deny that first-person reports are *reports* and to insist that, rather, they are *expressions* of emotion in order to get around the Cartesian claim that a person has "privileged access" to his or her own mental states. But whatever the merits of the Cartesian case, it is certainly no good argument that denies the obvious: that sometimes people recognize and acknowledge their emotion, and that acknowledgement becomes part of the emotion.

24. I have discussed the complexity of such verbal expressions in "I Love You," in my *About Love* (Lanham, Md.: Rowman and Littlefield, 2001) sec. 12b.

25. One could throw in here a general set of qualifications, beginning with the assumption that I actually love you, and depending on my general demeanor—just "being" is surely not enough if the particulars of my behavior are for the most part contemptuous or resentful. And, one might add, in the absence of any overwhelming need—say, to hold on to my rights to the apartment in a tight real estate market—such that my continuing to be with you can be wholly explained by motives that have nothing to do with love.

26. I, too, would want to reject what Peter Goldie calls the "avocado pear" metaphor, which he uses to criticize "basic emotions" talk, here regarding the idea of a "hardwired" core of expression surrounded by the soft and malleable fruit of cultural display rules.

27. See, here, Jerry Neu's excellent essay "A Tear Is an Intellectual Thing," reprinted in his book of the same title (op. cit.).

28. Jon Elster, *Alchemies of the Mind* (Cambridge: Cambridge University Press, 2000), esp. pp. 307ff.

29. Ibid., p. 312.

30. Ibid., p. 310.

31. George Downing, "Emotion Theory Reconsidered," in J. Malpas and M. Wrathall, eds., *Heidegger, Coping, Cognitive Science: A Festschrift for Hubert Dreyfus*, vol. 2 (Cambridge, Mass.: MIT Press, 2000) esp. pp. 265ff.

32. Ibid., p. 265.

33. Ibid., p. 266.

34. Ibid., p. 267.

Bibliography

Aristotle. *De Anima* ("Of the Soul") in *Complete Works*, Vol. 1, Jonathan Barnes, ed. Princeton, N.J.: Princeton University Press, 1984, pp. 641–691.
Arnold, Magda, ed. *The Nature of Emotion*. Harmondsworth: Penguin, 1968.
Averill, James R. *Anger and Aggression: An Essay on Emotion*. New York: Spring-Verlag, 1982.
Averill, James R. "The Social Construction of Emotion, with Special Reference to Love." In K. Gergen and K. Davis, eds., *The Social Construction of the Person Emotion*, pp. 89–109. New York: Spring-Verlag, 1985.
Averill, James R., and Elma P. Nunley. *Voyages of the Heart*. New York: Free Press, 1992.
Baier, Annette. "Davidson on Hume on Pride." *Journal of Philosophy* 73, no. 19 (1976): 758ff.
Baier, Annette. *A Progress of Sentiments*, Cambridge: Harvard University Press, 1991.
Baker, Gordon, and Katherine Morris. *Descartes*. Oxford: Oxford University Press, 1996.
Barbalet, Jack. "William James' Theory of Emotion." *Journal for the Theory of Social Behavior* Vol. 29 no. 3 (Sept. 1999) pp. 251–266.
Bedford, Errol. "Emotions." *Proceedings of the Aristotelian Society* (1957). Repr. in D. Gustafson, ed., *Essays on Philosophical Psychology*. New York: Doubleday-Anchor, 1963.
Bentham, Jeremy. *An Introduction to the Principles of Morals and Legislation*. New York: Hafner, 1948.
Ben-Zeev, Aaron. *The Subtlety of Emotions*. Cambridge, Mass.: MIT Press, 2000.
Ben-Zeev, Aaron, and Keith Oatley. "The Intentional and Social Nature of Human Emotions: Reconsideration of the Distinction between Basic and Non-Basic Emotions." *Journal of the Theory of Social Behavior*, Vol. 26 (1996).
Blackburn, Simon. *Ruling Passions*. New York: Oxford University Press, 1998.
Briggs, Jean. *Never in Anger*. Cambridge, Mass.: Harvard University Press, 1975.
Buss, David. *The Dangerous Passion*. New York: Free Press, 2000.
Calhoun, Cheshire, and Robert C. Solomon, eds. *What Is an Emotion?* New York: Oxford University Press, 1984.
Calhoun, Cheshire. "Cognitive Emotions." In C. Calhoun and R. C. Solomon, *What Is an Emotion?* New York: Oxford University Press, 1984.
Calhoun, Cheshire. "Emotional Work" in *Explorations in Feminist Ethics*, E. Cole and S. Coultrap-McQuin, eds. Bloomington: Indiana University Press, 1992.
Calhoun, Cheshire. "Subjectivity and Emotion." *Philosophical Forum* 22 (1989): 195–210.
Cannon, W. B. "The James-Large Theory of Emotions" *American Journal of Psychology*, 39 (1917): 115–124.
Carroll, Noel. *The Philosophy of Horror*. London: Routledge, 1990.

Chalmers, David J. *The Conscious Mind: In Search of a Fundamental Theory*. New York: Oxford University Press, 1996.
Charland, Louis. "Reconciling Cognitive and Perceptual Theories of Emotion: A Representational Proposal" *Philosophy of Science*, 64 (December 1997): pp. 555–579.
Charland, Louis. "The Natural Kind Status of Emotion." *British Journal for the Philosophy of Science* (December 2002).
Clark, Lee Anna, and David Watson. "Distinguishing Functional from Dysfunctional Affective Responses." In Paul Ekman and Richard J. Davidson, eds. *The Nature of Emotion*, pp. 131–136. New York: Oxford University Press, 1994.
Damasio, Antonio. *Descartes' Error*. New York: Putnam, 1994.
Damasio, Antonio. *The Feeling of What Happens: Body and Emotion in the Making of Consciousness*. New York: Harcourt Brace, 1999.
Darwin, Charles. *The Expression of Emotions in Animals and Men* (1862), ed. Paul Ekman. New York: Oxford University Press, 1998.
Davidson, Donald. "Hume's Cognitive Theory of Pride." *Journal of Philosophy*, 73, no. 19 (Nov. 4, 1976): 744–757.
De Rivera, Joseph. *A Structural Theory of the Emotions*. New York: International Universities Press, 1977.
De Sousa, Ronald. *The Rationality of Emotion*. Cambridge, Mass.: MIT Press, 1987.
De Waal, Frans. *Chimpanzee Politics*. London: Cape, 1982.
Dennett, Daniel C. *Consciousness Explained*. Boston: Little, Brown, 1991.
Descartes, René. *The Passions of the Soul*, trans. S. H. Voss. Indianapolis: Hackett, 1989.
Dixon, Thomas. "The 'Emotions': The Creation of a Secular Psychological Category." Unpublished manuscript.
Downing, George. "Emotion Theory Reconsidered." In J. Malpas and M. Wrathall, eds., *Heidegger, Coping and Cognitive Science: A Festschrift for Hubert Dreyfus*. Vol. 2, pp. 245–270. Cambridge, Mass.: MIT Press, 2001.
Ekman, Paul. *Darwin and Facial Expression*. New York: Academic Press, 1973.
Ekman, Paul. *Approaches to Emotion*. Hillsdale, N.J.: Erlbaum, 1984.
Ekman, Paul, Wallace V. Friesen, and Ronald C. Simons. "Is the Startle Reaction an Emotion?" *Journal of Personality and Social Psychology* 49, no. 5 (1985): 1416–1426.
Ekman, Paul. "An Argument for Basic Emotions." *Cognition and Emotion* 6 (1992): 169–200.
Ekman, Paul. "Are There Basic Emotions? A Reply to Ortony and Turner." *Physiological Review*, 99 (1992): 550–553.
Ekman, Paul. "All Emotions Are Basic." In Paul Ekman and J. Davidson, eds., *The Nature of Emotion*. New York: Oxford University Press, 1994.
Ekman, Paul, and Richard J. Davidson, eds. *The Nature of Emotion*. New York: Oxford University Press, 1994.
Ekman, Paul, and Klaus Scherer, eds. *Approaches to Emotion*. Hillsdale, N.J.: Erlbaum, 1984.
Ellsworth, Phoebe. "William James and Emotion." *Psychological Review*, 101, no. 2 (1994): 222–229.
Ellsworth, Phoebe. "Appraisal Processes in Emotion." In R. Davidson, H. Goldsmith, and K. Scherer, eds., *Handbook of Affective Science*. New York: Oxford University Press, 2002.
Elster, Jon. *Alchemies of the Mind*. Cambridge: Cambridge University Press, 2000.
Frank, Robert H. *Passions Within Reason*. New York: Norton, 1989.
Frank, Robert H. and Philip J. Cook. *The Winner Take All Society*. New York: Free Press, 1995.
Frankfurt, Harry. "Freedom of the Will and Second Order Desires." In Harry Frankfurt, ed., *The Importance of What We Care About*. New York: Cambridge University Press, 1988.
Freud, Sigmund. *Project for a Scientific Psychology* (1895). Vol. 3 of *The Standard Edition of the Complete Psychological Works of Sigmund Freud*, trans. and ed. James Strachey. London: Hogarth, 1953.

Frijda, Nico. *The Emotions*. Cambridge: Cambridge University Press, 1986.
Frijda, Nico. "The Politics of Emotion." *International Society for Research on the Emotions Proceedings*. Storrs, Conn.: ISRE Publications, 1994.
Frijda, N., B. Mesquita, J. Sonnemans, and S. van Goozen. "The Duration of Affective Phenomena, or Emotions, Sentiments, and Passions." In K. Strongman, ed., *International Review of Emotion and Motivation*, pp. 187–225. New York: Wiley, 1991.
Frijda, N., A. Ortony, J. Sonnemans, and G. Clore. "The Complexity of Intensity." In M. Clark, ed., *Review of Personality and Social Psychology*. Vol. 2, pp. 60–89. Newbury Park, Calif.: Sage, 1992.
Gardiner, H. N., *Feeling and Emotion*. Westport, Conn.: Greenwood Press, 1970.
Goldie, Peter. *The Emotions*. Oxford: Oxford University Press, 2002.
Goleman, Daniel. *Emotional Intelligence*. New York: Bantam, 1995.
Gordon, Robert. "The Passivity of Emotions." *Philosophical Review*, 95, no. 3 (July 1986).
Gordon, Robert. *The Structure of Emotions*. New York: Cambridge University Press, 1987.
Gordon, Robert. "Emotions." In *The Cambridge Dictionary of Philosophy*, 2nd ed. R. Audi, ed. Cambridge: Cambridge University Press, 1999.
Greenspan, Patricia. *Emotions and Reasons*. New York: Routledge, 1988.
Greenspan, Patricia. *Practical Guilt*. New York: Oxford University Press, 1995.
Griffiths, Paul E. *What Emotions Really Are*. Chicago: University of Chicago Press, 1997.
Harré, Rom. *The Social Construction Theory of Emotions*. Oxford: Blackwell, 1986.
Hobbes, Thomas. *Leviathan*. Indianapolis: Hackett, 1994.
Hochschild, Arlie. *The Managed Heart*. Berkeley: University of California Press, 1983.
Horkheimer, Max. "Traditional and Critical Theory." In *Critical Theory: Selected Essays*, trans. M. O'Connell. New York: Continuum, 1992.
Hume, David. *A Treatise of Human Nature* (1739). Oxford: Clarendon Press, 1973.
Izard, C. E. "Basic Emotions, Relations Among Emotions, and Emotion-Cognition Processes." *Psychological Review*, 99, no. 3 (1992): 561–565.
James, William. *Principles of Psychology* (1890). New York: Dover, 1950.
James, William. "What Is an Emotion?" *Mind* (1884). Repr. in Cheshire Calhoun and Robert C. Solomon, eds., *What Is an Emotion?* New York: Oxford University Press, 1984.
Johnson-Laird, P. N., and Keith Oatley. "The Language of Emotions." *Cognition and Emotion*, 3 (1989):81–123.
Johnson-Laird, P. N., and Keith Oatley. "Basic Emotions, Rationality, and Folk Theory." *Cognition and Emotion*, 6 (1992): 201–223.
Kenny, Anthony. *Action, Emotion, and Will*. London: Routledge and Kegan Paul, 1963.
Kraut, Robert. "Love." Repr. in G. Myers and K. D. Irani, eds., *Emotion: Philosophical Studies*, pp. 42–56. New York: Haven Press, 1983.
Lane, Richard, and Lynn Nadel, eds. *The Cognitive Neuroscience of Emotion*. New York: Oxford University Press, 1999.
Lazarus, Richard S. "Thoughts on the Relation Between Emotion and Cognition." *American Psychologist*, 37 (1982): 1019–1024.
Lazarus, Richard S. "On the Primacy of Cognition." *American Psychologist*, 39 (1984): 124–129.
Lazarus, Richard S. *Emotion and Adaptation*. New York: Oxford University Press, 1994.
Lazarus, Richard S., J. Averill, and E. Opton. "Towards a Cognitive Theory of Emotion." In Magda B. Arnold, ed., *Feelings and Emotions*. New York: Academic Press, 1970.
LeDoux Joseph. *The Emotional Brain: The Mysterious Underpinnings of Emotional Life*. New York: Simon and Schuster, 1996.
Levi, Robert. *The Tahitians*. Chicago: University of Chicago Press, 1973.
Lewin, Kurt. *A Dynamic Theory of Personality*. New York: McGraw-Hill, 1936.
Lewis, M. and J. Haviland, eds. *Handbook of Emotions*. New York: Guilford Press, 1993.

Lyons, William. *Modern Philosophy of Mind*. London: Penguin, 1996.
Malcolm, Norman. "The Private Language Argument." In D. Gustafson, ed., *Essays in Philosophical Psychology*. New York: Doubleday-Anchor, 1963.
Manstead, A., and A. Fischer, eds. *Feeling and Emotion: The Amsterdam Symposium*. Cambridge: Cambridge University Press, 2002.
Mesquita, Batya, and Nico Frijda. "Cultural Variations in Emotion: A Review." *Psychological Bulletin*, 112 (1992): 179–204.
Mesquita, Batya, and Hazel Markus. "Culture and Emotion: Models of Agency and Relationship as Sources of Cultural Variation in Emotion." In *Feelings and Emotions: The Amsterdam Symposium*. Cambridge: Cambridge University Press, 2002.
MIll, John Stuart. *Utilitarianism*. Indianapolis: Hackett, 1979.
Mowrer, O. H. *Learning and Behavior*. New York: Wiley, 1960.
Murphy, Jeffrey G., and Jean Hampton. *Mercy and Forgiveness*. New York: Cambridge University Press, 1988.
Nehamas, Alexander "Pity and Fear in [Aristotle's] Rhetoric and Poetics." In Amélie Rorty, ed., *Aristotle's Poetics*. Princeton, N.J.: Princeton University Press, 1990.
Neu, Jerome. *Emotion, Thought, and Therapy: A Study of Hume and Spinoza and the Relationship of Philosophical Theories of the Emotions to Psychological Theories of Therapy*. Berkeley: University of California Press, 1977.
Neu, Jerome. "Jealous Thoughts." In Amélie Rorty, ed., *Emotions*. Berkeley: University of California Press, 1980.
Neu, Jerome. *A Tear Is an Intellectual Thing*. New York: Oxford University Press, 2000.
Nietzsche, Friedrich. *Beyond Good and Evil*. New York: Random House, 1967.
Nietzsche, Friedrich. *On the Genealogy of Morals*. New York: Random House, 1967.
Nietzsche, Friedrich. *Daybreak*, trans. R. J. Hollingdale. Cambridge: Cambridge University Press, 1982.
Nussbaum, Martha. "Non-Relative Virtues." In Peter French, ed., *Midwest Studies in Philosophy*. Vol. 13. Notre Dame, Ind.: University of Notre Dame Press, 1988.
Nussbaum, Martha. *Upheavals of Thought*. Cambridge: Cambridge University Press, 2000.
Oatley, Keith. *Best Laid Scheme: The Psychology of Emotions*. Cambridge: Cambridge University Press, 1992.
Ortony, Andrew, G. Clore, and A. Collins. *The Cognitive Structure of Emotions*. New York: Cambridge University Press, 1988.
Ortony, Andrew, and T. J. Turner. "On 'What's Basic About Basic Emotions?'" *Psychological Review*, 97 (1990): 315–331.
Panksepp, Jaak. *Affective Neuroscience*. New York: Oxford University Press, 1998.
Parrott, Gerald. "The Role of Cognition in Emotion Experience." In W. Baker, L. Mos, H. Rappard, and H. Stam, eds., *Recent Trends in Theoretical Psychology*, pp. 327–337. New York: Spring-Verlag, 1988.
Pennebaker, James. *Opening Up*. New York: Guilford Press, 1997.
Peters, R. S. *The Concept of Motivation*. London: Routledge and Kegan Paul, 1963.
Peters, R. S., and C. A. Mace. "Emotions and the Category of Passivity." *Proceedings of the Aristotelian Society*, 62 (1961–1962): 117–142.
Plutchik, Robert. *Emotions: A Psychobioevolutionary Synthesis*. New York: Harper & Row, 1980.
Robinson, Jenefer. "Startle." *Journal of Philosophy*, 92, no. 2 (February, 1995): 53–74.
Rorty, Amélie, "From Passions to Emotions and Sentiments" *Philosophy*, 57: 157–172.
Rorty, Amélie, ed., *Emotions*. Berkeley: University of California Press, 1980.
Rorty, Amélie, ed. *Aristotle's Poetics*. Princeton, N.J.: Princeton University Press, 1990.

Royzman, Edward R., and John Sabini. "Something It Takes to Be an Emotion: The Interesting Case of Disgust." *Journal for the Study of Social Behavior,* 31, no. 1 (March 2001): 29–60.
Russell, James and J. Fernandez-Dols, eds. *The Psychology of Facial Expression.* Cambridge: Cambridge University Press, 1997.
Ryle, Gilbert. *The Concept of Mine.* New York: Barnes and Noble, 1950.
Salovey, Peter, and J. D. Mayer, "Emotional Intelligence." *Imagination, Cognition, and Personality.* 9: 185–211.
Scherer, Klaus. "Appraisal Theory." In T. Dalgleish and M. Power, eds., *Handbook of Cognition and Emotion,* pp. 637–663. London: Wiley, 1999.
Shaffer, Jerome. "An Assessment of Emotion," *American Philosophical Quarterly,* 20, no. 2 (April, 1983).
Shields, Stephanie. *Speaking from the Heart: Gender and the Social Meaning of Emotion.* Cambridge: Cambridge University Press, 2002.
Solomon, Robert C. *The Passions.* New York: Doubleday-Anchor, 1976. Rev. ed., Indianapolis: Hackett, 1993.
Solomon, Robert C. "Getting Angry: The Jamesian Paradigm in Anthropology." In A. Levine and R. Schweder, eds., *Culture Theory.* Cambridge: Cambridge University Press, 1984.
Solomon, Robert C. "On Emotions as Judgments." *American Philosophical Quarterly,* 25, no. 2 (April 1988): 183–191.
Solomon, Robert C. "The Politics of Emotion." In Peter French et al., eds., *Midwest Studies in Philosophy.* Vol. 22, pp. 1–20. Notre Dame, Ind.: University of Notre Dame Press, 1998.
Spinoza, Baruch. *Ethics.* Malibu, Calif.: J. Simon, 1981.
Stearns, Peter. "History of Emotion." In M. Lewis and J. M. Haviland, eds., *Handbook of Emotions.* New York: Guilford, 1993.
Stearns, Peter and C. Stearns. *Anger.* Chicago: University of Chicago Press, 1986.
Stocker, Michael. "The Schizophrenia of Modern Ethical Theories." *Journal of Philosophy,* 73 (1976): 453–466.
Stocker, Michael, and E. Hegeman. *Valuing Emotions.* Cambridge: Cambridge University Press, 1996.
Tavris, Carol. *Anger: The Misunderstood Emotion.* New York: Simon and Schuster, 1982.
Turnbull, Colin. *The Mountain People.* New York: Simon and Schuster, 1972.
Wierzbicka, Anna. *Lexicography and Conceptual Analysis.* Ann Arbor, Mich.: Karoma, 1985.
Wilson, Edward O. *Sociobiology: A New Synthesis.* Cambridge, Mass.: Harvard University Press, 1975.
Wittgenstein, Ludwig. *Philosophical Investigations,* trans. G. E. M. Anscombe. Oxford: Blackwell, 2002.
Zajonc, Robert. "Feeling and Thinking: Preferences Need No Inferences." *American Psychologist,* 35 (1980): 151–175.
Zajonc, Robert. "On Primacy of Affect." In Paul Ekman and Klaus Scherer, eds., *Approaches to Emotion,* pp. 259–270. Hillsdale, N.J.: Erlbaum, 1984.

Index

A Clockwork Orange (Burgess), 51
act, (mental) 43, 55, 59, (intentional) 69
Action Emotion and Will (Anthony), 18
actions, 6, 11, 14–16, 31, 35–37, 40, 89, 92, 108
actual events, 7
affect, 145, 155
affect program, 117, 132–133, 138, 142, 171
agency, 204–206
Alice in Wonderland (Carroll), 21, 87, 154
altruism, 131
amae (Ifaluk), 136
American culture, 139
Anaximenes, 116
anger, 80–82, 84, 86–89, 92, 106, 109–111, 118, 123–125, 136, 138–140, 142–143, 150, 153–154, 159, 164, 170–174, 227
angst, 142
anthropologists, 84–86, 88
anthropology, 76–78, 83, 89–90
anxiety, 142
apatheia, 18, 93
appraisal, 171–173
appraisal theory, 99
approval, 171, 173
Aquinas, Thomas, 125, 128, 164
Aristotle, 18–19, 25–26, 57, 61, 88, 92–93, 96, 105–106, 109, 124–126, 128–129, 132, 143–145, 163–165, 173, 201, 205, 214–215, 217, 223, 227
Armstrong, David, 6
Arnold, Magda, 99
"An Assessment of Emotion" (Shaffer), 160
atomism, 45, 48, 50, 53–54, 58, 71–72
attitudes, 42, 67, 87, 89
Augustine, 96

Austin, J. L. 16, 100
authenticity, 152
autonomic responses, 221
avocado-pear model, 118, 128, 133
Ayer, A. J. 98

Babel, Isaac, 227
bad faith, 152, 198, 210
Baier, 51
basic actions, 215
basic emotions, 115, 117, 123–124, 126, 128–130, 132–133, 136–140, 142, 157, 164
Bedford, Errol, 6,117, 135
behavior, 61, 73, 78, 82–87,
behavioral expressions, 131
behaviorism, 27, 119, 149, 151, 216
behaviorists, 122
belief, 48–56, 60–61, 64–69, 71, 79, 87–88, 112, 184–185
Bentham, Jeremy, 167–168
Ben-Zeev, 166–167
biological thesis, 130
biology, 78
Blackburn, Simon, 133, 213
blame, 88
bodily humours, 116
body, the 189–191
Bohr, Niels, 130
Bourdieu, Pierre, 191
Boyle, Robert, 129
Brentano, Franz 43, 60–61
Briggs, Jean, 82–83, 86, 90, 138, 140, 156
Broad, C. D. 101, 205
Brown, Thomas, 127
Bruner, Jerome, 232
"building block" metaphor, 129

Burroughs, Edgar Rice, 118, 122
Buss, David, 138

Calhoun, Cheshire, 180, 185
Camus, 41, 72
Cannon W. B. 26, 27, 29, 86, 213
Carroll, Lewis, 21, 87, 100, 154
Cartesian dualism, 144–145, 161
Cartesian tradition, 144
Cartesianism, 145, 150
catharsis, 10
cause, 6, 7, 9–10, 18, 28, 42–44, 45–51, 53, 56–59, 61–67, 73–74, 77–78, 86–87, 90
Chalmers, David, 144
choice, 17, 21–22,194–196, 212, 222–223, 230, 232
choice theory, 231
Chryssipis, 93
Church, Jennifer, 108
Clark, 162
Clore, Gerald, 117, 171
cognition, 92–93, 99, 131, 179, 192, 198
cognitive elements, 112
The Cognitive Structure of Emotion (Ortony, Clore, Collins), 162, 172
cognitive theory of emotions, 87–89, 99, 100, 105, 145, 178, 189, 210
cognitivism, 103
Collins, Allan, 117,171
communication, 120
Communist Manifesto (Marx), 37
compassion, 127
Concept of Mind (Ryle), 6
concept, 87–90
consciousness, 3, 10, 25, 29–30, 54, 144, 181, 187
constitutive judgments, 100
contemplation, 68
contempt, 99
control (of emotions), 13
Critique of Pure Reason (Kant), 97
culture, 77–80, 87–90

Dalton, John, 116, 129
Damasio, Antonio, 124, 178
Danto, Arthur, 193, 199
Darwin, Charles, 116, 118, 131, 223, 226
Davidson, Donald, 47–55, 58, 60–64, 66–67, 72, 74, 107–108, 162
De Anima (Aristotle), 125

De Sousa, Ronald, 101, 108, 155, 180, 184–186, 205
definite description, 49
Democritus, 129
Dennett, Daniel, 49, 144
dependency, 80
Derrida, Jacques, 136
Descartes, René 18, 20, 25, 29, 41, 42, 51, 57, 92, 116, 123, 126–127, 129–130, 137, 144, 151, 158, 163–164, 170, 180, 188–189, 214
descriptions, 59, 60, 64–66, 71–75, 87–89
desires, 20–22, 49, 51, 87, 93, 105–107
Dewey, John, 93,146, 148, 161, 185
dialectic, 122
disapproval, 173
disgust, 121
dispassionate judgments, 109
display rules, 119
Downing, George, 191, 222, 229–232
Dreyfus, Hubert, 191
drive, 130
"Duchenne" smile, 220

eidetic, 142
Ekman, Paul, 79,116, 118, 120–124, 129, 139, 154, 159, 162, 189–190, 197, 199, 214, 217, 220, 226
elective affinities, 130
Elster, Jon, 133, 199, 203, 222–230
embarrassment, 30–31, 99, 101
emergency paradigm, 97, 203
emotion felt, 27
Emotion and Object (Wilson), 62
Emotion: Philosophical Studies (Myers and Irani), 94
emotion, positive and negative, 164–167, 170, 172
emotional judgments, 102
emotional object, 8, 19
emotional opposites, 163, 176–177
"Emotions and Choice" (Solomon), 18–23, 186
empathy, 77, 83–84
enervating, 127, 165–166
engagement, 108
envy, 36, 38, 101, 140, 142
epinephrine, 29, 77, 82
epiphenomenon, 26–27
episodic mental concept, 32
epistemology, 88
Ethics (Spinoza), 127, 163, 188

etiology, 83
eudaimon life, 18
evaluative judgments, 99, 180
event, 63
evidence, 10–11
excuses, 28
existentialism, 18
experience, 3–4, 37–38, 40, 53–56, 58–59, 64–65, 68–69, 74–76, 87
expressions, 11 (of a judgment), 23, 40, 79–80, 83–84, 90

facial expressions, 118–124, 145, 159, 190, 217, 219–220
fact, 4, 8–9, 12, 28, 65–67, 70
fago, 136
fear, 80, 82, 107, 118, 123, 125, 137–138, 140, 153, 159, 171
feelings, 3–6, 20, 30–31, 33, 35, 39, 52, 54, 57–60, 71, 74–77, 80, 83, 85–88
fidgeting, 220
finalité, 147
first and other person, 8–9
fitness (Nietzsche), 148
flight, 171
Fodor, Jerry, 179
folk psychology, 134, 146, 157, 172
folk wisdom, 167
Frankfurt, Harry, 204, 208–209, 215
Freedman, 77
freedom, 204–205
Frege, G. 182
Freud, Sigmund 8, 10, 12, 15, 18–19, 30, 33, 35, 39, 64, 70, 79, 97, 107, 109, 130, 157, 187, 205–207, 211
Frijda, Nico, 123, 146, 149, 153–154, 162, 167, 171, 190, 201, 228
functions, 65–66

Geertz, Clifford, 90
Genealogy of Morals (Nietzsche), 155
generalizations, 65
genuine, 229
Gidé, Andre, 16–17
God, 14
Goethe, Johann, 130
Goldie, Peter, 118, 128, 133, 171, 183, 189, 203, 207–208, 218, 221
Gordon, Robert, 62, 184, 199, 201
Gorgias (Plato), 18

Greenspan, Pat, 175
grief, 147
Griffiths, James, 192
Griffiths, Paul, 117, 132, 178, 188, 199
guilt, 37, 46, 164

Hamlet (Shakespeare), 38–39
happiness, 168
happiness calculus, 168
happiness culture, 136
Harris, Marvin, 83–84
hate, 162–164, 170
hatred, 3
hedons (utilitarians), 167
Hegel, G. 204
Heidegger, Martin 4, 5, 20, 54–55, 142, 146, 191, 232
Heraclitus, 116, 130
hierarchy of desires, 209
Hobbes, Thomas, 89, 116, 122, 127, 129–130, 188
Hochschild, Arlie, 197, 229
Horace, 195
human nature, 128
Hume, David, 19, 42–58, 60, 62–64, 66–67, 71, 73–74, 80, 89, 92, 94, 98, 103, 105, 107–108, 110, 112, 116–117, 127–129, 145–146, 167, 182, 204
Husserl, 5, 43, 52, 54–55, 59, 109, 142, 185
hydraulic metaphor, 76, 79
hydraulic theory, 26, 30, 79–80, 157
hypercognated, 119

id, 18
idea, 37, 43–51, 53–55, 57, 58, 71
identity, 53, 71
Ifaluk, 79
Ik, 140
imagination, 68
impressions, 43–44, 45–46, 48, 50, 52–54, 57–58, 60, 71, 73–74, 167
inference, 69, 85
innervating, 127, 165, 166
instinct, 130
intellect, 90
intensionality, 59–60, 65
intensity, 12, 104–105
intention, 3, 4, 6, 18–19, 35–37, 42–44, 47, 50–63, 67–71, 73, 75, 149
Intentionality (Searle), 106

interpretation, 17, 77–78, 85–87, 89, 90
intimidation, 153
intuition, 35
investment metaphor, 107
involuntary nature, 227
Irani, 94
irrationality, 14, 34–36, 41, 92,93
Izard, Carroll, 122–124, 129, 154

"The James-Lange Theory of Emotion" (Cannon), 27
James, William, 3, 18, 26–27, 30, 64, 76–77, 79, 81, 86, 92–93, 100, 106, 108, 116, 119, 122, 130, 133, 143–145, 148–149, 152, 161, 182, 185, 189, 193, 197, 199, 201, 214, 217, 219–221, 229
Jamesian theory, 77, 79–80, 83, 85–86, 88, 90
jealousy, 3, 28,101, 137–138, 141–142
judgment theory, 185
judgments, 8, 10–15, 17–18, 20–21, 35–36, 39–40, 50, 54–56, 58, 74, 88, (emotional) 92–95, 97, (kinesthetic) 98, (evaluative) 100, 113, 146, 151, 187–188, (kinesthetic and aesthetic) 210, (kinesthetic) 211, 215
Jung, Carl, 79–80

Kafka, Franz, 95
Kant, Immanuel, 20, 92, 95, 97, 99, 204, 211, 213
Kemper, 123
Kenny, Anthony, 18–20, 60–63, 65, 67–69, 71, 74
Kierkegaard, Sorren, 3
kinesthetic judgment, 187, 190
klesas, 126
knowledge, 10, 11, 28–29, 34, 88
Kraut, Robert, 92

La Bruyère, Jean de 224
La Rochefoucald, F. 224
labeling, 150, 156
Lange, C. G. 26–27, 76
Langer, Suzanne, 89
language, 25–30, 77, 80–81, 88–89
Lazarus, 186
Le Doux, Joseph, 124, 159, 178, 184
Leibniz, G. 92, 100
Levi, Robert, 81–82, 86, 89–90, 119, 139, 156
Lévi-Strauss, Claude, 136
Lewin,Kurt, 162
Lewis, David, 106

logical relationship, 47
love, 3, 17, 36–37, 56–57, 70, 92, 101, 112, 127, 130, 156, 160, 162–164, 170, 173, 203, 218
Lutz, Catherine, 79
Lyons, Richard, 97

Mace, 199
MacIntyre, A. 15
manipulation, 153
Marx, Karl, 36
materialism, 152
matrix, 135–136
matrix theory of emotions, 134, 140
Mead, Margaret, 83–84, 141
meaning, 20, 75
Meaning (Schiffer), 103
Meinong, 56, 61
Malebranche, Nicholas, 92
memory, 68
Mendeleev, Dmitri, 115
mental acts, 5
mental concepts, 31 (episodic and dispositional)
Merleau-Ponty, Maurice, 54, 120, 191, 199
Mesquita, Batya, 136
metaphors, 79, 81–82
Meyer, Julius, 115
Mill, John Stuart, 106, 168
Molière, Jean–Baptiste,152
moods, 3–4, 8, 23, 146
moral philosophy, 18
morality, 8
Morrison, 82
motives, 12, 14
Mowrer, 167,
Murphy, Jeffrey, 179
Myers, 94
myopic, 14, 17
myth, 82, 136
myth of the passions, 35
Myth of Sisyphus (Camus), 72

names (of emotions), 78
The Nature of Emotion (Ekman and Davidson), 162
negative affect, 162
nema, 55
Neu, Jerome, 108, 141, 179–181, 185–187, 206
neurology, 25, 27–28, 76, 78
Never in Anger (Briggs), 82, 138
Newton, Isaac, 54, 57, 117, 127, 129, 130

Nicomachean Ethics (Aristotle), 106, 163–164, 201
Nietzsche, Friedrich, 14–15, 17, 34, 96, 108, 130, 148, 154–155, 176, 180, 183, 204–207, 211
node, 134–135
node in a nexus, 134
noesis, 55
nonvalenced appraisals, 175
Nussbaum, Martha 100, 128

Oatley, 123
object, 18, 42–43, 46–47, 48–75, 86, 89
occurrences, 4, 6–7, 9, 11, 33, 64, 66
offense, 111, 125
ontology, 44, 53, 56, 59, 61, 63, 67–75, 115, 150
opposite emotions, 164
oppositional thinking, 176
    Othello (Shakespeare), 38
Ortony, Andrew, 104, 117, 122–124, 129, 130, 135, 162, 171, 188

pain, 168–170
panic, 214–215
Panksepp, Jaak, 122, 123–124, 129, 133, 171, 178
paradigm of deliberate judgment, 98
paradigm scenarios, 155
paradoxes, 9
Passions of the Soul (Descartes), 126, 144, 158, 188, 163
The Passions (Solomon), 18–20, 54, 101, 134, 135, 186, 189, 192, 195, 225
passions, 42, 44, 47–48, 51, 80, 89, 92–93, 116, 126, 158, 162
passive mode, 199
passivity, 212, 216, 227
pathology, 109
Pears, D. F. 4–5
perceptions, 36, 59, 64, 66, 68, 76, 87–89, 92–93
personality, 30, 35
Peters R. S. 15,199
phenomena, (cultural) 77, 88
phenomenology, 18–19, 59–60, 65, 67–69, 74, 77, 131, 146, 151–152
philosophy, 42, 74, 76, 93
philosophy of mind, 6
physiology, 25, 27–29, 31, 42, 57, 63, 76–77, 85–87, 90, 92, 131
Pincoffs, Edmond, 96
Pitcher, George, 99

plasticity, 133
Plato, 18–19, 195
pleasure, 45–47, 168–170
Plutchik, Robert, 80
political (emotions), 148–150, 152, 155, 161
Pope Gregory, 125, 164
positive affect, 161
power, 152–153
Practical Guilt (Greenspan), 175
pragmatic paradoxes, 9
pragmatism, 41
precognitive, 123
prereflective, 97
pretense, 16–17
pride, 44–55, 57, 61, 66–68, 70, 72, 74, 107, 164, 166
primitivism, 160
Principles of Psychology (James), 198
privacy, 9
private language argument (Wittgenstein), 85
properties, 43, 50, 53, 60, 64, 68–70, 73, 75
propositions, 48–55, 58, 60–61, 63
proto-emotions, 133, 229
psychology, 53, 64, 68, 93, 122, (Buddhist) 126
purpose, 12

Quine, W. V. O. 53–54, 78

rage, 156, 214–215
rasas, 126
rationality, 14, 23, 35–36, 39–41, 93
Rationality of Emotion (De Sousa), 155, 186
Rawls, John, 192
reality, 35–37, 40–41
reason, 14, 26, 42, 89, 92–93
reductionism, 129–132, 134
reference, 54, 68, 79, 88
reflection, 109
Reik, 108
relations, 50–52, 58, 61–63, 68, 71, 73
relationship, 173
The Republic (Plato) 195
resentment, 99, 155
response, 12–14
responsibility, 22, 204–206
Rey, Georges 83
Rhetoric (Aristotle), 88, 92, 109, 124, 163
riri (Tahitian), 139, 156
Rise of Anthropological Theory (Marvin), 83
Roberts, Robert, 180

Robinson, Jenefer, 105–107, 157–160, 214
Rorty, Amélie, 188
Rorty, Richard, 225
Rosaldo, Michelle, 82
Rousseau, J .J. 89, 116, 120
Rubin, 108
Ryle, Gilbert, 6, 39, 106, 146, 151

sadness, 81, 151
Sartre, Jean Paul, 4, 13, 17, 36, 40, 56, 97, 145, 146, 148, 155, 158, 195–197, 209, 212, 225–226, 229–231
Saussure, Ferdinand de, 136
scenario, 108
Schachter S. 29–30, 101, 156
schadenfreude, 168
Schafer Roy, 196, 224–225
Scheler, Max, 142
Scherer, Klaus, 173, 186
Schiffer, Stephen, 103
Schoeck, 140
Schopenhauer 37, 130, 204, 211
Searle, John, 106, 144
second order desires, 208–209, 215
self, 35, 44–46, 48, 55, 57, 173
self-awareness, 17
self-deception, 23, 152, 231
self-esteem, 22–24, 37–38, 40–41, 46, 108, 224, 228
self-interest, 35
self-involved, 103
self-reference, 48–49
semantics, 61
Seneca 18, 93
sensations, 30–31, 33, 46, 48, 60, 87
sentimentality, 89, 157
seven deadly sins, 125,164
seven theological virtues, 164
Shaffer, Jerome, 94, 112, 160, 230
Shakespeare, 38–39
shame 30–31, 37, 99, 101, 166
shock, 158
Singer, Peter, 101, 135–136, 226
Skinner, B. F. 119, 151
Smith, Adam, 116, 127
Smith, Michael, 213
social context, 131
Socrates, 129, 168
Solomon, Robert, 100
Sorabji, Richard, 216

speech acts, 100
Spinoza, Baruch, 57, 71, 93–94, 116, 123, 127, 129–130, 146, 162–167, 180, 186, 188, 206
spontaneity (of emotions), 96–97
startle, 158, 160
startle response, 120, 148, 157, 159
status, 175
Stendhal, 37, 97, 100, 201
Stocker, Michael, 109, 180, 187, 189
Stoics, 94, 127, 145–146, 155, 180, 186, 216, 228, 230–231
strategies (emotional), 40–41,147–148, 153, 229
stress, 166
structural judgments, 112
structuralism, 134, 136
subjectivity, 38–41, 54, 151
substances, 151
suffering, 169
surreality, 20, 28
sustaining judgments, 112
syllogism, 50–52, 55, 58
systematic judgments, 101

Tahitian culture, 81, 82, 86, 89, 139, 156
Tarzan, 118
"A Tear Is an Intellectual Thing" (Neu), 108
Thales, 116
Theory of the Moral Sentiments (Smith), 127
"therapeutic" views of emotion, 216
thinking, 182, 183
thoughts, 93, 112
Tompkins, Sylvan, 116
Treatise of Human Nature (Hume), 44, 57, 98, 127
truth, 15
Turnbull, Colin. 140
Turner, T. J. 117, 122–124, 129

the Unconscious (Freud), 30
unintentional actions, 15, 16
Upheavals of Thought (Nussbaum), 100
utilitarians, 167–168
Utku Inuits, 81–84, 138, 140–141, 156

valence,162–164, 167, 170, 173, 176
valenced reactions, 180
values, 36, 70
vices, 163, 164, 165

violence, 169
virtue, 18, 45–47, 50–51, 68, 70, 74, 92, 128, 163–165
voluntary actions, 219

Walton, Kendall, 179
Watson, John, 80, 123, 124,150, 162
weeping, 221
What Emotions Really Are (Griffiths), 132
"What Is an Emotion?" (James), 26, 76, 197

will, 206
Will (Kant), 204
Will (Schopenhauer) 130
Will to Power (Nietzsche), 130
Williams, Bernard, 223
Wilson, J. R. S. 62–64, 67, 68, 71
Wittgenstein, Ludwig, 48, 85, 86, 108, 117, 146, 151

Zajonc, Robert, 92,159

Printed in the United Kingdom
by Lightning Source UK Ltd.
124250UK00001B/280/A